COMPARATIVE
POLICING

COMPARATIVE POLICING

The Struggle for Democratization

WITHDRAWN

M. R. HABERFELD

John Jay College of Criminal Justice, New York, NY

IBRAHIM CERRAH

Institute for Security Sciences, Turkish National Police Academy, Ankara, Turkey

EDITORS

SAGE Publications
Los Angeles • London • New Delhi • Singapore

For information:

Sage Publications, Inc.
2455 Teller Road
Thousand Oaks,
   California 91320
E-mail: order@sagepub.com

Sage Publications Ltd.
1 Oliver's Yard
55 City Road
London EC1Y 1SP
United Kingdom

Sage Publications India Pvt. Ltd.
B 1/I 1 Mohan Cooperative
   Industrial Area
Mathura Road, New Delhi 110 044
India

Sage Publications Asia-Pacific
   Pte. Ltd.
33 Pekin Street #02-01
Far East Square
Singapore 048763

Printed in the United States of America

Library of Congress Cataloging-in-Publication Data

Comparative policing : the struggle for democratization / M. R. Haberfeld, Ibrahim Cerrah, editors.
    p. cm.
Includes bibliographical references and index.
ISBN 978-1-4129-0547-3 (cloth: alk. paper)
ISBN 978-1-4129-0548-0 (pbk.: alk. paper)
   1. Police—Cross-cultural studies. 2. Law enforcement—Cross-cultural studies.
3. Democratization. I. Haberfeld, M. R. (Maria R.), 1957– II. Cerrah, Ibrahim.

HV7921.C6443 2008
363.2—dc22   2007029724

This book is printed on acid-free paper.

07   08   09   10   11   10   9   8   7   6   5   4   3   2   1

Acquisitions Editor:	Jerry Westby
Editorial Assistant:	Melissa Spor
Production Editor:	Catherine M. Chilton
Copy Editor:	Cate Huisman
Typesetter:	C&M Digitals (P) Ltd.
Proofreader:	Annette R. Van Deusen
Indexer:	Naomi Linzer
Cover Designer:	Candice Harman
Senior Marketing Manager:	Jennifer Reed

Contents

Preface

This book presents the reader with a unique insight into the struggles of police forces—from 12 different countries—as they move toward the democratization of their operations and responses.

Although we aimed to compile a list of countries that would represent a minitour around the world, it is still more of a sample rather than an ultimate and perfectly balanced portrayal of the existing situation.

The idea of presenting 12 different countries in a certain rank order representing the "Continuum of Democracy" is rooted in the presumption that policing is a profession that could and should be evaluated based on a number of parameters or qualifiers, regardless of its geographic location. Therefore, the level of adherence to these characteristics could and should be an indicator of the level of its democratic structure and operations.

A police force, being by its true nature an arm of the ruling government, will project not just the level of its democratic development as an institution but first and foremost the state of the democratic union in any given country. It is truly impossible to envision a democratic country with a nondemocratic police force or, vice versa, a democratic police force in a nondemocratic country. Based on this presumption, we created the Continuum of Democracy scale that allows for the differentiation between the levels of development or the current state of the struggle.

While it is always feasible to dream about the perfect Table of Contents, it is rarely possible to translate it into reality. As much as we attempted to reach out to many possible contributors, we were not always successful in securing the chapter contributions we wanted. However, we feel confident that the medley of countries and continents presented in the volume represents a quite balanced approach to comparative policing—balanced enough to allow us to identify the rank order of the countries on the Continuum of Democracy, or in more simple terms, the rank order represents what we feel is the placement of the country on a somewhat artificial scale that spans from the least to the most democratic approach to policing.

The most important function of a book preface is to explain to the readers the concepts and ideas behind the book they are going to peruse. Although the introduction in essence serves as a true explanation of the ideas presented in this volume, there is a very crucial aspect that the chapters do not address, and therefore it needs to be presented here.

We have attempted to explain the criteria that guided us—our decision-making process—in placing a given country at a certain place on the continuum from the least to the most democratic police force. These criteria included the following:

1. History of a democratic form of government

2. Level of corruption within governmental organizations and the oversight mechanisms in place

3. Scope of and response to civil disobedience

4. Organizational structures of police departments

5. Operational responses to terrorism and organized crime

In this introduction we outline the rationale for choosing the above set of criteria and the considerations that guided us in the selection process. However, we would be remiss if we didn't mention that none of our chapter contributors were involved in the decision-making process, and the editors are solely responsible for the placement of the countries on the Continuum of Democracy. It is important to acknowledge that the chapter contributors were provided with the set of criteria around which we would make the placement, and we asked them to provide us with an overview of the respective countries' policing systems, but we did not identify the projected place of the country with respect to its struggle toward democratization.

It might appear as a somewhat arbitrary decision that it was our *a priori* assumption that it would be almost impossible to get a decent contribution from our authors if they were told, ahead of time, that the country they would be writing about would represent, for example, the lowest rank on the Continuum of Democracy. This decision was not based on fear of some resentment that the authors might display but rather on the premise that such an artificial and rather arbitrary placing, prior to the overview of all the countries, would possibly skew the more objective depiction of the conditions.

After the chapters were submitted, similar considerations led us to feel that an open and democratic discussion with all the contributors would not render a consensus about where each country should be placed on the Continuum, as the editors themselves had some doubts about the ultimate place of certain countries on it. Hence, in this less than democratic manner, we decided that the ultimate responsibility for the placement would rest on the shoulders of the editors. Whatever argument the chapter contributors might have with this order will remain in the sphere of a more democratic exchange between the authors and the editors in the privacy of e-mail or verbal communication.

In light of this and similar considerations, the readers of this book, be they students of comparative policing or the academics already involved in the research on democratic transformations, will make their own decisions about the appropriateness of our choices. It is important to note that the criteria chosen to depict the struggles toward democracy are not the only possible parameters one could use to assess the stage of democratic policing in any country. There is no doubt that a host of other variables may possibly reflect and highlight the struggles and errors a country goes through in the transformation process. Nevertheless, it is imperative to identify the contours or baselines of the most potent variables, and we are confident that we managed to identify them.

We wish you, the reader, a pleasant journey through nearby or more remote places, depending where you come from and an intellectual journey that will leave you further pondering about the idea of policing.

—Maria (Maki) Haberfeld

—Ibrahim Cerrah

Acknowledgments

It is always a distinct pleasure to acknowledge people who were the inspiration and the driving force behind the book. We would like to start with one of the original three editors, Dr. Heath Grant, who for personal reasons needed to withdraw from the project.

Heath was one of the authors of the prospectus submitted to Sage outlining this project, and it was his skillful writing and talent that contributed, immensely, to the contract we received and to the product in front of the readers. His ideas, enthusiasm, and drive are unparalleled, and we missed his input and contributions.

The rather long list of peer reviewers was invaluable and helped us shape the contours and thoughts that were loosely dispersed in our academically oriented minds; each editor and author pulled toward a different direction; all were fully convinced that we would arrive at the same destination. Were it not for our insightful colleagues who reviewed the chapters, we would, undoubtedly, still be looking for the alternative detours. Therefore, in no particular order in terms of their contributions, we would like to express our profound gratitude to JoAnn Della-Gustina from Bridgewater State University, Charles L. Dreveskracht from Northeastern State University, Steven Engel from Georgia Southern University, Barry Goetz from Western Michigan University, Hidetoshi Hashimoto from University of Maryland, Otwin Marenin from Washington State University, Eugene McLaughlin from Open University, Steve Owen from Radford University, Peter Puelo from William Rainey Harper College, Phil Reichel from University of Northern Colorado, and Stanley Swart from University of North Florida. This book is the result of a truly peer-reviewed effort, and for this we are indeed very grateful.

Needless to say, all this would have not been possible without the amazing leadership of Jerry Westby, Sage's executive editor, and his assistants Melissa Spor and Vonessa Vondera as well as the editorial team. In addition, we would also like to thank our copy editor, Cate Huisman, who provided us with the most invaluable support, professional insight of the highest quality, and masterful editing that contributed greatly to the chapters' read-ability and comprehensibility. We are indebted to you for all your support and faith in our endeavors.

The last paragraph belongs to our family and friends, who should always realize that they are the real enablers behind our efforts to make a tiny dent in the struggle toward democratization.

1

Introduction

Policing Is Hard on Democracy, or Democracy Is Hard on Policing?

Maria (Maki) Haberfeld and Lior Gideon

Conceptual Framework

Global trends in terrorism and transnational crime have direct effects in both local *and* international contexts. Although the problems of terrorism, organized crime, and corruption are not new phenomena anywhere in the world, governments have shifted the nature of their law enforcement structures, functions, and practices in manners that reflect local internal and external political and socioeconomic forces. In many countries, responses to serious threats have typically resulted in an increasingly centralized and specialized force, even to the extent of merging police and military responsibilities. Such responses in times of threat have occurred in even strongly democratic societies, such as the United Kingdom, even though it has long been taken for granted that the roles of the military and police should be clearly separated in societies built upon the basic tenets of democratic governance (Kraska, 2001).

Issues of national security involving threats from other nations fall clearly within the domain of military responsibility, whereas those surfacing as a result of general criminality or lawlessness are the responsibility of local law enforcement. Where the functions and responsibilities of the military and police have merged, governments are characterized as repressive by those claiming to operate according to the principles of the rule of law. Within a changing global context, the difficulty of balancing due process and public safety needs is a paramount issue that challenges the very legitimacy that is fundamental to the effectiveness of law enforcement. Drawing upon the lessons learned and best practices of comparative policing systems is particularly important in contemporary times.

The extent to which changes in perceptions of the legitimacy of authorities affect the level of compliance with the law in everyday lives is an important question, particularly where we are dealing with countries at different levels of democratization (Cohn & White, 1997). Much of this perceived legitimacy is based on notions of government transparency and citizens' beliefs that they can participate in the establishment of a lawful society both on an individual community level and at the level of national social change.

For example, although democratic rule has returned to many countries in Latin America, "Relations between governments and society, particularly the poor and marginalized members of society, have been characterized by the illegal and arbitrary use of power" (Pinheiro de Souza, 2006, p. 1). While the end of dictatorships brought hopes of human rights and a rule of a lawful society, the reality is that there is a significant disparity in many of these countries "between the letter of the bill of rights, present in many constitutions, and law enforcement application and practice" (Pinheiro de Souza, 2006, p. 1). Access to "justice" in many cases is bought with money, a tool more available to narcotraffickers than the average citizen.

Many countries throughout the world have accepted a semimilitary model of policing in which police administrators see their role as fighting the enemy (crime) regardless of the constraints on arbitrary enforcement meant to be offered by the law and the criminal justice system. Although decreasing, this military ethos has helped to maintain a legal context in which the practices of torture and use of deadly force to suppress social movements has not disappeared. The use of special squads is common throughout Latin America, with many of them becoming the law unto themselves. Specifically this is illustrated in the Brazilian case.

A driving force behind the abuses and citizen perceptions of police impunity in general stems from corruption, beginning with low-level bribes and extending to include protection rackets. Chevigny (1999, p. 62) argues that corruption and police brutality are interrelated because "together they show the power of the police, their independence from the rest of the criminal justice system, and their ability to administer justice as they see fit." Paying bribes is a common practice in countries such as Mexico, not just as a means of bypassing the criminal justice system but also for avoiding a potential beating at the hands of officers for those who refuse to pay.

The above legal context will obviously not go a long way toward socializing citizens as to the value of rules and laws and their enforcement in society. The importance of this cannot be underestimated; legislation is meaningless unless the government is able to "anticipate that the citizenry as a whole will . . . generally observe the body of rules promulgated" (Fuller, 1964, p. 201). Given the fact that laws are created to enforce behavior that many people would often rather avoid, legal authorities are best served by "establish[ing] and maintain[ing] conditions that lead the public generally to accept their decisions and policies" (Tyler, 1990, p. 19). A government that needs to rely on coercion as a means of maintaining compliance with the law will be faced with an insurmountable task, both in terms of resources and practicality.

In a climate of global change, in which traditional boundaries and the presence of a clearly defined enemy are no longer realities, law enforcement has also tried to evolve internationally. For example, from a U.S. perspective, turning points such as the passage of the Patriot Act and the continued reexamination of the Posse Commitatus Act have led to the further blurring of military/police lines that began after the Cold War with the military taking on some drug enforcement responsibilities.

As policing moves away from its traditional responsibilities related to the control of local disorder, it will become increasingly less effective in meeting its objectives. Although it is easy to see how local law enforcement has seen a need to change its practices—viewing itself as the front line and first responder in the war on terror—the danger of further building a military ethos for policing is that it challenges the very legitimacy that makes it effective as noted above. Countries that have battled issues of terrorism for many years, such as Israel, recognize this distinction, seeing law enforcement as a support function to the "takeover" and engagement units responding to terror.

A growing body of useful comparative policing texts introduces the diversity and complexity of policing systems around the world. Important works such as *Policing Change, Changing Police* (Marenin, 1996) provide an overview of selected policing systems, highlighting the relationship between police and the state. Works such as Mathieu Deflem's *Policing World Society* (1998) explore the challenges and issues involved in cross-national cooperation and international policing. Recent efforts such as Das and Lab's *International Perspectives on Community Policing and Crime Prevention* (2002) contrast community policing models in countries as diverse as Canada, Israel, India, and Mexico. Other approaches, such as Ebbe's *Comparative & Criminal Justice Systems* (1996) and Dammer, Fairchild, and Albanese's *Comparative Criminal Justice* (2006) examine police systems within the context of the entire criminal justice system.

These efforts have provided important foundations for the fields of comparative policing and international policing studies, yet the following chapters will offer still new directions. In addition to providing a comprehensive comparative context of policing in the selected countries that will serve as a basic introduction to new students to the field, the material is presented in such a way as to highlight the critical global trends discussed, and thus link the comparative framework with current developments in the fields of democratic governance, legitimacy, human rights, and transnational crime.

The book will also provide some important political, social, and historical contextual information, so that connections between external authorizing environments and police responses can be introduced to the readers.

Topics introduced and discussed through the chapters circle around the following themes:

- Level of democratization
- Police professionalism, including preparation to perform the police function, merit recruitment, formal training, structured career advancement, systematic discipline, full-time service, extent to which police operations are conducted in public, and specialization
- Community oriented policing
- Use of force
- Accountability
- Human rights
- Forces for change and success/failure of these responses
- Responses to terrorism and organized crime, including the effects of such responses on legitimacy of the police force
- The extent of collaboration between the military and local policing

Countries have been selected for inclusion in the volume across a continuum of the democratization of policing practices. The country chapters are presented in a certain order that reflects their position on what the editors defined as the "Continuum of Democracy." By introducing the placement of countries on a continuum, the editors illustrate how no country can operate perfectly within a perfect rule of law. Social forces and the negative actions of human agents can move a country's law enforcement agencies away from democratic governance operating with community consensus and toward more coercive, autocratic practices. Being cognizant of these factors in the context of emerging responses to global terrorism and crime is a necessity and a key ingredient of the current volume.

The Continuum of Democracy: An Innovative Approach

To facilitate cross-fertilization of best practices and lessons learned with respect to policing, a democratization continuum is operationalized, and each country is analyzed along the continuum. Again, each country was selected based on its potential applicability to the continuum and the degree to which best practices and/or lessons learned could be drawn according to the book's themes, as described above.

A country's position on the Continuum of Democracy is therefore operationalized as its overall score based on the following five dimensions: the history of a democratic form of government, the level of corruption within governmental organizations and the oversight mechanisms in place, the scope of and response to civil disobedience, organizational structures of police departments, and operational responses to terrorism and organized crime.

On the scale of 1 to 12 (based on the number of countries represented in this book) the editors assigned a rank order to each country as a representation of the number they scored, measured on the five practical dimensions representing the operationalized definition of the Continuum of Democracy. Therefore, they identified China as the country that scored the lowest on each of the five dimensions, because it has no history of a democratic form of government, a high level of corruption in governmental organizations, and a history of a violent response to civil disobedience, representing a rather archaic structure of policing and a repressive response to problems of terrorism and organized crime. On the other end of the spectrum, representing the highest level on the continuum, they placed the United States, followed closely by or even competing for first place with Canada. Although the history of its democratic government is not as long as the United Kingdom's, the decentralized nature of the U.S. police force, the oversight mechanisms in place to deal with instances of corruption, the accountability required when dealing with civil disobedience, the structure of police organizations, and the modalities of response to the phenomenon of organized crime and terrorism earned the country its first place on the Continuum. It is imperative to note that the five dimensions are measured within the context of policing in the most recent years; therefore, the history of a democratic form of government (the first dimension) provides a context for the other four dimensions.

Additional Dimensions of the Innovative Comparative Approach

It is with the above framework in mind that international scholars have written chapters examining the differing contexts and police practices throughout the world. Although this edited work will allow for the traditional international comparisons common to current collections in the field, it is unique in that it is presented from an analytical context that challenges readers to critically assess global trends in policing. Based upon a review and operationalization of the contents provided throughout the chapter, readers and students of policing can attempt to identify the best universal practices (applicable to any democratic setting) for dealing with newly emerging issues based on the best practices and issues of the discussed countries. However, the need to clearly separate the roles of police and military, and the continued transparency and accountability of local law enforcement, will remain a central focus in international challenges to attain legitimacy. The reader will also be introduced to the basic principles of human rights law and practice in order to frame all of the above discussion.

Another central innovation of this work's conceptual framework is that it highlights how global trends in terrorism and transnational crime affect both local and international policing contexts. For example, departments internationally are rapidly trying to deal with the new threat posed by terrorism on the local level through first response, investigation, and coordination with other local and federal jurisdictions. Coordination with international policing efforts will also be essential. Therefore, rather than treating comparative and international policing as wholly separate fields as found in the rest of the literature, the volume's editors draw these linkages; the final section of the text thus offers an overview of current trends in international policing as a possible, partial, and practical solution to the democratization of the police process across the world.

Countries represented in this volume have been selected based upon both geographical location and underlying issues that can inform the larger analytical context of the work. By taking a brief look at some critical issues and concepts outlined in the following chapters, it is possible to compile a list of fundamental themes that shape and influence the democratization process of policing in each of the depicted countries. The same list however can be easily applied to many other countries struggling to reconcile the notion that democracy is hard on policing and that policing is hard on democracy.

The globalization process exposes many countries that have had marginal exposure to the Western world to rapid and demanding social change and thus new social and governmental challenges. Consequently, law enforcement, as one of the greatest social experiments, is a crucial indicator of the level of democratization.

In very concrete and operational terms, a country's level of democracy can be assessed by examining its law enforcement system(s) and its *modus operandi*. Similarly, the key to the level of developmental and economic success of the Western nations is their adoption of democracy. Within such nations, the police operate under internationally recognized democratic principles to ensure a harmonious society in which political, social, and economic life can flourish (Crawshaw et al., 2006, as cited in Chapter 5).

Cullen and McDonald (2008) argue in Chapter 5 that "democratic civilian policing is an essential component of good governance operating under a range of basic principles" (p. 121). Further argument advances the place of the military as having the primary role in securing the state from external threats, while the civilian police is destined to have "a primary and accountable role in citizen security and serving the law" (p. 121). Extraordinary circumstances, they argue, may require the military personnel to provide assistance to the civilian police in joint public safety operations.

In many countries, responses to serious threats have typically resulted in an increasingly centralized and specialized force, even to the extent of merging police and military responsibilities. When criminal threats, such as those in Israel, Brazil, Mexico, and Sierra Leone, become associated with national threats, the due process model tends to lose its validity, making room for a more centralized rigid police force with special engagement units that respond to terrorist activities.

Law enforcement does not operate in a vacuum. As becomes quite apparent from the pages of this volume, law enforcement reflects the level of democracy in a country, and the democracy of the country is reflected in its organizational structure and operations. Consequently, countries with very long histories of democracy, like the United States, United Kingdom, Canada, and France, will have more democratic policing that cherishes due process over crime control. In fact, as outlined in Chapter 13 on the U.S. police systems, law enforcement in the United States was created on the basis of separating civilian police forces from the central government. Although law enforcement in the United States now is connected to the local government (i.e., the local police) and shares information with other federal agencies, the overall perception is that of democratic policing and the due process model. On the other hand, in countries in transition, like Sierra Leone, Russia, Brazil, and Mexico, it becomes apparent that law enforcement struggles in its attempt to digest and assimilate the concepts of democracy in general, and in particular the ideas embedded in democratic policing, into the standard operating procedures of daily enforcement.

As argued by Gideon and colleagues in Chapter 9 on Israel, law enforcement agencies reflect the priorities, divisions, and social economic conditions of societies in which they exist. Consequently, police forces will demonstrate adaptation to the changing and growing needs of their respective societies. Similarly, Dupont ends Chapter 10 on the French police arguing that "police organizations respond and their reforms are responses to contextual stimuli" (p. 272). Frequently, as argued in the cases of the United Kingdom, United States, France, Turkey, and Russia, such adaptations are also an outcome of a growing concern about threats to homeland security by broadly defined terrorist activities. Such adaptations will shift the pendulum of democratic policing toward a more centralized and thus less democratic police force, departing from due process as can be seen in the Russian Republic, the United States in the days following September 11, Israel, the United Kingdom, Turkey, and France. However, it is not just the threat of assorted terrorist activities that influences and changes the shapes of democratic policing. Countries like Mexico and Brazil that struggle constantly with organized crime, drug cartels, and high violent crime rates experience similar transformations. These are good examples of times where adaptation and customization to an event, a series of events, or a more institutionalized challenge take over the noble cause of protecting civil rights, and the need to maintain public order and safety gains an elevated priority—no matter what the cost.

The primary duty of the police is to maintain social control within the community. What distinguishes the police from the public is their ability to use coercive force to control any given situation. However, such force will be displayed in its most benign version if the public complies with the demanded status quo. In Chapter 5 on the Sierra Leone police, Cullen and McDonald present President Tejan-Kabbah's vision of the role of the public vis-à-vis police work: "In order that . . . police officers can successfully fulfill our expectations, it is essential that all people of Sierra Leone help and support them at all times" (p. 129).

It is important to remember, in this context, that although the primary goal of the police is to maintain social control, the extent and nature of this control is guided by the governing body of any given country. As Haberfeld (2002, p. 15) notes, "Police forces, throughout the history, served and protected the ruler, the king, the politician, and never the public. The safety and security of the public was always secondary to the safety and security of the ruler, king, politician." This is the case in well-established democracies as well, and it can be better understood by examining the origin of the word *police,* which stems from the Greek word *polis,* meaning government center (see Haberfeld, 2002, p. 15). Consequently, while a law enforcement agency may operate in a democratic society, it is by definition not a democratic organization, and its goals are thus not democratic. Yes, it may serve democracy and its goals by maintaining public order, social control, and—more important—the status quo, but it should not be perceived as a democratic institution. Specifically, protecting the status quo suggests that law enforcement serves the government and its purposes. This is essential to understanding the swing of the pendulum of democracy with the challenges it faces: the shift in perception from a civilian police to a more militaristic organization with militaristic goals departing from due process and thus departing at times from the democratic principles.

As portrayed in the following chapters, and also mentioned in the onset of this chapter, responses to serious threats have typically resulted in an increasingly centralized and specialized force, even in the context of merging police and military responsibilities.

In this time and age, the public's demand and expectations of the criminal justice system may seem contradictory. Demands for more control are constantly rising versus demands for less violation of privacy. It is in this context that we raise the question: Is policing hard on democracy, or is democracy hard on policing? One good example of this query is the New York City Police Department's random checks at subway stations after the terror attack on the underground in the United Kingdom in 2005. The overall consensus, at least on the part of the operational police response, seemed to require an aggressive response to secure the subway system, while on the other hand a large segment of the public was infuriated with the police invading their privacy by searching their belongings.

"Democratic Policing"

Democratic policing is "a form of policing in which the police are accountable to the law and the community, respect the rights and guarantee the security of all citizens in a non-discriminatory manner" (de Mesquita Neto, 2001, p. 2). Furthermore, democratic police organizations function within and are accountable to the rule of law. The rule of the law refers to the idea that equality and justice are inseparable and that laws are applied equally to everyone. It is the standard that guides decision making throughout the criminal justice system.

In comparison to any other group in a democratic society, law enforcement personnel are supposed to symbolize tolerance and acceptance of diversity. Teaching officers how to enable their views and beliefs to coexist with the different views and beliefs of other citizens—and other officers— is one of the greatest challenges in law enforcement training. With that in mind and on similar levels, it is argued that teaching officers to preserve democratic principles while displaying firearms is a difficult task that needs to be carefully and constantly balanced. Indeed, Cullen and McDonald argue in Chapter 5 that "unfortunately, democracy is a complicated and often elusive phenomenon" (p. 122). When such balance is not achieved, then corruption may emerge, pushing democracy aside, as demonstrated in Chapters 3–6 on Brazil, Mexico, Sierra Leone, and Russia, respectively.

A police force is a paramilitary organization by nature and is expected to be highly professional. Therefore, an important notation that readers need to keep in mind throughout this volume is that more frequently than not, police forces are a by-product of military regiments, where police officers are recruited directly from the military or have some military training in their background. This is a phenomenon that can be traced to the Roman Empire; it has its roots in the Praetorian Guard created by Augustus Caesar and follows through until the establishment of the first modern police force by Sir Robert Peel. Similar developments can be traced in the case of police forces in Israel, Sierra Leon, Mexico, Brazil, Russia, France, India, and many other countries that are not covered in this volume.

As an outcome of such historical developments, frequently law enforcement agencies are viewed as centralized, paramilitary organizations. As such, their ability to adapt and change this image in the face of changing social and political environments presents a formidable challenge, not just for the organization itself but also for the individual police officer.

Law enforcement officers have evolved into ever-broadened generalists who must instantly answer a wide range of difficult questions and take prompt and correct action, all in the name of social control and public safety. Therefore, the public expects its police to handle almost any problem that surfaces. While police officers must respond to situations within the parameters of the law, they should have the freedom to make a decision based on the circumstances of a particular case. Decisions by police officers are likely to have profound implications for the people with whom they come in contact and for the officers themselves. These decisions often affect people's liberty and personal safety. Often it is precisely during this critical, split-second decision-making process that democracy becomes hard on policing.

On the other hand, police response to society's needs, and more specifically during the times of increased public order and security needs, may hit a brick wall when it faces the challenge of Haberfeld's question: "To enforce or not to enforce, that is the question" (2002, p. 4). Once we agree to the fact that laws should be enforced to maintain public order and safety, a different question needs to be asked: "How to enforce?" Such a question is critical to the discussion of democratic policing and the ways in which law enforcement agencies in different countries interpret the need and magnitude of desired enforcement. It is here that we pose the question: Is policing hard on democracy? Or maybe democracy is hard on policing? As Haberfeld posits, "I don't know the key to success but the key to failure is trying to please everybody" (2002, p. 153).

As previously mentioned, the primary duty of the police is to maintain social control within the community. This rationale has its long roots in the early days of policing, when police officers served the king, the ruler, and the politician. It is within this historical context that the pendulum shifts between crime control and due process or democratic policing, as illustrated in Chapters 2–6 on China, Brazil, Mexico, Sierra Leone, and Russia, respectively. As demonstrated in all the 12 countries whose police forces are presented in this volume, police react to social change. In fact, policing is known to be one of the greatest social experiments ever to exist. Even in countries that can be referred to as strong and established democracies, when the need to maintain public safety and protect against internal and external threats becomes a main priority for its governing bodies, some basic civil rights are being abandoned, and new policing practices emerge to adjust to the new priorities. The emergence of the new deployment techniques and police practices is justified for the sake of maintaining public safety and social order, or at least this is how it is presented to the larger audience on the receiving end.

Within the context of crime globalization, law enforcement agencies around the world became exposed to new challenges that include new forms and scopes of criminal activities, which mandate new methods of crime investigation, collaboration, and intelligence sharing, in particular with regard to terrorism and organized crime. These developments become apparent in countries like China, Russia, Sierra Leone, and Turkey. Additionally and independently, globalization came along with democratization, the ambition to leave behind (in the past) the nondemocratic or less democratic forms of government, and a desire to transition to the principles of democracy. This transition, as depicted in Chapters 3–6 on Brazil, Mexico, Sierra Leone, and Russia and in many ways in Chapter 2 on China (although it is not a democracy), is a long and complex process that frequently causes law enforcement leadership to stray, sometimes unintentionally, from the democratic principles that the country declared in its new hymn, one which usually espouses it ambitions and goals.

The attempt to examine law enforcement organizations by placing them on the Continuum of Democracy is a disputable challenge. As mentioned, a law enforcement force by itself is a nondemocratic organization.

Although on the surface the police aims to serve the public through order maintenance, it is always subjected to the ultimate vision of the current governing body, which is also the body that creates and passes the laws and the rules. This point is best demonstrated by Benoît Dupont in Chapter 10, who argues that France often placed the interests of the state above those of the public. A law enforcement agency begins as a centralized organization that shifts toward decentralization as a result of exposure to globalization and the need for change; however, it rapidly and almost happily regresses to the centralized model to adapt to the newly emerged challenges in the face of increasing crime, terrorism, and threat to the regime/government.

By examining the following chapters, it becomes more apparent how the pendulum of democracy swings back and forth between the historically defined military designation and the present and future idealistic orientation of democratic policing. In the process of transition from totalitarian regimes toward a democratic form of government, all the newly emerged democracies, such as Sierra Leone, Russia, Brazil, and Mexico (and in many ways also China in the era of globalization) are experiencing rising levels of crime due to the vacuum created during the shifting processes. During such transitions, police are perceived as lacking the ability to function, corrupt, and consequently dysfunctional and almost an obstacle to the democratization process.

Frequently, such sentiments cause a reverse reaction. As an adaptation, law enforcement operations shift back into a more centralized model with stricter and more invasive governmental oversight and intervention. This in turn may be viewed as nondemocratic.

To summarize, when reading through the chapters of this volume, readers are asked to consider five dimensions that will assist them to critically evaluate and analyze the countries placed on the Continuum of Democracy. The editors argue that the level of democratic policing can and should be defined by the factors associated with the five dimensions. It is by no means an empirically grounded assertion but rather a testimonial approach to sociopolitical and economic features researched by the volume's contributors. The editors are open to arguments and criticisms related to a given country's place on the democratic scale of policing. It is, however, imperative to look at these five dimensions:

1. History of a democratic form of government

2. Level of corruption within governmental organizations and the oversight mechanisms in place

3. Scope of and response to civil disobedience

4. Organizational structures of police departments

5. Operational responses to terrorism and organized crime

Readers must recognize and acknowledge the relative contribution of these five dimensions to the idea of democratic policing. Rather than imposing on the reader a strict and inflexible ranking order, the authors have opted for a tentative placement of the countries on the Continuum of Democracy, and have opened the floor for an academic discussion that will, undoubtedly, change and be heavily influenced by the current events at any given time and place that will accompany the reading of the chapters.

References

Chevigny, P. (1999). *Defining the role of the police in Latin America: The (un)rule of law*. Notre Dame, IN: University of Notre Dame Press.

Cohn, E. S., & White, S. O. (1997). Legal socialization effects on democratization. *International Social Science Journal, 49,* 151–171.

Dammer, H. R., Fairchild, E., & Albanese, J. S. (2006). *Comparative criminal justice* (3rd ed.). Belmont, CA: Thomson/Wadsworth Publishing.

Das, D. K., & Lab, S. P. (2002) *International perspectives on community policing and crime prevention.* Upper Saddle River, NJ: Prentice-Hall.

Deflem, M. (1998). *Policing world society: Historical foundations of international police cooperation.* New York: Oxford University Press.

Ebbe, O. N. (1996). *Comparative & international criminal justice systems, policing, judiciary and corrections.* Boston: Butterworth-Heinemann.

Fuller, L. (1964). *The morality of law.* New Haven, CT: Yale University Press.

Haberfeld, M. R. (2002). *Critical issues in police training.* Upper Saddle River, NJ: Prentice-Hall.

Kraska, P. B. (Ed.). (2001). *Militarizing the American criminal justice system: The changing roles of the armed forces and the police.* Boston, MA: Northeastern University Press.

Marenin, O. (1996). *Policing change, changing police: International perspectives.* London: Routledge.

de Mesquita Neto, P. (2001, March). *Paths toward democratic policing in Latin America.* Paper presented at the International Workshop on Human Rights and the Police in Transitional Countries, Copenhagen, Denmark.

Pinheiro De Souza, A. (2006). Narcoterrorism in Latin America: A Brazilian perspective. Retrieved May 25, 2007, from http://handle.dtic.mil/100.2/ ADA456509

Tyler, T. (1990). *Why people obey law.* New Haven, CT: Yale University Press.

2

The Chinese Police

Yue Ma

History of the Police

The modern Chinese police did not come into being until the late nineteenth century. Primitive forms of order maintenance, however, can be traced to China's very first dynasty that existed more than 4,000 years ago. The first emperor of the Xia dynasty (2100 to 1600 BCE) named an official known as the *Si Tu* to be responsible for maintaining order in the tribal state. Emperor Shun is reported to have said that if people were not friendly with each other and did not use restraints in their relationship, hatreds would develop and social disturbances would follow. The emperor therefore instructed the Si Tu to maintain order by eliminating hatreds and mediating disputes among tribal members. In addition to the Si Tu, a post of *Shi* was also created. The Shi was given the responsibility of operating jails and investigating crimes committed by tribal members (Yu, 1985b).

The next significant development of law enforcement came in the Qin and Han dynasties. During the Qin dynasty (221–206 BCE), China became a unified country. To strengthen the rule over the newly unified country, the Qin emperors developed various law enforcement mechanisms. The Qin dynasty, however, was a short-lived one. It lasted only 15 years. In contrast to the short life of the Qin dynasty, the Han dynasty (206 BCE–220 CE) lasted for more than 400 years. The Han dynasty was characterized by unprecedented economic prosperity and political stability. The law enforcement mechanisms originated in the Qin dynasty gained significant development in the Han dynasty.

During the Qin dynasty, an official known as *Zhongwei* was given the responsibility for maintaining law and order in the capital. The responsibilities of Zhongwei included patrolling city streets, investigating crimes, and handling emergency situations. Zhongwei was assisted in his duties by subordinate officers (Liu, 1985). By the time of the Han dynasty, the capital city, *Changan*, had developed into a populous city with about 80,800 households and 246,200 inhabitants.[1] It was estimated that Changan's population at its peak reached 500,000 (Gao, 1985a). As the population rose, crime increased. According to historical records, there were numerous criminal gangs in the city. The criminal gangs were engaged in all kinds of crimes, including theft, robbery, burglary, contract killings, and assassinations (Gao, 1985a).

The Han emperors took various measures to strengthen the law enforcement mechanisms in the capital and at the local levels. The chief administrative official in the capital was called *Changanling*. Maintaining law and order was one of the main responsibilities of Changanling. Changanling appointed an official called *Xianwei* to be the chief law enforcement officer of the capital. Under the command of Xianwei, there were officers known as *Xianyu*. Xianyu were responsible for patrolling city streets, maintaining order, investigating crimes, and apprehending offenders. To ensure that Xianyu perform their duties diligently, the Han emperors on several occasions raised the rank and the salaries of Xianyu (Gao, 1985a). In the capital, there were also security agencies in charge of protecting the emperor, the royal family, and the high-ranking government officials.

Outside the capital, it fell upon the administrative official of each prefecture to maintain the peace and order within his jurisdiction. The chief administrative official usually appointed a deputy administrative official to be in charge of maintaining law and order. *Ting*, the basic law enforcement agency, was established in villages, towns, marketplaces, ports, and along post roads. Ting was headed by a Ting chief. The Ting chief was usually selected from among retired army officers. To qualify for the position, the candidate had to be literate, have military knowledge, and know how to operate weapons. The Ting chief had line officers under his command. The responsibilities of Ting included patrolling streets to prevent the breach of peace, apprehending criminals, and producing apprehended criminals before the local court for adjudication (Gao, 1985b).

During the Qin and Han dynasties, the household registration system and the frank pledge system began to develop. The law required that all people be registered with the government. A person must be registered shortly after his birth, and the registration remained in effect until his death. If a person moved away from his original place of registration, he had to report his movement to the government, so that he could be registered in the place to which he moved. The household registration system was developed originally to facilitate the government's efforts to collect taxes and recruit laborers. It later became a social control mechanism. The government took the household registration seriously. Under the law of both Qin and Han dynasties, failure to register under the household registration system was an offense punishable by criminal penalty. In the Han dynasty, the government conducted a census annually to ensure the accuracy of the household registrations.

Under the frank pledge system, every five families were grouped into a unit called *Wu*. Wu was based on the principles of self-help and collective responsibility. Wu members were responsible for policing each other to ensure that no members would commit crime. If any Wu member committed a crime, it was the responsibility of other members to apprehend the offender and present him before the court for punishment. The law imposed a stiff penalty for Wu members' failure to fulfill their obligation. Failure to apprehend the offender would subject Wu members to the same punishment that would have been meted out for the offender. Historical records show that because of the severe penalty stipulated, Wu members were quite diligent in their efforts to report crimes and apprehend offenders. Wu was not only a self-policing but also a self-help system. The law imposed on Wu members the duty to protect each other and assist each other at the time of crime victimization. Wu members were subject to criminal punishment for failure to render assistance to their fellow members at the time of crime victimization (Liu, 1985).

After the Qin and Han dynasties, in the ensuing 1691 years, China was ruled by several different dynasties before the end of the era of imperial dynasties in 1911. The system developed in the Qin and Han dynasties, with some variations, remained the basic law enforcement system in all dynasties (Cao & Qi, 1985; Dutton, 1992; Han & Cao, 1985; McKnight, 1992; Yu, 1985a, 1985b, 1985c). The next significant development in law enforcement did not come until the late nineteenth century, when the concept of modern police was introduced to China.

The Qing dynasty (1644–1911 CE) was the last dynasty in China's history. The law enforcement system of the Qing dynasty bore remarkable resemblance to the system that had been developed nearly 2000 years before in the Qin and Han dynasties. In the capital, various security agencies were established to perform duties ranging from protecting the emperor and high-ranking government officials to maintaining law and order and apprehending criminals. Outside the capital, provincial and county administrative chiefs were given the primary responsibility for maintaining law and order in their localities. The frank pledge and the household registration system remained the main control mechanisms at the local levels. The frank pledge in the Qing dynasty was known as *Bao-Jia*. In the tightly knit Bao-Jia system, every ten households formed a *Pai*, which was headed by a Pai chief. Every ten Pais formed a *Jia*, which was headed by a Jia chief. Every ten Jias formed a *Bao*. The Bao chief was the chief law enforcement officer at the local level.

The traditional law enforcement system remained in force until the end of the nineteenth century. The nineteenth century saw Western powers' invasion of China and China's turning into a semifeudal and semicolonial society. The Western powers, after a series of aggressive wars, forced the defeated Qing government to sign numerous unequal treaties. A notable clause in these treaties was the demand to establish concessions in China. By the end of the nineteenth century, England, France, Germany, and Japan all had established concessions in major Chinese cities and ports. Concessions could not be reached by Chinese law. There the Western powers acquired the authority to exercise the extraterritorial jurisdiction. Under the authority, the Western powers set up their own judicial systems and applied their homeland laws. To maintain law and order within the concessions, the Western countries introduced the modern police system that had emerged not long before in their homelands. The model of modern police thus was introduced to China as a result of imperialist aggression and colonialization.

At the beginning of the twentieth century, the Qing dynasty entered its waning days. To save the disintegrating dynasty, the Qing government was in urgent need of finding new tools to suppress rebellions against the regime. Inspired by the police system established within concessions, the Qing government began to establish its own modern police after the model of Western police. In 1901, the Qing government established the first modern police agency, the Capital Police Bureau. The Capital Police Bureau was placed directly under the command of the emperor. Shortly after the establishment of the Capital Police Bureau, the Qing government ordered that police agencies be established in all provinces and major cities. In 1905, the Ministry of Police, which was given the responsibility of directing the police operation throughout the country, was established.

Though the dynasty was soon to expire, the police system gained quite noticeable development in the remaining days of the dynasty. By 1911, when the Qing dynasty was overthrown, the Capital Police Bureau had developed into a fairly sophisticated force. The bureau boasted of 418 high-ranking officials and 3,843 police officers; it had a number of specialized divisions, including patrol division, detective division, police training division, and police disciplinary division. Notably there was even a police academy established in the capital (Chang, 1985a).

After the demise of the Qing dynasty in 1911 and before the founding of the People's Republic in 1949, China was ruled by the Northern Warlords (1911–1927) and the Guomintang government (1927–1949). The modern police gained further development in this period. A centralized police system emerged. A ministry responsible for police affairs was established in the central government. Police bureaus were established at the provincial and county levels and in major cities. Apart from the regular police force, special police were also established. For instance, under the rule of the Guomintang, there were mine police, railroad police, fishing zone police, highway patrol police, taxation police, and forest police (Chang, 1985a, 1985b; Wakeman, 1995).

The Guomintang government was overthrown in 1949. After the founding of the People's Republic of China, the communist government abolished the old police system and declared that it would establish a police system of its own. The government established the police system by referring to the police model developed by the Communist Party in the revolutionary base areas. Despite the government's claim that it had created a brand new system, the police system established bore resemblance to the police systems that existed before. At the top of the police hierarchy was the Ministry of Public Security. Under the ministry, police bureaus were established at the provincial and county levels. The Ministry of Public Security was responsible for directing and coordinating the police operation throughout the country. In the 1950s and early 1960s, the police did an impressive job in crime control and prevention. The crime rate was low. There was, however, hardly any law governing the police operation. There was neither criminal law nor criminal procedure law. The police operation was governed mainly by party policies and nonpublished internal documents. During this period, the National People's Congress, the Chinese legislature, enacted the Police Regulation of 1957. But the regulation contained only 11 provisions, falling far short of providing necessary guidance to a police force that shouldered the responsibility of policing the world's most populous country.

Police Organization

The current framework of the police organization is laid down in the Police Law of 1995. The Police Law of 1995 is a comprehensive piece of legislation that contains provisions governing almost all aspects of policing, including police organization, police functions, police recruitment, police training, police administration and management, police powers, police disciplinary procedures, and police civil and criminal liability. According to the Police Law, the Chinese police consists of five components or five police forces. The five components are public security police, state security police, prison police, judicial police of the people's courts, and judicial police of people's procuratorates. (The terms *procurator* and *procuratorate*, as used in official translations of Chinese legal documents, refer to a prosecutor and prosecution service respectively.) Each police force performs specific functions prescribed by the law and each has its own organizational hierarchy.

Public Security Police

Public security police are the largest component of the Chinese police. Public security police perform a wide range of ordinary police functions, including investigating crimes, maintaining public order, directing traffic, conducting patrols, administering the household registration system and the citizen identification card system, providing guidance to mass-line crime prevention and security organizations, and providing services to community residents. (The *mass line* refers to a long-standing Chinese policy, especially in Mao's era, that the police must rely on the cooperation of the masses in their work. The so-called mass-line crime prevention organizations are organizations like neighborhood committees and security committees participated in by ordinary citizens.) Public security police are the most visible component of the Chinese police. When people talk about the police they usually think of public security police.

The organizational structure of public security police is set up within the framework of administrative structure of the government (see Figure 2.1). In the current government administrative structure, there are 22 provinces (not including Taiwan), five autonomous regions, and four municipalities directly under the central government.[2] Within each province and autonomous region, there are counties and municipalities directly under the provincial government. Within each municipality directly under the central government, there are counties and districts. The police hierarchy is set within this administrative structure.

At the top of the police hierarchy is the Ministry of Public Security, representing the central control by the national government. The ministry is responsible for directing and coordinating the police operation throughout the country. Under the Ministry of Public Security, in each province, autonomous region, and municipality directly under the central government, there is a provincial-level public security bureau. Under the provincial level public security bureau, in provinces and autonomous regions there are municipal and county public security agencies; in municipalities directly under the central government there are district and county public security agencies. At the bottom of the police hierarchy are numerous police stations that are set up in larger communities across the country.

Each local public security agency is accountable to the immediately higher public security agency and the corresponding local government. For instance, a provincial public security agency is accountable to the Ministry of Public Security and the provincial government, whereas a county public security agency is accountable to the provincial public security agency and the county government. There is no legislation specifically allocating the responsibilities of the central government and local governments in the police administration. In practice, the Ministry of Public Security is responsible for setting professional standards, making rules and regulations, directing and coordinating major criminal investigations, and providing assistance such as crime detection and forensic analyses to local police agencies. Local governments are responsible for determining the size of the police force needed in their localities, providing budgets for the police, and setting local law enforcement priorities. According to Chinese police experts, the dual leadership structure has the advantage of keeping the nation's police under centralized control and meanwhile permitting local governments the autonomy to determine local law enforcement priorities and how to best use law enforcement resources to address the local law and order concerns (Ma & Tian, 1995; Xu, 1995).

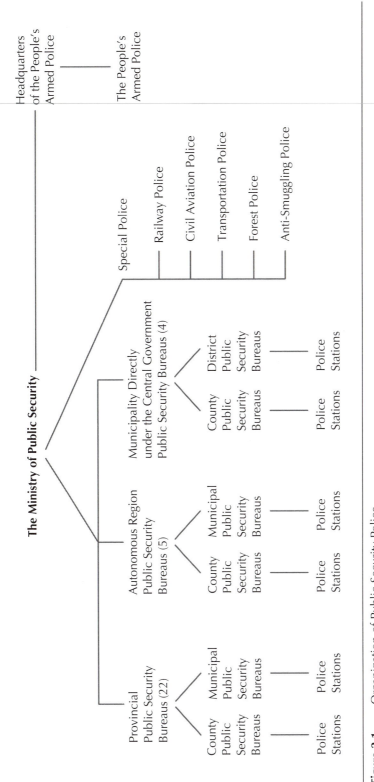

Figure 2.1 Organization of Public Security Police

In addition to regular public security police, there are also five special public security police. The five special police are railway police, transportation police, civil aviation police, forest police, and antismuggling police. The special police bear the responsibility of enforcing the law in their special professional fields. Railway police are responsible for maintaining order on trains and in train stations and investigating crimes committed in relation to railway transportation. Civil aviation police maintain order in airports and provide security for civilian air transportation. Forest police patrol national forests to prevent forest fires, poaching, illegal cutting, and other activities prohibited by the State Forest Law. Transportation police are responsible for providing security in waterway transportation. Antismuggling police are responsible for preventing smuggling.

The joint administrative structure applies to the special police as well. Administratively, the special police are organized within relevant government ministries. Railway police are organized within the Ministry of Railways. Transportation police are organized within the Ministry of Transportation. Civil aviation police are organized within the Bureau of Civil Aviation. Forest police are organized within the Ministry of Forests. The special police receive instructions for their day-to-day operation from respective ministries with which they are affiliated. They are also accountable mainly to their respective ministries. But the special police must follow the regulations and guidelines issued by the Ministry of Public Security and report their work periodically to the Ministry of Public Security. The special police may also seek professional assistance from the Ministry of Public Security. To deal with the increasingly rampant crime of smuggling, a special antismuggling police force was established in 1999. The antismuggling police are under the joint leadership of the Customs Administration and the Ministry of Public Security.

The Police Law contains no specific provisions regarding the organization and functions of the People's Armed Police. The People's Armed Police nonetheless is an important component of public security police. In 1983, the government converted 1 million soldiers from the army to form the People's Armed Police. The Police Law mentions the People's Armed Police very briefly. It states simply that the People's Armed Police perform the tasks given by the state with regard to protecting public safety. In practice, the duties performed by the People's Armed Police include border patrols, maintaining law and order at the border areas, providing security for high-ranking government officials and foreign dignitaries, guarding prisons and reform-through-labor facilities, guarding important government buildings such as radio stations and television stations, and guarding important facilities such as civil airports, bridges, and tunnels. The headquarters of the People's Armed Police are set up in the Ministry of Public Security. The force is under the joint command of the Ministry of Public Security and the Central Military Committee.

State Security Police

The state security police is a relatively new police force. It was established in 1983. The main functions of state security police are protecting national security and preventing and detecting foreign espionage, sabotage, and conspiracies against the state. State security police are under the leadership of the Ministry of State Security. Under the Ministry of State Security, a state security bureau is established in each province, autonomous region, and municipality directly under the central government. Subordinate state security agencies are established in selected municipalities directly under the provincial governments (see Figure 2.2). The lower-level state security agencies are usually set up in municipalities and coastal areas that have frequent contacts with foreign countries (Du & Zhang, 1990; Yuan & Sun, 1986).

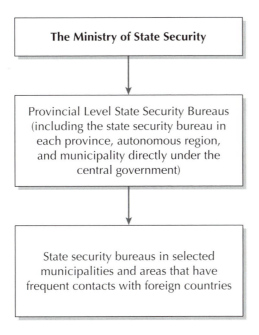

Figure 2.2   Organization of State Security Police

Prison Police

A noticeable feature of the Chinese police is that the police take full responsibility for supervising convicted offenders. The responsibility is divided between public security police and prison police. Public security police are responsible for supervising offenders serving community sentences; whereas prison police are responsible for supervising incarcerated offenders. Prison police are under the leadership of the Ministry of Justice. The Bureau of Prison Management within the Ministry of Justice has the overall responsibility for supervising the administration and operation of the country's prison system. The bureau sets general correctional policies and makes rules and regulations with regard to the prison administration. In each province, autonomous region, and municipality directly under the central government, there is a provincial-level Bureau of Justice (see Figure 2.3). A department of prison management is set up in each provincial-level Bureau of Justice. The department of prison management is directly responsible for the administration of prisons located within its jurisdiction (Xu, 1995).

Figure 2.3   Organization of Prison Police

Judicial Police

Judicial police are responsible for providing security for people's courts and people's procuratorates. According to the Organic Law of the People's Court and the Organic Law of the People's Procuratorate, each people's court and people's procuratorate has the authority to establish its own judicial police. The functions of judicial police include providing security for the court and the procuratorate, serving subpoenas, conducting searches ordered by the court or the procuratorate, and executing court orders and judgments. Judicial police affiliated with the people's courts are also responsible for carrying out the death sentences meted out by the courts.

Recruitment and Training

The Police Law sets forth the basic recruitment standards. To become a police officer a candidate must have the following qualifications:

1. Be 18 years old or older

2. Support the constitution

3. Have good moral character

4. Be in good health

5. Have an education level no less than high school graduation

6. Be willing to serve as a police officer

The Police Law prohibits people with criminal records and people who have been expelled from public employment from becoming police officers.

The Police Law specifies only the minimum qualifications. A regulation issued by the Ministry of Public Security sets forth more conditions for police candidates. The regulation enumerates six categories of people that are disqualified from becoming police officers. The six categories are the following:

1. People who have been criminally punished, and people who, either as adults or juveniles, have been sent to camps of reeducation through labor

2. People who are suspected of a crime and for whom the suspicion has not yet been cleared

3. People who have been discharged from public employment

4. People with bad moral character or who have displayed immoral conduct, such as being a hoodlum or a thief

5. People with family members or relatives who have been sentenced to death or are still serving criminal sentences

6. People with family members or relatives who have been, either at home or abroad, engaged in activities aimed at overthrowing the Chinese government

To complement the Police Law's minimum age requirement, the ministry's regulation sets the maximum age limit for police candidates. The regulation states that to become a police officer a candidate cannot be older than 25 years of age. As a preferential treatment for candidates from ethnic minority groups, the regulation extends the maximum age limit to 30 for ethnic minority candidates.

China is a country composed of 56 nationalities. The Han people compose more than 90 percent of the total population, an overwhelming majority. The 55 other nationalities are considered minority nationalities. The population of the minority nationalities makes up about 9 percent of the total population. The central government has long carried out a policy that emphasizes the equality and unity of all nationalities. There is in general a harmonious relationship between the Han nationality and the minority nationalities. There is no problem such as particularly tense relations between police and the minority nationalities. The government encourages members of minority nationalities to join the police force. This is so especially in the five autonomous regions, where there is a relatively large population of minority nationalities. There is a national policy that members of minority nationalities should be given preferential treatment when they seek higher education or employment in government agencies. As required by this policy, police agencies similarly must give preferential consideration to candidates of minority nationalities when recruiting police officers.[3]

Qualified police candidates must take written examinations and go through strength and agility tests. To ensure that new recruits meet the recruitment standards, the Ministry of Public Security requires that the examinations and tests be organized and administered by a provincial police agency. Applicants must take provincewide examinations and tests. In making selection decisions, police agencies consider the scores a candidate receives in the examinations and tests and the information obtained by the police regarding a candidate's past experience and moral character. Once selected, the new recruits are required to go through a one-year probationary period. During the one-year period, the new recruits receive education and training at police academies. Only those who perform satisfactorily and pass the end-of-term examinations will be formally hired as police officers.

The Police Law sets out higher educational requirements for officers holding leadership positions. To be promoted to a leadership position, an officer must be college educated, have the necessary legal knowledge and practical experience in police work, and have administrative talent and skills. The candidate must also complete required in-service training in a police university or academy. The officially stated policy is that no officer can be promoted unless he or she completes the required in-service training.

To raise the level of professionalism among police, in 1992 the Chinese government established the police ranking system. According to the People's Police Ranking Regulation, there are five ranks in the Chinese police:

1. General superintendent (conferred on individuals who hold posts at the level of government minister) and deputy general superintendent (conferred on individuals who hold posts at the level of deputy government minister)

2. Superintendent (first, second, third grade)

3. Inspector (first, second, third grade)

4. Sergeant (first, second, third grade)

5. Officer (first, second grade)

A new recruit usually starts from the lowest rank. After a few years of service, the officer can apply for promotion. To be promoted, the officer must meet the promotional requirements, which include higher educational attainment and completion of required in-service training.

The leadership of the Chinese police has attached great significance to police education and training. Many police education and training facilities are established to accommodate the increasing demand of police education and training. It is estimated that there are now more than 300 police universities, colleges, and academies. The police educational level has improved significantly in recent years. In 1984, police officers with college education made up only 4.3 percent of the total police force. By 1991, this figure had risen to 19.2 percent. The percentage of police officers with a high school education rose as well, from 35 percent in 1984 to 57 percent in 1991 (Luo, 1995; Ma & Tian, 1995). According to figures released by the Ministry of Public Security, in 1999 police officers who had educational attainment of two years of college or higher already made up 44 percent of the total police force (Ministry of Public Security, 1999).

Police Functions

Police Functions in General

In comparison with the police of other countries, the Chinese police perform much broader functions. The Police Law stipulates 14 functions to be performed by the police. The 14 functions are the following:

1. Preventing and investigating crimes

2. Maintaining the public order and preventing activities that endanger the social order

3. Maintaining traffic order and handling traffic accidents

4. Organizing and administering fire prevention work

5. Controlling firearms, ammunition, and knives as well as flammable, explosive, and radioactive materials

6. Supervising the operation of certain types of professions and industries[4]

7. Providing security for high-ranking government officials, foreign dignitaries, and important buildings and facilities

8. Controlling and managing mass rallies, parades, and demonstrations

9. Administering the household registration system and handling affairs of conferring or revoking citizenship, entry into and exit of the country, and foreigners' residence and travel in China

10. Maintaining order and security at border areas

11. Supervising offenders sentenced to control, detention, and deprivation of political rights as well as offenders serving prison sentences outside prison, offenders serving suspended sentences, and offenders on parole

12. Supervising the operation of and providing security for the computer information network

13. Providing guidance to and supervising the work of security units in government offices, social organizations, and enterprises; providing guidance to mass-line security and crime prevention organizations

14. Performing other duties prescribed by laws and regulations

The functions listed in the Police Law are only the tasks of public security police. The Police Law contains no provisions with respect to functions of other police. The functions of other police are specified in other relevant legislation. For instance, the duties and functions of state security police are provided for in the State Security Law; the duties and functions of prison police are contained in the Prison Law; and the duties and functions of judicial police are specified in the Organic Law of the People's Court and the Organic Law of the People's Procuratorate.

Public security police are a highly specialized force. Within the Ministry of Public Security, there are directorates responsible for various types of police work. For instance, there are directorates responsible for ordinary criminal investigation, for investigating economic crimes, for public security, for border control, for exit-and-entry control, for fire-fighting, for traffic control, for drug law enforcement, for guarding high-ranking government officials, for jail administration, for supervision of the public information network, for internal supervision, for officer education, etc. Police specialization exists at lower-level police agencies as well. In lower-level police agencies, there are usually criminal investigation police, public order police, household registration police, traffic police, foreign affairs police, and fire-fighting police. Moreover, China became a member of Interpol in 1984. Within the Ministry of Public Security, the China National Central Bureau of Interpol serves as the liaison agency with Interpol. The Chinese police have ever since actively cooperated with Interpol in exchanging information and apprehending internationally wanted criminals (Ministry of Public Security, 1999).

Antiterrorism Function

Terrorism is not a new phenomenon in China. Over the past several decades, China has had its share of terrorist attacks. How to deal with terrorist attacks has long been a concern of the Chinese police. The September 11 attacks, however, have further alerted the Chinese police about the danger of terrorism. Since the September 11 attacks, the Chinese police have taken a series of measures to strengthen the police ability to deal with and prevent terrorist attacks. The Chinese government has also taken steps to improve its cooperation with the world community in the struggle against terrorism.

In the early 1980s, in response to several incidents of hijacking of civil aircraft, a special antihijacking police force was established within the public security police. In China, the threat of terrorist attacks comes mainly from an Islamic separatist organization operating in Xinjiang Uighur autonomous region located in the northwest part of the country. The separatist group is known as East Tujue (Turk) Islamic Movement. Xinjiang autonomous region has a relatively large Muslim population. The aim of the East Tujue group is to separate the region from China. The group has organized and carried out numerous terrorist attacks, including bombings, kidnappings, assassinations, and arson in the region. The group is connected with international terrorist networks. Members of the group used to train in bin Laden's terrorist camps in Afghanistan. On September 11, 2002, the UN Security Council passed a resolution declaring the East Tujue Islamic Movement a terrorist organization. ·

After the September 11 attacks, an antiterrorist bureau was established within the Ministry of Public Security. The main functions of the bureau are to conduct research, collect and analyze intelligence, and direct and coordinate antiterrorist work in the country. Following the tradition of mass-line policing, the police leadership emphasizes the importance of combining the work of professional antiterrorist experts and the efforts of mass-line crime prevention organizations. The government calls for waging a people's war against terrorism. Under the direction of the antiterrorist bureau, the antiterrorist police units in Beijing and other cities have worked out anti–terrorist-attack plans and carried out anti–terrorist-attack exercises. For instance, the antiterrorist unit in Beijing carried out exercises to rescue hostages taken by terrorists in seized foreign embassies. Various types of anti–terrorist-attack exercises have also been carried out in other cities.

Since September 11, the Chinese government has significantly stepped up its cooperation with other countries in the global war against terrorism. Soon after September 11, the Chinese police began to share intelligence with the U.S. law enforcement agencies. The Chinese government has reached similar cooperative agreements with a number of other countries as well. Most notably, China, Russia, and four other central Asian countries signed the "Agreement Concerning the Establishment of Regional Antiterrorist Institutions Among Members of the Shanghai Cooperation Organization." The agreement calls for close cooperation of member states in combating and preventing terrorist attacks. It establishes a six-country antiterrorist institution with its headquarters located in the capital city of the Republic of Kyrgyzstan. At the bilateral level, the Chinese army and the army of Kyrgyzstan in 2002 even carried out a joint anti–terrorist-attack military exercise.

Policing Strategies

In the first 30 years of the People's Republic, China adopted a policing strategy that was markedly different from that commonly seen in Western countries. China during this time had little contact with the outside world and was largely a closed society. The government imposed tight restrictions on people's movement. Corresponding to this social condition, the police adopted a strategy suitable for policing a static and stable population. In most Western countries, routine patrols are the mainstay of the police work and are called the backbone of policing. The Chinese police, however, over a time period of more than 30 years conducted no regular patrols. Routine patrols were not essential or necessary to the Chinese police. For the Chinese police, the key to successful policing was not the deterrent effect of routine patrols but their ability to keep a tight control over the subject population through restrictions upon travel and the extensive surveillance system of the mass-line crime prevention organizations.

The household registration system provided the police with the tools of restricting people's travel and monitoring people's movement. The law required that all people be registered under the household registration system. Shortly after a person's birth, parents or guardians of the person had to have the person registered at the local police station. The registration remained in effect until the person's death. Most people remained in the place of their original registration. Relocation due to job transfer was not common. If a person needed to move to another city, he or she had to notify the local police. The police would revoke the person's household registration and give the person a certificate so that he or she could register with the police at his or her new residence. Registration with the police was required not only of permanent residents, it was required of temporary residents as well. If a person came from another city to visit relatives or friends, he or she had to notify the police and register as a temporary resident. The person had to specify with whom he or she was staying and how long he or she would stay there.

The police were assisted in their efforts to monitor the movement of the population by neighborhood committees that were established across the country. Neighborhood committees were the most important mass-line organizations in the urban area. The law required that a neighborhood committee be established for every 100 to 600 households. The neighborhood committee performed a variety of functions related to community's well-being. For instance, the neighborhood committee organized informal patrols around the neighborhood to prevent theft or burglary, organized community residents to clean up the neighborhood, informed residents of crimes that had occurred in or near the neighborhood, reminded residents to take precautions against crime, and mediated disputes among community residents.[5]

The neighborhood committee worked under the guidance of the police. In the urban area, a police station was established in each larger community. A police station was headed by a chief and one or two deputy chiefs.

There were three types of police officers in a police station: household registration officers, public security officers, and internal affairs officers. Internal affairs officers were administrative officers who stayed in the police station to handle all office-related police work. Among the duties of internal affairs officers were processing household registration applications, handling revocation and transfer of household registration, receiving residents who came to the police station with their concerns, and handling citizens' complaints. Public security officers were in charge of maintaining law and order at the locality. Their duties included assisting higher-level police agencies in conducting criminal investigations, apprehending wanted criminals, locating stolen property, detaining people not properly registered under the household registration system, and investigating people engaged in suspicious activities.

Not all police stations were staffed with public security officers. Public security officers were staffed only in police stations located in areas with complicated security situations. In police stations that had no public security officers, the tasks of public security officers were performed by household registration officers.[6] A police station usually divided its jurisdictional area into several subareas, with each subarea consisting of several communities. A household registration officer was assigned to each subarea. The general guideline was that each household registration officer was responsible for 700 households. The household registration officer visited the communities under his or her control frequently and kept close ties with the neighborhood committees in the communities. Due to their frequent contacts with community residents, household registration officers were the most visible police officers in the eye of the public. Because household registration officers played such a key role in policing, it is no exaggeration to say that the work of household registration officers constituted the backbone of policing in that era.

A neighborhood committee in most cases was composed of retired workers or housewives. Members of the neighborhood committee conducted informal patrols in the neighborhood, stood guard against theft and burglary, and reported suspicious people and activity to the police. The neighborhood committee served as the eyes and ears of the police. Under its watchful eye and with its intimate knowledge of the community, any strangers and suspicious activity would be quickly noticed and promptly reported to the police.

Apart from neighborhood committees, internal security units at workplaces formed another link in the extensive network of mass-line crime prevention organizations. Within each work unit, be it factory, department store, hospital, or school, an internal security unit was set up. The internal security unit was responsible for providing security for the work unit and assisting the police in investigating crimes committed at the workplace or by employees of the work unit.

The policing strategy characterized by reliance on mass-line crime prevention organizations worked well for the police in the 1950s and the early

1960s. The crime rate in China was low. According to figures released by the government, the crime rate during this period was about 30 to 40 per 100,000 inhabitants (He, 1992). Apart from the low crime rate, the Chinese police, thanks to the work of household registration officers, in general maintained a close and positive relationship with community residents. The academic study of criminal justice did not exist in China then. It would not be hard, however, to find reports in Chinese newspapers about the harmonious relationship between police and community residents and stories about how police officers provided much needed help to community residents and how community residents helped police solve crimes and catch criminals. Police at this time were called by the Party to carry out a mass line in policing.

The police relied on mass-line policing until the late 1970s; then the situation began to change. Since the implementation of the policy of economic modernization, Chinese economy and society have undergone profound changes. In the past 25 years, China has maintained one of the fastest rates of economic growth. Economic development has brought about prosperity, and in its wake an unprecedented rise in crime. Western criminologists have long observed that modernization is often accompanied by an increase in criminality (Clinard & Abbott, 1973; Rogers, 1989; Shelly, 1981; Wilson & Herrnstein, 1985). China proves to be no exception to the pattern. In 1980 China's crime rate stood at 77.2 per 100,000 inhabitants, which was already much higher than the low crime rate in the 1950s and 1960s. By 1990 the figure had risen sharply to 200.2 per 100,000 inhabitants. There was especially an upward trend in serious and violent crimes. Between 1980 and 1990 the overall crime rate increased 160 percent, whereas the number of serious crimes increased 240 percent.[7] In addition to the sharp increase in the official figures, both government officials and scholars acknowledge that because of inaccuracy of the statistics taken by the police, the actual crime figures could be much higher (see Dutton & Lee, 1993; He, 1989; and Wang, 1989).

Faced with the sharp rise in crime, the police seemed to be at loss in finding effective ways to curb the upsurge in crime. The police found that the old policing strategies were no longer working, and they had yet to find new ones. The introduction of a market economy transformed the Chinese society. The changed socioeconomic conditions in turn resulted in the erosion of the basis of the past effective policing strategies. The opening up of the labor and commodity market created an ever-increasing demand for labor and commodities in urban areas. Tens and thousands of people from the countryside flooded to cities and coastal areas in search of work. These people moved on a temporary basis and usually were not registered in places where they were working. In the 1980s, it was estimated that there were about 80 million migrant workers constituting a floating population in large and coastal cities (Dutton & Lee, 1993).[8]

The presence of the sizable floating population reduced the ability of the police to monitor the urban population. Taking advantage of the weakened police control, criminals, especially criminal gangs, mingled with migrant workers to commit crimes, moving from one place to another. Studies noted a close connection between the increase in crimes and the growth in the floating population. Criminal gangs and the transient criminals committed a large number of ordinary street crimes. They were also responsible for the emergence of a variety of new types of crimes, for instance, drug trafficking, smuggling of cultural relics, the manufacture and sale of illicit arms, and the kidnapping and sale of women and children (He, 1992; Huang, 1991; Li, 1993).

With the erosion of the basis of the past policing strategies, the police were faced with the challenge of developing new strategies to deal with the upsurge in crime. To quickly reverse the upward trend in crime, the Chinese police adopted campaign-style policing. The campaign-style policing was characterized by launching short, sharp assaults upon particular types of crime for a limited period. China for a long time had a relatively low police-to-population ratio. In the early 1990s the police-to-population ratio was estimated to be between 1:745 and 1:1400, which was much lower than that in major Western countries (Dutton & Lee, 1993; Ma & Tian, 1995).[9] The modest police force, relying on the surveillance system of mass-line organizations and the restrictions placed on people's travel, seemed sufficient to police a largely stable and static population. As the basis of the closed system of social control eroded, the police line was suddenly stretched thin. Faced with the unprecedented rise in crime, the police realized that they did not have resources to target all crimes at once. The police thus adopted a strategy of concentrating their forces against particular categories of crimes. It was hoped that striking hard on certain types of the most harmful crimes would result in an overall crime reduction (Dutton & Lee, 1993; Tanner, 2005).

In the 1980s and early 1990s the government launched several "severe-strike" campaigns. The campaign against the "six evils" launched in the late 1980s illustrated this campaign-style policing. Convinced that moral decay was the root cause of the rise in crime, the government launched a campaign against the six evils. The six evils were prostitution; producing, selling, and spreading pornography; kidnapping women and children; planting, gathering, and trafficking in drugs; gambling; and defrauding people by superstitious means. The government claimed that the campaign was a success and achieved its desired goal. It was estimated that in a matter of months the police throughout the country ferreted out 213,000 cases of the six evils that involved 770,000 people. Of the people involved in the six-evil cases, 6,129 were arrested and prosecuted, 5,650 were sent to reeducation-through-labor camps, and 586,000 were punished by the police under public security regulations (Jiang & Dai, 1990).[10]

To maximize the effect of the severe-strike campaign, the National People's Congress substantially increased the penalty for targeted crimes. The legislature also amended the Criminal Procedure Law to make it easier for police to arrest and detain and for prosecutors to prosecute and convict offenders who had committed the targeted crimes. For instance, "The Decision on Severely Punishing Offenders Engaged in Offenses that Greatly Endanger the Public Security," issued by the Standing Committee of the National People's Congress, authorized the courts to punish certain types of offenders more severely than permitted by the Criminal Law. Offenders subjected to the enhanced punishment included those who committed serious violent crimes; those involved in the illicit manufacture, sale, and transportation of firearms and explosives; those involved in smuggling people; and those involved in inducing, permitting, and forcing women to engage in prostitution. According to the Decision, in cases involving the specified crimes, not only could the courts sentence offenders to longer imprisonment terms than were stipulated in the Criminal Law, but also, when there were aggravating circumstances, the courts could even sentence the offenders to death regardless of whether the death penalty was stipulated for the crime in the Criminal Law.[11]

In a companion decision, "The Decision on Expediting the Trial of Cases Involving Crimes that Greatly Endanger the Public Security," the Standing Committee of the National People's Congress relaxed the procedural requirements in cases involving certain serious crimes. The Criminal Law provided that after being sentenced to death, a defendant had 10 days to appeal the death sentence. The Decision of the Standing Committee, however, substantially shortened the appeal period for offenders convicted of certain types of crimes. According to the Decision, in cases involving crimes such as murder, rape, robbery, and sabotage by using explosives, the appeal period was reduced from 10 days to 3.[12] The legislative intent was to maximize the shocking effect of the death penalty. With the relaxed procedural requirement, offenders charged with crimes that fell within the stipulated category could be convicted, sentenced, and executed within days of their arrest. Because of the relaxed procedural protections, curtailed trial procedure, extensive imposition of the death penalty, and fast execution became notable features of severe-strike campaigns.

Despite the fanfare surrounding each severe-strike campaign and the government's claim that the campaigns substantially improved the public security situation, evidence suggests that the campaign-style policing achieved only marginal success. Crime statistics indicate that the overall crime rate dropped precipitously while each campaign was on but shot up once the campaign was over. The fluctuation of the crime rate indicates that the campaigns at best produced only a short-term effect. Commentators, both Western and Chinese, have also noted various side effects of the campaign-style policing. The most serious among them are police recourse to arbitrary and extralegal measures to accomplish the goal of a campaign, for instance, the use of torture to obtain confessions, falsification of crime statistics to exaggerate the effect of the campaign, extensive use of the death penalty, and abusive use of the death penalty, i.e., imposition of the death penalty on offenders who did not commit the targeted crimes (Dutton & Lee, 1993; Tanner, 2005; Zhou, 1999).

When severe-strike campaigns were first organized, the government and the police expected that the severe punishment would produce dramatic deterrent effect and result in a long-term reduction in crime. As the campaigns have fallen short of their goals, the police have tended to routinize them. Whenever the public security situation worsens, the police select certain target crimes and launch a severe-strike campaign. Apart from several nationwide severe-strike campaigns, there also have been provincewide campaigns. The routinization of campaigns seems to have taken a toll on police officers. Lower-level police agencies and police officers are exhausted by the continuation of campaigns. Many officers no longer regard severe-strike campaigns as special struggles but rather only part of routine police work. They know that campaigns will come periodically. After one campaign is over, they should get ready for the next. Even some police officials have become concerned about the costs of constant campaigns. Not only do police officers become mentally and physically exhausted, ongoing engagement in the campaigns has also compromised the accomplishment of other long-term force development goals, for instance, police education, police training, and the development of police professionalism in general (see Tanner, 2005).

Although there are no signs that the police will end the campaign-style policing, the government realizes that it cannot rely on severe punishment alone to accomplish the goal of crime reduction. The government has long advocated an overall crime reduction strategy known as "comprehensive management." The central idea of the comprehensive management strategy is to mobilize all social forces and take all-around measures to accomplish the goal of crime control. The government emphasizes the importance of strengthening mass-line crime prevention organizations, reducing recidivism, and intensifying education of young people. In the 1980s, while launching severe-strike campaigns, the government doubled its efforts to strengthen the mass-line crime prevention organizations. With the growth of the Chinese economy, there emerged quite a number of new towns and cities. The government emphasized that neighborhood committees must be established in the newly emerged towns and cities. The government record showed that between 1986 and 1989 the number of neighborhood committees increased by 10.9 percent nationwide (*Law Yearbook of China*, 1990). In the new era of economic reform, however, the police relied more on monetary incentive than the traditional appeal to people's revolutionary enthusiasm in recruiting people who would like to be part of the mass-line crime prevention efforts (Dutton, 2005).

Realizing that it was no longer possible to restrict people's travel and movement by using the old household registration system, the government in 1986 established the resident identification card system. The identification card system was designed to supplement the traditional household registration system. The law requires that all residents attaining the age of 16 apply for and thereafter carry a resident identification card. The police are given the authority to request people to show their identification cards.

Failure to produce the card is a cause for detention and investigation. The identification card system helps the police continue to maintain certain control over the subject population.

No systematic studies have been conducted to evaluate the effect of various policing and crime reduction strategies. It is hard to tell how effective these strategies actually are. As far as the crime rate is concerned, it has maintained an upward trend. According to the crime figures reported in the *Law Yearbook of China*, the crime rate in 1980 stood at 77.2 per 100,000 population. The rate rose to 200.9 per 100,000 population in 1990. In the mid-1990s the crime rate declined slightly, but it shot up again in the late 1990s. In 2001, the crime rate reached 360 per 100,000 population.[13] Effectiveness of policing apparently is not the only factor that may affect the increase or decrease of crime rate. The crime rate, as noted by criminologists, in China as well as in other parts of the world, could be affected by many different factors (Bakken, 2005; Siegel, 2003; Vold & Bernard, 1986). Theoretically, it is possible to argue that despite effective policing the crime rate may still be pushed up by other factors. In China's context, however, due to the lack of empirical evidence, it is impossible to judge whether and how effective various policing strategies actually are in reducing and preventing crimes.

Campaign-style policing and comprehensive management are not the only strategies the Chinese police have tried. Operating in a dynamically changing society, the police leadership is aware that police must constantly adapt themselves to the changing social conditions and look for more suitable policing strategies. In that respect, the Chinese police leadership is willing to look beyond the national borders and learn from other countries' policing experiences. A noticeable development in the past several years is the police leadership's embrace of the idea of community policing.

Since the late 1990s, community policing has captured the attention of the Chinese police. Inspired by its presumed success in Western countries, the Chinese police leadership embraces community policing as a new way to accomplish the goal of effective policing. After several years of experimenting, community policing has become an officially endorsed policing strategy. The Ministry of Public Security requires that community policing programs be established in all large and medium-sized cities. The whole-hearted acceptance of community policing by the Chinese police is due in no small measure to the resemblance of community policing to China's traditional mass-line policing. Though the term *community policing* is imported from the Western policing community, the central idea of community policing—namely, seeking community cooperation in crime control and prevention—is hardly new to the Chinese police.

As in Western countries, community policing in China is not clearly defined. There are no officially endorsed models of community policing. Community policing programs differ from one community to another. The top police leadership makes no attempt to create a single community policing model for all communities. It sets the basic tune and leaves it to the lower police agencies to experiment and determine what kind of community policing programs will work best for them. The Ministry of Public Security broadly specifies the duties of community policing officers:

1. Gathering information from the community

2. Monitoring the population movement in the community

3. Maintaining order in the community

4. Helping residents take precautions against crime victimization

5. Providing service to the community[14]

Within the broad framework set by the Ministry, community policing officers in practice perform a wide range of duties, including educating community residents about the importance of observing the law, conducting patrols and maintaining order in the community, monitoring the public facilities that are likely to be frequented by criminals (for instance, hotels and public entertainment facilities), monitoring the floating population in the community, and providing guidance and assistance to mass-line security organizations (Feng & Zhang, 2003; Liu, Li, & Guo, 2002; Ni, 2003; Xiong, 2002).

Police agencies at various levels understand that community policing means more than implementing direct action programs. Community policing is a new philosophy of policing that requires police agencies to reconsider their organization and operating procedures. To ensure that police officers adapt themselves to the new policing strategy, the police leadership sets forth new standards to evaluate officers' performance. The basic standards to evaluate community policing officers are to see whether community residents are satisfied with the police and whether there is a good police-community relationship. From the perspective of crime control, developing positive relations with community residents is seen as a means to accomplish the goal of crime reduction. Correspondingly, an important factor in evaluating community policing officers' performance is to see whether the officers have mobilized the community residents to actively participate in crime-fighting efforts, whether community residents have provided more leads and information to the police, and whether the crime rate in the community has decreased.

According to the guidelines issued by the Ministry of Public Security, one community policing officer in general should be responsible for 1,000 to 3,000 households. The local police station, depending on the specific situation of the community, may decide to assign one, two, or more community policing officers to each community. The Ministry of Public Security directs that a police box staffed by community policing officers should be established in each community. To help community residents identify police boxes, it is required that police boxes in each county and city must have the same design and recognition symbol.[15]

Convinced by the promise of community policing, the top police leadership has made vigorous efforts to implement community policing programs. The centralized command structure of the Chinese police has made it possible for the police leadership to push community policing programs quickly to the entire country. Community policing did not capture the attention of the Chinese police until the late 1990s. By the end of 2001, however, there were already more than 200,000 community policing programs established in the country. Of the total of 380,000 police officers employed by local police stations nationwide, more than 200,000 of them were involved in community policing programs.[16] Without passing a judgment on the quality and the impact of the programs, one has to admit that it is truly remarkable for the police leadership to push the community policing programs to the entire country in such a short period of time.

Despite the lack of empirical data on the effect of many different types of community policing programs now existing in the country, police officials from the Ministry of Public Security on down have praised community policing as a success. They claim that community policing has produced the effect of reducing crime and strengthening the relationship between police and community residents. The official claims notwithstanding, objectively speaking, it seems that more empirical studies are needed before one can form a judgment on the merit and effect of various community policing programs. Because community policing in China is still at its initial stage of development, how various community policing programs will evolve and the real impact of community policing still remain to be seen.

Police and the Rule of Law

The significance of the criminal procedure law in the criminal justice administration is well recognized in all democratic countries. For every government that is not totally authoritarian or anarchistic, it is essential that there be a body of law designed to balance the public interest in crime control against the individual interest in freedom from state coercive authority. Criminal procedure is the law designed to serve that purpose. Despite the significance of criminal and criminal procedure laws in ensuring a fair administration of criminal justice, China's criminal justice system in the first 30 years of the People's Republic operated without the guidance of either criminal law or criminal procedure law. The system of criminal justice, like many other aspects of life in China during this time, operated to a large extent in a "lawless" state. The Chinese leadership downplayed the role of law out of concern that codified law might restrain the Communist Party's pursuit of revolutionary goals (Keith, 1994; Lee, 1997; Turner, Feinerman, & Guy, 2000). The police operation was guided mainly by nonpublished and often changing party policies. Guiding the police operation by nonpublished internal documents undoubtedly provided the Party with the flexibility to use the police as a tool to carry out its policies, but the drawback of the practice was obvious. It placed the police beyond the reach of law. Without promulgated rules to regulate police behavior, neither police nor ordinary citizens could judge whether police acted within the bounds of law.

The promulgation of the Criminal Procedure Law in 1979 marked a significant step forward in the direction of establishing a comprehensive legal system in China. Police power for the first time in the history of the People's Republic was defined in the form of written law. Given its symbolic and substantive significance, the original Criminal Procedure Law was quite rudimentary. In the course of its implementation, legal commentators noted various deficiencies of the law. Apart from deficiencies in provisions governing the trial proceedings, commentators noted especially the insufficient procedural safeguards at the stage of police investigation. In 1996 the National People's Congress amended the Criminal Procedure Law. The amended Criminal Procedure Law (CPL) substantially expands the procedural protections of defendants and suspects and contains more provisions governing police behavior. The progress made notwithstanding, legal commentators have noted quite a few new problems in the amended law and have recommended that the law be further revised.

Power to Arrest and Detain

The CPL makes a distinction between the power to arrest and the power to detain. The CPL imposes strict restrictions on the police power to arrest. To make an arrest, the police must in all circumstances seek approval from the people's procuratorate. The law grants police no authority to make arrests under any circumstances without approval of the people's procuratorate. However, despite the restrictions on the power to arrest, it would be wrong to assume that the Chinese police have less power to restrict people's freedom. In contrast to restrictions placed on the power to arrest, the CPL contains few restrictions on the police power to detain.

According to the CPL, police do not need to seek approval from either a judge or a procurator when exercising the detention power. The CPL enumerates seven circumstances under which police may detain a person:

1. When a person is about to commit a crime, is in the process of committing a crime, or is found to have just committed a crime

2. When a person is identified by the victim or eyewitnesses as the one who has committed a crime

3. When criminal evidence is found on a person or in his or her residence

4. When a person, after committing a crime, attempts to commit suicide or flee the jurisdiction or has already fled;

5. When it is possible that a person may destroy or tamper with evidence or collude with others to give false testimony

6. When a person refuses to give his or her real name or address and makes it impossible to establish his or her identity

7. When there is grave suspicion that the person is a transient criminal, a repeat offender, or an offender who commits crimes in conspiracy with others

The CPL in general permits the police to detain a person for three days. Within three days, the police must either gather sufficient evidence to arrest the person or have the person released. If the police believe that sufficient evidence exists for the person's arrest, they must submit a written request for arrest to the people's procuratorate. The people's procuratorate is required to make a decision either to approve or disapprove the request within seven days. If the people's procuratorate does not approve the police request for arrest, the police must release the detained person immediately. To ensure that the police have enough time to collect evidence, the CPL permits the police to extend the three-day time limit from one to four days if they cannot complete the investigation within three days. Because the police may have a maximum of seven days to collect evidence and the prosecution has seven days to decide whether to approve the police request for arrest, in ordinary cases the maximum time a person may be detained by the police prior to arrest is 14 days.

The maximum seven-day police investigation period, however, may be further extended in cases involving crimes committed by transient criminals, repeat offenders, or offenders who commit crime in conspiracy with others. In such cases, the CPL permits the police to detain a suspect for as long as 30 days. The extended investigation and detention period is justified on the ground that cases of this nature are more complicated, and the police need more time to complete the investigation. The CPL itself contains no definitions of transient criminals, repeat offenders, or offenders committing crimes in conspiracy with others. The definitions are supplied in a regulation issued by the Ministry of Public Security. According the regulation, transient criminals are those who commit crimes repeatedly by crossing city and county borders, repeat offenders are those who have committed more than three crimes, and offenders committing crimes in conspiracy with others are those who commit crimes with one or more other offenders.[17]

The regulation was issued with the intent to facilitate the implementation of the CPL by providing the police with a guideline as to how to determine whether a particular suspect should be subject to extended detention. In practice, however, the police often ignore the distinction between ordinary offenders and offenders that fall within the special categories. Many officers seem to think that because the CPL permits extended detention for certain offenders, they are justified in subjecting all suspects to extended detention. Research studies indicate that the seven-day detention limit is often flouted. It is common for police to detain suspects that do not fall within the special categories for more than seven days (Chen, 2000; Chen & Song, 2000).

An issue that arises after a person's arrest is when the police must complete the investigation so that the case can be brought to trial. To prevent prolonged postarrest detention, the CPL provides that in ordinary cases the police must complete the investigation within two months. In complicated cases, if the police cannot complete the investigation within two months, with the approval of the people's procuratorate at a higher level, they may extend the postarrest investigative detention for another month. In normal cases, the maximum duration of postarrest detention is three months. After three months, the police must submit the case to the people's procuratorate for prosecution consideration. There are, however, exceptions to the general rule.

The CPL provides that in cases involving crimes committed in outlying areas to which transportation is inconvenient, in cases involving organized crime, and in cases involving serious crimes committed by transient criminals, if the police cannot complete the investigation within three months, they may apply to the people's procuratorate at the provincial level to have the detention period extended for another two months. With the added extension, if the police still cannot complete the investigation and if they believe that the arrested person if convicted would be subject to more than 10 years of imprisonment, they may apply to the people's procuratorate at the provincial level to have the investigative detention extended for another two months. Thus, under exceptional circumstances the police may detain an arrested person for as long as seven months before they are required to refer the case to the people's procuratorate for prosecution consideration.

Awaiting trial in police custody for seven months certainly is not a welcome aspect for suspects, but this kind of detention is statutorily permitted and subject to approval by the people's procuratorate. A more troubling aspect of the police detention practice is the circumstances under which police may extend detention without seeking approval from the people's procuratorate. The CPL under two circumstances permits police to extend investigative detention without seeking approval from the people's procuratorate. First, the CPL provides that while conducting an investigation, if police find that the suspect has committed a crime other than the one under investigation, they may recalculate the detention time limit from the date that they discover the new crime. Second, if police cannot establish a suspect's identity after his or her arrest because of the suspect's refusal to give a name or address, the police do not need to commence calculating the detention time limit until they can establish the person's identity.

Granting the authority to the police to decide when detention duration should commence creates a great uncertainty as to how long a suspect may be detained in police custody. The broad grant of discretion in practice has resulted in widespread abuse. A tactic often used by the police is that even though they know a suspect has committed more than one crime, they name only one crime in the request for arrest. After the suspect is arrested and at the time when the detention limit is about to run out, they declare that they have "discovered" another crime committed by the suspect. The police thus can restart the detention time limit at the time that they "discovered" the new crime. Moreover, the police sometimes simply pretend that they cannot establish a suspect's identity. This practice similarly allows them to subject suspects to extended detention. Police commentators have noted that this broad discretion, coupled with the skeptical attitude of the police toward providing procedural protections for suspects, has made unlawful extension of postarrest detentions one of the most serious problems in the implementation of the amended CPL (Chen & Song, 2000; Sun, 2000).

The police tendency to disregard the law for law enforcement convenience underscores the difficulty in implementing a comprehensive legal system in China. As acknowledged by both government officials and legal commentators, promulgation of law alone would not assure police compliance with the law. As noted by some commentators, while it is laudable that the amended CPL grants more rights to individuals due to the lack of a culture of respect for the law among the police, it is likely that the gap between the law and practice may actually grow wider (Lawyers Committee for Human Rights, 1996). To ensure proper implementation of the CPL, commentators and government officials agree that the police leadership needs to make more efforts to educate officers about the legal procedures prescribed in the CPL and to instill in officers the concept that police must keep their actions within the bounds of law (Chen, 2000; Chen & Song, 2000; Liu, 2001a, 2001b).

Power to Search and Seize

Police have broad power to conduct searches. The CPL grants police the authority to conduct searches and seizures without the need to seek approval from either the people's court or the people's procuratorate. The CPL provides that police must have a search warrant before a search can be conducted, but it contains no provision as to who has the authority to issue a search warrant. The void is filled by a regulation issued by the Ministry of Public Security, which provides that the authority to issue search warrants rests with police themselves. According to the regulation, any police officers with the rank of county police chief or above have the authority to issue search warrants.[18]

The warrant requirement in the CPL, as supplemented by the regulation issued by the Ministry of Public Security, creates essentially a self-policing mechanism to ensure the reasonableness of police searches. In Western countries, the authority to issue warrants usually resides with judicial branch officials. The judicial branch official can be a judge or a procurator. The rationale behind the practice is that only a judicial branch official, neutral and detached from immediate investigations, can objectively evaluate the situation and make a fair judgment as to whether sufficient grounds exist for a search. With regard to police, it is concerned that police, at the forefront of the fight against crime and under the pressure to ferret out crime, are unlikely to be objective in judging whether a search is warranted.

To assure objective evaluation of the grounds for searches does not seem to be the concern of the CPL. To the drafters of the CPL, the risk of unreasonable searches appeared to come mainly from street-level officers. Along this line of thinking, the assumption behind the warrant requirement of the CPL is that so long as police officers are required to obtain a search warrant from a high-ranking officer, the risk of unreasonable searches will be reduced. Since the implementation of the amended CPL, no systematic studies have been conducted to evaluate the effectiveness of the self-policing mechanism. Despite some documented cases that high-ranking officers in exercising the warrant authority have prevented low-ranking officers from conducting illegal searches (Liu & Wei, 1999), the overall effect of the self-supervisory system remains unknown. Apart from the potential conflict of interest in the system of permitting police to issue warrants to themselves, the lack of evidentiary criteria necessary to sustain the issuance of a search warrant presents another difficulty. The CPL contains no provision concerning the evidentiary standard necessary to justify the issuance of a search warrant. The practical effect of the lack of evidentiary criteria is that high-ranking officers are more likely for act arbitrarily when deciding whether a search warrant should be issued.

Power to Interrogate

One of the most noticeable revisions in the amended CPL is the grant to suspects the right to counsel at the police investigation stage. The old CPL afforded defendants the right to counsel at the trial stage but contained no provision with respect to legal representation at the police investigation stage. The extension of the right to counsel to the police investigation stage by the amended CPL represents a significant step forward in the development of criminal procedure in China. The effort to extend the right to counsel, however, met with resistance from the police both before and after the promulgation of the amended CPL. At the legislative debate, most legal experts were in favor of extending the right to counsel to the police investigation stage, but the police were against the idea. The Ministry of Public Security submitted a report to the National People's Congress contending that lawyers' involvement would hinder police investigations and undermine the police ability to solve crime.

The final version of the right to counsel contained in the amended CPL is a product of compromise between the two opposing views. The amended CPL grants the right but attaches several restrictions. The restrictions attached, as shown in the course of implementation of the law, seem to have had quite a negative impact on the proper exercise of the right. The statutory restrictions, coupled with police reluctance to faithfully implement the law, have in many cases rendered it impossible for lawyers to provide meaningful service to their clients.

Under the CPL, the police may interrogate a suspect in two circumstances. First, the police may summon a suspect to a police station for interrogation.

This form of interrogation is known as a summons for interrogation. Second, the police may interrogate a suspect after he or she is taken into police custody. The CPL provides for several procedural safeguards for suspects subjected to police interrogation. In a summons for interrogation, the CPL provides that the duration of interrogation cannot exceed 12 hours. The purpose of the provision is to prevent the police from turning a summons for interrogation into a *de facto* detention. To ensure that the police do not proceed from the premise that a suspect is guilty, the CPL requires that prior to interrogation the police must afford the suspect an opportunity to make a statement to profess his or her guilt or innocence. The police may interrogate a suspect only after he or she is given the opportunity to make such a statement. The noble intention of the provision notwithstanding, research studies indicate that police often ignore the procedural requirement and interrogate suspects directly without giving them the opportunity to make a statement. Not only do the police often deprive suspects of the right to make a statement, it is also common for the police to apply psychological pressure on suspects to make them talk. An often-used tactic is for the police to tell the suspect that they have already obtained solid evidence against him or her and that it would be in his or her best interest to confess (Liu, 2001a, 2001b). Tactics of this nature apparently are contrary to the letter and the spirit of the CPL.

Police interference with a suspect's exercise of the right to counsel represents one of the most troubling aspects in the implementation of the amended CPL. The police abuse, however, is at least in part attributable to the legislative regime itself. The CPL states that after completion of the first police interrogation, the suspect has the right to retain a lawyer to represent him or her. The retained lawyer, according to the CPL, has the right to inquire of the police about the crime of which the client is suspected, the right to meet with the client, and the right to ask the suspect about the circumstances of the case. The CPL then sets out several restrictions. It provides that in cases involving state secrets, lawyers must seek approval from the police before meeting with detained suspects. The CPL further provides that the police, when necessary, can be present at meetings between suspects and their lawyers.

The CPL grants suspects the right to counsel, but at the same time it gives police the power to supervise suspects' exercise of the right. The supervisory power given to the police in practice has led to widespread abuse. The police often deny suspects' requests to seek legal advice in the name of protecting state secrets, regardless of whether a case actually involves state secrets. It is also common for police agencies to set time limits on meetings between lawyers and suspects. The time permitted for each meeting is usually from 15 to 45 minutes, and in each case lawyers are permitted to meet with their clients only twice. The restrictions placed on the free communication between lawyers and suspects have greatly hampered lawyers' ability to represent their clients.

The CPL does not mandate the police presence at the meetings between lawyers and suspects. It only gives police the discretion to determine whether a police presence is necessary. Although this is not indicated in the CPL, regulations issued by the Ministry of Public Security make it clear that the police presence is for the purpose of preventing lawyers' wrongdoing, for instance, colluding with suspects to obstruct the police investigation. The intent of the CPL is that the police are not supposed to be present at all meetings between lawyers and suspects. They can be present only when there are reasonable grounds to believe that such a presence is necessary to prevent the possibility of wrongdoing by lawyers. In practice, because there are no guidelines as to under what circumstances the police presence is justified, the police tend in almost all cases to decide that the police presence is necessary.

After the promulgation of the CPL, the Ministry of Public Security issued two regulations concerning the police authority to supervise lawyers' meetings with suspects.[19] The regulations in many aspects further expand the police supervisory authority. The CPL states only that the police may be present at meetings between lawyers and suspects whenever necessary. The regulations provide that the police not only have the right to be present but also the power to suspend the meetings. The regulations state that if the supervising officer believes that a lawyer has violated the law or the rules of the meeting place, the officer is obligated to persuade the lawyer to stop such unlawful conduct. If necessary, the officer may suspend the meeting and report the lawyer's misconduct to relevant lawyers' management agencies. Theoretically, it seems quite incomprehensible to allow police officers, in most cases not legally trained, to judge a lawyer's behavior, including the legality and appropriateness of the advice a lawyer provides for his or her clients. But the real concern is not the theoretical soundness of the regime but the rampant police abuse of the supervisory power.

The Ministry regulations provide that police may suspend meetings between lawyers and suspects on two grounds: One is when lawyers violate the law when providing legal advice; the other is when lawyers violate the rules of the meeting places. Police cannot make the law, but they are in charge of making the rules of the meeting places, which in most cases are jails or other holding facilities. This power to define the rules of the meeting has thus become the main weapon of the police in restricting suspects' exercise of the right to counsel and in suspending lawyers' meeting with their clients. Some police agencies ask lawyers to submit outlines before meetings with suspects and then permit lawyers to ask only the questions contained in the outlines. In the name of ensuring proper conduct of police investigation, some police agencies prohibit lawyers from asking suspects any questions related to the case. Lawyers are permitted only to read statutory provisions or explain the meaning of the law to their clients. When present at the meetings, officers often show little respect for lawyers. They willfully interrupt consultation sessions or simply turn consultation sessions into a police interrogation. Some police agencies install recording devices or video cameras at the meeting place to monitor lawyer's behavior. More outrageously, under the pretense of preventing escape, some police agencies even ask lawyers to prepare handcuffs for their clients. Lawyers are permitted to proceed with the consultation only after they handcuff their own clients (Chen 2000; Chen & Song, 2000).

Despite the offensive nature of these measures, many police agencies seem to feel justified in imposing such restrictions. The police contend that the measures are necessary to prevent lawyers from colluding with suspects to undermine the police investigation. With respect to lawyers, the police seem to hold an us-versus-them mentality. The police regard themselves as crime fighters and guardians of the public interest. They view lawyers as people associated with and speaking for criminals. In their view, what lawyers intend to do is nothing more than attempt to undermine the police efforts to solve crime. With this kind of mentality prevailing in the ranks of the police, it is not surprising that many officers take an uncooperative or hostile attitude toward lawyers. Furthermore, a lawyer's fate in China is far from that of only being distrusted by the police. There is no lack of stories that lawyers are arrested and sentenced to jail for providing legal service for suspects and defendants.

The police distrust of lawyers in part is attributable to the low regard traditionally held by the Chinese for law and lawyers. The origin of the distrust of lawyers can be traced to the very first day when the Western style legal profession was introduced to China. The Western style legal profession appeared in China in the late Qing dynasty. The profession met with official disapproval as soon as it emerged. In an edict issued in 1820, the emperor deplored the trend toward "unbridled litigation" incited by a growing corps of "litigation tricksters." The emperor described these "litigation tricksters" as "rascally fellows" who intended to "entrap people for the sake of profit." The emperor directed that those who made a profession of preparing legal petitions for others be severely punished. The legal annuals of the Qing dynasty reveal numerous cases in which legal draftsmen were punished by penal servitude (Bodde & Morris, 1967). In modern times, the lack of interest in establishing a comprehensive legal system further deepened the disrespect for the legal profession. Because of the deeply entrenched distrust of the legal profession, there probably is a long way to go before lawyers can gain respect and become a truly functional component in China's criminal justice process.

Police use of torture is another serious problem in the current police operation. The CPL prohibits the use of torture as a means to obtain confessions. The statutory prohibition, however, has not prevented torture. Like the low regard for lawyers, there is also a long historical tradition of using torture as a means to extract confessions. Torture was an officially sanctioned method of obtaining confessions in all imperial dynasties. The feudal law gave overwhelming weight to confessions. Regardless of the existence of other evidence, a person's guilt was not certain until the person confessed to the crime. Because of the weight attached to confessions, the feudal law authorized the use of torture as a means to obtain confessions.

The official sanction of the use of torture and its frequent application marked one of the most distinctive features of the centuries-old Chinese feudal legal tradition (Bodde & Morris, 1967; Cohen, 1968; Dutton, 1992; Xiao, 1987; Zeng, 2000).

The remnant influence of the feudal tradition undoubtedly plays a role in the police tendency to resort to torture. But the difficulty in solving the problem is attributable more directly to the permissible and tolerant attitude of some police agencies and officials toward police use of torture. Faced with the demand from the government leadership and the public to bring crime under control, many police officials share the view that forcing suspects to talk offers the most efficient way to solve crimes. It should be noted that torture is not only a prohibited way to obtain evidence, it is also a criminal offense punishable by long-term imprisonment. In serious cases the offense is punishable even by the death penalty. The stiff penalty nevertheless has hardly produced any deterrent effect. This is largely because many police agencies take a hands-off policy toward officers' use of torture. Officers who resort to torture are rarely prosecuted or disciplined. On the contrary, they are praised, rewarded, and promoted for their ability to crack difficult cases (Chen, 2000; Chen & Song, 2000; Zhou, 1999). With the mentality that the end justifies the means prevailing among police officers and officials, it is not surprising that the statutory ban has produced little effect.

Educating police officers, including high-ranking police officials, about the importance of enforcing the law within the bounds of law and cultivating a culture of respect for the law among officers undoubtedly remain key in the effort to overcome the police tendency to use torture. Legal scholars meanwhile also argue that revision of the CPL is necessary to prevent police use of torture. Since the promulgation of the amended CPL, there has been a heated debate in Chinese legal circles as to whether Chinese law has recognized the principle of presumption of innocence. The amended CPL contains no clear language stating that an accused is presumed innocent until proven guilty. The relevant provision of the CPL states that, "Without adjudication by the people's court in accordance with the law, nobody should be determined as guilty of a crime" (Art. 12, CPL). Some scholars are of the view that Chinese law has in effect recognized the principle of presumption of innocence. Others argue that the provision states nothing more than that only the people's court has the authority to determine a person's guilt or innocence (see Lu, 1998; Song & Wu, 1999; Wang, 1996; Yang, 1998; Yue & Chen, 1997b, 1997c).

In contrast to the controversy surrounding the issue of presumption of innocence, scholars seem to agree that Chinese law does not fully recognize the privilege against self-incrimination. Article 93 of the CPL provides that a suspect must answer questions asked by interrogators truthfully. A reasonable interpretation of the provision is that if suspects are innocent, they are certainly entitled to insist on their innocence; but if they are in fact involved in the crime, they are under legal obligation to admit their guilt. To some police officers, the imposition of such obligation provides the justification to resort to torture. Because of the lack of the idea that a person should be presumed innocent until proven guilty, many officers operate on the premise that a suspect is guilty upon arrest. When a suspect refuses to admit guilt, the police naturally feel justified in resorting to torture to make the suspect fulfill the legal obligation to reveal the truth. Concerned that the provision may have contributed to the police tendency to use torture, many legal scholars suggest that the provision be revised. They argue that it is time for Chinese law to formally recognize the principle of presumption of innocence and grant suspects and defendants the full privilege against self-incrimination, including the right to remain silent (Chen, 2000; Chen & Song, 2000; Song & Wu, 1999; Yue & Chen, 1997a). It is not clear, however, whether the Chinese legislature is ready to make such legislative moves.

Police Accountability

The Chinese police in general have a positive image in the eye of the public. However, they are not immune from misconduct. Police misconduct in China, as in other countries, takes different forms. Some often-mentioned forms of police misconduct include corruption, brutality, making wrongful arrests, conducting unreasonable searches and seizures, unjustifiable use of weapons, and illegal use of police vehicles and equipment. Before the adoption of the new economic policy, China was a closed society. Out of concern that discussing police misconduct openly would tarnish the police image, the government dealt with police misconduct internally without public knowledge. Since the implementation of the policy of economic reform, the government has taken a more open view with regard to police misconduct. The government recognizes that police, like other government agencies, should be subject to citizens' and society's supervision. In the past 20 years, the government has made considerable efforts to establish a police accountability system. The basic structure of the police accountability system is provided for in the Police Law of 1995. This law specifies four types of police supervision mechanisms. They are procuratorate supervision, administrative supervision, internal supervision, and citizen supervision.

Procuratorate Supervision

The people's procuratorate has general oversight authority over the police. It has power to review and approve police requests for arrest. If necessary, it may participate in, direct, and provide guidance to police criminal investigations. The people's procuratorate has the duty to assure that all police actions be in compliance with the law. It may receive citizens' complaints against the police and investigate alleged police misconduct. In serious cases of police misconduct, the people's procuratorate has the authority to bring criminal prosecutions against infracting officers.

Administrative Supervision

To ensure that all government agencies abide by the law when performing their duties, the government established an administrative supervisory system in the 1980s. In the administrative supervisory system, all government agencies are subject to the oversight of the Ministry of Supervision. Police, as the government's law enforcement body, are also subject to the administrative supervision. The Ministry of Supervision and its subordinate agencies have the authority to receive citizens' complaints against the police and to send agents to police agencies to inspect their work. Upon receiving citizens' complaints, the supervisory agency has the authority to investigate the alleged police wrongdoing. The law requires that police agencies cooperate with the supervisory agency in its investigation. Upon finding misconduct of a police officer, the supervisory agency may impose sanctions prescribed in the Police Law against the infracting officer or recommend that the police agency take appropriate disciplinary action against the officer.

The disciplinary sanctions prescribed by the Police Law include warning, record of a demerit, record of a major demerit, demotion, dismissal from the post, and expulsion from the police force. The Police Law provides no procedural protections for officers facing disciplinary actions. Certain procedural protections are provided by regulations issued by the Ministry of Public Security. According to the regulations, a hearing is required before disciplinary actions may be imposed on an officer. The officer involved has the right to be notified of the hearing and has the right to defend him- or herself at the hearing. The officer has the right to tell his or her side of the story and produce evidence to aid his or her defense. Once a decision with regard to the disciplinary actions is made, the officer must be notified of the decision in writing. If the officer is not satisfied with the decision, he or she has the right to ask the agency to reconsider the decision or to ask a higher-level agency to review the decision. According to the Administrative Litigation Law, the officer can also request the administrative tribunal of the people's court to review the disciplinary decision rendered against him or her.

Citizens' Supervision

The Police Law provides that in performing their duties, police must voluntarily accept citizens' and society's supervision. The law specifies three ways in which citizens may exercise the right of supervision:

1. The right to make recommendations and suggestions to the police

2. The right to file complaints against the police

3. The right to bring lawsuits against the police

Citizens may file complaints against the police in several ways. They may file complaints with the people's procuratorate, with the Ministry of Supervision or its subordinate agencies, with the police agency involved, or with higher-level police agencies. The law requires that agencies that receive citizens' complaints investigate the alleged police wrongdoing and notify complaining citizens of the result of the investigation and the disposal decisions in a timely fashion.

Citizens have the right to file administrative or civil lawsuits against the police. Cases filed in the administrative tribunals usually involve police imposition of administrative sanctions. Under Chinese law, the police have the authority to impose various forms of administrative sanctions. The police may subject a person to administrative detention or send a person to a camp of reeducation through labor for disorderly conduct that falls short of a crime. These administrative offenses typically include transgressions such as disturbing social order and obstructing public security. For minor administrative offenses, the police may subject offenders to administrative detention for up to 15 days. In serious cases, the police may send offenders to camps of reeducation through labor. The duration of confinement in the camps may run from one to three years.

The police power to impose administrative sanctions has long been surrounded by controversy. Some commentators believe that granting police the power to subject people to administrative detention and to long-term confinement in camps of reeducation without judicial proceedings creates a great potential for abuse (Biddulph, 1993; Fu, 1994). The government nonetheless is not prepared to take away the power from the police. Although the law does not require police to seek judicial approval for imposing administrative sanctions, it does grant citizens the right to ask the administrative tribunal of the people's court to review the legality and appropriateness of the police decisions to impose such sanctions. To a certain extent, the postsanction court review provides some judicial supervision over this broad police power.

Upon reviewing a citizen's complaint, if the administrative tribunal believes that the sanction imposed is inappropriate, it may annul the sanction or order the police to enter into a new decision. Available research indicates that supervision by the administrative tribunal has produced a positive effect on police decision making. To avoid unfavorable court rulings, many police agencies have tightened the internal review of decisions to impose administrative sanctions. Stricter agency reviews have significantly reduced the number of litigations brought against the police in the administrative tribunal and lowered the overall rate of court rejection of police decisions to impose the sanctions (Chen, 2000; Ma & Tian, 1995).

In addition to seeking relief from the administrative tribunal, citizens may sue the police in the civil courts for monetary damages. The State Compensation Law specifies the circumstances under which the police may incur civil liability. According to the law, the police are civilly liable if they unlawfully subject citizens to criminal or administrative detentions, arrest citizens without reasonable grounds, cause citizens to suffer bodily injury or death by beating or instigating others to do so, or cause citizens to suffer bodily injury or death by illegal use of weapons or other police equipment.

Giving citizens the right to sue the police represents a significant development in China's legal reconstruction. In the first three decades of the People's Republic, it was unthinkable that ordinary citizens could bring the police to court. Even after the adoption of the new economic policy, citizens were not given the right to sue the police right away. The State Compensation Law, which was promulgated in 1994, formally gives citizens the right to sue the police. Since the law came into force, many citizens have exercised their rights and brought lawsuits against the police. Imposition of civil liability was not only to assure that citizens be compensated when police violate their rights. More significantly, the system was created to shape police behavior. It is expected that civil liability will increase police awareness of the importance of respecting citizens' rights when performing their duties.

To ensure that citizens receive timely compensation, the State Compensation Law requires the police agency to bear the primary responsibility for satisfying the monetary damages awarded by the court. On the other hand, to make responsible officers learn a lesson from the lawsuit, the law also requires that the police agency order the responsible officers to reimburse wholly or partially the damages paid by the police agency. There is evidence indicating that the civil liability system has produced the effect of making police agencies take more measures to strengthen officers' education and training. Since the law mandates that the infracting officers bear at least partially the cost of the compensation, the system has also created an incentive for individual officers to show more respect for citizens' legal rights (Lang, 1995; Luo, 1995).

Internal Supervision

The Police Law provides that higher-level police agencies must oversee the work of lower-level police agencies. Higher-level police agencies have the authority to inspect the work of lower-level police agencies and correct the wrong or improper decisions made by lower-level agencies. The Police Law further provides that an internal supervisory committee must be established in all county- and municipal-level police agencies. The internal supervisory committee is responsible for receiving and handling citizens' complaints against the police. It has the authority to investigate the alleged police wrongdoing and to discipline infracting officers.

A notable feature of the police internal supervision is that the authority of the supervisory committee goes far beyond handling citizens' complaints. The internal supervisory committee has the obligation to ensure the legality of all police actions and the efficiency and effectiveness of police performance. It has the authority to review all police action decisions, including decisions to arrest, to search, to detain, and to impose administrative sanctions. It is incumbent upon the committee to correct all police irregularities, for instance, wrongful arrests, illegal searches, prolonged detentions, improper imposition of administrative sanctions, etc. The supervisory committee also has the duty to assure overall police efficiency. The committee should inspect police work regularly to ensure that policing plans and strategies are properly implemented. Officers from the supervisory committee conduct routine supervisory patrols. They may follow officers on duty around to provide on-site supervision, or they may pay surprise visits to see whether officers on duty are performing their tasks properly and diligently.

The Chinese police authority does not regularly release police statistics. However, at the fiftieth anniversary of the founding of the People's Republic, the Ministry of Public Security compiled a report to celebrate the accomplishments of the police. The report, published in 1999, offers a glimpse of the work done by the police internal supervisory committees. The report shows that in 1999 the internal supervisory committees in police agencies nationwide corrected more than 300,000 incidents of unlawful or improper police actions and issued more than 20,000 supervision and inspection decisions and recommendations. The supervisory committees took various disciplinary actions against officers found of wrongdoings, including suspending 2,556 officers from active duty and subjecting 1,366 officers to administrative confinement (Ministry of Public Security, 1999).

Most police commentators agree that the establishment of the internal supervision system has played a positive role in maintaining police discipline and raising police professionalism. Some preliminary studies conducted shortly after the implementation of internal police supervision showed the positive effects of the new system. The studies showed that because of the oversight exercised by the internal supervisory committee, there was a significant decline in the rejection rate by the people's procuratorate of police requests for arrest and a noticeable reduction in citizens' complaints against the police (Lang, 1995; Ma & Tian, 1995). Research studies on the subject, however, are in general lacking. Before more empirical studies are conducted and more evidence comes to light, one can only assume that the system is playing a positive role in making the police a more disciplined force.

In comparison with the situation in the first 30 years of the People's Republic, when the concept of police accountability did not even exist, the establishment of the police accountability system marked a significant step forward in China's police development. In the first three decades of the People's Republic, the police were regarded as a tool of the Communist Party to suppress class enemies and to consolidate the dictatorship of the proletariat. Because the police were so intimately related to the exercise of political power, the government not surprisingly would not allow any public criticism of the police, let alone permit lawsuits against the police.

As China enters an era of economic development, there is a change in the perception of the police role. The police are no longer seen as a tool of the

Communist Party to carry out class struggle but a professional force that shoulders the responsibility of maintaining law and order to assure public security and a stable environment for economic development. As China marches to modernity, the government realizes that it must modernize its police. The establishment of the system of police accountability shows that the government is willing to move in the direction of bringing the police operation within the purview of law. The police accountability system in China is still at its initial stage of development. It will take time for the system to reach its maturity. But the establishment of such a system undoubtedly will play a positive role in making the Chinese police a more disciplined force.

Conclusion

Policing in China has undergone significant changes in the past 25 years. Economic development has brought China prosperity it has never seen before. Prosperity, however, is not the only product of the economic growth. Crime has been a partner in China's march to modernity. The sharp increase in crime, coupled with the erosion of the basis of the past policing strategies, presents an unprecedented challenge to the Chinese police. To police an increasingly modern society, the Chinese police must modernize the force and look constantly for new policing methods and strategies. As China becomes an open society, the Chinese police are willing to learn from the policing experiences of other countries. In the past two decades, the Chinese police have introduced to China numerous policing methods that are commonly used in Western countries. Most notable among them are the introduction of routine motorized patrols, the establishment of a 110 emergency number system, and the implementation of community policing in recent years.

Developing new policing strategies, however, is not the only challenge faced by the Chinese police. Because of the influence of the traditional low regard for law and the failure to establish a comprehensive legal system in a long period of time, many police officers have yet to develop and internalize the idea that police must enforce the law within the bounds of law. The use of torture and other violations of citizens' rights continue to be serious problems in police operations. Since the late 1970s, the Chinese government has made great efforts to establish a comprehensive legal system in China. The promulgation of the Criminal Law and the Criminal Procedure Law in the late 1970s marked the beginning of China's legal reconstruction. Since then, the National People's Congress has passed several police-related laws, most notable among them the Police Law and the amended Criminal Procedure Law. The Ministry of Public Security and other government agencies have also issued numerous police-related regulations. While these laws and regulations are not perfect, it is nonetheless fair to say that there are laws and regulations to govern almost all aspects of police operations.

Admittedly, promulgation of law alone would not change the ingrained patterns of police behavior. In China's context, the police leadership faces an arduous task of cultivating a culture of respect for the law among police officers. The passage of various police-related laws and regulations has set up a framework for making the police live up to a higher professional standard. The police leadership in the past two decades has also made considerable efforts to raise the level of professionalism among police. Great progress has been made; more remains to be made. Despite many problems that still exist, one should be confident that the Chinese police are moving in the direction of becoming a modern, more professional, and more disciplined force.

Appendix: The Hong Kong Police

Hong Kong had been a British colony for more than 100 years before Great Britain handed Hong Kong's sovereignty back to China in 1997. Under the British rule, the Hong Kong police were called the Royal Hong Kong Police Force. The force was modeled after the British police and followed British laws and procedures. After Hong Kong was returned to China, the Royal Hong Kong Police Force was renamed the Hong Kong Special Administrative Region Police Force.

Since regaining sovereignty over Hong Kong, the Chinese government has granted Hong Kong the status of Special Administrative Region. Under this system, Hong Kong enjoys a high degree of self-rule and self-governance. The Hong Kong Police Force is under the leadership of and accountable to the Government of Hong Kong Special Administrative Region. The Hong Kong police are not a police agency under the Ministry of Public Security, and the force is not a part of the Chinese police. The Hong Kong police and the Chinese police, however, have maintained a close working relationship in detecting crimes and apprehending criminals.

As of the end of 2004, the Hong Kong Police Force consisted of 27,754 sworn officers and 5,232 civilian employees. The force is headed by a commissioner and two deputy commissioners. The police perform a wide range of duties, including patrol, order maintenance, crime investigation, directing traffic, providing security for government officials and visiting dignitaries, providing emergency services to residents, controlling illegal immigrants, etc.

The Hong Kong police boast of a high degree of specialization. There are six major regional formations. Each regional formation is commanded by an assistant police commissioner. Under the regional formation, there are police districts. The regional police perform the basic police functions within the region. The regional police are responsible for conducting routine patrols, order maintenance, investigating crimes, and providing service to the residents. While the regional police force has the authority to investigate crimes committed within its region, it usually hands more complicated cases to specialized bureaus in the police headquarters.

In the police headquarters, there are five major departments: the Department of Operation and Support, the Department of Crime and Security, the Department of Personnel and Training, the Department of Management Service, and the Department of Finance, Administration, and Planning.

The Department of Operation and Support is responsible for police antiterrorist operations and operations of special-duty police units. It conducts regular reviews of tactics used in crowd management and riot control and handles matters such explosives and bomb disposal.

The Department of Personnel and Training is responsible for recruitment of police officers and for their entry-level and in-service training. There is a police training school under the direction of this department.

The Department of Management performs the logistics function. It is responsible for developing and maintaining the police information and communication system, including various computer facilities for the force. It coordinates all matters concerning police administration, for instance, the relationship between departments in the police headquarters and the relationship among different regional formations. It has the duty to ensure the efficiency and quality of police work and service. To accomplish this goal, it regularly reviews and evaluates the work of various police departments and formations. This department conducts research aimed at finding better and more effective policing strategies. It is also responsible for receiving and handling citizens' complaints against the police.

The Department of Finance, Administration, and Planning is responsible for financial management of the force. Its tasks include internal audit and management of civilian employees of the force.

Of the five departments, the one that attracts a lot of attention is the Department of Crime and Security. This department consists of several bureaus. The Commercial Crime Bureau is responsible for investigating commercial crimes, for instance, commercial fraud, computer crime, counterfeiting, forgery, credit card fraud, etc. The Narcotics Bureau is in charge of antidrug operations. In Hong Kong, organized crime, such as crimes committed by triads and secret societies, has long been a concern of the police. To effectively deal with the crimes committed by triads and criminal gangs, there is a bureau in the department in charge specifically of investigating crimes committed by organized crime figures. To enhance the department's ability to solve crime, it has several special bureaus. The Criminal Record Bureau is the repository of all criminal records. The Criminal Intelligence Bureau is responsible for collecting and analyzing crime-related information and intelligence. The Forensic Bureau is responsible for forensic examination of firearms and ammunition used in crimes. The Identification Bureau performs the task of analyzing fingerprints and photographs. Apart from criminal investigation, the department is also responsible for providing security for high-ranking government officials and visiting dignitaries.

The basic requirements for becoming a police officer in Hong Kong are that the candidate must be a permanent resident of Hong Kong and have lived in Hong Kong for at least seven years. The educational requirement for becoming a police constable is that the candidate must have some high school education. To become an inspector, the candidate needs to have an associate degree from a college. To be selected as a police officer, a candidate needs to take a written examination, go through an interview, and pass a physical fitness test, a medication examination, and a psychological screening. It is required that the candidate must be proficient in speaking both Chinese and English. Once selected, the candidate must go to the Police Training School to receive training.

The training requirements are different for police constables and inspectors. An inspector needs to complete 36 weeks of basic training that covers police procedure, law, foot-drill, physical training, and weapon handling. Training for police constables is the same as that of inspectors, except that constables are required to complete only 27 weeks of training. Additionally, since constables are usually the first to be on the scene of crimes, emergencies, or other unexpected situations, they are required to receive first aid training. Both inspectors and constables must pass a professional examination before they can graduate from the Police Training School.

A police constable must complete four years of service before being eligible for promotion to the rank of sergeant. If promoted, the officer must serve in the rank of sergeant for three years before he or she can be promoted to the rank of station sergeant. Apart from the years of service required, to be promoted, an officer must also pass a professional examination and be recommended by the Selection Board. After certain years of service, regardless of his or her rank, be it constable, sergeant, or station sergeant, an officer can apply to be promoted to the rank of inspector. To become an inspector, the candidate must have higher educational attainment, pass a professional examination, and be recommended by the Selection Board. The police ranking system in Hong Kong is similar to that of the British police. The highest rank is superintendent. Below superintendent there are chief inspector, senior inspector, station sergeant, sergeant, and police constable.

Notes

1. *History of Han: Book of Geography.* This is a history book written by Bangu (32–92 CE), a historian of the Han dynasty. See p.1543 of the copy printed by the China Publication Bureau in Beijing in 1962.

2. An autonomous region is the same as a province. It is established in regions with relatively large ethnic minority populations. In theory, an autonomous region has more autonomy and independence in its administration, because it needs to take into consideration the special needs of ethnic minority groups. In reality, the administration of an autonomous region is similar to that of a province. Municipalities

directly under the central government are major municipalities that the central government considers necessary to keep under its direct control. The capital city, Beijing, and China's most important industrial and commercial city, Shanghai, are both municipalities directly under the central government.

3. For China's policy with respect to minority nationalities, see *The White Paper on China's Policy and Practice with Respect to Minority Nationalities* issued by the Press Office of the State Council of the People's Republic of China, 1999.

4. The industries and services that come under regular police supervision include hotels, car rentals, pawn shops, and printing and carving houses. These services are believed to be often used by criminals. Police supervision of these businesses is perceived as necessary to track down criminal offenders' criminal activity.

5. See "Organic Regulation of the Urban Neighborhood Committees," promulgated by the Standing Committee of the National People's Congress, December 31, 1954.

6. The organizational structure of the police station and the functions of the three types of officers were specified in the "Organic Regulation of the Public Security Station" promulgated by the Standing Committee of the People's National Congress, December 31, 1954, and the "Detailed Regulation on the Work of Public Security Station" issued by the Ministry of Public Security in November, 1962.

7. See *Law Yearbook of China, 1981–1991*.

8. Today, it is estimated that the size of the floating population is about 114 million. See Fang (2005).

9. In the same period, the police-to-population ratio was higher in all other major Western nations. For instance, the police-to-population ratio in the United States was 1:377; in Germany it was 1:505; in France it was 1:333; and in Japan it was 1:555 (see Dutton & Lee, 1993; Ma & Tian, 1995).

10. Both authors of the cited article were high-ranking Chinese police officials. Bo Jiang was director of the Department of Legal Affairs of the Ministry of Public Security, and Yisheng Dai was acting director of the Institute of Public Security.

11. See "The Decision on Severely Punishing Offenders Involved in Offenses that Greatly Endanger the Public Security," issued by the Standing Committee of the National People's Congress, September 2, 1983.

12. See "The Decision on Expediting the Trial of Cases Involving Offenders Who Have Committed Offenses That Greatly Endanger the Public Security," issued by the Standing Committee of the National People's Congress, September 2, 1983.

13. See *Law Yearbook of China, 1981–2001*.

14. "Towards Implementing Community Policing in All Large and Medium-Sized Cities by 2004." Speech by Luo Feng, deputy minister of public security, at the national meeting of police stations. Xinhua News Agency, March 20, 2004.

15. "On Strengthening the Community Policing Programs," a directive issued jointly by the Ministry of Public Security and the Ministry of Civil Administration. *Legality Daily*, August 20, 2002.

16. See note 14.

17. "Regulation on Procedures of Handling Criminal Cases by Public Security Agencies" (1996), issued by the Ministry of Public Security.

18. See note 17.

19. The two regulations issued by the Ministry of Public Security are "Regulation on Procedures of Public Security Agencies" (1997) and "Regulation on Lawyers' Participation in Criminal Procedure Activity at the Investigation Stage" (1997).

References

Bakken, B. (2005). Comparative perspectives on crime in China. In B. Bakken (Ed.), *Crime, punishment, and policing in China* (pp. 64–99). Lanham, MD: Rowman & Littlefield.

Biddulph, S. (1993). Review of police powers of administrative detention in the People's Republic of China. *Crime & Delinquency, 39*(3), 337–354.

Bodde, D., & Morris, C. (1967). *Law in imperial China.* Cambridge, MA: Harvard University Press.

Cao, P., & Qi, J. (1985). Security agencies and security system in the Ming dynasty. In China Social Science Research Institute, the Legal History Section (Ed.), *Introduction to China's police system* (pp. 233–247). Beijing: The Masses Publishing House.

Chang, Z. R. (1985a). The police system and its characteristics during the time of Northern Warlords. In China Social Science Research Institute, the Legal History Section (Ed.), *Introduction to China's police system* (pp. 318–336). Beijing: The Masses Publishing House.

Chang, Z. R. (1985b). The police system under the rule of Guomintang. In China Social Science Research Institute, the Legal History Section (Ed.), *Introduction to China's police system* (pp. 337–357). Beijing: The Masses Publishing House.

Chen, G. Z., & Song, Y. H. (2000). *Research on issues in implementation of the Criminal Procedure Law.* Beijing: China Legality Publishing House.

Chen, R. H. (2000). *The frontier issues of criminal procedural law.* Beijing: China People's University Press.

Clinard, M., & Abbott, D. (1973). *Crime in the developing countries.* New York: John Wiley.

Cohen, J. A. (1968). *The criminal process in the People's Republic of China: 1949–1963.* Cambridge, MA: Harvard University Press.

Du, X. C., & Zhang, L. Y. (1990). *China's legal system.* Beijing: New World Press.

Dutton, M. (1992). *Policing and punishment in China.* Cambridge, UK: Cambridge University Press.

Dutton, M. (2005). Toward a government of the contract: Policing in the era of reform. In B. Bakken (Ed.), *Crime, punishment, and policing in China* (pp. 189–233). Lanham, MD: Rowman & Littlefield.

Dutton, M., & Lee, T. (1993). Missing the target: Policing strategies in the period of economic reform. *Crime & Delinquency, 39*(3), 316–336.

Fang, B. (2005). The floating people. *U.S. News & World Report, 138,* 47–48.

Feng, W. G., & Zhang, W. (2003). *A practical course in community policing.* Beijing: People's Procuratorate Publishing House.

Fu, H. L. (1994). A case for abolishing shelter for examination: Judicial review and police powers in China. *Police Studies, 17*(4), 41–60.

Gao, H. (1985a). Social conditions and security management in the capital of the west Han dynasty. In China Social Science Research Institute, the Legal History Section (Ed.), *Introduction to China's police system* (pp. 74–88). Beijing: The Masses Publishing House.

Gao, H. (1985b). *Thing*—the local police agencies during the Qin and Han dynasties. In China Social Science Research Institute, the Legal History Section (Ed.), *Introduction to China's police system* (pp. 98–105). Beijing: The Masses Publishing House.

Han, Y. L., & Cao, P. (1985). Security agencies and security regulations in the Qing dynasty. In China Social Science Research Institute, the Legal History Section (Ed.), *Introduction to China's police system* (pp. 261–280). Beijing: The Masses Publishing House.

He, B. S. (1989). The crime trend, causes and penal policies in our country. *Political Science and Law Forum, 5,* 1–11.

He, B. S. (1992). Crime and control in China. In Heiland, H.-G., Shelly, L. J., & Katoh, H. (Eds.), *Crime and control in comparative perspective* (pp. 241–251). Berlin: Walter de Gruyter.

Huang, W. (1991, July 29–August 4). Crackdown on abduction of women and children. *Beijing Review,* 24–27.

Jiang, B., & Dai, Y. H. (1990). Mobilizing all possible social forces to strengthen public security—A must for crime control. *Police Studies, 13,* 1–9.

Keith, R. C. (1994). *China's struggle for the rule of law.* New York: St. Martin's Press.

Lang, S. (1995). *Questions and answers in regard to the Police Law of the People's Republic of China.* Beijing: China Democracy and Legality Publishing House.

Lawyers Committee for Human Rights. (1996). *Opening to reform? An analysis of China's revised Criminal Procedure Law.* New York: Lawyers Committee for Human Rights.

Lee, T. V. (Ed.). (1997). *Law, the state, and society in China.* New York: Garland.

Li, B. (1993, August 9–15). China cracks down on armed criminals. *Beijing Review,* 16–17.

Liu, G. J., & Wei, Y. N. (1999). *Cases of Criminal Procedure Law.* Beijing: China University of Political Science and Law Press.

Liu, H. N. (1985). The security agencies and the laws and regulations regarding security management during the Qin dynasty. In China Social Science Research Institute, the Legal History Section (Ed.), *Introduction to China's police system* (pp. 59–73). Beijing: The Masses Publishing House.

Liu, J. C. (2001a). *Interpretations of provisions of the new Criminal Procedure Law.* Beijing: People's Court Publishing House.

Liu, J. C. (2001b). *New interpretations and new explanations of the Criminal Procedure Law and relevant regulations.* Beijing: People's Court Publishing House.

Liu, J. G., Li, B. J., & Guo, F. H. (2002). *Community policing and policing norms.* Beijing: Public Security Press.

Lu, Q. Z. (1998). Exploring issues concerning the establishment and implementation of the principle of presumption of innocence in China. *Law Science, 10,* 36–43.

Luo, F. (1995). *Interpretation of the Police Law of the People's Republic of China.* Beijing: The Masses Publishing House.

Ma, Z. Y., & Tian, M. Q. (1995). *Interpretation and explanation of the Police Law of the People's Republic of China.* Beijing: China People's Public Security University Press.

McKnight, B. (1992). *Law and order in Sung China.* Cambridge, UK: Cambridge University Press.

Ministry of Public Security. (1999). *Policing in China.* Beijing: The Ministry of Public Security.

Ni, H. Y. (2003). *Community policing.* Beijing: Public Security University Press.

Rogers, J. (1989). Theories of crime and development: An historical perspective. *Journal of Development. 3,* 315–318.

Shelly, L. (1981). *Crime and modernization*. Carbondale, IL: Southern Illinois University Press.

Siegel, L. J. (2003). *Criminology*. Belmont, CA: Wadsworth/Thomson.

Song, Y. H., & Wu, H. J. (1999). The principle against compulsory self-incrimination and its procedural guarantees. *China Legal Science 1999* (2), 117–128.

Sun, Q. (2000). Some thoughts on perfecting the law of arrest in our country. *China Legal Science 2000* (4), 93–98.

Tanner, M. S. (2005). Campaign-style policing in China and its critics. In B. Bakken (Ed.), *Crime, punishment, and policing in China* (pp. 171–188). Lanham, MD: Rowman & Littlefield.

Turner, K. G., Feinerman, J. V., & Guy, R. K. (Eds.). (2000). *The limits of the rule of law in China*. Seattle: University of Washington Press.

Vold, G. B., & Bernard, T. J. (1986). *Theoretical criminology*. New York: Oxford University Press.

Wakeman, F. (1995). *Policing Shanghai 1927–1937*. Berkeley: University of California Press.

Wang, F. (The Minister of Public Security) (1989). Reform and strengthen the public security work in order to serve the need of establishing a market economy. In *Law Yearbook of China—1989* (pp. 813–816). Beijing: Law Yearbook of China Publishing House.

Wang, J. M. (1996). From "guilt by adjudication" to "presumption of innocence." *Law Science, 5,* 13–15.

Wilson, J., & Herrnstein, R. (1985). *Crime and human nature*. New York: Simon & Schuster.

Xiao, Y. Q. (1987). *A course in Chinese legal history*. Beijing: Law Publishing House.

Xiong, Y. X. (2002). *Community policing in China*. Paper presented at the International Symposium of the Trend and Counter-Measures of Crimes in the 21st Century, Beijing, 2002.

Xu, X. Y. (1995). *On the Police Law of the People's Republic of China*. Beijing: Officers' Education Publishing House.

Yang, M. (1998). On the implementation of and the departure from the principle of presumption of innocence in our country's Criminal Procedure Law. *Law Science, 3,* 21–25.

Yu, L. N. (1985a). The frank pledge system and the security at the local levels in the Song dynasty. In China Social Science Research Institute, the Legal History Section (Ed.), *Introduction to China's police system* (pp. 188–204). Beijing: The Masses Publishing House.

Yu, L. N. (1985b). The origin and development of the ancient Chinese police functions. In China Social Science Research Institute, the Legal History Section (Ed.), *Introduction to China's police system* (pp. 3–4). Beijing: The Masses Publishing House.

Yu, L. N. (1985c). Security agencies and security management in the Tang dynasty. In China Social Science Research Institute, the Legal History Section (Ed.), *Introduction to China's police system* (pp. 145–163). Beijing: The Masses Publishing House.

Yuan, H. B., & Sun, X. N. (1986). *China's judicial system*. Beijing: Beijing University Press.

Yue, L. L., & Chen, R. H. (1997a). International standards on criminal justice and the amended Criminal Procedure Law in our country. *Law Science, 1,* 21–25.

Yue, L. L., & Chen, R. H. (1997b). International standards on the fair criminal process and the amended Criminal Procedure Law (Part I). *Tribune of Political Science and Law, 3,* 44–56.

Yue, L. L., & Chen, R. H. (1997c). International standards on the fair criminal process and the amended Criminal Procedure Law (Part II). *Tribune of Political Science and Law, 4,* 37–45.

Zeng, X. Y. (2000). *The legal history of China.* Beijing: China People's University Press.

Zhou, G. J. (1999). Exploring certain issues concerning the prohibition of extracting confessions through torture. *Tribune of Political Science and Law, 1,* 82–95.

3 Neofeudal Aspects of Brazil's Public Security

Benjamin Nelson Reames

A subtle but perhaps profound shift in the study of Brazilian public security is underway. The dominant scholarly tradition has detailed authoritarian legacies that have shaped public security—e.g., the repertoires of brutal state repression, the state institutions often seen as failing or illegitimate, and the stark spatial segregation of classes. This approach was crucial in calling attention to the institutional holdovers of authoritarianism that (in Brazil and elsewhere) undermine the justice system, weaken citizenship, criminalize the poor, and give rise to repressive styles of policing.

More recent studies of public security tend to portray contemporary urban Brazil as increasingly fractured and stratified by privately secured spaces as well as being webbed together at the political level by networks of corruption and criminality. The notion of "authoritarian atavisms" is becoming less useful, while the idea of neofeudal power structures explains more. Here I use *neofeudal* loosely and generally to refer to various theories that identify growing extra-legal violence, shrinking spaces for public life, the privatization of security, and the absence or illegitimacy of state presence in many areas as alterations in the power relations that determine the Brazilian public security situation.

This shift in focus may lead to a better understanding of how public security and power dynamics have developed in the past 25 years in Brazil. Ultimately, it may also lead to an approach that relies less on the notion of authoritarianism to explain the deficiencies and maladies that plague the developing and modernizing world in an era of prevalent democratization, globalization, and fractured state boundaries. Instead, a more powerful explanation may rely more on relationships among transnational corporations, social networks, private enterprises, and criminal organizations in the context of weakening state control.

Three core problems with the Brazilian police—brutality, corruption, and ineffectiveness—undermine confidence in democracy and degrade the value of it.[1] Analysts have long placed blame for these problems on severe social and economic stratification, the durable legacy of authoritarian regimes (most recently, 1964–1985), the lack of resources and training for the police, a culture of vigilantism and violence, and ingrained racial and class prejudices. All of these factors, which range from the structural to the cultural, surely contribute to police violence, corruption, and poor performance. However, the government and the nature of federalism have much to do with holding these defects in place by inhibiting reform.

Furthermore, there are at least two institutional problems that can easily be overlooked. First, there is the Janus face of Brazil's justice and security system, which projects one reality and recognizes another. Second, the increasingly institutionalized criminal and extra-legal organizations in Brazil have formed networks that embed the entire public security system in connections that weaken its independence and authority. On the first point, one can identify a fundamental institutional paradox that slows progress toward democratic policing. In Brazil, as in many countries, there is the proper way the law is supposed to be enforced on the one hand and the way that justice is commonly meted out on the other. These contradicting realities coexist in Brazil with remarkable resiliency, starkness, and severity—a fact that merits special attention and a term for the phenomenon, "institutional duplicity."[2] On the second point, criminal networks have become so strong, wealthy, embedded in *favelas* (Brazilian slums) and into rich society, not to mention armed to the teeth, that they affect public security institutions by corrupting them and depleting them of legitimacy. One cannot understand the dynamic of crime and public security responses to it without considering the dynamic that I call neofeudalism, in which corrupt groups and organized criminal organizations both reap the benefits of disorder and cripple the ability of the state to maintain order.

Institutional duplicity grows out of dichotomies embedded in the Brazilian justice system: Written rules and regulations do not permit police to achieve the goals and expectations that are placed on them; police mandates outstretch their capacity; the political system is expressly egalitarian but overlays a socioeconomic system that is extremely hierarchical; and multiple agencies share responsibility for law enforcement, often leaving no single agency accountable. Often the prescribed means do not lead to the intended ends, so detours and shortcuts are invented to subvert the system; the shortcuts then stay in place and the two systems—one legitimate, the other illegitimate—operate side by side. The result is a confusing justice system, which serves different people differently, conceals commonplace corruption, and is inefficient and resistant to reform.[3]

However, institutions that are accountable to civilian authorities are precisely what is needed both to improve public security (Agüero, 1997; Frühling, 1998; de Mesquita Neto, 1999) and to consolidate democracy in the region (Dominguez & Lowenthal 1996; Linz & Stepan, 1996; Ungar, 2002). Given the waves of crime and police violence that swept the country with impunity in the 1990s, it would be easier to marshal evidence showing that the arrival of democracy has degraded more than improved policing in Brazil.[4]

So if democracy did not improve public security on its own, the pressing question is the reverse: Can a more transparent, accountable police system be used as leverage to achieve a deeper, consolidated democracy?[5] The evidence for optimism from Brazil is that as civil society groups have gained a more mature and informed understanding of police institutions, they have proposed and implemented practical reforms and improvements. In the last 10 years there have appeared civilian complaint centers (*ouvidorias*), community policing programs, less repressive municipal police services, some functional unification of police forces, witness protection programs, and police stations staffed by and attending to women, to mention a few prominent reforms. These innovations have aimed not only to improve the justice system but also to expand citizenship, and though recent, many reforms have been credited with increasing transparency, responsiveness in government, and the public's sense of participation. The future of policing, crime control, and perhaps democratic consolidation may be chartered by civil society experts and reformers who are engaged and well informed.

This chapter starts with a historical overview and analysis of institutional arrangements of the police, from the meta- to the intrainstitutional features. After defining the Brazilian police, the chapter takes a critical look at the public security apparatus in the context of crime, violence, human rights abuses, organized crime, and the growth of uncivil society. The concluding section uses the thus elaborated institutional framework and context to consider the police reforms that have been implemented or proposed. Throughout this analysis, three outstanding features of the Brazilian public security system are stressed: the nature of federalism, the presence of ingrained institutional duplicity, and the influence of privatized security and criminal organizations that generate a type of neofeudalism.

Brazilian Institutions and Public Security

From the end of the 1970s through the 1980s, Brazil, like most countries of South America, underwent a democratic transition; the transition achieved the basic democratic benchmarks: the legalization of political parties, the popular vote, the end of censorship, and freedom of labor union activity. However, the justice and public security sectors—also essential for democracy—lagged behind.

Part of the reason for Brazil's inability to revamp its police forces is its political structure and size. Brazil contains roughly 180 million people and almost half of the land area of South America and as a federal democracy consists of 26 states and one federal district. The job of policing this vast territory has, for the most part, always been delegated to the states. The 1988 Constitution neither unified police forces nor facilitated further decentralization; instead, it made some of the contradictory or dysfunctional traits of the policing system harder to charge. Brazil exhibits a strong type of "demos-constraining" federalism, which means that reforms at the national level are difficult to pass if a small minority resists them (Stepan, 2000). A number of constitutional amendments have been proposed, typically to unify police forces or make them more accountable to civilian authorities; all have failed due to a strong police lobby or conservative elements in smaller states.[6]

To understand what demos-constraining federalism means at the federal level, one must begin with the fact that Brazil's political parties are nonprogrammatic, inconsistent, and numerous, and they vary over time and from state to state. Thus the policy lobby does not behave like an ordinary interest group, because they are the opposite of political parties. The policy lobby has few ostensive leaders, and it requires little political organization, because its rank and file are already organized, informed of relevant legislation, and reasonably united in their agenda. Police institutions—particularly the rigidly hierarchical military police—are explicit that they oppose unification, infringements on rights and privileges, and civilian trials for police officers (all reforms that are explained below). Further, police threats are not considered empty in Brazil, because police have used their power to disrupt: Police strikes, though illegal, have crippled various states over 60 times since the 1990s and have often resulted in the military being called in to control order. As a result, elected officials rarely admit that the police lobby influences them. Yet reform does not pass. Legislators demonstrate their shades of allegiance or compliance not through discourse or action, but by *not* acting.

Moving to the state level, where the police are organized, managed, and funded, Brazil's federal institutions do not help reform efforts. Governors ostensibly control the police by appointing a Secretary of Public Security (SPS) to manage policing. However, despite a governor's power to appoint and remove officials and control their budgets, the police institutions enjoy a great deal of autonomy because of their constitutional protections (explained below), which they use strategically. Because the police are insulated, armed, and constitutionally protected, and because their cooperation is necessary to achieving core parts of any governor's agenda, they feel emboldened to wait out governors or an SPS that they do not agree with. Police know (and admit) as much (Salles & Lund, 1999). Rather than bend police to their will, governors must strike compromises and develop working relationships with police departments. They do not simply command them. Nor do the Secretaries of Public Security. There is frequent animosity (or at least, institutional competition) between the civil police and the military police. The leadership personnel of the former are trained lawyers, while a militarized hierarchy leads the latter. Thus, an SPS drawn from either corporation has difficulty uniting the two groups. To avoid that bureaucratic loggerhead, the chosen SPS might be a public prosecutor or a retired army official instead. Yet in such an instance the SPS runs the risk of becoming a marginalized figure that knows neither institution well. For all these reasons, it is necessary to take an institutional look at Brazilian public security arrangements.

Primary Police Institutions

Brazil's primary public security institutions are its police, most of which are required by mandate of federal law but organized at the state level. There are two main types—an investigative police force and an ostensive police. Additionally, there are multiple municipal guards (which lack special arrest or investigative powers), two federal forces, and firefighters who also fulfill public safety functions. These forces are presented in Table 3.1, and this chapter analyzes them from a variety of perspectives: constitutional, historical, intra- and interinstitutional.

Each state (including the federal district) has a civil police for judicial investigations and a military police for maintaining order.[7] These organizations are considered "half polices" by some, because the civil police (PC for *polícia civil*) investigate possible crimes and the military police (PM for *polícia militar*) are charged with suppressing and preventing crime, but the activities involved in investigating and controlling crime are not made to coincide. In fact, the Constitution of 1988 requires each state to have these two functionally and organizationally different police forces, but the federal government does not require mechanisms for the PC and PM to share information, resources, planning, or jurisdictions. As a result, the dual police system has created divergent command systems, pay scales, and rules that regulate conduct. Infamous rivalries, competitiveness, and conflicting institutional cultures often further complicate the ability of the PM and PC to work together. This functional duality has exacerbated the problem of institutional duplicity by impeding cooperation and doubling the number of police institutions needed.

Military Police

The 27 corporations of the PM form the largest, most visible type of police force in Brazil with 450,000 officers. The state of São Paulo alone has at least 89,000 military police officers; the states of Rio de Janeiro and Minas Gerais both have over 40,000. The military no longer commands them, but the PM still composes "an auxiliary and reserve force of the Army."[8] This specific responsibility to support the military, though unused, still significantly affects policy, training, and ethos. For instance, the PMs are structured internally according to a military model in which there are

Table 3.1   Police Forces of Brazil

Government Level and Number of Forces	Main Police Forces and Attributes	Personnel (estimate)
Federal (2 forces)		16,000
1	Federal Police (PF)	8,000
	Few in number, highly trained, less corrupt, overextended; responsible for border and immigration control, federal crimes, protection of sensitive areas and important officials.	
1	Polícia Rodoviára (Highway Police)	8,000
State (54 forces)		600,000
27	Military Police (PM)	450,000
	Ostensive, order-maintenance policing; numerous, well-armed; some military training.	
27	Civil Police (PC)	150,000
	Investigative or judicial policing, plain-clothed, have legal training.	
Local (357+ forces)	Municipal Guards	60,000
	Provide security in public parks, schools, and transit; increasingly common in larger cities; generally lack firearms; have few powers, but are the focus of police developments given their proximity to citizens and less violent history.	
Total police forces by jurisdiction: 415+	Total police forces by type: 5	Total police personnel: 676,000

SOURCES: Mariano, 2004; Proença, 2004; de Souza Leal, 2004. Estimates are used, because the actual numbers constantly fluctuate, due to turnover and expanding police forces.

two main hierarchical domains—officers and soldiers (*oficiais* and *praças*) (Lemgruber, Musumeci, & Cano, 2003). As often follows in such bureaucracies, the fundamental values transmitted in regulating conduct are those of hierarchy and discipline.[9] Also, the PM frequently create elite units to deal with specific types of crimes or problem areas, a tendency that has much in common with the military. Further, the PM inherited from the military an excessive number of ranks (12, to be exact) that makes advancement very difficult and creates an elite group of insulated and well-paid brass at the top.[10] In short, the Brazilian approach to policing has created a structural dichotomy within the PM: It performs a civil function with a militarized institution.

Civil Police

The PC are considered judicial police forces, because they carry out investigations of crimes (except those committed by the PMs) under the supervision of the courts and the attorney general (*Ministério Público*). The PC's function is to establish causal connections between the crime, the circumstances, the perpetrators, and the accomplices. The PC also assemble crime reports; perform arrests, seizures, and searches by court order; and manage grossly overcrowded jails and holding cells. In theory, they do not patrol the streets in uniform or do ostensive policing, though this too is an example of institutional duplicity.[11] Much about the PC is dated. For example, most forces were formed during the First Republic (1889–1930); the Penal Process Code (*Codigo de Processo Penal*), which dictates the PC's functioning, has not changed since 1941. A major problem is the paralyzing weight of bureaucratic duties due to the legally mandated *inquérito policial* (formal police inquisition). It has been blamed for contributing to low morale, inefficiency, corruption, and the brutal extraction of confessions (Lemgruber et al., 2003).

The PC constitute the second most important of the police forces, because they are fewer in number and more dependent on other public officials than the PM. Nationally, there are roughly 150,000 members of the PC. Of these, a good estimate is that there are 10,000 *delegados* or high-ranking officials (a *delegado titular* is a chief of a precinct); the rest include investigators, detectives, specialists, and clerks. In many states, all *delegados* have law degrees, which confer a higher status in Brazilian society, but the competitive hiring process with new educational requirements has not yet cleared out a very stagnant body of personnel in other states: Despite the new law, it is estimated that nationwide only 60 percent of delegados have bachelor's degrees in law (Mariano, interview, 2004).

Federal Police

The PF (Polícia Federal) are few in number and overloaded with responsibilities. Most estimate that the federal police personnel numbers 15,000, but the best Brazilian estimate of actual police *agents* is 8,000 (Proença, interview, 2004).[12] The PF are responsible for controlling entry and exit via land, sea, and air frontiers and ports—during a strike in 2004, they managed to slow down all international travelers because of their airport responsibilities. The PF also guards key members of the government, foreign diplomats, and major federal government installations throughout the country. Officials who have received death threats—even from other police forces— are often placed under the protection of the PF. This relatively small force is also charged with finding and destroying hidden airfields, controlling territorial and crime problems with native groups in the Amazon, and investigating sophisticated financial and political crimes. With passport and other bureaucratic duties occupying much of their time, the PF's efforts to control corruption and contraband (arms and drugs) may be pushed onto the back burner, making it easier for organized crime to act with impunity.

Besides protecting Brazil's territorial integrity and public officials, the PF is responsible for managing national security threats. In this capacity, it liaises with international police organizations, including Interpol. The PF provides a central intelligence collection and disseminating service for the various state police forces. In many respects the work of the PF parallels the activities of the Federal Bureau of Investigation (FBI) in the United States. The PF maintains specialized units, such as the Division of Organized Crime Control and Special Investigations (*Divisão de Repressão ao Crime Organizado e Inquéritos Especiais*—DECOIE), which specializes in financial crime; the Tactical Operations Command (*Comando de Operações Táticas*—COT), a SWAT-like force officially formed in March 1990 that has over 50 agents trained in hostage negotiation and rescue, tactical operations such as rapid entry into aircraft and buildings, and of course special weapons training and snipershooting; and the Antinarcotics Division (*Divisão de Repressão a Entorpecente*—DRE*)*, which works mainly to intercept illegal drugs sales and drugs in transit. A unique institutional trait of the PF is that the marshals (high-ranking officers of limited number) can form these special units and divisions ad hoc and informally, and very little hierarchical control or approval is needed. The adaptability and the public confidence that the PF enjoys is unique among Brazilian police. Ironically, despite their solid reputations, the size of the PF remains limited due to trepidations about a centralized, federal police amassing too much power, as happened during authoritarian periods.

Municipal Guards

The *Guarda Municipal* is a low-key type of public security force that exists in more than 357 of Brazil's 5,561 municipalities.[13] The characterization of the municipal (or civil) guards as less extreme than the PMs is reflected in their training, weaponry, powers, deployment, activity, and pay. If armed, they typically carry only a nightstick and a radio or more rarely a 38-millimeter revolver. They earn a salary of R$700–800 a month (about US$250–275). On average, training lasts four months. The municipal guards patrol parks and schools and in that sense relieve PMs of some basic order maintenance policing.

Other Forces

On the state level, the departments of *bombeiros* perform functions that include fighting fires, so these services are usually translated as "fire departments"; however this definition leaves out a variety of public safety and civil defense services they provide. For example, in most states bombeiros respond to emergencies such as floods, bomb threats, crowd control for special events, collapsed buildings, rescue operations, and natural disasters—typical police responsibilities in many countries. If there is not a specific suspect to apprehend or a crime underway, the PMs often do not respond to emergency calls, leaving the bombeiros to attend to many public order and safety problems. Many departments of bombeiros are being separated from the PM, into which they had been incorporated; currently, 16 of the 26 states have independent bombeiros.

Other forces at the federal level do policing, but they are either very new or very limited. The National Secretariat of Public Security (SNSP or SENASP—*Secretária Nacional de Segurança Pública*) announced the creation of a National Guard (*Força Nacional*) on August 5, 2004. Luiz Fernando Corrêa, national secretary of public security at the time, announced that 300 officers had been trained and another 1,500 would commence training by the start of 2005. So far, the troops have been recruited from the PM's special operations forces. The National Guard is meant to be deployed when states ask for emergency help, presumably when police strikes or serious crime problems threaten public order. It is almost certain that their first deployment will be in Rio de Janeiro, where the governor has already requested federal help in battling drug traffickers. The forces will be under the command of state authorities. They will wear symbolically important black uniforms like the Tactical Operations Troops of the PF. Two other small, federal, law-enforcement agencies include the federal railway police and a dock police force that guards warehouses and other infrastructure at national ports.

Meta-Institutions: The Current Police System in Federal Law

The police system is needlessly burdened with dualities, some of which are embedded in the Constitution. Besides the bifurcation of police activity into two "half polices," there are three other dualities: First, the PC and PM have national-level protections and mandates, but state-level control, funding, and organization. The Constitution defines policing as a state-level responsibility, while national laws and norms dictate the structure and disciplinary systems of the police. In short, indirect control of the police is centralized, yet direct control is decentralized to the states. This duality of control burdens the police with multiple political masters and impedes reform in the following specific ways: Given that the state-level PM and PC represent about 97 percent of the public security system in terms of personnel,[14] and the states lack the exclusive power to reform and regulate these police forces (and, as mentioned above, the national government has proved crippled in doing so), it seems the nation's main public security forces remain disturbingly insulated from interference by elected representatives.

The second duality is that the 1988 Constitution sustains institutional duplicity by cementing a confusion of policing responsibilities. The responsibility for criminal investigation falls both to the federal and civilian police (Article 144, paragraphs 1 and 4). Order maintenance and crime prevention is the job of the PM (Article 144, paragraph 5), but the armed forces also have the responsibility to guarantee "internal security" and order maintenance (Article 142). As a result, there are conflicts over power and confusion over responsibility among the police forces.

Third, the Constitution preserves an unnecessary link between the civilian-controlled police and the military. Even though the police are subordinate to state governors, the Constitution defines the police as ultimately responsible to the army.[15] The police also won the guarantee of a privileged forum for the trial of police officers. Before 1988, only a few states had military tribunals. With the current Constitution, any state with more than 20,000 active military police officers is authorized to create a State Military Court (Article 125, sections 3 and 4). The upshot is that for an official of the PM to lose his or her job for administrative misconduct or crimes, only military courts and, in effect, commanding officers can order dismissal. As a result, military police officers are—in terms of responsibility to civilians and public officials—the most insulated public servants. The policing system that emerges from the Constitution is confused, insulated, military-minded, and difficult to change.[16]

In sum, when Brazil became a democratic republic again, it adopted a throwback police system that solidified the decentralized structure, functional duality, and complex legal authority in which conditions for corruption and ineffectiveness are fertile. The police have privileges, protections, and overlapping responsibilities in the national ambit yet come under decentralized control at the state level. They are militarized and resistant to change. They are bifurcated into functionally distinct and often redundant and uncooperative police forces whose responsibilities are intertwined without being shared. Paulo Sérgio Pinheiro, not only a noted Brazilian political scientist but an expert on human rights and policing, summarized that the 1988 Constitution reinscribed the repressive apparatuses that were formulated during the dictatorship by reinscribing what the military governments had put into practice, creating a clear continuity in place of a true transition (1994). In other words, though the rules for policing have changed, most of the institutions, mechanisms, and systems for how policing is actually conducted have not changed.

Historical Development of Police Institutions

Most historical analyses of the Brazilian police imply that a sort of ineluctable path-dependency has produced the dire situation of today. Given the enduring patterns of abuse, impunity, and inefficiency, it is easy to see why. Both the ostensive policing that the PM conducts and the PC's investigative practices developed over more than a century and a half. But rather than point to such facts as evidence of cultural continuity or unresolved class conflict, which they may be, I focus on the institutional practices and relationships that became embedded over time.

The PM grew out of a national force that operated in the nineteenth century to protect ruling groups. In the imperial period (1822–1889), Brazil's primary police force was the National Guard (*Guarda Nacional*). Created on August 18, 1831 (reformed significantly in 1841) and composed only of voting citizens (those who earned a minimum income), the National Guard's main function was to repress a majority population of socially and economically excluded people—slaves, former slaves, native people, racially mixed, and other poor groups. The National Guard was organized separately within each province (what would become "states") and used brutal and racist tactics of suppressing disorder. As their size and influence grew, the National Guard forces came to rival the army. So, principally after 1841, the imperial government assigned the army to protect borders, put down revolts, and maintain general stability; the National Guard was left to protect ruling groups and public spaces (Fausto, 1999).

Other inchoate police forces took shape. The Ministry of Justice appointed a chief of police in each provincial capital; parishes and municipalities then had deputies and subdeputies who took on duties as "justices of peace" (Fausto, 1999). These men investigated and, in some cases, tried and sentenced criminal cases. In this sense, they were forerunners of the PC. The imperial government created the Municipal Guards (*Corpo de Guardas Municipais*) in the capital city, Rio de Janeiro, also in 1831, and permitted other provinces to do the same. Many cities followed suit, including São Paulo in that same year. Finally, the provinces developed their own Public Forces (*Forças Públicas*) much in the mold of the National Guard, to protect their own interests and in some cases their sovereignty.

Important traits formed during the imperial period inform the present day policing situation (Mariano, interview, 2004). First, competition between national and provincial powers was a major factor, because the National Guard and state-level Public Forces competed against each other in terms of loyalty and active strength; this state-federal tension persists today. Second, the imperial period inaugurated a "judicial policing" approach in which the chiefs of police, responsible to judges, conducted investigations with an "inquisitorial approach" that easily gave way to torture. Third, order maintenance policing was conducted by armed forces, and therefore ostensive policing became associated with the structure, rules, disciplinary approach, and strategies of military institutions; these police were prepared to confront internal and external "enemies" rather than "citizens." Those same police are not around today, and it is unclear if their ethos is, but their titles, techniques, and divisions still are. Also, following from the second and third points, it is notable that the bifurcation of police activity developed early on and never ceased.

Over the course of the First Republic (1889–1930), the task of ostensive policing remained a state-level activity and, depending on the state, was divided among Public Forces and Municipal or State Civil Guards. The Public Forces grew significantly. For example, in São Paulo the force started with 3,940 officers in 1891 and reached 14,079 in 1924; French advisors were contracted to help train and structure the police in 1906. They developed an infantry, an artillery division, a cavalry, and, by 1926, even a small air force. On the other hand, a State Civil Guard was created in São Paulo on October 22, 1926, to conduct ostensive policing of a nonmilitary variety (Mariano, interview, 2004). By 1964, São Paulo's Civil Guard had 15,000 officers.

Authoritarian regimes left durable legacies on the Brazil's police institutions. During the era of the populist dictator GetúlioVargas (1930–1945), police operations became centralized and militarized, because the police were used to suppress dissent and maintain order. Nonmilitary ostensive policing began to disappear, along with the potential for the state's sovereignty. With the death of Vargas came the ascension of Juscelino Kubitschek, the election of Jânio Quadros, and the brief government of João Goulart. After this mostly democratic reprieve, public security arrangements abruptly changed again under the bureaucratic authoritarian federal government of 1964–1985. It became especially severe after December 13, 1968, when Institutional Act 5 dissolving the Congress was handed down. Civil Guards and Public Forces around the country were merged. Decree 1,072 of December 30, 1969, extinguished Civil Guards in 15 states and annexed them to state military forces.[17] This fusion resulted in the end of the Civil Guards and Municipal Guards (though these were to be reincarnated later) and in the creation the Military Police. The ruling military apparatus then placed the PM under the direction of the Ministry of the Army (Law Decree 667/69, Article 1).

Thereafter, two changes had an enormous impact on policing: The federal government assigned the responsibility of maintaining order to the PM—a responsibility that had been previously shared by a uniformed and active PC (Law Decree 667/69, Article 3; Law Decree 1,072/69). Second, the military exerted greater influence over the PM by creating a special army division to oversee the PM and by appointing military officers to direct the PM and to the state secretariats of public security. As a result, the PM became stronger, singular, and more militarized.

Interinstitutional Problems With Public Security

Taken together, the weaknesses in the justice and public security systems mean that Brazil lacks a coercive state apparatus to protect the rights of the general population (Linz & Stepan, 1996; Stepan, 2000). A state cannot have a coercive apparatus without a law enforcement system, which requires the core institutions of public security to cooperate. As a meta-institutional matter as argued above, the Constitution impedes the ability of the PC and PM to work together. Though that dysfunction manifests itself as an interinstitutional problem, it will not be repeated here; instead this section highlights two other problems: the involvement of the military in policing operations and the difficulty police have in working with the courts.

Relations between the military and the police are a traditional focus of concern in developing democracies. But in that context Brazil is a relatively stable and advanced democracy, and it does not provoke many worries about the military taking over the well-entrenched and sizeable police forces. On the other hand, the armed forces have never been entirely removed from policing operations, because they may be—and have been on numerous occasions—used to preserve internal security and maintain law and order, according to Article 142 of the Constitution. Two main justifications are invoked when using the military in public security: the deployment is either temporary or exceptional (or both). Due to a wave of police strikes starting in the mid-1990s, President Fernando Henrique Cardoso deployed armed forces to control order in a number of states, even though the troops had no arrest powers. Armed forces have also been used in response to "exceptional" crime problems—perhaps most famously in Operation Rio (from November 1994 to May 1995). This joint operation of the armed forces and state government involved controversial invasions into the favelas (or *morros*, the hilly, impoverished areas of Rio) in an attempt to disarm drug traffickers and interrupt organized crime. The media success of Operation Rio and subsequent statements by public officials suggest military incursions into slums and poor neighborhoods to combat arms and drug trafficking will continue. Overall, the federal government employed the military at least 50 times from 1985 to 1997 and numerous times thereafter due to police strikes (de Mesquita Neto, interview, 2004).

A key question that arises is how these cooperative arrangements will be structured. Some experts have called for ongoing arrangements in which the military would support the police in setting up blockades and checkpoints and would have judicial powers in frontier areas to better control criminal activity (Braudel Institute of World Economics, 2003). The trends indicate an interest in and a willingness to blend police and military functions, which if it continues should require legislation and demand careful planning and strict civilian supervision.

The Brazilian justice system is chronically slow and impedes the legal application of justice. The environment of impunity contributes to police brutality and corruption; the frail justice system also contributes to inefficiency, which creates incentives for people to go around the justice system, thus reinforcing the cycle of vigilante justice and institutional duplicity. Consider the fact that the state São Paulo maintains a PC of 36,000 members to investigate crimes, and there were 523,396 officially filed reports of crime in 1999, but only 84,519 police investigations were opened (16 percent of all reported crimes, which usually have a better chance of being solved than the majority that go unreported). Based on these *inquéritos*, the Public

Ministry formally processed 25,300 cases, of which 12,102 began by capturing a suspect in the act, which does not require much investigative activity. In short, only 2.5 percent of all reported crimes reached a judge as the active result of police investigations (Institute of Citizenship, 2002). Ironically, without this filter of investigative ineffectiveness, the court system would be swamped. There is roughly one judge for every 23,000 inhabitants, while the United States has one for every 9,000 (da Silva Filho, 2000).

Questions of control over public security institutions at the state level also exacerbate problems with institutional duplicity. Governors ultimately direct the police, but in most states a Secretary of Public Security (SPS) manages both forces. During the authoritarian regimes, this official would be from the military. Since the country was democratized, the selection of secretaries of public security has been problematic, as both the PC and PM bitterly resent one having "command" over the other. Therefore, an official is often selected who has no experience with either force. Further, the SPS often has little direct control over the two forces; the PM in some states are effectively insulated from the SPS. The SPS's purpose is to harmonize strategies, budgeting, and operations, yet as long as both police maintain separate jurisdictions and operate separate databases and systems of telecommunications, the SPS's capacity to do so is extremely limited, even when welcome. The result is a muddled system of political and operational control.

Intrainstitutional Factors: Internal Problems With the Police

Brazilian police institutions are frequently undermined from within by corruption, impunity, and bureaucratic privileges. These tendencies are often ill-defined and overlapping but clearly contribute to brutality and inefficiency and impede progress toward democratic policing (da Silva Filho & Gall, 1999). Institutional duplicity allows these deficiencies to persist because they are rarely confronted directly, and even reformers who would tackle such problems are often disheartened by their seemingly intractable nature.

Police corruption is a serious problem in Brazil. It not only erodes the rule of law, but police corruption is frequently connected to torture, the excessive use of force, and brutality (Costa, 2004). Petty forms of corruption (or *parasitismo*) that include petty bribes, shirking, and passive corruption (turning a blind eye) are common. More troubling for democracy, however, is serious corruption, which is evident in criminal activities so pervasive that they could not exist without police cooperation or complicity: The rise of drug trafficking; the sale not only of guns, but of heavy artillery like antiaircraft missiles and landmines; theft and robbery of vehicles; the frequent escape of prisoners; and the unstoppable network of *jogo do bicho* (a type of underground gambling) are all testaments, in their own ways, to the involvement of police in organized crime. These problems are examined in greater detail below in the section on uncivil society (Braudel Institute of World Economics, 2003).

Corruption and brutality impede the application of accountability within the public security institutions. Neither the judicial system nor the internal disciplinary systems of the police effectively punish individual police officers, and this creates the problem of impunity. There is some confusion about what agency should exercise responsibility for oversight of the PC and PM. The *Ministério Público* (translated with some ambiguity as the public prosecutor's or attorney general's office, but here as the "Public Ministry") is ultimately responsible for investigating and trying cases of police misconduct, but the Public Ministry is not fulfilling this function (Global Justice, 2003). Some blame ambiguity in the 1993 law (Institute of Citizenship, 2002). At least 10 states have developed *ouvidorias*, or external civilian oversight offices. *Ouvidorias* have proved very effective (in most states) in increasing transparency of police operations, tracking trends of police violence, exposing serious problems, and involving civil society in police planning; however, despite having the ability to "follow" the investigation of police abuse cases, *ouvidorias* cannot investigative or impose accountability on individual police officers.

Internal discipline is the responsibility of *corregedorias*, the Brazilian version of internal affairs offices. In some states, like Rio de Janeiro, there is a corregedoria for both of the police departments and a third, recently created "unified" corregedoria that takes over some investigations from either the PC's or the PM's corregedoria. Crimes and misconduct are supposed to be investigated and handled by corregedorias, whose resources are limited (in terms of budgets, manpower, and geographic reach) and whose procedures are not transparent. Alleged crimes are investigated by members of the same force accused of committing them, often in the very same precincts (*delegacias*); then the cases are tried in special courts. For instance, crimes committed by the PM (except murders, explained below) are sent to military tribunals, which have earned a paradoxical track record by throwing out cases of homicide and severely punishing disciplinary matters such as desertion and insubordination.[18] This is partly explained by the authoritarian regime's legacy: Internal control systems of both police forces were used to maintain hierarchy and discipline. This tendency was marked in the PM, but it affected the PC as well. To this day it is much more likely that a PM officer will be punished for not having shined shoes than for using excessive force to detain a suspect.

Investigations of the most severe forms of police brutality—murder and torture—have only recently begun to approximate principles of democratic policing. The public court system (*Justiça Comun*) cannot try cases against PM officers. However, in 1996, a federal law was passed to make an exception in the case of murders committed by police officers.[19] Further, torture was finally defined as a crime in 1997.[20] Impunity persists, because the two police forces tend not to characterize the crimes of torture or homicide as such. In the case of torture, investigations are often opened as a case of assault (*lesão corporal*) or not opened at all, alleging lack of evidence of a crime or lack of evidence of the authorship of the crime. In the case of homicide, the tendency is to open an investigation into a crime committed by the victim and a case of "resistance to police action followed by death." Since "resistance to police action followed by death" is not a legally defined crime, homicide can fall under this category and escape investigation. This practice, as confirmed by recent research of the police ombudsman, is frequently tolerated by the Public Ministry and the judiciary, and it contributes to the closure of investigations and to the failure to initiate judicial proceedings in cases of homicide committed by police officers.

The policing system is beset by bureaucratic dysfunctions. The retirement system demonstrates the weight that bureaucratic privileges put on the policing system. Approximately two-fifths of the budget for the Secretary of Public Security of São Paulo is spent on retirees. The PM of São Paulo alone supports about 35,000 retirees, or almost one for every two active service members. The privilege of higher-ranking officers is a significant factor here: It is easier for them to retire at a higher salary, so that São Paulo has 1,400 active first sergeants and 14,000 on pension. There are 53 active colonels, while 1,000 receive pensions. Also, active police are deployed in positions that nonsworn personnel fill in many other countries, such as cooks, barbers, and pharmacists. For reasons of military esthetics, 11,000 police officers (including 620 musicians) of the PM of São Paulo fulfill tasks irrelevant to policing. Possibly 25 to 30 percent of active duty PMs never hit the streets (Mariano & Bicudo, 2004).

Training and education of the police are widely considered to be a cause of police-society conflict. Experts agree that education is lacking and training is excessively militarized, which conditions police officers to "engage enemies" rather than "serve citizens" (see Costa, 2004; Mariano & Bicudo, 2004; de Mesquita Neto, 1999; de Mesquita Neto, interview, 2004). Proposed reforms center around providing continuing education and training, teaching human rights and citizenship, and extending formal education requirements. Though government increasingly demands higher educational standards, civil society is assisting, because funds and innovative ideas are limited.[21] Such strategies do not replace the specific training that could be provided by a police academy, but they are intended to raise the educational level of the police forces while diminishing the social stigmatization and segregation that can lead to conflict. Other reforms under consideration would create a single National Police Academy to develop a cohesive curriculum for all police officers. As it stands, training varies from state to state and police force to police force. The PM's training reinforces military values of rigid discipline, centralization of decisions, emphasis on special or tactical units, and an aggressive approach to confronting an "enemy" (da Silva & Gall, 1999; de Souza Leal, interview, 2004). The training for the PC is largely absorbed with the technical details and proper mechanisms for undertaking an *inquérito policial* (specialized police investigation) as defined in the penal process code, which most observers consider outmoded and burdensome (Costa, 2004).

In terms of strategy and deployment, the police of Brazil utilize approaches that are almost exclusively reactive and suppressive rather than proactive and preventive. There are signs that this is starting to change as the PM in most states have some type of community policing programs in place. But isolated community policing programs will not necessarily "put more cops on the street" or put them in better touch with society. Further, preventive policing achieves less of its potential impact in Brazil than elsewhere, because resources that might be applied to assign officers to the street are instead applied to maintaining an excessive number of ranks, hiring military cooks and barbers because of the preoccupation with military esthetics, and providing special privileges for public officials. Cutting useless bureaucracies and outsourcing tasks to nonsworn personnel would increase police presence and allow preventive policing to be more effective.

In terms of pay and benefits, there are two outstanding features: disparities and shortfalls. There is remarkable disparity between different ranks, states, and police forces in terms of what police officers earn; also, today police are underpaid, whereas previously they were absurdly underpaid. In recent years, the police have received salary hikes in most states. This followed a wave of police strikes and demonstrations in 1996–1997 and 2002. Strikes by the police, which are constitutionally forbidden, are overt examples of problems that low pay causes. Less tangibly, low pay also makes police officials more susceptible to corruption and bribery, and many are compelled to work second jobs (*bicos*) to support their families. These illegal and dangerous jobs, usually in the clandestine security sector (discussed further below) tire police officers and frequently deplete their ranks: The Ouvidoria of São Paulo found that out of every 10 police officers that were killed (including in traffic accidents), 8 died while off duty, likely working their second or third jobs. The chart in Table 3.2 is based on 2001 data from selected states and lists monthly salaries in the Brazilian currency (the *real*) followed by a U.S. dollar estimate, which includes *gratificações* (or "benefits," such as health insurance and travel allowances).

Context of Public Security Problems: Neofeudalism

An institutionally duplicitous environment, as described above, creates the following paradox: There is a revered legal mechanism to achieve something, and then there is the way it actually gets done (Muniz, interview, 2004; Proença, interview, 2004). The hierarchically rigid fiefdoms of Brazilian bureaucracy are ventilated by shortcuts to or diversions from justice. Police death squads, which persist today, provide a horrifying example of shortcuts to vigilante "justice" (Caldeira, 2000; Huggins, 1998). Investigations that rarely yield enough evidence to prosecute crimes against the poor serve as a more common example of diversions down dead ends; as

Table 3.2   Selected Monthly Police Salaries in 2001

| | Civil Police | | | | Military Police (increasing ranks) | | | | | | | | | | |
| | Detective/ Investigator | | Delegado | | Soldier | | First Lieutenant | | Captain | | Colonel | |
State	real	$	real	$	real	$	real	$	real	$	real	$
Alagoas	550	196	4,000	1,429	464	166	1,063	380	1,612	576	3,657	1,306
Bahia	689	246	1,653	590	764	273	963	344	1,259	450	1,758	628
Federal District	3,009	1,075	6,480	2,314	1,250	446	2,950	1,054	3,500	1,250	NA	NA
Espírito Santo	800	286	2,000	714	300	107	NA	NA	NA	NA	NA	NA
Goiás	905	323	4,204	1,501	650	232	1,384	494	1,822	651	4,980	1,779
Pará	770	275	2,611	933	557	199	1,228	439	1,609	575	2,422	865
Paraná	728	260	6,031	2,154	558	199	2,012	719	3,779	1,350	5,594	1,998
Pernambuco	773	276	3,183	1,137	803	287	2,020	721	2,850	1,018	4,360	1,557
Rio de Janeiro	1,100	393	3,600	1,286	500	179	1,810	646	2,155	770	4,112	1,469
Rio Grande do Sul	644	230	4,800	1,714	524	187	1,259	450	1,674	598	4,172	1,490
São Paulo (city)	894	319	1,750	625	757	270	1,750	625	4,264	1,523	5,962	2,129

NOTE: It is important to keep in mind that because of exchange rate fluctuations, consistent inflation, the ambiguity of what constitutes a "benefit," and pay raises of almost 50 percent in some states, these numbers are not accurate. They are meant to give a general idea of police salaries. Data come from secretaries of public security and police unions and were published in *Folha de São Paulo*, p. C1 (July 22, 2001).

a result, people living in the impoverished favelas often seek justice from local crime bosses rather than from the police. The cumulative result is cynicism and lack of confidence in the police, which only makes their job harder when they try to do it properly.[22] Institutional duplicity, like the old expression, *para inglês ver,* is a tacit situation that can both explain and cause stagnancy.[23] This stagnancy not only slows institutional progress toward a model of democratic policing, it distorts other aspects of public security.

This section briefly explores how policing interacts with the Brazilian context of public insecurity. A major paradox has been that the return to democracy coincided with the increase in violent crime and the spread of criminal organizations (Pinheiro, 1994; Zaluar, 2000). Nor has the fear of crime subsided. In search of ever more security, urban Brazilians have built fortified enclaves for homes and offices that are strewn with barbed wire and surrounded by fences, cameras, and guards; these built structures, as physical reminders of hostility, seem to justify the paranoia that built them (Caldeira, 2000). On average, crime, criminal organizations, the fear of crime, violence, and violent responses from police have all risen over the past 15 years; all of these problems involve the police.

Moreover, there has been stark spatial segregation at the urban level, and increased networking among criminal groups at the transnational level. Feudalism, as an economic and political order, can be characterized by the decentralization of political authority (to lords and barons) in the midst of globalizing forces (such as mercantilists and the Catholic Church) and the use of brutality to extract rents and raise armies. In neofeudalism, mafias, private armies, and barons of international trafficking also collect tributes, administer justice, and muster soldiers from the squalid territories that they control. Private security in Brazil is beginning to outmatch public police forces as the rich contract their own armies of security companies, often illegitimate. If this vicious cycle spins out of control, the legitimacy of the Brazilian state will be compromised, and its ability to establish hegemony, either through coercion or compliance, will be weakened. For these reasons, a dynamic that is justifiably called neofeudalism has the power to bankrupt the public security institutions of Brazil.

Crime and Violence

Crime and violent crime rates rose during the 1990s and remain at very high levels, leaving much of the populace terrorized by fear. According to the Brazilian census, the rate of homicide grew by 130 percent between 1980 and 2000, going from 11.7 for each 100,000 inhabitants to 27. For a span of 10 years after democratization (1991–2000), official data show a steady rise in intentional deaths (not necessarily homicides), going from just over 40,000 per year to just under 60,000. Of these, about 40,000, or about 88 percent of all murders, are homicides committed with guns. Murders outnumber death by diseases such as AIDS. According to one estimate, one of every 20 inhabitants of the city of São Paulo was a victim of armed robbery in 2002; there were 1,704 such incidents daily (Braudel Institute of World Economics, 2003). In 2001, Brazil's homicide rate reached 27.8 per 100,000, based on 47,899 murders; for point of comparison, the United States is a relatively violent country, and its murder rate is usually between 5 and 6 (Lemgruber, 2004).

In favelas and poor communities in the peripheral areas, homicide rates exceed 100 per 100,000 people, among the highest in the world. In general, young, dark-skinned males are the most likely to be killed or suffer violence. In 1999 in the city of Rio de Janeiro, for every 100,000 males between the ages of 15 and 29, 239 were murdered (Institute of Citizenship, 2002). Men are much more likely to be murdered than women, yet nearly one in five Brazilian women has been the victim of violence perpetrated by a man (Global Justice, 2002). Nonetheless, the pattern is for people of African descent as well as the poor, the young, and the male to be the disproportionate victims of intentional death. The disturbing result, often overlooked by considering just demographic data, is a marked concentration of violence in areas of poverty and social exclusion (Cano & Santos, 2001). This concentration of violence, including police violence, and concomitant apathy in wealthy, privately secured enclaves, feeds the dynamic of neofeudalism.

How do police figure into this picture? First and foremost, the ineffectiveness of the police contributes to the public security problem: A May 2003 analysis of homicides in Rio de Janeiro showed that only 2.2 percent of the killers were apprehended at the crime scene, and only 1 percent of all other murders were solved by the police (Braudel Institute of World Economics, 2003). Second, corruption and brutality have allowed some areas of Brazil to develop into zones where drug trafficking, organized crime, and police violence run rampant; the reprisals and friction between police and gangs have produced geographical pockets that resemble war zones.

Police Violence and Human Rights

The history of human rights abuses by Brazilian police is well established and long. Research from the imperial period (Holloway, 1993) through the Cold War (Huggins, 1998) demonstrates a tradition of arbitrary, racist, and brutal police action that informs the present situation. The most extreme abuses are of two types: torture (committed especially by the PC in the investigation of crimes) and summary executions and aggression (more often committed by the PM). After 1990, when the first democratically elected president since the 1960s took office under the new democratic constitution, the trend of police violence rose along with violent crime in general. The numbers of civilians killed by the police in São Paulo and Rio de Janeiro reached 868 and 1195, respectively, in 2003 (Global Justice, 2003). In São Paulo that works out to an average of 2.37 citizens killed by the police each day; in Rio de Janeiro, the average is 3.2.

Widely publicized police killings in the past 14 years have increased conflict and violence between police and society: After Carandiru, the 1992 prison massacre in São Paulo that left 111 dead, prison riots are still commonplace. In Eldorado do Carajás, 19 landless workers in the state of Pará were executed by police; as of late 2003, the case has not been closed, and rural violence continues. Police killings in Corumbiara and Vigário Geral have given way to ongoing drug wars in these peripheral communities; these are marked by periodic police invasions. Many years after the infamous execution of street children in front of a famed church, Candelária, one of the mentally disturbed survivors went on to hijack bus number 174 in Rio de Janeiro, leading to more public fright, international outrage, and an acclaimed documentary ("Onibus 174"). The televised scenes of police brutality and executions in the 1997 cases of Favela Naval in Diadema (outside São Paulo) and of Cidade de Deus in Rio de Janeiro caused international outrage. Rather than foreswearing such tactics, São Paulo's PM formed yet another elite unit that performs raids such as "Operation Castelinho" that killed 12 members of the PCC ("First Command of the Capital") gang in Sorocaba on March 5, 2002.

Organized Crime and Uncivil Society

The power of drug traffickers has become a major problem, especially in Rio de Janeiro and São Paulo. Drug gangs operate with a command hierarchy capable of mobilizing well-armed "soldiers," as they are called, in the winding, hilly streets of Rio's favelas or the suburban satellites of São Paulo. Police estimated Rio drug gangs had an arsenal of 10,000 weapons in 2003. In 2004, they discovered caches that included automatic rifles, landmines, grenades, and shoulder-launched antiaircraft rockets. During the early 2000s, powerful narco-trafficking bosses, such as Paulo César Silva dos Santos ("Linho") or "Fernandinho" Beira-Mar, controlled multiple favelas and armies of more than 500 "soldiers" in their early 20s (in fact, they rarely live into their 30s); sometimes, they carried on this control from jail. Favela residents know corrupt police to be complicit in fomenting unrest when certain criminal bosses escape or are released from jail and then wage war on other gang leaders. Newspaper accounts regularly report on police officials and army officials who have been arrested for selling weapons to drug traffickers, their reputed enemies. The strength of organized crime corrupts the police institutions and escalates the level of violence.

Even uncorrupt police can indiscriminately terrorize favelas. Police violence is often labeled as an authoritarian atavism or the result of sheer savagery, but unfortunately such police officers might be responding to a "rational" desire to shore up their authority.[24] As police feel their power diminish, credible threats and violent shows of force are intended to extend their authority in regions where state hegemony is eroded.

The police seem better able to manage mutual and cooperative existence with lower-key criminal organizations such as the *jogos do bicho* (an illegal numbers game), but this so-called petty crime has led to extreme violence and has funded corruption at high levels.[25] José Carlos Gratz used funds from the *jogo* to finance control of the state government of Espírito Santo. By early 2003, Gratz was president of the State Legislative Assembly, controlled the machinery for electing assemblymen, and had appointed allies as judges and prosecutors (Miranda, 2003).

Networks of criminality, like those cited above, link organized criminal groups and the state by way of corruption. Growing evidence from Brazil, and scholarly work in general, suggests that "uncivil society" can be treated as a conceptually distinct and significant actor.[26] Uncivil society consists of organized groups that are not legitimate economic organizations, but are "rent-seeking" in the sense that they extract duties in exchange for access to the goods, territories, and privileges that they control. They reject the rules of civil society; for example, they use violence to resolve conflicts. They rarely seek to overthrow the state; rather, they seek to co-opt or corrupt it. Research on the robust spread of violent drug and arms traffickers in Brazilian slums demonstrates perhaps the strongest dimension of these networks of criminality (Arias, 2004; Zaluar, 2000). A growing set of examples includes organized criminal organizations, gangs, vigilante groups, illegal security firms, death squads, mafias, and militias.[27]

Death squads perfectly capture the problem with uncivil society and the police: Death squads can be well organized (even registered as philanthropic organizations; see below) and frequently operate extra-legally with the collaboration or complicity of the police. There are two types of death squads: the informal squads (typically off-duty police officers engaged in vigilante killings) and organized groups of on-duty police who hide their actions, not their identities. Two experts trace the modern incarnation of these two types to the mid-1960s under the ruling military regime.[28] Though the activities of torture and death squads slowed after the decline of the repressive regimes of the 1970s, groups such as Amnesty International and Human Rights Watch have testified to their presence today.

The informal type of death squad more clearly involves uncivil society. The case of *Scuderie Detetive Le Coq* (SDLC) and one human rights group that has denounced them, Global Justice (*Justiça Global*) demonstrates the civil/uncivil tension. SDLC was a death squad formed in 1964 during the military dictatorship and named after a legendary detective (Le Coq) from Rio de Janeiro. The group became legally recognized as a "non-profit philanthropic institution engaged in community service" (at least in the state of Espírito Santo, neighboring Rio), and by the 1990s SDLC had 3,800 directly or indirectly involved members (Global Justice, 2002). As street children were found dead on public streets with bullet holes in the backs of their heads, intense public pressure forced Espírito Santo to create a special commission composed of representatives from the PC, PM, and attorney general's office. The commission found police officers affiliated with the SDLC to have been involved in the executions. The commission further found that the SDLC was connected to drug trafficking, arms trafficking, gambling, prostitution, fraud, public embezzlement at all levels of government, and coercion and bribery of public officials. Global Justice, as a civil society actor, has used its international connections (including with the Inter-American Human Rights Court of the Organization of American States) to strongly denounce the SDLC, but the SDLC is not simply a criminal organization. It is an example of a well-organized, officially recognized network of public officials, police officers, and private citizens that cannot be classified as a political party, a gang, or a part of government, and the SDLC rejects the ethics of civil society and the peaceful resolution of conflict. The conflict between Global Justice and SDLC is an instance of a contest between civil society and uncivil society over the nature of public security.[29]

Private security is another realm of activity characterized by duplicity, mixing the criminal with the legal and the private with the public. Private security firms appear as one of the fastest-growing sectors of Brazil's economy. The Federal Police registered some 4,000 private security firms with 540,334 employees in 2000; there were another 811 firms registered to provide their own security ("organic security"). However, most estimates suggest that the number of people working for unlicensed providers is easily double that: 1 million to 1.5 million, not to mention unlicensed organic security firms (Institute of Citizenship, 2002). Teresa Caldeira, a Brazilian anthropologist, traces a number of connections that implicate private security firms with criminality. For example, *justiceiros* (vigilante hitmen) hide behind the façade of private security enterprises; most of these clandestine security services employ police officers or former police officers, and many are involved with gangs and drug dealers. She summarizes: "In fact, although private and public policing may . . . look like opposites, they share a matrix of relationship and structures. In Brazil, the matrix is of unstable relationships between legal and illegal, of abuses and violence" (Caldeira, 2000, p. 206).

Besides overt connections to criminality, private security in Brazil is troubling in two other ways: the demonstrable inability to regulate the industry and the risk of deepening inequality. Most private security goes unregulated. There are approximately 25,000 guards working in Rio de Janeiro's condominiums alone, but there are only 30 authorized entities to work in condominiums (Amora, 2004). Unregistered security services can range from the simply illegitimate to the elaborately clandestine; they can serve as fronts for death squads or the more routine neighborhood vigilante groups.

At the very least, unregistered private security creates a dangerous black market with perverse incentives: Guards are regularly underpaid, undertrained, and drawn from the ranks of off-duty police officers looking for second jobs (*bicos*) to augment their small salaries. Having police officers work second jobs in private security is both illegal and widely recognized: "[Bicos] cause duplicity in functions, physical exhaustion of police troops, besides delegitimizing the nature of public security, since public employees provide services for businesses whose interests come to collide with police functions" (Institute of Citizenship, 2002, p. 28). In addition, poor Brazilians are increasingly likely to suffer double discrimination with the unfettered growth of private security. Because Brazil has one of the largest income gaps between the rich and the poor worldwide, private security in Brazil will continue to create fortified enclaves for the wealthy. Impoverished citizens may continue to suffer disproportionately the cruelty of brutal policing as well as new forms of control and humiliation at the hands of private security.

Civil Society and Prospects for Reform

The institutional problems with the police and the broader context of criminality does damage to Brazilian society. Violent crime, organized crime, and uncivil society—especially when exacerbated by police brutality, corruption, and incompetence—undermine Brazilians' faith in their public security system. A 1999 victimization study in Belo Horizonte (the fourth or third largest and perhaps safest of the major cities) revealed that 66 percent of robbery and assault victims did not report crimes to the police; the lack of confidence was the principal reason (32 percent). Furthermore, when asked to express their opinion of the police, 39 percent of respondents said they did not trust the PM, and 46 percent said the same about the PC (Beato Filho, 2002). Such victimization studies and public opinion surveys regularly reinforce the impression that the Brazilian public has little faith in the police and that this lack of confidence impedes police work by limiting the assistance and information that the PC and PM can count on from society.

Yet organized civil society has not been a passive victim, and it has responded with growing expertise, which can be seen especially in its involvement with public security reforms that may help consolidate democracy by creating a functional justice system and by slowly bridging the disjunctive nature of Brazilian citizenship. Civil society organizations helped dismantle the authoritarian regime in the 1980s, and instead of disappearing under democracy with nothing to resist, these organizations have established "new connections between the autonomous spheres of society and political institutions" (Pinheiro, 2000, p. 134). For instance, the National Movement for Human Rights, formed in 1982, worked to set up research centers on violence in the national universities; in 1987, the University of São Paulo (USP) inaugurated the first Center for the Study of Violence (*Núcleo dos Estudos de Violência*, NEV). Throughout the 1990s, the press, nongovernmental organizations, universities, labor unions, professional associations (like the Brazilian Bar Association), and social movements have worked together to create footholds in government in the form of commissions, congressional inquiries, and ombudsmen. These modest steps allowed civil society organizations (CSOs) to gather more information about police actions and increase the visibility of human rights problems. The National Congress created the Human Rights Commission in 1995, and between 1995 and 1997, 13 states likewise created human rights commissions in their legislative bodies.[30] Today, traditional human rights organizations like the Teotonio Vilela Commission and the *Centro Santos Dias* in São Paulo work with research centers like NEV at USP, the *Instituto Superior de Estudos da Religião*, and the Center for the Study of Security and Citizenship in Rio, and they collaborate with newer organizations like *Movimento Viva Rio* and Global Justice, also both in Rio. In this way, CSOs have been able to accumulate experiences and share knowledge through better networks—some of which, like the Third Sector Information Network, are explicitly designed for that purpose (Pinheiro, 2000).

Civil society organizations have served as a nexus for proposing police reforms, such as community policing programs, civilian oversight, and community councils on public security. Early on, Governor Franco Montoro (1983–1987) created community security councils in São Paulo (by decree 23.455 and by resolution) and women's police stations. In Rio de Janeiro, Governor Leonel Brizola (1983–1987) established a mechanism of civilian oversight called the State Counsel of Justice, Public Safety, and Human Rights, on which CSOs had a seat. Both were left-leaning politicians with significant ties to the democratic resistance. Governor Mário Covas took office in 1995 in São Paulo, was reelected in 1998, and inherited the progressive tradition of working with CSOs. In 1995 Covas created the country's first civilian oversight office of the police (*ouvidoria*) at the request of the archdiocese and staffed it with a trusted activist from the church and civil society, Benedito Domingos Mariano. In 1997, Covas launched the State Program for Human Rights, modeled after the national program inaugurated in 1996 by President Cardoso. Likewise, Brizola returned to office in 1991, restored dismantled projects, established community-oriented policing in Rio de Janeiro, and created working relationships with civil society.

Community Security Councils

Many different forms of the *Conselhos Comunitários de Segurança* (CONSEPs) have appeared throughout the country. A critical assessment is that these local, unpaid citizen groups "tend to be mere meetings to hear complaints from the populace, which always receives the same excuses [from officials]: lack of resources" (da Silva Filho, 2000). Others hold a much more optimistic view. Community forums are a related innovation that allow more input from citizens and have been credited with helping reduce violent crime.[31] Officials in the northern state of Ceará, for example, explain that CONSEPs do a number of things: put police officers in touch with citizens (which is a necessary step in community policing), resolve minor conflicts, defuse tension between groups and between police and citizens, give citizens a sense of empowerment and participation in public affairs in general, and alert police officials to crime trends (Freitas Lopes, interview, 2004). In Minas Gerais, CONSEPs are seen as part of a paradigm shift in policing. As part of the fundamental overhaul, CONSEPs in Minas Gerais broaden the idea of police services, make it possible for community policing programs to function, develop partnerships in the community and with civil society, and allow for decentralization and regionalization of policing (Beato Filho, 2002).

Women's Police Stations

The first police station staffed mostly by women was created, by law, in the state of Santa Catarina in 1985. The state of São Paulo, however, copied the idea and created its own women's station on April 6, 1985, before Santa Catarina's capital city of Florianopolis was able to bring the idea to fruition (Global Justice, 2002). Such stations usually have male officers available, but must have female receptionists and women on staff (officers and psychologists) with whom victims can file complaints and give testimony and from whom victims can receive support. The best stations have day care rooms as well. There are 307 women's police stations in Brazil; this number is growing despite funding cutbacks. Of these, 40 percent are in São Paulo, and 13 percent are in Minas Gerais. They have been successful in raising the number of reported crimes. In 2001, women registered 334,589 cases of violence at São Paulo stations.

Women's police stations, by attending mostly to women and youth, represent an innovation in accessibility. Proponents conceived of these stations as tools to combat domestic violence and sexual assaults, because they would focus on investigating these crimes, be less psychologically and physically intimidating to female victims of sexual violence who wanted to report such crimes, and thus provide greater visibility and reporting accuracy to crimes of sexual, domestic, and gender-specific natures. Reportedly, a substantial number of women have received greater attention, have not had to suffer in silence, and have felt empowered knowing they could denounce such crimes (Global Justice, 2002). However, many activists have withdrawn support from these stations, because they provide such poor services due to lack of funding and resources.[32]

Community Policing

This approach concept calls for regular, nonthreatening contact with the members of a community or neighborhood. Typically police officers leave their vehicle and attempt to build trust with civilians; they treat citizens as partners in preventing crime. This not only reduces fear, it allows police to gain better information about criminal activities. First introduced in Rio de

Janeiro in the 1980s, this concept has now spread to virtually every state PM department and works best when used in conjunction with citizen-based public security councils (Beato Filho, 2002).

Witness Protection Programs

Witness protection programs led and managed by civil society allow police to root out corruption and prosecute organized criminal organizations and drug traffickers. This is a special concern of civil society, because witness protection involves saving the life and ensuring the rights of intimidated and gravely threatened people—often completely innocent bystanders. In Brazil, the provision of this service began with civil society and later received the belated help of government. In 1995, a broad-based human rights movement and other civil society groups formed the PROVITA *(Programa de Proteção a Vítimas e a Testemunhas)* in the northeast. Now part of a national system, PROVITA had protected over 500 witnesses in 17 states as of 2004 (Amnesty International, 2005). (Another version, PROTEGE, started in Rio Grande do Sul, but it does not rely on a civil society to function.)

Ouvidorias

Since 1995, after Brazil's first civilian oversight mechanism for the police was created in São Paulo, the innovation of ouvidorias has spread throughout the most populated and developed states. There are six fully independent and fully functioning ouvidorias and another four inchoate versions. They have created a national forum and have garnered funds from the various foundations and even the European Union to continue their project of diffusing external oversight of the police (see Lemgruber et al., 2003).

Conclusion: In Search of Consolidation

The study of postauthoritarian Brazil has been threaded together by analyses of the cruel legacies of oppressive policing, widespread impunity for state agents, privileges for the rich, and criminalization of the poor. Historians (e.g., José Murillo Carvalho, Thomas Holloway, etc.) and the social scientists mentioned in this chapter have documented these problems and traced their genealogies. The consensus is that the roots of this family tree extend down at least to the colonial period. Though the most recent authoritarian regime (1964–1985) sounded its death knell over 20 years ago, the abuses and social maladies that persist are commonly linked to authoritarian holdovers. These theoretical relationships seem likely to continue evolving.

One Brazilian think tank argues that if problems with crime, violence, and public security institutions are not "addressed constructively, they

ultimately will undermine the stability and legitimacy of democratic government" (Braudel Institute of World Economics, 2003, p. 1). Democratic
theory is not needed to conjure three reasons why Brazilian democracy may
be threatened: First, police forces that act without accountability erode citizenship rights and undermine the rule of law. Second, without effective
freedom, the quality of democracy can be eroded. Finally, when the formal
institutions of democracy do not function fairly and effectively, the citizenry's faith in democracy fails. But as it happens, common sense coincides
with democratic theory.

After the transition (the installation of a democratic government) the
consolidation of democracy completes the process of democratization
(Valenzuela, 1988). Though less is known about how consolidation happens, one framework provides three dimensions for conceptualizing it: atti-
tudinal, procedural, and behavioral (Linz & Stepan, 1996). Police relate to
these three areas as follows: The functioning of the public security and justice systems affects citizen perceptions of the worth of democracy (attitudi-
nal), determines the efficacy of the rule of law (procedural), and influences
how police, civil society, and uncivil society decide to resolve conflicts
(behavioral). The three core police problems identified at the outset—
ineffectiveness, corruption, and brutality—degrade citizenship, weaken the
rule of law, and erode trust in democracy. Therefore, progress in police
reform is essential to consolidating democracy.

There are institutional reasons for the problems with democratic consolidation in Brazil. The public security system often does not modernize or
respond to democratic pressures, because police institutions, which are
somewhat insulated from political and civil society everywhere, are especially insulated in the Brazilian case. Further, the ends demanded of the
police are incompatible with police capacity and competence, not to mention their handicap of corruption, so there is little incentive for the police
to take initiative in tackling internal problems on their own. The result is
deadlock. The police may alleviate demands on the system by taking shortcuts or creating dead ends for certain citizens, but this also produces a type
of disjunctive democracy—that is, a polity beset by unequal rights and citizenship (Holston & Caldeira, 1998). Institutional duplicity in the police
deprives citizens of a fair and useable state, which is the bedrock of a consolidated democracy (Linz & Stepan, 1996). Therefore Brazilian democracy
must deal with institutional problems and contradictions to create the effective, accountable police forces necessary for consolidation.

In addition, Brazil is at risk of developing a neofeudal system of citizen
security, one that is privatized, spatially segmented, brutal, and subject to the
vagaries of warring factions in and outside of the state. In a neofeudal system,
nongovernmental organizations and international institutions like the
International Monetary Fund consistently make demands of the state, even as
the state is fractured and breached by corruption and loses territory to criminal elements. Sérgio Adorno writes: "The criminal justice system continues

to prove ineffective in containing violence within a democratic rule of law. Problems related to law and order have affected citizens' belief in the institutions of justice, instigating the not uncommon private solutions to conflict" (author's translation, Adorno, 2002, p. 1). The federal government of Brazil has not yet lost the monopoly on violence to the extent that Colombia's has, but the state's capacity to solve problems and respond to pressures from CSOs, ordinary citizens, human rights groups, and foreign investors is weak.

Democratization has not consistently led to improvements in the police of Brazil, and it seems that improvements in police institutions have yet to consolidate or deepen democracy on their own, though there are positive signs that civil society is engaging these issues with success. A major reason for stagnancy and backsliding is that Brazil, under democracy, has not done away with institutional duplicity and has not dismantled criminal networks that have their tentacles glued to the Brazilian state. The Brazilian state and its justice system go on functioning, but in some sense, informal and illegal activity give it the image of the emperor with no clothes, which the court's observers pretend not to see for the sake of keeping the court in order. Empty legal mandates risk becoming the imaginary threads of democracy with which the emperor cloaks himself. Achieving a more democratic model of policing in Brazil will require honest efforts to consolidate and unify Brazilian police institutions, facilitate cooperation, impose accountability, and bolster the legal mechanisms for achieving justice. It will also require tilting the balance of power in favor of the state and civil society and against the networks of criminality that corrupt and feed off it.

Notes

1. Though the problems with the police are myriad, corruption, brutality, and ineffectiveness stand out as the most severe and distinct. Dozens of prominent experts recently published a national plan for public security, "Projecto Segurança Pública para o Brasil" (from the *Instituto Cidadania* or Institute of Citizenship), which President Lula da Silva endorsed during his 2002 campaign. The report corroborates the above assessment, listing brutality (*práticas violentas*), corruption (*corrupção* and involvement with criminality), and ineffectiveness (actually, inefficiency) among the major problems facing the police, along with lack of public confidence (Institute of Citizenship, 2002).

2. "Institutional duplicity" is my invented term, but the notion is borrowed from Brazilian scholars of the police. Roberto Kant de Lima (1995), Domício Proença, Jr. (interview, 2004), and Jacqueline Muniz (1999; Muniz, interview, 2004), among others, have discussed this problem and are cited throughout this chapter. A crystallization of this phenomenon comes from three other experts, Lemgruber, Musumeci, and Cano (2003), when they observe that the difficulties in controlling the police of Brazil arise from the institutional context in which "on one side, there are laws and rules that formally delimit police action; on the other, there are arrangements and informal cultures that define the collection of practices through

which discretionary power is exercised on a daily basis" (p. 71, author's translation). Proença (2004) says more directly, "There is the way things are supposed to be done, and the way they are actually done."

3. Kant de Lima (1995, p. 1) describes something similar as the "Brazilian legal paradox": "In Brazil, a constitutionally egalitarian order is applied in a hierarchical way through the justice system. Different legal treatments are given for the same infractions, depending on the social or professional situation of the suspect. . . . Consequently, in clear disobedience of the law, the police judge cases and punish criminals."

4. The evidence from the democratizing world—Brazil, South Africa, Russia, Argentina, and Eastern Europe, for example—supports the pessimistic view that democracy does not bring better policing, but it is worth pointing out that these are merely correlations. In-depth studies are the best way to arrive at answers about causality.

5. The term "consolidated" means the establishment of an effective and functioning democracy that citizens have become accustomed to and accept as the "the only game in town"; "deeper" democracy implies effective improvements in rights and liberties, accountability, participation, and equality.

6. By 1998, there were four proposals to reform the police—from Fernando Henrique Cardoso, Mário Covas (former São Paulo governor), Hélio Bicudo, and Zulaie Cobra Ribeiro—all to separate the PM from the military or to change their duties. None of the constitutional amendments were voted on. Rather, in February 1998, the National Congress approved Amendment 18/1998 establishing the PM as "militaries of the states" and reinforcing their military status, making it more difficult to reform the public security system.

7. The customary translation for *polícia militar* is "military police." Hearing the term, many foreigners might mistake the PM for the police of the military (*polícia do exército*) or erroneously conclude that the PM are part of the military. Though the PM were made subordinate to the army during the military dictatorship (1964–1985), and though they remain a "reserve" of the army and maintain barracks and military training, these state police forces are not nationally unified and are functionally and institutionally separate from the military. The PM forces grew out of a separate tradition of state military forces, much in the way the states in the United States had state guards and militias before there was a regular federal army. Thus, a better translation would be the "*militarized* police." However, for the sake of convention, I will also refer to them as the "military police" or more often simply the "PM," which is their common moniker in Portuguese.

8. 1998 Constitution, Article 144, paragraph 6.

9. This observation about military behavior is relevant, because historically, minor disciplinary infractions have been more severely punished than have infractions involving the use of excessive force to detain a suspect. For example, skipping the chain of command in a simple administrative process is a serious offense to authority. As for discipline, appearing with even a too-large mustache would be seen as flippant or negligent and also an offense to immediate supervisors.

10. The ranks are, in order from lowest to highest: soldado; cabo; first, second, and third sargento; subtenente; first and second tenente; capitão; major; tenente-coronel; and coronel.

11. Perhaps out of institutional envy, the PC does maintain a visible fleet of patrol vehicles (*viaturas*), which are painted and bear institutional emblems and

sirens. Some argue that by increasing the number of visible police vehicles, the PC is making citizens feel safer; others argue that it more appropriate for these investigative police officers to use under-cover vehicles, in essence suggesting that the PC is sacrificing effectiveness for pride or public appearances. Whatever the case, this demonstrates that it is not entirely accurate to say that the PC does not do ostensive policing. On paper they are supposed to take investigative action on the orders from the Ministério Público. I have personally taken part in "blitzes" or random traffic stops with the PC and can attest that they were supremely ostensive actions and not investigative.

12. Jane's data most likely included the Federal Highway Police. The number of 8,000 updates the number of 7,000 from da Silva Filho's research (2000) and draws on the best estimates from various other experts (Benedito, interview, 2004; Proença, interview, 2004; de Souza Leal, interview, 2004).

13. The number of municipal guard forces may be as many as 400, according to The Braudel Institute of World Economics (2003). The estimate of 357 comes from Athias (2003).

14. Their numbers—600,000 together—make the state forces the most important law enforcement agencies: The combined federal police number about 16,000 and are extremely overextended in terms of responsibilities and territory. (This percentage calculation, however, does not include municipal guards, public defense forces [bombeiros], or military personnel, to be discussed later.)

15. Article 144, section 6 makes the police subordinate to both the military and state governors: "The Military Police and the *Corpos de Bombeiros Militares* [military firefighters and public defense force], being auxiliary and reserve forces of the Army, are subordinated, along with the Civil Police, to the governors of the states."

16. "The Union [federal government] shall have the exclusive right to legislate on: . . . general norms of organization, troops, military supplies, calling up and mobilizing the PM and Bombeiros [firefighters and rescue squads]" (Article 22, section 21).

17. The states included São Paulo, Rio Grande do Sul, Paraná, Rio de Janeiro, Espírito Santo, Minas Gerais, Bahia, Pernambuco, Paraíba, Rio Grande do Norte, Pará, Amazonas, Ceará, Goiás, and Sergipe (Mariano, interview, 2004).

18. Research conducted in 1987 by the Human Rights Center Santos Dias of the São Paulo archdiocese analyzed 380 cases. They found that officers were absolved in 90 percent of cases in the first category, while officers were punished in 85 percent of cases in the second category.

19. Law Decree 9,299 was passed in 1996 after being proposed by human rights advocates, most notably a federal deputy (congressman) from São Paulo, Hélio Bicudo. Originally the bill called for all crimes against the person to be transferred to the civil court system instead of the military courts (*Tribunal Justiça Militar*) but this definition was limited to ensure passage.

20. Law Decree 9,455, approved by Congress on April 7, 1997, almost 10 years after the country had redemocratized and signed international human rights treaties.

21. For instance, the Ford Foundation helped two universities in Rio de Janeiro develop courses on public security for members of the PM; new recruits and young officers take classes with other students. Federal universities in the states of Minas Gerais and Pernambuco, among others, have also developed coursework along these lines.

22. This analysis is mirrored in the *Projecto* to which President Lula ascribed: "Therefore, the path of the vicious cycle is painfully obvious: lack of investigation, lack of confidence, lack of information" (Institute of Citizenship, 2002, p. 33). It also

cites the "impossibility of applying rational public policies," which in turn leads to "public distrust, generating underreporting of crimes, which contributes to reduced investigative efficiency" (p. 36).

23. *Para inglês ver* translates typically as "for the English to see"; in colloquial terms it is an official mendacity for the sake of appearances, often to seem modern.

24. As Luiz Eduardo Soares, noted anthropologist and former national secretary for public security (SENASP), argued, "Random brutality is the easiest and strongest way for bad cops to impose their own conditions on the [drug] traffickers" (Soares, 2000).

25. See de Araujo Evangelista (2003). Police allow the gambling to persist probably because, as a lottery that is not state-sponsored, it seems like a petty and unstoppable crime, but it can become quite serious for a few reasons: First, police also take a cut of the profits. Interestingly, it is the PC that usually receives the payoffs, and the PM does not. Hence, the illegal betting can generate more friction between the two police forces than between police and criminal organizations. Second, the profits can go to fund political corruption at higher levels. Third, these numbers rackets can grow into larger criminal organizations.

26. Some have called the rise of uncivil society the "dark side" of democratization, because "an inexorable shadow of uncivil society follows the strengthening of civil society" (Pinheiro, 2000, p. 121). Others consider it the result of globalization, reasoning that "organized crimes such as smuggling, drugs, and trafficking in prostitution and children" have fed its growth (Mittelman & Johnston, 1999, p. 119).

27. See also Shelley (1995) and Williams (1994).

28. See Huggins (1998), pp. 136–140. More broadly, Pinheiro writes: "All classes of vigilantes in several Brazilian cities exist, in a certain way, as a continuation of the death squads and other repressive clandestine organizations and practices that prevailed during the dictatorship" (2000, p. 121).

29. This case is very much a conflict. Following a congressional investigation, Brazilian civil society actors, including human rights groups, the very influential Brazilian Bar Association (OAB), and unions, formed a movement to react against organized crime and serious human rights violations. Numerous members of this movement received death threats, and one attorney was killed on April 15, 2002 (Global Justice, 2002).

30. These states include Rio de Janeiro, Rio Grande do Sul, Santa Catarina, São Paulo, Espirito Santo, Bahia, Pernambuco, Rio Grande do Norte, Ceará, Pará, Acre, Maranhão, and the Federal District (de Mesquita Neto, 1999).

31. One research institute claims that a Public Security Forum formed in the São Paulo suburb of Diadema helped reduce the number of homicides by half in that extremely violent periphery (Braudel Institute of World Economics, 2003).

32. For instance, only 61 percent actually have firearms, and 77 percent have phone lines and vehicles, all of which seem essential for police work; in terms of helpful items, only 13 percent have a fax machine, and 12 percent have a copy machine.

References _____

Adorno, S. (2002). O monopólio estatal da violência na sociedade brasileira contemporânea. In S. Miceli (Ed.), *O que ler na ciência social brasileira 1970–2002* (Vol. IV, pp. 1–32). São Paulo: Editora Bertrand Brasil.

Adorno, S. (2004). O monopólio estatal da violência. *Revista da Oficina de Informações, 5*(52), 50–51.

Agüero, F. (1997). Toward civilian supremacy in South America. In L. Diamond, M. F. Plattner, Y. Chu, & H. Tien (Eds.), *Consolidating the third wave democracies* (pp. 177–207). Baltimore: Johns Hopkins University Press.

Amnesty International. (2005, December 2). *"They come in shooting": Policing socially excluded communities.* Retrieved August 7, 2006, from http://web.amnesty.org/library/Index/ENGAMR190252005.

Amora, D. (2004, August 5). A segurança privada cresce sem regulacao. *O Globo,* p. 16.

de Araujo Evangelista, H. (2003). *Rio de Janeiro: Violência, jogo do bicho e narcotráfico sengundo uma interpretação.* Rio de Janeiro: Editora Revan.

Arias, E. D. (2004). Faith in our neighbors: Networks and social order in three Brazilian favelas. *Latin American Politics & Society, 46*(1), 1–38.

Athias, G. (2003, November 9). Planalto quer fortalecer guarda municipal. *Folha de São Paulo,* p. C1.

Beato Filho, C. C. (2002, January). *Reinventar a polícia: A implementação de um program de policiamento comunitário.* Informative paper of CRISP, Universidade Federal de Minas Gerais, number 2. Belo Horizonte, Brazil: CRISP.

Braudel Institute of World Economics. (2003). *Segurança pública (A plan of action: Public security in Brazil).* Braudel paper number 33. São Paulo: Author.

Caldeira, T. P. R. (2000). *City of walls: Crime, segregation and citizenship in São Paulo* Berkeley: University of California Press.

Cano, I., & Santos, N. (2001). *Violência letal, renda e desigualdade social no Brasil.* Rio de Janeiro: 7 Letras.

Costa, A. T. M. (2004). *Entre a lei e a ordem.* Rio de Janeiro: Fundação Getúlio Vargas.

Dominquez, J. I., & Lowenthal, A. F. (Eds.). (1996). *Constructing democratic governance: Latin America and the Caribbean in the 1990s.* Baltimore: Johns Hopkins University Press.

Fausto, B. (1999). *A concise history of Brazil.* New York: Cambridge University Press.

Frühling, H. (1998). Policía y consolidación democrática en Chile. *Pena y Estado, 3,* 81–116.

Global Justice. (2002). *Human rights in Brazil: 2002.* Rio de Janeiro: Author.

Global Justice. (2003). *Human rights in Brazil: 2003.* Rio de Janeiro: Author.

Holloway, T. H. (1993). *Policing in Rio de Janeiro: Repression and resistance in a 19th century city.* Palo Alto, CA: Stanford University Press.

Holston, J., & Caldeira, T. P. R. (1998). Democracy, law, and violence: Disjunctions of Brazilian citizenship. In F. Aguero & J. Stark (Eds.), *Fault lines of democracy in post-transition Latin America* (pp. 263–297). Miami, FL: North South Center Press.

Huggins, M. K. (1998). *Political policing: The United States and Latin America.* Durham, NC: Duke University Press.

Institute of Citizenship. (2002). *Projecto segurança pública para o Brasil.* São Paulo: Author.

Kant de Lima, R. (1995). *A polícia da cidade do Rio de Janeiro: Seus problemas e paradoxos.* Rio de Janeiro: Editora Forense.

Lemgruber, J. (2004, October). *Violência, omissão e insegurança pública: O pão de nosso cada dia.* Presentation at the Academia Brasileira de Ciências, Rio de Janeiro.

Lemgruber, J., Musumeci, L., & Cano, I. (2003). *Quem vigia os vigias? Um estudo sobre controle externo da polícia no Brasil.* Rio de Janeiro: Editora Record.

Linz, J. J., & Stepan, A. (1996). *Problems of democratic transition and consolidation: Southern Europe, South America and post-communist Europe.* Baltimore: Johns Hopkins University Press.

de Mesquita Neto, P. (1999). Violência policial no Brasil: Abordagens teórics e práticas de controle. In D. Chaves Pandolfi, J. Murilo de Carvalho, L. Piquet Carneiro, & M. Grynszpan (Eds.), *Cidadania, Justiça e Violência* (pp. 129–147). Rio de Janeiro: Editora Fundação Getulio Vargas.

Miranda, R. (2003). *The organized crime in Espírito Santo State.* São Paulo: Braudel Institute of World Economics.

Mittelman, J., & Johnston, R. (1999). The globalization of organized crime. *Global Governance, 5*(1), pp. 103–127.

Muniz, J. (1999). *"Ser policial é, pobretudo, uma razão de ser":* Cultura e cotidiano da polícia militar do Estado do Rio de Janeiro. Rio de Janeiro: Instituto Universitário de Pesquisa do Rio de Janeiro.

Pinheiro, P. S. (1994). The legacy of authoritarianism in democratic Brazil. In S. Nagel (Ed.), *Latin American development and public policy* (pp. 237–253). New York: St. Martin's Press.

Pinheiro, P. S. (2000). Democratic governance, violence, and the (un)rule of law. *Daedalus, 129*(2), 119–143.

Salles, J. M., & Lund, K. (Directors). (1999). *Notícias de uma guerra particular (News from a private war).* Motion picture. Rio de Janeiro: Videofilmes.

Shelley, L. L. (1995). Transnational organized crime: An imminent threat to the nation-state? *Journal of International Affairs, 48*(2), 468–489.

da Silva Filho, J. V. (2000). Reflexões para uma política nacional de segurança pública. In J. P. dos R. Vellos, R. C. de Albuquerque, & A. C. Magalhães (Eds.), *Pobreza, cidadania e segurança* (pp. 234–248). Rio de Janeiro: José Olympio.

da Silva Filho, J. V., & Gall, N. (1999). *A polícia.* Braudel paper number 22. São Paulo: Braudel Institute of World Economics.

Soares, L. E. (2000, October). *Crime, violence and corruption in Latin America.* Paper presented at ILAS Forum on Latin America Policy, Columbia University, New York.

Stepan, A. (2000). Brazil's decentralized federalism: Bringing government closer to the citizens? *Daedalus, 129*(2), 145–169.

Ungar, M. (2002). *Elusive reform: Democracy and the rule of law in Latin America.* Boulder, CO: Lynne Rienner.

Valenzuela, J. (1988). Democratic consolidation in post-transitional settings: Notion, process, and facilitating conditions. In S. Mainwaring, G. O'Donnell, & J. Valenzuela (Eds.), *Issues in democratic consolidation: The new South American democracies in comparative perspective* (pp. 57–104). Notre Dame, IN: University of Notre Dame Press.

Williams, P. (1994). Transnational criminal organisations and international security. *Security, 36*(1), 96–113.

Zaluar, A. (2000). Perverse integration: Drug trafficking and youth in the *favelas* of Rio de Janeiro. *Journal of International Affairs, 53*(2), 654–671.

Interviews

Benedito, M. D. (2004, February). Interview. São Paulo.

Freitas Lopes, F. (2004, August). Interview, Fortaleza, Ceara.

Mariano, B. D. (July, 2004). Interview, São Paulo.

de Mesquita Neto, P. (2004, January). Interview, Núcleo de Estudos da Violência, University of São Paulo.

Muniz, J. (March, 2004). Interview, Secretaria Nacional de Segurança Pública (Senasp) Brasilia.

Proença, D., Jr. (2004, January). Interview, Rio de Janeiro.

de Souza Leal, P. C. (2004, September 13). Interview, Goiánia.

4

Paths to Fairness, Effectiveness, and Democratic Policing in Mexico

Benjamin Nelson Reames

Despite being a functioning democracy, Mexico has not established a strong rule of law. High rates of violent crime and routine police corruption were already serious problems in the early 1990s; then increased drug traffic, more active street gangs, high-profile cases of kidnapping and corruption, unrest in regions like Chiapas, and a string of unsolved murders in Ciudad Juarez added fuel to a fire of public insecurity. Police and justice institutions responded ineffectively in the late 1990s. As a result, Mexico's crisis of public insecurity also manifested itself as a crisis of confidence in democratic leaders. If a democratic government fails to provide a fair and effective justice system that guarantees public security and protects rights, then it risks forfeiting one of its core functions that properly defines it as a consolidated democracy. Thus the real and perceived problems with crime, policing, and justice have left Mexico an embattled democracy. The core question becomes, Will public security institutions in Mexico proceed along the path of democratic policing, or will public security continue to degenerate and weaken the lived experience of democracy?

Public insecurity in Mexico is the result of crime but also of corrupt and poorly functioning police forces, and this has been a primary public concern for many years. The good news is that the heightened sense of urgency has generated increased political will to effect reform. Other factors may also facilitate reform: The federal system has been decentralizing for many years, making it possible for public officials to be more responsive to local needs; the political parties have become competitive, making democracy a functional (albeit messy) reality; also, efforts to stanch public sector corruption and inefficiency are important items on the political agenda. In short, public officials increasingly appear to have motivation and capacity to push for improvements in policing and accountability.

Yet would-be reformers will continue to confront challenges within the prevailing patronage-based political system and the fractured federal governmental system. For instance, when trying to overhaul public security, Mexican institutions at the national level face the predicament of having to further decentralize power and resources to states and municipalities while simultaneously increasing centralized information gathering and oversight. Politically, they are called upon to vet police forces, sever links to organized crime, and reform legal codes. Further, those in government stand a better chance of surmounting these challenges if they leverage the resources and expertise of civil society, but civil society has long been ignored or co-opted. In some sectors, Mexican civil society is active and robust; in others, it lacks technical capacity and public confidence—public-security related non-governmental organizations (NGOs) usually belong to the latter camp. As a result, reform may hinge once again on personality and political will. To make real progress, political actors will probably need to juggle the politics of federalism and partisanship while managing civil society input and institutional inertia in government.

In short, I argue here that Mexico is at a fork in the path to democratic policing. Various governments around the world have done and do face the same predicament: an erosion of their monopoly on the legitimate use of force becomes coupled with rising crime rates, which requires legitimate state forces to contain. In that context, government officials in Mexico and elsewhere may perceive a choice between providing citizen security and protecting civil rights. However, it is now widely acknowledged that "rights versus security" is a false dichotomy and that the only way to provide both—in fact, the best way to provide either—is through comprehensive public security reform that integrates and invests in both. Furthermore, meeting this challenge at an important crossroads may reap extra rewards. In other words, for a government to reform the police in the face of pressures to further militarize and/or privatize public security could help to reassert the essential role that accountable, rights-respecting public institutions play in maintaining democracy.

Assessing the Mexican Public Security Situation

By the end of the century, the idea of *paths to democracy* had gained immense currency among Latin Americanists.[1] The path model suggested that a number of decisive variables could either impede or assist a country in achieving and consolidating democracy. Not surprisingly, at least one analyst noted that democratization of the police can also be modeled in terms of paths (de Mesquita Neto, 2001). To do so requires considering the impact of crime, civil society organizations, and most important, the defining features of the police, legal institutions, and state itself. The present analysis makes clear that the obstacles have so far outweighed the resources and capacity for change. The main obstacles include an ossified bureaucracy that is resistant to change and lacks good information about how to change, a political environment prone to sabotage and deadlock, and the lack of legal authority to make over-arching institutional changes. These features are unlikely to change in the short term. On the other hand, the capacity for reform derives from good information about police reforms and improvements, the concerted effort of civil society to propose practical reforms, and the availability of resources and individuals to actually implement such changes. When the scales tip in favor of capacity over obstacles, Mexico will approximate its promise of providing democratic, effective, and rights-respecting police.

With that framework in mind, this chapter gauges Mexico's progress on the path toward implementing democratic police procedures. In doing so, it is essential to make sense of the various police forces themselves and their mandates and powers through an institutional lens. This chapter begins with a profile of the police. The second part places the police in the context of challenges to public security: private security growth, organized crime, police corruption, and high crime rates. The final part assesses Mexico's prospects for achieving effective and just democratic policing in the context of the obstacles and capacities that the current conditions of Mexican fed-eralism and civil society present, which have gained increased expert scrutiny of late (Cornelius & Shirk, 2007).

_____ Institutional Introduction to the Police of Mexico

First, it is important to understand how Mexico is *not* unique. The legal structure of its police is like that of other large, federal democracies in Latin America—such as Brazil and Argentina—in that there are both federal and relatively autonomous state police forces, bifurcated into judicial (investiga-tive) and ostensive (order-maintenance or militarized) police departments. Mexican police also confront problems common throughout Latin America: low pay, poor training, disorganization, corruption, ineffectiveness, lack of public confidence, and ill-defined or unachievable mandates.

On the other hand, the exceptional features of Mexican institutions and police are instructive. Mexico has been a democracy on paper since 1917, but due to one-party rule, political competition only started to take hold in the late 1980s and was decisively affirmed with the election of President Fox (of the PAN, the National Action Party) in 2000. In short, because Mexico did not fall under military dictatorship in the latter half of the twentieth cen-tury like most countries to the south of it, the principal impediments to police reform in Mexico are *not* those of wresting civilian control over pub-lic security institutions or overcoming entrenched elements of hard-line con-servatives. That said, Mexico does not have the distant, long-standing experience in democracy that some of these same countries have (Argentina,

Brazil, Chile), which is seen as making Mexico's practice of democracy somewhat inchoate (not to mention fragile). For instance, Mexico's federal system has not truly functioned as such due to the seven-decade dominance of the PRI (the Institutional Revolutionary Party) that centralized power; in terms of policing, this has slowed the process of decentralization that might have given more discretion and power to authorities who better understand local crime problems. Finally, Mexico's strategic location between the United States and the rest of Latin America makes it the frequent focus of critical international attention to public security problems, especially issues related to drug trafficking and immigration. The upshot is that the police forces of Mexico are rife with both problems and potential.

Mexico is a large federation of 31 states and one federal district, and it maintains a range of police forces belonging to a variety of jurisdictions and functional separations. Estimates of the force size vary due to inadequate centralized data collection and frequent changes, but it is safe to say there are about 400,000 police officers in the country and about 3,000 different forces at municipal, state, and federal levels.[2] So there is a distinct multiplicity of police forces in Mexico. Other outstanding features include the institutionalized nature of corruption, growing militarization, poor preparation, and ineffectiveness in the face of increasingly severe crime.

With the election of Vicente Fox to the presidency in 2000, Mexico shed one-party rule and raised expectations for public sector reform. Fox experienced increasing pressure—domestically and abroad—to reduce corruption, confront organized crime, and develop modern, effective, rights-respecting police forces. Finally, on March 29, 2004, he presented his first cohesive police reform proposal (*Iniciativa de Reforma en Seguridad Pública y Justicia Penal*). Though fragmented reform efforts had been underway, the proposal was unique in aiming to unify some the nation's police organizations and to give investigatory power to a greater number of police officers. The range of forces means that there is no single police institution that defines Mexican policing. However, some of the more recent reforms, including those in three of the most significant police bodies, nicely demonstrates the kaleidoscopic picture of Mexican policing.

First, the federal attorney general's office (*Procuraduría General de la República*—PGR) established a new police force, the Federal Agency of Investigation (*Agencia Federal de Investigaciones*—AFI) which replaced the notoriously corrupt Federal Judicial Police (*Policía Judicial Federal*—PJF) by the presidential decree of Vicente Fox (2000–2006) on November 1, 2001. The efforts to develop the AFI into a professional, uncorrupted force for the investigation of federal crimes are ongoing.

Second, the Federal Preventive Police (*Policía Federal Preventiva*—PFP) was created in 1999 by the initiative of President Ernesto Zedillo (1994–2000) to prevent and combat crime throughout the country.[3] The PFP comes under the direction of the federal Secretariat of Public Security (*Secretaría de Seguridad Pública*—SSP) and has been assuming its authority in stages over time, as its budget has grown and it has combined and reorganized police departments from major agencies such as those for migration, treasury, and highways.

Third, the Secretariat of Public Security of the Federal District (*Secretaría de Seguridad Pública del Distrito Federal*—SSP-DF), unlike the previous two, does not have national reach, but it does manage a combined force of over 90,000 officers in the Federal District (DF). The SSP is charged with maintaining public order and safety in the center of Mexico City, where public insecurity and crime rates are highest in the nation. As a result, there have been concurrent efforts to increase accountability and improve police effectiveness. Beginning in 1996, authorities began a dramatic restructuring of the SSP-DF, which included replacing major officials with army officers. Recently, the most high-profile effort has been Mexico City Mayor Andres Lopez Obrador's decision in 2002 to contract the consulting firm of Rudolph Giuliani, former mayor of New York City, to advise the SSP-DF on public security policy.

The Mexican police, properly defined, are the public security forces charged with the prevention and investigation of crimes; these forces are therefore meant to support the Public Ministry (*Ministerio Público*, which prosecutes crimes) and the judiciary. Given the changing, complex nature of these police institutions, a clear description of what they actually do is best achieved by using two defining dimensions—function and jurisdiction.[4]

Functional Description of the Police

Mexico's police are divided into a dual set that includes preventive police (the order-controlling *policía preventiva*) and judicial police (the typically plain-clothed and investigative *policía judicial*). The preventive police do what is often called "ostensive policing" and thus maintain order and public security in cities and towns; they do not investigate crimes and assist the Public Ministry in doing so only at its request. They are empowered to act according to police and governmental regulations (Article 21 of the Constitution).

The judicial police are an auxiliary to the Public Ministry and act under its authority and command. The judicial police belong to institutions known as *procuraduría generales*, which are important justice institutions translated usually as attorneys' general offices. There are three key types of police actors in this type of law enforcement: the police officers (*policías judiciales*), investigating agents of the public prosecutor (often simply called *ministerios públicos*), and technical experts (*peritos*). Depending on their jurisdiction, judicial police enforce federal law (*fuero federal*) or local law (*fuero común*).

According to the National Public Security System (*Sistema Nacional de Seguridad Pública*—SNSP), municipal- and state-level police forces employed some 280,000 officers in 1999. The nearly 34,000 preventive police of the federal district and the federal preventive police raised the number to 319,600 preventive police in 1999. Today there are probably over 330,000 preventive police; judicial police officers number over 26,000.

Jurisdictional Description of the Police

There are four types of jurisdictions that affect the nature, activity, and organization of police institutions: the three levels of government—federal, state, and municipal, and the federal district.

Municipal Police

Preventive policing is the shared responsibility of the federal, state, and local authorities, according to the Constitution and reforms passed in 1999. The question is, How much and how well do local authorities manage policing? Mexico has been undergoing a process of decentralization since the 1980s. Police work often gets overlooked in the attention paid to health, education, and fiscal decentralization; however, local law enforcement is likely to increase its order-maintenance (if not investigative) activities for the years to come, and the federal government has not offered much help or guidance.

The *municipio* represents the local level of government and may contain many smaller towns and cities. Like counties in the United States that have sheriffs, a municipio can maintain a police force. Municipios have only preventive police, but not all have them. There are 2,395 municipios; 335 have no police forces. There are 2,000 municipios with fewer than 100 officers, which implies that the police departments are not very developed and probably not very modernized. However, 87 of the largest municipios account for 68.7 percent of preventive police at all levels of government, so some are quite complex.

Policing in the Federal District

The Federal District (DF) covers a territory of 1,500 square kilometers and contains the heart of Mexico City and the seat of federal government. There are 9 million residents in the DF and about 19 million people in the metropolitan region (depending on where one draws the boundaries). The DF has a directly elected mayor who has the power to appoint the heads of the law enforcement forces of the city: the public security secretary of the federal district and the attorney general of the federal district.

Preventive Police—DF: The DF stands out for having the highest crime rates in Mexico as well as a huge preventive police force of approximately 34,000 officers (not to mention 40,000 auxiliary police and 15,000 banking police). These nearly 90,000 officers work for the SSP-DF, which has five major divisions and an annual budget of over 10 billion pesos. [The initial salary for a patrol officer of the SSP-DF was raised to 5,000 pesos per month (about US$500) in 2004.]

Like most police departments of major cities, the DF's preventive police are divided into regional subgroups (a geographically defined police with specific jurisdictions) and into functional divisions with special responsibilities and resources. Slightly less than half of the preventive police are grouped into the geographical distributions of the Sectoral Police (*Policía Sectoral*). Within the Sectoral Police there are six main regions with usually three precincts in each (a total of 16 precincts) and a number of sectors within each precinct (a total of 70 sectors).

The Sectoral Police compose one of the five divisions; the remaining four divisions of the preventive police (over 17,000 of the 34,000) are organized into special divisions rather than geographic groupings. The second division, the Metropolitan Police (*Policía Metropolitana*), consists of six special units: the Public Transit Police, the Tourist Police, the Grenadiers (*Granaderos* protect the historic district), the Mounted Police, the Feminine Police (the *Policía Femenil* work in schools, with juveniles, at public events, and in public parks and gardens), and the Emergency Rescue Squad (ERUM).

The third division is a set of Special Squadrons (*Fuerzas Especiales*) consisting of four main groups: the Helicopter Squadron; the Special Unit, which specializes in motorcycles; the Task Force (*Fuerza de Tareas*), which deals with terrorist and bomb threats; and the Alfa Group, which is a secretive, ad hoc force that works with the Special Unit and fights drug trafficking. The fourth division is Roadway Security (*Seguridad Vial*), which maintains a force of brown-uniformed police that patrol the roads and highways. A chronically understaffed Internal Affairs is the final division.

Though the chain of authority is a source of common confusion, the SSP-DF is not synonymous with the preventive police. There are two other, separate forces—under the charge of the SSP-DF but not part of the preventive police—that compose the Complementary Police: the Auxiliary Police (approximately 40,000 strong), which guards official buildings and other specific locations like the airport, and the Banking Police (about 15,000 officers), which guards businesses, financial institutions, and banks. The complementary forces function in a more ostensive capacity than the police forces that investigate and apprehend suspects; in theory, they should allow for significant decentralization, better use of resources within the preventive police, and for the creation of reserve order maintenance forces when necessary.

Judicial Police–DF: The DF is also unique for maintaining its own force of judicial police, the Judicial Police of the Federal District (*Policía Judicial del Distrito Federal*—PJDF), which are organized under the office of the attorney general of the DF (the *Procuraduría General de Justicia del Distrito Federal*—PGJDF). The PGJDF receives complaints and reports of possible crimes and investigates them. They maintain 16 precincts (delegaciones) with an estimated 3,500 judicial police, 1,100 investigating agents for prosecuting attorneys (*agentes del ministerio público*), and 941 experts or specialists (*peritos*). The PGJDF budget exceeds 3 billion pesos each year. It is clearly a substantial force.

State Police

The 31 states maintain—like the DF, but unlike the cities—both preventive and judicial police. The state-level preventive police are over 90,000 strong. The judicial police, by definition, must enforce the states' local laws (commonly called *fuero común*). By infrequent estimates, there are over 21,000 state-level judicial police officers in the state judicial police forces (*Policía Judicial de los Estados*—PJE) organized under the offices of the attorneys general (*Procuradurías Generales de Justicia*).

Federal Police

PGR and AFI: The federal Public Ministry (*Ministerio Público*) has a separate judicial police force, which operates nationwide under the office of the federal attorney general (PGR), who is appointed by the president. When Attorney General Rafael Marcial Macedo de la Concha was appointed by Vicente Fox, concerns were raised about militarization of the police. The PGR's mandate is to investigate and prosecute federal crimes such as drug trafficking, arms trafficking, kidnapping, and environmental and public health crimes. The PGR under the Fox administration has seen its budget grow from 5.6 billion pesos in 2001 to 7.2 billion pesos in 2004; it employed a staff of 21,838 in 2004.

The PGR reconfigured and renamed the federal judicial police (PJF), which was much maligned for corruption and ineffectiveness. The AFI replaced the PJF and was probably intended to invite comparisons to the FBI of the United States. The AFI had a budget in 2004 of 2,622 million pesos, thus amounting to about a third of the PGR budget. The force consists of more than 5,000 judicial police officers, 1,600 investigators, and 450 specialists.

The rest of the PGR law enforcement activities (besides the delegations for each state) can be broken up into planning departments, internal controls, and more notably, deputy attorney general offices (*subprocuradurías*), which contain special units. Because the federal police are charged with some of Mexico's most vexing crime problems—stanching the flow of illegal drugs, solving kidnappings, and fighting other types of organized crime—it is worth mentioning two subprocuradurías that have evolved over time.

The PGR's first Special Anti–Organized Crime Unit (*Unidad Especial contra la Delicuencia Organizada*—UEDO) appeared as a response to organized crime, which was first defined in Mexico's legal code in February

1994 as "three or more persons organized under rules of discipline and hierarchy in order to commit, in a violent and repeated way or with the purpose of profit, any of the crimes legally defined." The Federal Law against Organized Crime (*Ley Federal contra la Delincuencia Organizada—*LFcDO) was passed in November 1996 to deal with the problem of drug trafficking, though other crimes, such as migrant smuggling, trafficking in arms or infants, and terrorism, were covered and targeted as well.

The Office of the Special Prosecutor for Crimes Against Health (*Fiscalía Especializada de Delitos Contra la Salud—*FEADS) appeared in 1997 after General Gutiérrez Rebollo, head of the National Anti-Drugs Institute (*Instituto Nacional de Combate a las Drogas—*INCD), was arrested on charges stemming from association with leaders of the Juárez cartel. So INCD, which previously dealt with drug trafficking, was dismantled, and FEADS was put under the direction of a civilian, Mariano Herrán, and the UEDO operated out of FEADS headquarters in Mexico City. Two other key units within FEADS were the Border Rapid Response Groups (*Grupos de Respuesta Rápida Fronteriza*) and the Special Anti–Money Laundering Unit (*Unidad Especializada contra el Lavado de Dinero—*UECLD). UECLD was created in January 1998 to implement anti–money laundering legislation, which dates from 1990. The problem of corruption in FEADS was not entirely solved, and agents in Tijuana and Monterrey were arrested for extortion and kidnapping. Both FEADS and UEDO have been reorganized; some examples of their new units are described below.

As it was organized, the Office of the Deputy Attorney General for Special Investigation of Organized Crime (*Subprocuraduría de Investigación Especializada en Delicuencia Organizada—*SIEDO) received 357 million pesos of the 2004 budget. SIEDO contains six special units (with smaller, separate budgets) intended for investigating specific types of crimes: crimes against public health; terrorism and arms trafficking; money laundering and counterfeiting; human trafficking, namely in minors, organs, and undocumented people; kidnappings; and robbery and auto theft. A second example is the Deputy Attorney for Special Investigation of Federal Crimes (*Subprocuraduría de Investigación Especializada en Delitos Federales—*SIEDF), which received about 16 million pesos of the 2006 budget. The four separate units under its direction cover crimes related to intellectual property, financial transactions, environmental damage, and public servants who obstruct justice.

Both examples demonstrate the general rule that Mexican policing institutions try to reorganize themselves in a rational way to respond effectively to specific crime problems. But actually, legislation must first address specific crime problems; most often only then can the police institutions themselves respond to the law. Without specific laws that enable them to act, public institutions in Mexico—police departments included—find it difficult to pursue particular goals, no matter how pressing. Another result of when legislative action is lacking and bureaucratic tinkering is used to address crime-fighting needs is that official reorganizations and departmental shuffles tend to be quite frequent. Ad hoc adjustments and internal regulatory changes in the Mexican type of bureaucracy are uncommon; each department or agency is created with a fixed set of procedures and powers. So when bureaucratic change is deemed necessary, this is often accomplished by renaming, reorganizing, and/or reconstituting a particular organization. An easier but less effective method of bureaucratic reorganization is to move the head of one department to another in an attempt to add a personal imprimatur or change the character of the second institution, though these changes are often largely cosmetic. In short, adjustments are difficult to make quickly and effectively in the Mexican system, making the law enforcement apparatus less nimble than would be desirable.

The SSP and the PFP: Sweeping reforms began to shake up the federal SSP in 2005, as President Fox created the Public Security Cabinet (*Gabinete de Seguridad Pública*) at the federal level with Fox as the nominal head and with the chief of the SSP coordinating activities. The SSP comes under the jurisdiction of the Interior Secretariat (*Secretaría de Gobernación*) and had a budget of 6,462 million pesos for 2004 and a total staff of 22,900, which included members of the police. As a gesture toward integration, the new cabinet will also include the attorney general as a permanent member, in addition to military officials. Fox also transformed an undersecretariat for prevention and citizen participation to work with the newly created Council of Citizen Participation (*Consejo de Participación Ciudadana*—CPC) that is intended to monitor performance, analyze police, and suggest courses of action in the area of public security. Miguel Angel Yunes was appointed to this undersecretary post.

Under President Fox, Alejandro Gertz Manero had been the Secretary of Public Security, which is a cabinet position, though it falls under the Interior Secretariat, which also holds a cabinet position. When Gertz stepped down in 2004, then-Deputy Interior Minister Ramon Martín Huerta replaced him. President Calderon has since made Genaro García Luna the Secretary. The sense of flux in the SSP, the push for reform, and the changing authorities mean that future organization of the SSP is uncertain. As it stands, however, the SSP houses two important public security institutions: the federal preventive police and the National Public Security System (SNSP, discussed further below). The entire SSP had a budget of 6,462 million pesos allocated to it in 2004.

The federal preventive police (*Policía Federal Preventiva*—PFP) is a force that was created in 1999 at the behest of the Zedillo administration (1994–2000) and the prompting of the SNSP to control crime throughout the country. The Mexican Senate passed legislation in December 1998 that called for the creation of a national law enforcement body that would combine the Federal Highway Police (*Policía Federal de Caminos*), the Federal Fiscal Police (*Policía Fiscal Federal*), and the Federal Immigration Police (*Policía Migratoria Federal*). Initially, concerns focused on the fact that the new police force could be politically repressive toward opposition parties, and then attention turned to the military training, service background, and ethic of the new recruits.

The PFP has technical and operative autonomy and is headed by a commissioner named by the president. In 2000, the SSP's PFP had 10,699 officers; 4,899 of these were from the military (3rd Brigade of the Military Police), about 4,000 came from the Federal Highway Police, 1,500 from the Federal Fiscal Police, and 600 from the Interior Secretariat's intelligence agency, the Center for Research and National Security (*Centro de Investigación y Seguridad Nacional*—CISEN). These new members were then trained by the military. In short, rather than creating an entirely new police force, the PFP has cobbled together a force with a decidedly militarized character.

Restructuring of the PFP left it with some notable attributes in 2004. Besides the typical training, development, and planning departments, there are unique coordinating departments (*Coordinaciones*). Reflecting both the military and police background of the incorporated personnel, the Department for Regional Security is organized into four types of deployment: ports and borders, federal highways, other federal zones, and regional commands (34 of them). There is also a Department of Intelligence for Crime Prevention, which is organized internally to mimic closely the PGR units for federal crimes such as trafficking, terrorism, kidnapping, analysis, information, and statistics. Finally, there are federal support forces intended for disasters, special operations, and strategic deployments. The budget of the PFP in 2004 was 3,598 million pesos, which is more than half of the SSP budget.

Security Institutions: It merits explaining at the outset that four bodies have developed over time, often intermingling and evolving in ways that have caused confusion: the National Security Council (*Consejo de Seguridad Nacional*), the National Security Cabinet (*Gabinete de Seguridad Nacional*), the National Public Security Council *(Consejo Nacional de Seguridad Pública)*, and the Public Security Cabinet (*Gabinete de Seguridad Pública*).

• President Salinas created the National Security Cabinet (*Gabinete de Seguridad Nacional*) in 1988. Under President Calderon, the Attorney General (or head of the PGR), Eduardo Medina-Mora Icaza, has been made the technical secretary of the cabinet. The cabinet also includes the secretaries of the defense, interior, public security, and the navy.

• The National Security Council was installed by Fox in February 2005, as required by the 2005 National Security Law. Fox tapped Santiago Creel, head of the Interior Secretariat, to be executive secretary of the council. The deliberative body brings together the heads of CISEN, Public Security, and National Defense among of other secretariats and has often been compared to the U.S. National Security Council; however, Mexico's version is especially focused on developing policies to address problems of organized crime and international drug traffickers. Calderon nominated Sigrid Arzt, who is an academic expert also active in civil society, to be the new technical secretary.

- The National Public Security Council (*Consejo Nacional de Seguridad Pública*) was established in 1995 and is currently headed by the Secretary of Public Security, Genaro García Luna. (This is explained further in the SNSP section below).

- The Public Security Cabinet (*Gabinete de Seguridad Pública*) was established in 2004 by the SSP to address public concern with rampant crime problems. (This is described above in the section on the SSP and the PFP.)

The Center for Research and National Security (Centro de Investigación y Seguridad Nacional—CISEN): Created in 1989, this is Mexico's principal civilian intelligence agency. CISEN is an instrument of the executive branch, subordinate to the Interior Secretariat (*Secretaría de Gobernación*). CISEN's primary function is to collect and process intelligence and security-related information.

Because drug trafficking organizations have proved successful in penetrating the security institutions, the anti–drug trafficking part of CISEN's intelligence and operations was transferred in 1992 to the newly created INCD and to its intelligence arm, the Anti-Drugs Center (*Centro de Planeación para el Combate contra las Drogas—CENDRO*). INCD did not solve corruption problems, and FEADS was subsequently created (see PGR, above).

SE-SNSP: Another important addition to the public security apparatus is the Executive Secretary for National Public Security System (*Secretariado Ejecutivo de Sistema Nacional de Seguridad Pública—SE-SNSP*), which began in 1994 with constitutional changes (Articles 21 and 73) that raised public security to the status of a state policy. The expressed idea was to coordinate public security efforts, plans, and data collection as well as to systematically fight crime and address demands for public security.

The Zedillo administration followed in 1995 with legislation formally creating the SNSP. A key decision was to locate the SNSP within the Interior Secretariat (*Secretaría de Gobernación*) rather than the PGR Secretariat. The law also created the National Public Security Council (*Consejo Nacional de Seguridad Pública*) as a coordinating body for the SNSP. The council included the secretary of public security, who presides, as well as the 31 state governors, the attorney general, the mayor of the DF, and the military chiefs. (In 2004, Fox announced that he would dramatically restructure the National Public Security Council, and the final outcome under President Calderon is not clear at this writing.) Also created was a series of coordinating councils at the state and local levels, emphasizing the central government's role in data collection, coordination, and planning, rather than direct control. The SNSP has grown in budgetary terms from 226.6 million pesos in 1996 to 366 million pesos in 2004. By 2000, the resources allocated by federal and state governments reached over 9 billion pesos.

Institutional Problems in Public Security

Ineffectiveness among Mexican police forces has proven durable, partly because the reasons for it are entrenched deep into police institutions. To break the cycle of poor performance and the lack of public trust and resources, police institutions need to develop information collection systems that regularly collect standard and accessible data on police and criminal activities. Most state-level police departments lack the capacity and technology to develop computerized information tracking systems that are necessary to perform large-scale crime-mapping, regularized data collection and sharing, and accountability monitoring, but police institutions of the PGR, PGR-DF, and AFI could develop this capacity and help others adopt it. Also, public resources must be allocated to increase the salaries of police officials if *mordidas* (small bribes) are going to be replaced by legitimate sources of income. Finally, the time and money spent on training and vetting police forces remain insufficient. Such investments are a first step in reforming institutions and chipping away at public distrust and corruption.

Corruption and Public Confidence

It is widely believed that corruption and inefficiency plague the Mexican police. Further, low pay and lack of resources have hindered efforts in improving police performance, battling corruption, and professionalizing the forces. A related lack of public confidence has eroded the ability of the police to respond to crime: Surveys regularly find that around 90 percent of respondents in Mexico City have "little" or "no" trust in the police. Such a lack of public confidence translates into a lack of support—that is, an unwillingness to report crimes or assist in investigations, which is crucial to solving crimes. Fox repeatedly stated, in presenting his reform initiative, that only 25 percent of all crimes are reported in Mexico, which is a high estimate.

Fox made reducing public corruption a key goal of his administration and gained some international recognition for his efforts. Mexico moved up several places to 51st—that is, improved—on the global corruption index published by Transparency International (TI), an advocacy NGO. However, that indication of progress was never sustained. A management consulting firm (A. T. Kearney) reported in 2002 that Mexico's attractiveness to foreign investors had dropped, from fifth to ninth place worldwide, due to concerns with corruption and crime (see the section on crime and public security, below). In 2007, Transparency International reported that 80 percent of Mexican respondents said in 2006 that their law enforcement and police institutions were "corrupt."[5]

Official corruption is prevalent within the police and common to the very practice of policing in Mexico.[6] TI estimated in 2002 that the median Mexican household spends 8 percent of its income on bribes (mordidas). Police officers are the officials frequently extracting these mordidas. Corruption within the

Mexican police force often takes on a pyramidal structure, with those at the bottom receiving low wages, and corrupt officials on the top sometimes taking in huge sums. The average police patrol officer in Mexico City earns an insufficient salary with which to support a family. It is frequently argued that mordidas allow police officials to augment their paltry salaries and avoid processing citizens for minor infractions.[7] However, a large percentage of these bribes flow upward, producing wealthy officers at the top and a wide base of still-impoverished patrol personnel at the bottom of the pyramid.[8]

Human Resources

Training, preparation, and institutional support for the police are generally poor. For the preventive police, academic and professional training are recent additions to policy. Of the 58 police academies, 25 began training operations in the last 23 years; most do not enforce a minimum educational requirement. Basic training lasts an average of four and one-half months; for example, in the DF, basic training lasts for six months. The majority of Mexican police officers have completed only elementary school or less. This situation has accelerated the erosion of institutional standards and postponed the modernization of the police. Police departments often lack: tools to evaluate job performance, guidelines for performance, methods to ferret out corruption, technical support, and understanding of human rights and community relations.

Legal System

Overload is a significant problem in the Mexican criminal justice system. When a complaint is received and a preliminary inquiry (*averiguacion previa*) begun, a criminal case is opened. Alternatively, cases can be initiated when a law officer detains a person caught in the act of committing a crime. The person can be detained for up to 48 hours before being brought before a judge for a preliminary hearing. The judge has up 72 hours to decide on one of three options: The person is jailed subject to trial, freed on bail, or freed due to lack of evidence. If the person is not freed due to lack of evidence, the judge may ask the police to gather more evidence. When the investigation is complete, the judge concludes the trial portion of the process and issues a sentence. Part of the overload problem arises because investigating officers, on average, receive a new complaint for each day of the year. Reported crimes practically doubled from 1991 to 1997, and reported crimes are only a small fraction of actual crimes. When districts (such as the DF) consider policing policies known as "zero tolerance," which require a high number of arrests, this administrative backlog could worsen.

Federalism

Mexico has yet to tap the potential dynamism that federalism offers in terms of innovation, reform, and decentralization. One strategy is to create federal grants that give states incentives to create mechanisms of accountability (such as external oversight), stronger internal affairs departments (which are often nonexistent or nonfunctional), and even experimental reforms (such as crime-mapping, women's police stations, or community policing). A second strategy to utilize federalism in the interest of professional policing is to mandate changes that simplify and streamline police work and information. All police departments might be required to adopt rather simple institutional procedures (such as weapons and evidence registries) and to use uniform crime reporting mechanisms that would make it possible to study crime trends and the effects of state and local police activities. Finally, federalism works best when the central entity disseminates results of research widely—to states, localities, and civil society—so that reforms and successes not only percolate up, but also diffuse throughout the country.

Mexico's main institutional mechanisms in achieving these tasks include INACIPE (*Instituto Nacional de Ciencias Penales*). INACIPE, however, lacks the ability to support local experimentation and study. Furthermore, there are no public entities that are autonomous or external to the police that can audit police performance, investigate misconduct, or impose accountability. Given Mexico's political situation, this movement might have to begin at the federal level.

Paths to Democratic Policing

President Fox presented a coordinated justice and security sector reform proposal on March 29, 2004 (*Iniciativa de Reforma de Seguridad Pública y Justicia Penal*). Though it could not have changed things overnight, citizens were not assuaged. In June 2004, millions of Mexicans marched on the capital wearing white and demanding more security. The president met with many of the groups' leaders on July 1, 2004. In early 2005, President Fox began to revamp the federal public security institutions yet again in response to a rising tide of kidnappings, a massacre in Cancún, and the murders of police officers and prison officials by narco-traffickers. So questions remain as to whether or not Mexico is on the path to democratic policing and what path that would be.

To begin, we should consider what is meant by "democratic policing." Defining democratic policing is a research topic unto itself, but the core idea is a set of public security institutions that increase accountability to the public and a set of police practices that require police to strive to be impartial and rights-respecting.[9] De Mesquita Neto has posited that there are at least five different paths to democratic policing, but none is exhaustive, and they

are not mutually exclusive, and therefore they should "open and not conclude a debate" (de Mesquita Neto, 2001, p. 2). Because two of these
paths—civil war and foreign invasion—can be safely ruled out for Mexico,
only three paths to democratic policing are likely in Mexico's situation:
reform led by the government, reform led by civil society, or reform caused
by political agreement.

Reform led by government happens when external events and pressure
lead political actors within the government to perceive a "significant increase
in crime and disorder in the society and/or a significant increase in police corruption and violence" and "initiate a process of police reform" (de Mesquita
Neto, 2001, p. 7). Civil society may influence the reform process along this
path, but government officials are much more capable of directing and co-
opting the process once they initiate it.[10] The overriding influence of elected
officials can have a downside, because they often have a shorter horizon for
reforms. Elected officials want credit for effective crime control, and they
make additional calculations about the police forces they are trying to reform
and the institutional structure of government itself. For example, Mexico
City's leftist mayor seemed to have embraced "tough on crime" measures,
partly because he reasoned he could have an immediate impact on police
activity but little impact on the character of police institutions themselves.[11]

The second path is largely hypothetical: An increase in crime and disorder sparks protests and pressures from civil society, which then leads the
reform movement. Though police violence and corruption top the agenda,
Mexico does not meet all of the criteria of the second path, because one
could not say that "civil society is strong and the government is weak" (de
Mesquita Neto, 2001, p. 11).

The third path is reform initiated by political agreement, and it might be
Mexico's best chance. In this scenario, crime, disorder, and/or police violence and corruption again motivate actors, but in this case government *and*
civil society become the actors who have an agreed interest to advance a
program of police reform. In such cases, "The nature of police reform
depends largely on the strength of the government and the civil society, the
position of the police . . . and the degree of public concern" (de Mesquita
Neto, 2001, p. 13). Such reform also depends on networks of policy experts
to provide some of the ideas that become policy innovations, a governing
structure that does not enable hard-line groups to block reform, and an
institutional structure of the police that is amenable to change.

In sum, it seems that a system of democratic policing in Mexico achieved
by motivated elected officials (the first path) may end up being shortsighted and prone to failure. If reform were achieved through explicit collaboration and partnership between civil society and the government (the
second path), it would be more durable and significant. Given that, at least
four factors affect how government and civil society respond to the political and institutional environment of public security: crime, organized crime,
private security, and civil society.

Common Crime

Crime rates and the perception of public insecurity grew substantially in the 1990s and the first half of this decade. Three major cities, Mexico City, Tijuana, and Ciudad Juarez, stood out with high rates. Kidnapping has gained the most media attention, but the most common crime is theft (*robo*), and it has increased the most since 1993; theft represents nearly 50 percent of reported crimes. Homicide rates also increased in Mexico, though not as severely as in other parts of Latin America. Based on victimization studies, it is clear that crime reporting is low. Surveys reveal that the main reason is lack of confidence in the police. According to official data (*Instituto Nacional de Estadistica, Geografia e Informatica*—INEGI), in 2001 there were 24,742 sentenced criminals and 28,619 people charged (*delincuentes presuntos*) in the federal jurisdiction (*fuero federal*) and 123,071 sentenced criminals and 163,995 people charged in local crimes. Thus, Mexico had a conviction rate of one person for every 10 crimes reported (from a total of about 150,000 convictions for over 1.5 million reported crimes, each of which may involve multiple people) in 2001. As crimes become more personally invasive and the mismatch between victimization and crime reporting continues, one can assume that the public is getting increasingly frustrated and desperate. Hard-line *mano dura* candidates, who neglect civil society, do well in such an environment. Civil society may have to rally the public to earn a place at the reform table.

Organized Crime and Challenges to the State

Another set of forces can bankrupt and sideline civil society, at the same time making the state respond more militantly. Such forces are evident in the growth "in drug trafficking and organized crime, the emergence of armed groups such as the Ejército Zapatista de Liberación Nacional (EZLN, the Zapatista National Liberation Army) and the Ejército Popular Revolucionario (EPR, the People's Revolutionary Army)" which is related to "the increase in public insecurity, and the great crisis in the country's judicial institutions" (Benitez Manaut, 2000, p. 127). Formerly in Mexico, the old National Security Police and the office of the attorney general served as structural intermediaries between traffickers and those in political power (Astorga, 2000, p. 61). When the old power structure began to deteriorate in the 1980s and throughout the 1990s, the political opposition gained ground; thus traffickers showed more autonomy. "Recent changes in the correlation of forces in Mexico have created a context in which democratic forces have not been able to consolidate or to impose the rule of law over the working agreements among power groups, including both established and new bands of traffickers, that do not respect democratic civility" (Astorga, p. 81).

Organized crime is considered a major security threat, because it exacerbates corruption, enables drug trafficking, and brings increasing amounts of violence and high-powered weaponry to Mexico. Criminal organizations began to restructure themselves in 2003, which led to open warfare in some parts of the country. These drug-trafficking gangs are competing to control the *plazas*, which are used as drug corridors into the United States. Seventy-four deaths among rival drug traffickers were registered in the first three months of 2004, with Sinaloa registering the highest number.[12] Though the death tolls and public disturbance are a security problem, should these fragmented drug cartels reunify, the crime problem may worsen.

Popular insurgency can also be considered an internal security threat for the state, though this threat has somewhat subsided since its peak in 2004. In January of that year, the EZLN announced its southern insurgency in an uprising in Chiapas meant to coincide with the implementation of the North American Free Trade Agreement. Though the threat to the state has subsided, reported human rights abuses, assassinations, political turbulence, and concerns about internal security have continued. In addition, other guerilla groups appeared in the south, such as the Insurgent People's Army (ERPI) and the more lethal EPR, which have inflicted casualties on police and army personnel in Guerrero and Oaxaca among several other states. President Fox stated in April 2001 that the guerrilla movements were finished, a claim that rang hollow when, four months later, another armed group called the FARP (*Fuerzas Armadas Revolucionarias del Pueblo*) set off bombs in three Banamex offices in Mexico City to protest its sale to U.S. corporate giant Citicorp. These popular insurgencies and globalization protests, like endemic corruption and the fight against drug trafficking, have led (and threaten to lead) to increased involvement of the military in police work and order maintenance, which troubles many.

Private Security

Mexican security companies have grown significantly in recent years in response to the state's failure to provide security, and this growth further erodes that capacity of the state. Mexico holds third place in the purchase of security equipment worldwide. Between 1998 and 1999, the number of private security companies in Mexico increased some 40 percent. The Mexican government has had serious problems in regulating these companies, most of which are illegitimate, because they lack the necessary legal permits. At least 10,000 private security firms operate in Mexico, yet only 2,000 had some form of official permit in 1999. According to official figures, in December 2000 there were 2,984 private security companies registered with 153,885 employees. The inability to regulate or control these forces creates potential security problems. Because many of these companies are unregulated, some will engage in criminality instead of (or as a means of) protecting their clients, thus exacerbating the problem of insecurity. According to a study by the Mexico City legislative assembly, in 1998 there were more private security guards than police. A substantial number of private security guards were formerly police officers or presently work as security guards while off duty as police officers; these dynamics increase the likelihood of police corruption.

Civil Society

Mexican civil society is becoming involved in public security matters. They have been involved in the creation and management of the *Comisiónes de Derechos Humanos* (Human Rights Commissions or CDHs) as a result of national legislation. Several state-level commissions have been created, but they lack extensive grassroots networks, broad civil society cooperation, and common methods of data collection. Long-term success depends on developing such networks, improving civil society, and allowing organs such as the CDHs to wield more power.

Policing strategies have not yet helped Mexican civil society deal with its deeply embedded crime and corruption problems. Two factors, social stratification and selective policing, everywhere serve to isolate a crime problem for a time, but often later these problems become more intense and spill over into protected areas, creating "national security problems." When national security is invoked as a response to transnational drug trafficking or gangs, all reform bets are off. Police responding to crime as a national security problem may invoke strategies that have actually been linked to "increases in urban gang violence, organized crime, and attacks in wealthy areas," not to mention the curtailing of civil rights (Ungar, 2002, p. 79). Social stratification is also a problem, because it serves as a hothouse for more resilient criminal networks and more violent policing strategies. Enclosed and violent neighborhoods can in turn increase fear and social isolation, limit movement, and curtail the openness of public space, all of which reinforces social stratification and limits the reach of civil society.

Conclusion

The relationship of policing to democracy is manifold in Mexico. As the front end of any judicial system, the police must function effectively and fairly for the legal system to do the same. Mexico's legal system is increasingly important as the country strives to rein in public corruption and grow its legitimate economic sector. Furthermore, Mexico needs accountable and rights-respecting public security forces as the backbone of democracy. Without these protections, Mexico could degrade into a bland, procedural democracy, where elections occur but active participation, due process, and civil rights are not a lived reality for most citizens. Last, where public security forces are incompetent or corrupt, citizens lose faith in public institutions and invest in private security, which sets off a cycle that further erodes the egalitarian nature of citizenship.

Besides the danger of democratic backsliding, there is an upside to consider that makes it possible to frame the challenge in a more positive way: Fair and efficient police earn the confidence of the public and thus serve to bolster the public nature of security, expand citizenship, create responsive public institutions, and legitimize democracy. Because their reach and numbers are so vast, the police institutions of Mexico have the potential to improve the substantive quality of democracy for Mexican citizens if they embrace principles of transparency, efficiency, and democratic policing. The path to doing so may have to be blazed by public officials and government bureaucrats who find a common interest in making the Mexican police fairer and more effective.

Glossary

Attorney General's Office	*Procuraduría General de la República* (PGR)
Attorney General's Office of the Federal District	*Procuraduría General de Justicia del Distrito Federal* (PGJ-DF)
Center for Research and National Security	*Centro de Investigación y Seguridad Nacional* (CISEN)
Experts, technical experts, or specialists	*peritos*
Federal Agency of Investigation	*Agencia Federal de Investigaciones* (AFI)
Federal District	*Distrito Federal* (DF)
Federal Judicial Police	*Policía Judicial Federal* (PJF)
Federal law	*fuero federal*
Federal Preventive Police	*Policía Federal Preventiva* (PFP)
Interior Secretariat	*Secretaría de Gobernación*
Judicial Police of the Federal District	*Policía Judicial del Distrito Federal* (PJDF)
Local law	*fuero común*
Office of the Special Prosecutor for Crimes against Health	*Fiscalía Especializada de Delitos Contra la Salud* (FEADS)
Public Secretariat	*Ministerio Público*
Secretary of Public Security of the D.F.	*Secretaría de Seguridad Pública* (SSP)

Notes

1. A brief tracing of this intellectual development can be seen in the following works: Berins Collier, 1999; Linz and Stepan, 1996; and O'Donnell, Schmitter, and Whitehead, 1986. See also the edited volume that revisited Rustow's 1970 *Comparative Politics* article, "Transitions to Democracy" of eponymous title (Anderson, 1999).

2. These estimates amount to a ratio of about 2.6 police officers per 100 citizens, assuming a population of 104 million and a police population of 400,000. Estimates of the actual number of police came from privately accessed pages from Jane's Information Group (http://www.janes.com) retrieved on October 30, 2004, the CIA fact book (CIA, n.d.), news reports following Fox's announcement of the proposal to reform the justice system (March 29, 2004), Vargas (2003), and data gathered from Mexican government Web sites (see suggested readings).

3. The PFP was created on December 13, 1998; for all intents and purposes, it did not come into existence until 1999.

4. This observation, like many others throughout, is owed to Ernesto López Portillo Vargas (2003).

5. Information can be found at the annual Global Corruption Reports at http://www.transparency.org

6. Police departments are not the only area of the criminal justice system where corruption is found. A recent UN Human Rights Commission special report on the independence of judges and lawyers warned that Mexico's justice system suffered widespread corruption. Based on testimonies, it estimated that 50 to 70 percent of federal judges were involved in acts of corruption and said that in some states, civil matters were not processed without the payment of a bribe.

7. A fascinating response to this reality was the mayor of Ecatepec's decision to abolish all parking and traffic violations so that police officers would have to stop shaking down citizens for bribes (Sullivan, 2003).

8. Since much of this corruption occurs in Mexico City, this practice raises the question of if and how the "zero tolerance" recommendations of the Giuliani consulting group will be effected. If mordidas function to exchange small bribes for not processing civilians through the criminal justice system, and if "broken windows" approaches to policing call for prosecuting minor crimes to prevent more serious ones, there is a necessary conflict.

9. De Mesquita Neto calls it "a form of policing in which the police are accountable to the law and the community, respect the rights and guarantee the security of all citizens in a non-discriminatory manner" (2001, p. 2). David Bayley identifies two main features: *accountability* and *responsiveness* (1997). Otwin Marenin focuses on six principles, two of the most important of which are *accessibility* and *accountability* (for citations and further explanation, see Stone and Ward, 2000). For their part, Stone and Ward concur and add that *accountability* to multiple structures at multiple levels is what makes policing democratic. Also see Charles Call's analysis of the creation of an international "norm" for democratic policing (Call, 2000).

10. Colombia, Chile, and Peru may serve as recent examples.

11. The argument to be made in more detail is that even when reform-minded officials face police institutions whose norms and ethos are notoriously hard to change, they will often adopt zero tolerance policies as a way of reducing crime, because reforming the institutions themselves seems more difficult. The *mano dura*

or *tolerancia cero* policing approaches of Carlos Ruckauf in Buenos Aires and Luis Fleury in Sao Paulo are examples.

12. These figures came from privately accessed pages from Jane's Information Group (http://www.janes.com).

References

Anderson, L. (1999). *Transitions to democracy.* New York: Columbia University Press.

Astorga, L. (2000). Organized crime and organization of crime. In J. Bailey & R. Godson (Eds.), *Organized crime and democratic governability: Mexico and the U.S.–Mexico borderlands* (pp. 58–82). Pittsburgh, PA: University of Pittsburgh Press.

Bailey, J., & Godson, R. (Eds.). (2000). *Organized crime and democratic governability: Mexico and the U.S.–Mexico borderlands.* Pittsburgh, PA: University of Pittsburgh Press.

Benitez Manaut, R. (2000). Containing armed groups, drug trafficking, and organized crime in Mexico: The role of the military. In J. Bailey & R. Godson (Eds.), *Organized crime and democratic governability: Mexico and the U.S.–Mexico borderlands* (pp. 126–158). Pittsburgh, PA: University of Pittsburgh Press.

Berins Collier, R. (1999). *Paths toward democracy: The working class and elites in Western Europe and South America.* New York: Cambridge University Press.

Call, C. (2000, March). *Pinball and punctuated equilibrium: The birth of a "democratic policing" norm?* Paper presented at the annual conference of the International Studies Association, Los Angeles, California.

Central Intelligence Agency (CIA). (n.d.). Mexico. In *CIA—The World Factbook.* Retrieved August 1, 2007, from https://www.cia.gov/library/publications/the-world-factbook/geos/mx.html

Cornelius, W., & Shirk, D. (Eds.). (2007). *Reforming the administration of justice in Mexico.* La Jolla, CA, and Chicago: Center for U.S.-Mexican Studies and University of Notre Dame Press.

Linz, J., & Stepan, A. (1996). *Problems of democratic transition and consolidation: Southern Europe, South America, and post-communist Europe.* Baltimore: Johns Hopkins University Press.

de Mesquita Neto, P. (2001, March). *Paths toward democratic policing in Latin America.* Paper presented at the International Workshop on Human Rights and the Police in Transitional Countries, Copenhagen, Denmark.

O'Donnell, G., Schmitter, P. C., & Whitehead, L. (Eds.). (1986). *Transitions from authoritarian rule: Comparative perspectives.* Baltimore: Johns Hopkins University Press.

Stone, C. E., & Ward, H. (2000). Democratic policing: A framework for action. *Policing and Society, 10*(1), 11–47.

Sullivan, K. (2003, September 8). Mexican town forgoes law for order. *Washington Post,* p. A15.

Ungar, M. (2002). *Elusive reform: Democracy and the rule of law in Latin America.* Boulder, CO: Lynne Rienner.

_____ **Interview**

Vargas, E. L. P. (2003, May). Interview at the Instituto Nacional de Ciencias Penales, Mexico City.

_____ **Further Reading**

Alvarado, A., & Arzt, S. (Ed.). (2001). *El desfío democrático de México: seguridady Estado de derecho*. México City: El Colegio de México, Centro de Estudios.

Attorney General's Office (Procuraduría General de la República—PGR). Retrieved August 1, 2007, from http://www.pgr.gob.mx

Bailey, J. & Chabat, J. (Ed.). (2002). *Transnational crime and public security*. San Diego, CA: Center for U.S.–Mexican Studies at the University of California San Diego.

Country briefing (n.d.). *The Economist* [Electronic version]. Retrieved August 1, 2007 from http://www.economist.com/countries/Mexico

Lawyers Committee for Human Rights and Centro de Derechos Humanos Miguel Agustín Pro Juárez. (2001). *Injusticia legalizada*. New York: Author.

Quezada, S. A. (Ed.). (2000). *El almanaque mexicano*. México City: Editorial Grijalbo.

Secretary of Public Security of the D. F. (*Secretaría de Seguridad Pública*—SSP). (n.d.). Pagina principal de la SSP. Retrieved August 1, 2007 from http://www.ssp.df.gob.mx

Smith, J. J. (1992). *Modernizing Mexican politics* (2nd ed.) New York: ISHI Press.

Valenzuela, J. (1992). Democratic consolidation in post-transitional settings: Notion, process, and facilitating conditions. In S. Mainwaring, G. O'Donnell, & J. Valenzuela (Eds.), *Issues in democratic consolidation: The new South American democracies in comparative perspective* (pp. 57–104). Notre Dame, IN: University of Notre Dame Press.

Vargas, E. L. P. (2002). The police in Mexico: Political functions and needed reforms. In J. Bailey & J. Chabat (Eds.), *Transnational crime and public security: Challenges to Mexico and the United States* (pp. 109–135). San Diego, CA: Center for U.S.-Mexican Studies at the University of California San Diego.

5

Postconflict Democratization of the Police

The Sierra Leone Experience

Stuart Cullen and William H. McDonald

Democracies are political systems characterized by popular participation, genuine competition for executive and legislative office, fostering of fundamental human rights, and institutional checks on power. While the actual democratic structure of government may vary, these fundamental concepts remain constant (Siegel, Weinstein, & Halperin, 2004).

The key to the level of developmental and economic success of the Western nations is their adoption of democracy. Within such nations, the police operate under internationally recognized democratic principles to ensure a harmonious society in which political, social, and economic life can flourish (Crawshaw, Cullen, & Williams, 2006).

Democratic civilian policing is an essential component of good governance operating under a range of basic principles. In ensuring that a police organization is civilian rather than military, there must be separate government ministers having control and oversight over the police and military. Similarly, the commander or chief of police and senior police posts should not hold military rank or be associated with the national armed forces. Whereas the military have a primary role in securing the state from external threat, the police should have a primary and accountable role in citizen security and serving the law. Extraordinary circumstances may demand military personnel having to assist the police in joint public safety operations (for example, in protecting the citizenry from terrorists or armed bandits). In these circumstances, it is essential for the police to have primacy in command and control of operations. Legislation or the constitution should prevent the police from being controlled by political parties or the military (Crawshaw et al., 2006).

The police should be accountable to government, for example, through a minister of citizen security or home or internal affairs, and to the citizens through community consultative groups representing all sections of society. The police should be able to respond to community needs and expectations. This can be facilitated by the organization of an independent civilian review board or commission comprising cross-party political appointees and other nonpartisan members. Their role is to oversee and monitor policing functions and senior police appointments and to ensure that matters of public concern are addressed (Crawshaw et al., 2006).

Democratic police organizations function within and are accountable to the rule of law. Their members have a duty to protect human rights. National legislation defines their authority and responsibility, rules of conduct for officers and officials, standards for the legitimate use of force, and similar practices. Torture and extra-judicial tactics are prohibited. Formal mechanisms should exist to investigate allegations of police misconduct and where necessary, to enforce the law (Code of Conduct for Law Enforcement Officers, 1979).

Unfortunately, democracy is a complicated and often elusive phenomenon. The establishment of democracy in postcolonial nations around the world, particularly Africa, has not ensured political, social, or economic development. In many African states, democracy has evaporated or been crushed in the path of intractable and destructive conflicts based on tribalism, race, religious and identity issues, corruption, wealth, and land issues. The sheer impoverishment and ruinous situation of much of Africa, never starker or more revealing, testifies to that reality.

The misappropriation of state and public assets and finances by the ruling or dominant elites have turned many of these democracies into "kleptocracies." The effects of the unattended HIV/AIDS pandemic throughout the continent have further added to political and economic disaster and the decline of civil society. And as citizens react, the unrepresentative and often unelected corrupt ruling cliques characteristically deploy the military and police against ordinary citizens. The resulting spiral of violence frequently leads to civil war.

Background

The political, social, and economic decline of the Republic of Sierra Leone from its independence in 1961 through its 1991 civil war provides a case study at its most brutal and raw. It is a classic example of the importance of the police to democracy. More important, it demonstrates the effects and consequences of the political transformation of a democratic police organization into a repressive and corrupt arm of a despotic government.

The Republic of Sierra Leone occupies 71,740 square kilometers on the west coast of Africa and has an estimated population of 6,017,643 (July 2005 estimate). It remains one of the world's poorest and least developed countries despite vast deposits of diamonds and other natural resources (CIA, n.d.).

Sierra Leone gained independence in 1961 following 150 years as a British protectorate. The nation was established as a constitutional democracy and a member of the British Commonwealth. The legal system and laws of Sierra Leone were based on those of England and Wales and customary tribal practices. The first general election under universal adult franchise took place in May 1962 (Cullen & McDonald, 2005).

The first police force in Sierra Leone, the paramilitary West African Frontier Force, was created in 1900 from the Royal Sierra Leone Regiment and commanded by the British officer corps. Its primary purpose was to protect British colonial interests (Lord, 2005). The Police Act of 1964, part of the national Constitution, established the Sierra Leone Police (SLP) as a national, armed, civil force. The Constitution separated the police from the military and charged them with specific responsibility for citizen security, the prevention of crime, and the detection, apprehension, and prosecution of offenders. The force generally follows the British police model in organization and rank structure (Cullen & McDonald, 2005).

During the five years following independence, the country possessed some critical structural features necessary for the development of a modern democratic state, including an educational system based on the British model, a modern economy, a multiparty political system, a professional civil service, and a Western style constitution. A modern military, police, and judiciary served society with a degree of professionalism and integrity. Despite positive beginnings, Sierra Leone quickly fell into ruinous decline brought about by endemic corruption (Thompson & Potter, 1997).

Political Decline, Corruption, and the Police

In a 1967, a coup d'etat brought Siaka Stevens and his All Peoples' Party (known by its acronym APC in the local language) to power. They quickly moved the nation from a multiparty constitutional democracy to a single-party executive presidency. With them came excesses of systematic corruption in the national government, particularly the police, and in every aspect of daily life (Thompson & Potter, 1997).

Like many African nations, Sierra Leone always experienced some level of government corruption as a by-product of modernization. Under Stevens and the APC, the extent of corruption grew to such proportions that the distinctions between the personal lives and the public roles of government officials and between personal and public finances blurred at every level of the administration (Thompson & Potter, 1997). They openly condoned and encouraged the looting of government funds at levels rarely seen. The adage, "A cow will graze on the land allotted to it for that purpose," often alluded to by Stevens himself, became their operative norm (Thompson &

Potter, 1997, p. 150). Few nations have experienced such a pattern of government corruption (Kpundeh, 1993). Eventually, that culture of corruption allowed economic domination of the entire country by members of the power elite. The entire government structure became a mechanism for profit and personal gain (Kpundeh, 1995).

Once in power, the APC quickly changed the civilian nature of the police and moved to exert complete control over their activities. That control became a critical element in their consolidation of power and the exploitation of society. The inspector general of police and the head of army were made part of the ruling cabinet, and the cabinet operated almost solely for the benefit of the dominant (though not majority) Limba tribe and its allies. Its policy was to divide and rule the nation for the personal gain of its members, and that was only possible through the neutralization of the police (Lengor, interview, April 14/15, 2005).

APC political appointees infiltrated the administrative machinery of the police force and brought with them the widespread corrupt practices of the ruling political party. The police leadership was purged of non-APC personnel (Lord, 2005). Transfers, promotions, and recruitment became APC economic and political opportunities. Promotion depended entirely upon APC membership, political loyalty, and bribes (Lengor, interview, April 14/15, 2005). Political favoritism allowed the recruitment of uneducated and illiterate APC supporters into the police ranks. Officers who failed to support these practices were quickly transferred to undesirable postings or dismissed on trumped up charges (Meek, 2003).

The ruling party soon controlled every aspect of SLP operations, and the police quickly became political agents of the APC (Lengor, interview, April 14/15, 2005). During the 1982 national election, for example, the APC used the police against its political opposition, the Sierra Leone Peoples Party, in a violent conflict known as the Bush Devil War. Its members were licensed to abuse their powers to protect and profit the ruling elite and to seize every opportunity for personal gain through bribes and criminal activity (Lord, 2005). Equally important, any resistance to APC authority from within the police service itself had been neutralized (Thompson, 1996).

Members of the SLP engaged in general policing duties directed by the APC through senior police officers, protected monopolies, collected bribes from sympathetic corrupt businesses, and harassed both the political and financial rivals of the APC. Targeted business people were arrested on fabricated charges, then convicted, imprisoned, or executed and put out of business. "Connected" competitors easily acquired the assets of these closed businesses at ridiculous prices (Lengor, interview, April 14/15, 2005).

Police agents provocateurs were employed to encourage and then reveal "crimes," either real or fictitious, allegedly committed by prominent citizens or political opponents. The accused were then publicly prosecuted, or in lieu of prosecution coerced into state-sponsored delinquency. SLP Special Branch officers, posing as bona fide university and college students, spied on students and professors, reporting back to a paranoid regime that feared subversion from its youth (Lengor, interview, April 14/15, 2005).

In the end, the SLP had been totally politicized. Opposition to the state-sponsored economic corruption that might normally arise from the police had been neutralized. The SLP role in the political, economic, and social fabric of the state had changed. The responsibility for citizen security and the protection of democracy had been replaced by the responsibility to manage and safeguard a national protection racket for the benefit of the ruling clique (Lengor, interview, April 14/15, 2005).

Corruption and an accompanying general systematic neglect of police services by the national government led to the decline of their constitutional role in society. Skills necessary for effective policing were not sought. Officers were untrained and lacked uniforms and even basic equipment. These problems were exacerbated by low wages, illiteracy, the lack of professional standards and ethics, and extremely poor morale. This situation quickly led to a breakdown in the quality of police service, and more important, a breakdown in public confidence in the police (Groenwald & Peak, 2004; Malan, Rakafe, & McIntyre, 2003; Meek, 2003). Restoration of that public trust became one of the critical elements for restoring the police and the society (Groenwald & Peak, 2004).

Widespread societal and political instability followed. By 1991 the country was economically and politically near collapse. Opposition to the APC from the political opponents and the disenfranchised business community reached explosive levels. What followed was one of the most violent and horrific internal conflicts in the history of Africa.

The Civil War

In 1991 a Liberian civil war spread northward into Sierra Leone. Foday Sankoh's Sierra Leone Revolutionary United Front joined with Charles Taylor's National Patriotic Front of Liberia (NPF) to overthrow the government and seize the country's diamond mines. Millions of dollars' worth of diamonds smuggled out of the country financed the rebellion (Lord, 2005). At the same time local militias and delinquent youth gangs such as the West Side Boys, fuelled by the influx of drugs, especially heroin, took control of large sections of the country, adding to the chaos (M. Lengor, interviews, April 14/15, 2005). At the height of the conflict, experts estimate more than 48,000 armed combatants, representing a variety of political and criminal organizations, participated in the civil war (Meek, 2003).

Atrocities committed by all parties to the conflict, but especially by rebel forces, terrorized the population (CIA, n.d.). The limbs of innocent citizens, police officers, and political opponents were systematically amputated. Captives were forced to murder and mutilate their own local political leaders, family members, and tribal officials. Enslavement, forced conscription of child soldiers, and systematic gang rapes of women and children plagued the nation. The Sierra Leone military and SLP proved powerless and lost control of large areas of the country to the various rebellious forces, violent gangs, and criminal thugs. Eventually, elements of the military rebelled, contributing to further chaos and disorder (Lord, 2005).

The Sierra Leone Police and Restoration of Democratic Rule

In March 1996, after considerable international pressure and military support, and despite continuing violence, free elections established a fledging democratic government under President Ahmed Tejan Kabbah (Lord, 2005). Kabbah's role in the reconstruction of Sierra Leone, and particularly in the rebuilding of the SLP in that process, has proven critical to the nation's reconstruction.

Educated at a private school in Sierra Leone, Kabbah earned his bachelor's and law degrees in Britain. His entire career had been in the public sector. He served as district commissioner in all the regions of Sierra Leone and as deputy chief of the West African Division of the United Nations Development Program in New York. During the 1970s he coordinated United Nations assistance to liberation movements that needed to be assimilated into legitimate governments following the cessation of conflicts in South Africa and Namibia. That experience convinced him of the critical importance a reorganized and democratic SLP would play in the restoration of social order and democracy ("State House," 2005).

Recent international experience in postconflict resolution efforts supported his position. Most experts agreed that, absent restoration and maintenance of the rule of law, all other investments in the peace process would prove meaningless (Malan et al., 2002).

Shortly after assuming office, Kabbah petitioned the government of the United Kingdom for assistance in the restructuring and development of the Sierra Leone Police. The United Kingdom authorized a preliminary project in 1997, but continuing internal conflict forced its early cancellation. A second program, the Commonwealth Police Development Task Force became operational in 1998. Led by a career British detective and former assistant chief constable, Keith Biddle, the task force included a small number of former United Kingdom police officers and police advisers from Canada, Malaysia, Sri Lanka, and Zimbabwe. All had considerable experience in command roles and a wide range of policing skills. Their charge included technical and financial assistance to support community safety through logistical support, the provision of professional expertise, and the delivery of wide-ranging training programs (Biddle, interview, April 13, 2005).

The selection of Biddle to command the project proved instrumental to its success. During his 32 years of service, he had served in a wide variety of ranks and assignments. He had a well-deserved reputation as a direct, tough, no-nonsense police officer with proven qualities of leadership and a sharp intellect (Malan et al., 2002; Meek, 2003).

The task force faced a ruined and demoralized SLP. More than 900 officers had been killed during the various internal conflicts. Many had been tortured, while others suffered amputation by the rebellious forces. Inept and corrupt personnel occupied leadership and other key positions. Much of the senior command staff and many of the middle-level officers were APC appointees. The force lacked even fundamental equipment and training. Most police facilities had been looted or destroyed during the conflict. Various warring factions and criminal elements had commandeered vehicles, communications systems, and weapons. Wages had not been paid in years (Biddle, interview, April 13, 2005; Malan et al., 2002).

Death, torture, and desertion had reduced the force from its prewar size of 9,300 officers to less than 6,600. And the task force faced a psychological crisis within the SLP. Years of war, corruption, and governmental neglect, the loss of public confidence, and the frequent abandonment of officers and police facilities to advancing rebel forces left the SLP a demoralized organization (Malan et al., 2002).

The SLP had little or no presence outside the capital. Remnants of the army and the quasi-official Civil Defence Force (CDF) maintained a semblance of aimless and undirected "security" around the country through a network of road checkpoints. The CDF was a ragtag collection of armed, ill-disciplined, and aggressive youths, often without uniform or identification, known locally as *Kamajors* (brave hunters). They came primarily from local armed militia groups that had earlier colluded with the army and loosely allied themselves with the government. Little more than armed thugs, they terrorized civilians; committed rapes, ritual murders and other violent crimes; and consistently interfered with the military, police, and peacekeeping operations. Their presence disrupted stability and citizen security (Hoffman, 2005).

The military was little better. Basically an armed mob, corrupt and with little organization or purpose, they continued to contribute to the national chaos and mayhem (Malan et al., 2002).

Amazingly, even though the SLP had virtually collapsed, Biddle found that many officers had served bravely under the most difficult of circumstances. Despite the destruction of most police facilities, many police officers still reported for duty and attempted to go through the motions of providing a police presence. Although it was at odds with the SLP's corrupt image and practices, there remained an underlying ethos of loyalty to the state, nation, and organization. As an institution, the SLP had not been involved in atrocities. Many officers had struggled to maintain constitutional order. The majority had remained loyal to the nation (K. Biddle, interviews, April 13, 2005). For example, in May of 1997 they had fought bravely to save the life of the newly elected President Kabbah by holding off attacking army elements bent on a coup (Malan et al., 2002).

The first priority of government and the international community was to restore law and order in a democratic model and to ensure that the SLP had primacy in all matters of citizen security. To do so, the new government had to aggressively address corruption within the force, restore police self-confidence, and most critical, to restore public confidence. That required an entire rebuilding of the SLP, a job made even more difficult by the continuation of the civil war in many parts of the country (Malan et al., 2002).

President Kabbah set the tone for the new SLP in August of 1997 in the official Government Policing Charter.

THE SIERRA LEONE POLICE

Government Policing Charter

Introduction

My Government wants to create a police service which will be a credit to the Nation.

The Role of the Police

The Sierra Leone Police will assist in returning our communities to peace and prosperity by acting in a manner which will:

- eventually remove the need for the deployment of military and para-military forces in our villages, communities and city streets
- ensure the safety and security of all people and their property
- respect the human rights of all individuals
- prevent and detect crime by using the most effective methods which can be made available to them
- take account of local concerns through community consultation
- at all levels be free from corruption

Equal Opportunities

The personnel policies of the Sierra Leone Police will be the same for all members, regardless of sex or ethnic origin. All recruitment, training, postings, promotions and opportunities for development will be based on a published equal opportunities policy.

The Role of My Government

The Government will do all in its power to ensure that the Sierra Leone Police is:

- directed and managed in accordance with The Constitution
- locally managed so as to ensure that community views are always taken into consideration

- adequately resourced and financed
- well equipped to undertake its duties
- professionally trained
- dynamically led and,
- that the terms and conditions of service for members of the Sierra Leone Police reflect the importance of the task they perform.

The Role of the People

In order that our police officers can successfully fulfill our expectations, it is essential that all people of Sierra Leone help and support them at all times.

Conclusion

Our aim is to see a reborn Sierra Leone Police, which will be a force for good in our Nation.

August 1998 His Excellency
The President Alhaji Dr Ahmed Tejan-Kabbah

SOURCE: *From Crisis to Confidence* (1998).

The charter called for a professional service-oriented police organization that would meet the needs and expectations of all citizens by working in partnership with the community. Moreover, it restored the civilian, democratic nature of the national police service. The SLP would become a "force for good"; this slogan became the unofficial motto of the new SLP.

From Crisis to Confidence

Biddle, his task force colleagues, and members of the SLP command staff quickly adopted the theme set by the president. Senior members of the SLP suspected of corruption or of political affiliations with prior regimes were retired or suspended (Malan et al., 2002). Biddle and his team summoned the remaining senior officers to a master planning session in December of 1998. The seminar, entitled "From Crisis to Confidence," was a historic turning point for the SLP and produced a strategic blueprint for it (Biddle, interview, April 13, 2005).

The working group began by identifying the key values and aims of the new police service. From that they formulated a mission statement based on the president's "force for good" concept.

A Force for Good

Our Duty

We will provide a professional and effective service which:

- Protects Life and Property
- Achieves a peaceful society
- Takes primacy in the maintenance of Law and Order

Our Values

We will respect Human Rights and the freedoms of the individual
We will be honest, impartial, caring and free from corruption

Our Priorities

We will respond to local needs
We will value our own people
We will involve all in developing our policing priorities

Our Aim

To win public confidence by offering reliable, caring and accountable police services

---

SOURCE: *From Crisis to Confidence* (1998).

The master plan identified a wide range of operational and organizational needs. These included human resources and welfare, organizational structure, training, policy making and support, planning, operational management, rules and regulations, ethical standards, recruiting, command and control, and roles and responsibilities. But their main energy focused on restoring the corroded public trust and confidence in the police as quickly as possible. The plan called for the immediate application of community policing principles to the particulars of Sierra Leone's recent history and complex social structure. Organizational changes in support of that objective would start with individual officers and units. The new SLP would then be built up from that foundation (Groenwald & Peak, 2003).

Local Needs Policing

In the months prior to the planning session, the SLP, under the guidance of the task force, had piloted a Sierra Leonean version of community policing in several urban districts and one rural community called local needs policing (LNP). LNP focused on local needs as defined by specific communities. Key issues included victim services, domestic violence, crime prevention, and the needs of those most victimized by the war, especially women and children (Groenwald & Peak, 2003).

These decentralized units delivered police services to meet the expectations of the local community. And with the absence of a meaningful national police service, they became, in effect, independent neighborhood based police forces, addressing immediate local needs in full view of and in close scrutiny by the community. The model allowed for flexibility, enabling local LNPs to develop in different ways to match the pluralist needs of different communities throughout Sierra Leone. Equally important, the model allowed for the restoration of the rule of law and of public confidence in the police at the very foundations of the society (Groenwald & Peak, 2003; Lengor, interview, April 13/14, 2005).

The pilot projects met with considerable success. The idea was adopted as the main mechanism for the restoration and rebuilding of the SLP. Local Needs Policing became the cornerstone of the force strategic plan. LNP would expand as elements of the countryside came under control of the national government. In support of that effort, and in face of the disastrous lack of training, the blueprint called for an aggressive Field Training Officers Program to provide relevant and effective training services (Biddle, interview, April 13, 2005).

Under the LNP initiative, SLP headquarters would continue to be responsible for the strategy and direction of the police force and for managing organizational needs, but police services were decentralized through the LNP units. Neighboring LNP units were clustered into Local Command Units (LCUs) under the direction of a police superintendent. Each LCU worked in collaboration with a Local Policing Partnership Board made up of citizens and local tribal leaders (Moigbe, interview, 2005). Superintendents' authority extended beyond the delivery of routine police services and included the management of local police resources and equipment, training and the development of personnel, job descriptions, and staff assessment (K. Biddle, personnel communication, April 13, 2005).

The LNP concept met another important need of the police force. Because the senior members of the SLP had formulated the program, its success promised to restore self-confidence within the force itself. It was, in effect, their property, their plan, the first organized effort to restore the force and its fundamental role in a democratic society. They had designed it and were accountable for its success or failure (Biddle, interview, April 13, 2005).

By 2002, policing primacy had been established throughout the whole of Sierra Leone. By April 2005, 27 LCUs provided local police services nationwide, each with its own Local Policing Partnership Board (Lengor, interview, 2005).

But a major problem presented itself in the early stages of the plan's implementation: the issue of force leadership. The incumbent acting head of the police, the inspector general of police (IGP), and other senior officers eligible for the position faced both political and practical problems. Politicians and local community leaders threatened to derail the appointment of anyone other than their own political or tribal allies. Considerable infighting between senior police officers over control of the force made matters worse and threatened the potential effectiveness of the reorganization effort (Biddle, interview, April 13, 2005).

President Kabbah addressed the issue immediately. He approached the government of the United Kingdom and asked that Biddle be appointed to head the SLP. The appointment of an outsider had advantages. The candidate would be seen as unsullied by state and institutional corruption and neutral in matters of tribal and kinship allegiances. International donors were more likely to support the nation-building process if the IGP had no connection with previous allegations of corruption or human rights abuses. With permission of the United Kingdom and after approval by the Sierra Leone Parliament, President Kabbah swore Biddle in as inspector general of police on December 1, 1999 (Biddle, interview, April 13, 2005).

Biddle immediately became a member of the Police Council, a statutory body made up of the inspector general of police, the deputy inspector general, the vice president of the republic, the minister of internal affairs, a representative of the Civil Service Commission, a representative of the bar association, and two eminent citizens appointed by the president. The council advised the president on all major matters of policy relating to internal security, including the role of the police, budgeting and finance, administration, and any other matter as dictated by the president (Biddle, interview, April 13, 2005).

United Nations Assistance

At about the time of Biddle's appointment, the promise of United Nations assistance to the SLP arrived. The United Nations Observer Mission in Sierra Leone (UNAMSIL) was to maintain peace and restore a trained, legitimate military and citizen security. Based on the experience of more than 20 such postconflict missions in recent years, the United Nations understood the critical importance of establishing a civilian democratic police service. The UNAMSIL civilian police element, the Commissioner of Civilian Police (CIVPOL), was charged with improving the professional standards of the SLP.

By the year 2004, 9,400 UNAMSIL troops and 119 international civilian police (CIVPOL) were deployed throughout the country; that force was scheduled to be downsized to 3,300 by June of 2005 (Refugees International, 2004). Unfortunately, the initial relationship between the Commonwealth task force and the CIVPOL was somewhat confused and at times difficult (Malan et al., 2002).

A number of problems hampered the relationship. The initial CIVPOL deployment took place 15 months after the British task force was formed and became fully operational only in 2000. By the time CIVPOL arrived, the British contingent had been deeply involved with the SLP for almost three years. A strategic reorganization plan had already been prepared and initiated. At times, however, CIVPOL appeared to ignore or disregard the work that had been done (Biddle, interview, April 13, 2005).

CIVPOL, for example, reported a need for community policing while overlooking the fact that the inspector general and his senior staff had already initiated a progressive model of community policing through the Local Needs Policing program that met the needs and expectations of the communities of Sierra Leone. A community policing command staff had been appointed, and Local Policing Partnership Boards established. And an aggressive Field Training Officers Program in support of the community policing initiative was under way (Biddle, interview, April 13, 2005; Malan et al., 2002). In another incident, CIVPOL's complaints about the British lack of cooperation in providing them accommodations in a rural war-torn district simply failed to recognize that neither the government nor the SLP had the necessary resources to do so (Malan et al., 2002).

CIVPOL demands that the SLP conform to "international best practice" based on the experience of other similar missions around the world, particularly those in the Balkans, complicated matters further. The Balkan experiences were considerably different from those of Sierra Leone (Malan et al., 2002). CIVPOL appeared to have little appreciation that different nations emerging from conflict require different solutions, solutions specific to their circumstances. "Off the shelf" programs were not always appropriate or welcomed by the SLP. Sierra Leone had its own unique history, and the SLP required unique solutions (Biddle, interview, April 13, 2005).

Bureaucratic reporting procedures and CIVPOL accountability to United Nations headquarters in New York made efficient decision making difficult and constrained the provision of promised United Nations funds. Changing and emerging international priorities, especially in the form of international humanitarian disasters, diverted funds initially committed to the SLP, thereby damaging CIVPOL credibility (Biddle, interview, April 13, 2005).

The CIVPOL personnel selection process, directed from United Nations headquarters, caused further difficulties. A number of totally inappropriate officers had been assigned to the project. Many were inexperienced, with less operational practice or knowledge than their SLP counterparts. One had served only 18 months in his home force (Malan et al., 2002). Some came from nations with authoritarian regimes and had little experience of civilian, service oriented policing, modern policing styles and methods, or concepts of institutional reform within the democratic process, while others had gained experience only in countries with questionable human rights records and endemic corruption within government and society (Biddle, interview, April 13, 2005). Many spoke no English and were unable to communicate directly with the English-speaking SLP (Malan et al., 2002).

In time, however, CIVPOL made important contributions to the democratization and rebuilding of the SLP. Among their accomplishments, they played a key role in the reestablishment of the Police Training School, provided a variety of specialized training programs, developed a force evaluation program, conducted important needs studies, designed a human rights manual for SLP officers assigned to election duties and Human Rights issues, provided badly need equipment, and built several new police stations (K. Biddle, interviews, April 13, 2005; Malan et al., 2002).

Combating Corruption

Over the next few years, the SLP and the national government, with the assistance of its international partners, initiated a wide range of programs and changes to move the force and the nation closer to their democratic goals. Donor funding enabled the purchase of equipment, vehicles, training, and a modern radio communications system as well as the building of new police stations and the important refurbishment of the Police Training School (Malan et al., 2002).

The problem of corruption, especially in the midlevel ranks, continues to threaten progress (Malan et al., 2002). To facilitate more rapid and expeditious removal of corrupt officers from the organization, SLP administrative policies have been reformed. Existing practices allowed such officers to remain in the police services until the outcome of the criminal prosecution against them was determined. The new regulations require the SLP to dismiss officers charged with a criminal offense under administrative disciplinary procedures regardless of the outcome of the criminal case. At the same time, effective mechanisms have been introduced to investigate, expose, and prosecute misconduct and to boost public confidence in the organization's ability to deal openly with allegations of misconduct, poor discipline, and inefficiency within the police service (Biddle, interview, April 13, 2005).

In 2000, the government of Sierra Leone passed an anticorruption bill creating the Anti Corruption Commission (ACC). Headed by an independent commissioner and staffed with lawyers, former SLP officers, and Commonwealth task force, the ACC investigates a range of corruption complaints. A toll free anticorruption hotline allows for and encourages anonymous reporting. The 2003–2005 five-year ACC strategic plan contains specific programs for the prevention of corruption, including public education, more effective investigation and prosecution of offenders, and research and intelligence gathering (Biddle, interview, April 13, 2005). A Truth and Reconciliation Committee modeled on that of South Africa has been in operation since 2003 (Dougherty, 2004; Lengor, interview, April 14/15, 2005). In August 2000, at the urging of the Sierra Leone government, the United Nations Security Council established the Special Court for Sierra Leone to try those responsible for the crimes committed during the civil war (Special Court for Sierra Leone, 2005).

The New Sierra Leone Police

The task force, with the help of local journalists, trained police personnel in public and media relations in order to further improve the image of the SLP. A formal press office has been established (Moigbe, interviews, April 14/15, 2005).

The SLP suffered from internal inertia. Because of political corruption and government neglect, all decision making within the organization had become the sole domain of senior officers. Consequently, supervisors and managers abrogated their responsibilities, passing even simple matters to senior management. Political favoritism compounded the problem by creating an illogical and cumbersome rank structure of 21 ranks, many with duplicate roles and responsibilities. The official duties, for example, of constables, corporals, sergeants, sergeant majors, and subinspectors were identical. The organization had become top heavy, a steeply pyramidal and stagnant bureaucracy, where decision-making and organizational communications were impossible. In 2003, the SLP leadership addressed the problem. They reduced the number of ranks to nine and clarified the duties of each. The following year, the SLP collapsed the 15 posts of senior assistant commissioner and assistant commissioner into a single rank of assistant inspector general (AIG).

The current rank structure of the SLP is shown in Table 5.1.

Table 5.1   Current Rank Structure of the Sierra Leone Police

Rank	Number
Deputy Inspector General	1
Assistant Inspector General	15
Chief Superintendent	18
Superintendent	33
Assistant Superintendent	198
Inspector	417
Sergeant	1838
Constable	4251
Total	6771

SOURCE: Moigbe (interview, April 14/15, 2005).

In order to improve the quality of supervision and leadership, a comprehensive promotional system based on merit and performance has been implemented (Biddle, interview, April 13, 2005). SLP officers of the rank of assistant superintendent and above attend the prestigious 10-week International Commanders' Program at the Police Staff College, Bramshill, England. The course, designed specifically to meet the needs of the SLP, provides training in operational planning and command skills, leadership, strategic planning skills, ethical policing, human rights, and the political, social, and economic context of policing. Participants are attached to English police forces, assigned to units specific to their regular SLP duties. On return to Sierra Leone, they design and conduct relevant training programs for middle managers and supervisors based on their Bramshill experiences (Cullen & McDonald, 2005).

Vigorous organizational reforms have moved the police force toward decentralization of resources and greater operational authority for local commanders. The entire organizational structure has been revamped. Under its current structure, the SLP maintains four major operational regions: Western Province Divisions, Northern Province Divisions, Southern Province Divisions, and Eastern Province Divisions. Central headquarters control includes the following key organizational elements (Moigbe, interview, April 14/15, 2005):

- Criminal Investigation Department (CID)
- Complaints, Discipline, and Internal Investigations Department
- Special Branch
- Operations Support Division (Public Order)
- Media and Public Relations Department
- Estates Department
- Marine Department
- Equal Opportunities Department
- Research and Planning
- Police Training School
- Transport
- Communications
- Family Support Unit
- Community Relations Department
- Inspectorate
- Change Management

The force continues to be understaffed, down from its preconflict staffing of more than 9,000, and the problem of illiteracy interferes with progress. To address these issues, the SLP has raised recruiting standards and initiated an aggressive recruiting campaign. Special efforts have been made to bring women and university graduates into the force. Women currently occupy two of the AIG positions, and graduates are joining the force in increasing numbers (Moigbe, interview, April 18, 2005). Current applicants for the SLP must be citizens of Sierra Leone between 18 and 30 years of age, of good health and without criminal convictions. They must possess a minimum of five General Certificates of Education and complete a multifaceted selection process. All applicants, irrespective of education, join at the constable rank. There is no direct entry at officer rank (Cullen & McDonald, 2005).

When Biddle left the SLP in late 2003, the force had clearly achieved measurable and qualitative success in a very short period of time under extremely difficult circumstances (Groenwald & Peak, 2004). His replacement, Deputy Inspector General of Police Brima Acha Kamara, a career Sierra Leone police officer, continues the work begun by Biddle and the Commonwealth task force (Biddle, interview, April 13, 2005).

The SLP and the nation are very much works in progress. Serious problems still exist, and the future remains uncertain. Large numbers of citizens have migrated from rural areas to the major cities. Wide-scale poverty and unemployment, the repatriation of large numbers of refugees and combatants, political and regional instability, the tradition of corruption, and similar issues remain threats to progress. Nonetheless, the country and the SLP continue to move toward democracy. While some increase in robbery and automobile-related crime as well as problems with urban traffic congestion and road safety have been noted, the national crime rate remains low, with an annual national homicide rate of less than 1 per 100,000 (2003). A duly elected democratic government remains in place. Civil war has been avoided.

The successful rebuilding of the SLP to date can be attributed to many factors, but two stand out. First, and perhaps most important, the reform of the Sierra Leone Police was led from the very top of the government and the society. President Kabbah made it a priority for his administration. He personally penned the Government Policing Charter, sought international support, and took the bold step of appointing a well-qualified foreign national to head the force. He endorsed the SLP strategic plan, and his authority made it national policy.

Second, the SLP reorganized itself. Rather than struggling to retrofit tactics and programs developed in other postconflict societies, the force took charge of its own rebuilding by developing Sierra Leonean solutions to its problems. With the help of the British task force and support from the United Nations, the SLP designed its own strategic plan around the specific needs and expectations of the citizens of Sierra Leone and within its existing political system, history, and criminal justice system. And they did so from the bottom up rather than from the top down. The operational success of the SLP is largely a factor of its unique decentralization of police services to the community level in a community-policing framework as the starting point for the force rebuilding process. Only after police returned to the community both physically and philosophically did the formal reorganization begin.

References

Central Intelligence Agency (CIA). (n.d.). Sierra Leone. In *World factbook*. Retrieved April 18, 2005, from http://www.cia.gov/cia/publications/factbook/goes/sl.html

Code of conduct for law enforcement officers. (1979). In *Resolutions adopted by the general assembly during its thirty-fourth session* (Resolution 34/169, pp. 185–187). Retrieved March 18, 2005, from http://www.un.org/documents/ga/res/34/ares34.htm

Crawshaw, R., Cullen, S., & Williams, T. (2006). *Human rights and policing. The Raoul Wallenberg Institute professional guide to human rights*. Boston: Martinus Nijhof.

Cullen, S., & McDonald, W. H. (2005). Sierra Leone. In L. Sullivan (Ed.), *Encyclopedia of Law Enforcement* (pp. 1297–1299). Thousand Oaks, CA: Sage.

Dougherty, B. (2004, Fall). Searching for truth: Sierra Leone's truth and reconciliation commission [Electronic version]. *African Studies Quarterly, 8,* 1–21. Retrieved May 15, 2005, from http://www.africa.ufl.edu/asq/v8/v8ila3.htm

From crisis to confidence. (1998). (Brochure). Freetown, Sierra Leone: Royal Sierra Leone Police.

Groenwald, H., & Peak, G. (2004). *Police reform through community-based Policing: Philosophy and guidelines for implementation*. New York: International Peace Academy.

Hoffman, D. (2005). *The Kamajors of Sierra Leone*. Retrieved 15 Sept 2005 from http://www.ssrc.org/fellowships/gsc/fellowship_and_grant_awardees/individual pages/

Kpundeh, S. (1993). Prospects in contemporary Sierra Leone. *Corruption and Reform, 7,* 237–247.

Kpundeh, S. (1995). *Politics and corruption in Africa: A case study of Sierra Leone*. Washington, DC: University Press of America.

Lord, D. (2005). *Paying the price: The Sierra Leone peace process*. Retrieved April 1, 2006, from http://www.c-r.org/accord/sleona/accord9/intro.shtml

Malan, M., Rakafe, P., & McIntyre, A. (2002). *The restoration of civil authority— Peacekeeping in Sierra Leone—the UNAMSIL hits the home straight*. Retrieved March 29, 2005, from http://www.iss.co.za/Pubs/Monographs/No68/Chap. 8.html

Meek, S. (2003). Policing Sierra Leone. In *Sierra Leone, building the road to recovery*. Retrieved April 21, 2005, from http://www.issafrica.org/Pubs/Monographs/No80/Content.html.

Refugees International. (2004). *Spotlight on Sierra Leone: Continued investments required to sustain peace*. Retrieved August 27, 2007, from http://www.refugeesinternational.org/content/article/detail/3904

Siegel, J. T., Weinstein, M., & Halperin, M. H. (2004). Why democracies excel. *Foreign Affairs, 83*(5), 57–61.

Special court for Sierra Leone. (n.d.). Retrieved April 18, 2005, from http://www.globalpolicy.org/intljustice/sierraindx.htm

State house on line. (2005). Retrieved April 10, 2005 from http://www.statehouse-sl.org

Thompson, B. (1996). *The constitutional history and law of Sierra Leone (1961–1995)*. New York: University Press of America.

Thompson, B., & Potter, P. (1997, September). Governmental corruption in Africa: Sierra Leone as a case study. *Crime Law and Social Change, 28,* 137–154.

Interviews

Biddle, K. (2005, April 13). Interview in Cheshire, UK.

Lengor, M. (2005, April 14 & 15). Interview at Police Staff College, Bramshill, UK.

Moigbe, M. (2005, April 14, 15, & 18). Interview at Police Staff College, Bramshill, UK.

6 Policing the Russian Federation

Peter Roudik

Russia belongs to the civil law tradition of continental Europe. Its present legal system is defined by the 1993 Constitution, which provides for a federation of 86 constituent components with a strong executive branch of power. Federal laws and codes constitute the most commonly encountered sources of law in Russia. The difference in name is largely based on how long and how comprehensive the statute is. The president may issue decrees and directives, and the government and federal agencies are authorized to adopt regulations in the areas of their general competency. The current Russian police force is called the *militia*.[1] This name originated during the time when the Soviet people's militia and system of internal affairs were created immediately after the Bolshevik Revolution of 1917. The structural and functional operations of the Soviet police force and the police force during the Russian empire were mainly equivalent. Nevertheless, the Soviet government, due to the extensive politicization of government systems, renamed the police force as the militia. This name was preserved in the course of the democratic reforms that occurred during the last 15 years, because the essence of this institution has not been changed.

Historical and Political Background

In Russia, the police force never was a body responsible for crime control only. It was always a vital component of the state regardless of who was at the top of state bureaucracy. Under all regimes, the police force's main task was to maintain the government's rule over an ethnically diverse population

---

AUTHOR'S NOTE: Views expressed in this chapter are solely those of the author and do not reflect the position of the U.S. Library of Congress.

spread over large geographical areas. Instead of serving the people, the militia always sought to keep them submissive. Forms and means for implementing this task varied with the times depending on the political atmosphere; however, the basic features of Russian policing are and have been that it is political, arbitrary, and limited in actual effectiveness.

The first regular police institutions were created in the late sixteenth century. For the next 100 years, public order was controlled by local guards and night watches drawn from among the citizenry. Reforms initiated by Peter the Great (1672–1725) introduced the European concept of police in Russia and increased the role of a centralized force fighting crime and supporting public order. The office of the policemaster general was created in St. Petersburg in the early eighteenth century. He subordinated provincial police chancelleries in other large cities. During the reign of Catherine the Great (1729–1796) the authority of central police bodies was continuously expanded beyond the largest cities to the provinces. The creation of a centralized force made up of soldiers transferred for police duty did not obviate the employment of local population in the police force. Following the 1775 administrative reform, police service remained in the jurisdiction of provincial and local authorities until 1802, when the national Ministry of Internal Affairs (MIA) was created by Czar Alexander I. The jurisdiction of the MIA was very broad, because this new institution combined functions of six separate preexisting agencies of state power. The Czar's decree assigned the minister the duty to "take care about the well-being of [the] population, calmness, tranquility, and improvement of the Empire" (Adrianov, 1902, p. 54). The ministry controlled activities of local government offices and managed the police force nationwide. Later, special police departments were created in large military equipment plants, mines, and train stations.

During the nineteenth century, the regular system of police hierarchy was built. In 1837, the central authorities established the appointive office of constable, for the first time extending the state police presence below the district level. In 1862, the district police chief, hitherto elected by the nobility, was converted into a centrally appointed subordinate of the provincial governor. The establishment, in 1879, of a force of sergeants to assist the constables completed the system. In the 1860s, in order to increase police effectiveness, the force was relieved of its tax collecting duties, and its investigative and trial authority was cancelled. At the same time, in addition to regular police functions, the authority of the Ministry of Internal Affairs was extended to control the mass media, postal service, labor and economic data, military draft, and secret service. The extended authority made the police force, which continued to be governed under 1862 guidelines for staff size and pay, extremely overstretched. At the end of the nineteenth century, a total cadre of 47,866 police officers handled a population of nearly 127 million (Weissman, 1985). This made the ratio of police personnel to population in St. Petersburg and Moscow comparable with those of Berlin and Vienna. However, these figures reflected establishment rather than actual strength. They made no allowances for vacancies and included policemen used as clerks, messengers, and servants. Unlike officers in Europe, Russian officers remained most of the time at stations awaiting a public call or a summons by a fellow officer. Also, Russian police were burdened with an unusually wide array of additional duties, from monitoring sanitation to ensuring public respect for the Russian Orthodox Church.

This wide scope of authority was preserved after the fall of the Russian Empire. After the czar's abdication in February 1917, the provisional government supported the development of local self-rule and a democratic people's militia; however, police functions were never transferred to the municipalities, and the police remained a major pillar within the Ministry of Internal Affairs, which exercised strong control over police activities. Government-appointed police inspectors were dispatched to all provinces and administrative districts. They were entitled to make appointments, issue decrees, and intervene in routine police work. This militia was dismantled after the October 1917 Bolshevik Revolution, which marked the beginning of a 64-year Communist regime known as Soviet period. On the third day after the Communists took control of the government, a workers' militia aimed at supporting the revolutionary order was established.

The revolution inspired novel approaches to policing, such as the transfer of police duties to social organizations and the introduction of a mandatory police duty. These proposals were not implemented, and in the mid-1920s, Soviet police structures were finally formed. Newly established police departments were incorporated into the system of internal affairs, which recreated the previously existing multifunctional government agency. In 1922, the functions of the secret police—with jurisdiction over informer networks, concentration camps, internal troops, frontier guards, and crimes against the state and existing political system, including terrorism and serious crimes committed by high-level government officials—were given to the notorious State Security Committee (KGB). The KGB was formally an executive government agency and was subordinate to the Communist party leadership. In theory, the KGB was expected to investigate only a very specific range of criminal offenses, but the politicization of the Soviet state had always ensured its use according to the instructions given by the party leaders focusing on fighting real, potential, and imaginary political threats and destroying the foes of the regime (Gerson, 1976). In early 1990s, the KGB expanded its authority through involvement in combating crime.

Regular Soviet police were simultaneously subordinate to relevant representative bodies, which formed a strong, centralized system of state power, and to higher police departments, which were led by the national Ministry of Internal Affairs. During the Soviet period, the militia moved from being a paramilitary body responsible for suppressing political opposition to a law enforcement body in charge of maintaining social and economic order. Numerous divisions were created within the militia's bureaucracy in order to regulate diverse aspects of people's lives. Even though the degree of centralization varied during different historical periods and the organization of the Ministry of Internal Affairs has been subject to many changes, the police system was always a part of the all-encompassing Soviet regime (Shelley,

1996). Operational changes reflected shifts in policies and power at the highest level and, thereby, the vital role of all police functions in Russia. Until 1990, Russia's regular militia was under the direct supervision of the Ministry of Internal Affairs (MIA) of the Soviet Union. At that time, the Russian Republic established an MIA, which assumed control of the republic's police. The transformation of the Soviet political system in the late 1980s and early 1990s had a low impact on the daily activities of the police, who were neither ready to cope with the crime unleashed by the transition nor prepared to assume their new role as defenders of democracy. Leadership of the Russian police force, which performs a wide range of functions though its accountability to the citizenry remains minimal, continues to view the preservation of the nation's political stability as the most important component of law enforcement activity in all territories of the country (Rushailo, 2001).

The Ministry of Internal Affairs: Status, Structure, Functions

In 1991, Russia obtained its independence from the Soviet Union, endorsed democracy, and implemented principles of the rule of law. However, old Soviet methods have been carried forward by the police, which, unlike other law enforcement agencies, did not undergo extensive reorganization after 1991. After President Yeltsin's unsuccessful attempt, in 1991, to combine all security, intelligence, and police services into a unified system under presidential control (this was outlawed by the Constitutional Court because of the lack of mechanisms to monitor and control such an organization), a separate Ministry of Internal Affairs and the Federal Security Service were created. The Federal Security Service became responsible for the state's internal security; it covers counterespionage and the fight against terrorism, although concerns were raised that it operates like the old KGB, monitoring the telephones of opponents of the regime, spreading misinformation, and intercepting mail. Given that the Federal Security Service was essentially formed from the old KGB, these allegations are not groundless.

The current legal status of the Ministry of Internal Affairs was established by the Presidential Decree of July 18, 1996, which defined the ministry as a federal agency of the executive branch of government charged with "protecting the rights and liberties of the persons and citizens, preserving law and order, and guaranteeing public security" as well as "perfecting the legal basis of its activities." The ministry is subordinate to the president of Russia, and its functions, as defined by legislation, include identifying and forecasting security threats and taking measures for their prevention and neutralization. Within the bounds of its jurisdiction, the MIA manages regular police activities and provides for professional training, legal defense, and social security of MIA personnel.

The ministry operates at both the central and local levels and administers from its main office in Moscow. Its system of internal affairs consists of structural links at various levels within all 98 of the constituent components of the Russian Federation, several administrative districts and municipalities, sections of railway, air, and water transport, so-called regime objects, and regional administrations for fighting organized crime. The ministry also has an investigative committee, supply administrations, a network of educational and training institutions, scientific and research facilities, and special units formed for special tasks. The MIA has its own armed forces to perform designated tasks; these forces are completely separate from the regular army. MIA forces are equipped with heavy weapons and are organized in a way similar to that of military units. After many years of secretiveness, the organizational structure of the ministry is now open and can be viewed on its Web site. The Minister of Internal Affairs and the heads of all regional internal affairs departments are appointed and dismissed by the president of the Russian Federation.

During the last 10 years, in response to an increase in the size of the criminal community and structural changes to it, new services and departments were created within the MIA. These departments are the Main Department for the Fight Against Economic Crimes, the Main Department for the Fight Against Organized Crime, the Committee for Combating Illegal Drug Trafficking, the Main Department for Special Technical Operations, the Federal Migration Service, Special Purpose Detachments, and the National Central Interpol Bureau. These services are integral parts of the MIA system and independently cooperate with foreign partners. In 1993, Russia joined Interpol. The MIA is also involved in regional cooperation between law enforcement authorities of other former Soviet republics. However, it has been reported that, to avoid long and cumbersome bureaucratic procedures associated with reporting operations in territories of the newly independent states to national authorities, Russian police have performed arrests of suspected criminals hiding abroad and transported them to Russia without informing police authorities in the countries where the operations were conducted (Khinstein, 2003). Russian police receive significant foreign assistance, especially from the United States.

Prior to November 1997, the MIA had command over all penal institutions, which were then placed under the Ministry of Justice's authority in response to recommendations from the Council of Europe. Fire protection also was among the MIA's functions before 2002, when this responsibility was transferred to the Ministry for Emergency Situations.

During the last 15 years, the government has attempted to improve training, tighten discipline, and decentralize the administration of the police throughout the Russian Federation so that it might respond better to local needs and deal more effectively with drug trafficking and organized crime. In 1997, President Yeltsin of Russia signed a new Anticrime and Corruption Law presented by the Interior Minister. The law simply poured more money into archaic structures, leaving police as ineffective as before but in greater numbers. The redirection of MIA resources to internal troops during the Chechnya war and to the MIA's new local riot squads, which were often used as a personal military for regional governors, undercut police reform. President Vladimir Putin of Russia recognized in his 2005 State of the Nation address that Russia's system of internal security was "chronically ill and is in need of reforming" (Putin, 2005).

Crime Statistics

After being freed from the control of the Communist party, the overstretched and underresourced police force concentrated on issues of importance to itself, and the effectiveness of police actions diminished while crime rates, which during the Soviet period were lower in Russia than other countries with comparable levels of economic development, skyrocketed. Among the factors contributing to the still growing criminality in Russia are the conflicts that frequently accompany changes of ownership and an increased struggle for power along clan and ethnic lines or between national interests. The lack of an effective system in society for preventing legal infringements, inadequate legal and logistical support for the battle against terrorism, legal nihilism, and the departure of qualified personnel from law enforcement agencies led to the increased criminal threat. After a 33 percent increase in reported crime between 1991 and 1992, the annual crime rate has continued to increase at a much lower rate (5–8 percent annually) during the last 10 years as the economic and political situation in the country has become more stable.

In 2004, 2.9 million crimes were registered in the country of 142 million residents (2,100 crimes per 100,000 population). About 35 percent of them constituted serious and most serious crimes, which are equivalent to first and second degree felonies. About half of all crimes were property related (i.e., stealing, swindling, theft). Every tenth crime was committed by the illegal intrusion into another's residence. About 500,000 reported crimes were business related. During the last five years, the number of registered crimes rose annually by 5 percent. Only one half of all crimes were solved. Among the unsolved crimes are 6,000 killings and attempted killings. In 2004, 1.3 million individuals who had committed crimes were identified. One quarter of all crimes were committed by a previously convicted person. Every fifth crime was committed by a drunkard; every tenth by a minor. The percentage of foreigners among documented criminals is insignificant, and almost all of them are citizens of neighboring former Soviet republics (MIA, 2004).

As the prosecutor general of the Russian Federation reported, while existing criminal statistics do not reflect the real number of crimes committed, these statistics do reflect the erroneous method by which crimes are registered. Presently, reporting crimes is a police function and is often used to adjust statistics. As evaluation of police work is based on the percentage of crimes that police solve, police are interested in registering only crimes that are easily solved (petty crimes and misdemeanors) or that cannot be avoided (most dangerous crimes). Police officers often decide not to initiate criminal proceedings when the case seems difficult to prove. "The pursuit of statistics has given rise to a whole generation of detectives who when they arrive at the scene of crime think about how to conceal a crime rather than how to clear it up" (Thomas, 2000). Their superiors condone and, perhaps, even encourage this practice, because it enhances the department's record by increasing the percentage of successful investigations. Despite the fact that almost all ministers of internal affairs since the mid-1990s have been quoted on many occasions as calling for an end to "deception" in crime statistics, nothing has changed. Perhaps, until crime statistics begin to be received through non-MIA channels, it will be almost impossible to make even an approximate assessment of the scale of crime in Russia.

The police have invented sophisticated techniques to refuse the acceptance of statements from individuals. Unreasonable denials to register crimes are so widespread that in 2000, the Constitutional Court issued a ruling stating that individuals have the right to review police materials substantiating a refusal when a request to initiate police proceedings is rejected. Another reason for the denial of crime registration is the existing system for officer performance evaluations. According to this practice, an officer's number of solved crimes must increase with each year. Even if all the officer's criminals are caught and future crimes are prevented, a police officer's work is unsatisfactory if the officer does not solve at least one more crime each year than he or she solved the previous year. To cope with this practice, policemen have invented so-called paper crimes, where they register and investigate crimes allegedly committed by imaginary people. Another method of inflating a clearance rate is to plant drugs or gun cartridges on innocent people. The consequences of these actions are the concealment of real crimes and the falsification of statistics. However, without the artificial minimization of registered crimes, police workload would increase several fold to a level where they could not handle all cases. According to the prosecutor general, only one-third of crimes committed in Russia are registered and taken into account by police. That statistic means the true number of crimes committed annually in Russia is equal to 9 million (Ustinov, 2005). Independent experts estimate the crime rate at 10–12 million (Galeotti, 2002).

Police Legislation

As soon as Russia became independent from the Soviet Union and started to build a law enforcement system, researchers recommended the adoption of a police code to function as a consolidated legal act that would combine legal norms of police law regarding the protection of public order, public security, and citizen rights and freedoms. The supporters of this idea claimed the application of police related legal norms was complicated, because they were spread over numerous legislative acts. Supporters recommended the code include both procedural and material norms (Belskii, 2004). This idea appears from time to time in Russian legal publications, but it is strongly opposed by police leadership and lacks wide support from legislators.

Presently, Russian police (militia) are governed by the federal Police Law adopted on April 18, 1991. The law was the first to regulate police agencies comprehensively, an event Russian scholars described as part of the democratization process (Peyser & Vitsin, 2005). The law defines the organizational structure of the police force and prescribes its rights and duties. Unfortunately, amendments to the law do not reflect changes in criminal procedure and do not enhance democratic standards in police activities.

Organizational Structure of the Police

The Police Law divides the force into criminal police and public security police. Criminal police prevent and detect crimes and search for persons who have fled from agencies of inquiry, investigation, or a court. Public security, or local, police maintain public order; prevent, suppress, and investigate minor crimes; and assist citizens and legal entities. Public security units run local police stations, temporary detention centers, and the State Traffic Inspectorate. They deal with crimes outside the jurisdiction of the criminal police and are charged with routine maintenance of public order. Local police compose about 60 percent of the total number of police (Butler, 2003).

Even though the Russian police are divided between criminal and public security police, all police are subordinate to the Ministry of Internal Affairs of the Russian Federation. While the criminal police are the centralized federal structure, the public security police are dually subordinate and report to the ministry as well as to the executive authorities of their relevant constituent component of the Russian Federation. The Minister of Internal Affairs oversees the work of the entire police force all over Russia. However, the minister is not a national police chief, as his deputies, the chief of the criminal police and the chief of the public security police, directly head their respective services. Within each constituent component, the police are headed by the chief of the component's internal affairs department, who is appointed and dismissed by the president of the Russian Federation upon joint recommendation of the federal Minister of Internal Affairs and the governor of the relevant constituent component. Police chiefs in towns, districts, and other municipal establishments are heads of their respective internal affairs departments and are appointed by the chiefs of the components' internal affairs departments. All police units have the same government-approved gray uniforms with red piping. Public security police units created by local and municipal governments may have their own insignia.

Criminal Police

The duty of the criminal police is to stop, discover, and prevent crimes that require preliminary investigation, conduct searches for wanted and missing individuals, and assist public security police. The government of the Russian Federation determines the structure of the criminal police. The criminal police force is divided into organizations responsible for combating particular types of crime. For example, the Main Directorate for Organized Crime works with other agencies, such as the MIA's specialized rapid-response detachment offices. In 1995, special units were established at the directorate to deal with contract killings and other violent crimes against individuals. Government Regulation No. 925 of December 7, 2000, states that the criminal police force consists of the following divisions: criminal search, economic crimes, taxation crimes, organized crime, operations and technical activities, internal security, and police detachment for special purposes. The National Central Bureau of Interpol and its territorial branches are included in the criminal police. Chiefs of the criminal police and public security police for the components of the federation are appointed by the Russian Federation Minister of Internal Affairs. The criminal police force is financed from the federal budget.

Public Security Police

The main duty of the public security police force is to secure the personal safety of Russian citizens, maintain public order, and protect property. Public security police prosecute administrative misdemeanors and investigate crimes when preliminary investigation is not required. The public security police manage detention centers and are divided into two parts—federal and local.

The organizational divisions in the public security police extend to its financing. The federal government defines the budget and structure for public security police programs that are financed through the federal budget. Regional and local authorities may create additional detachments or units of public security police. These detachments are financed by local and regional budgets according to the norms established by the federal government. All regional MIA departments have special purpose detachments, commonly known as the Black Berets, which are aimed at combating terrorist and serious criminal activities. They are similar to U.S. SWAT teams and are deeply involved in fighting drug trafficking and tax evasion. Special detachments of police also are created for cities with populations exceeding 300,000 persons.

As part of the trend toward decentralization, some municipalities, including Moscow, have formed their own militias, which cooperate with their MIA counterparts. The Moscow contingent, with reportedly 2000 officers receives support from the mayor's office and the city's internal affairs department as well as from the MIA budget. Municipal police units have the best and most up-to-date weapons and combat equipment available. Furthermore, they enjoy a reputation for courage and effectiveness. Although the law on self-government supports such local law enforcement agencies, the federal government attempted to restrict further moves toward independence by strictly limiting the powers of such formations. For example, municipal police do not carry guns or other weapons except in emergency situations. Public security police include traffic police, area officers, and officers of the street patrol service; they inspect the affairs of minors, and they staff police stations, detention centers, centers for keeping drunkards and vagrants, passport and visa departments, departments on licensing weapons and protection services, and services for escorting criminals.

Internal Troops

The police force also includes military units called Internal Troops who participate in emergency military operations, disperse crowds, and fight public disobedience. Internal Troops are permanently assigned to this duty, as opposed to the regular armed forces, which are also periodically called up for law enforcement duties. The legal status and responsibilities of the force are similar to those of the National Guard in the United States; they are determined by the Law on Internal Troops of the Ministry of Internal Affairs of the Russian Federation of February 6, 1997. Under this law, the MIA maintains armed units whose responsibilities are to assist police in protecting public order, important state objects, and special cargoes; to participate in the territorial defense of the Russian Federation; and to render assistance to the federal Border Service in protecting the state boundary.

Internal Troops have a militaristic structure and appearance and are estimated to number 200,000. They are divided into three mobile groups with five divisions (Jamestown Foundation, 1998). These troops are better equipped and trained than the regular police. The size of the force, which is staffed by both conscripts and volunteers, has grown steadily during the last years, although the troop commander has reported serious shortages of officers. Russia's Internal Troops, by law, are charged with assisting various agencies of Russia's MIA, which, in turn means they are assigned only a support role. These forces are equipped with guns and combat weapons to deal with serious crimes, terrorism, and other extraordinary threats to public order. During the last few years, the crime rate among the troops doubled. A contributing factor to this change was a steep increase in desertions that coincided with service in Chechnya, where Internal Troops are routinely used for street patrol.

Police Rights and Duties

General functions of the police are stipulated by the 1991 Police Law. The law states that the police's duties are to

- Prevent, stop, and discover crimes and administrative misdemeanors
- Assist people suffering from crimes and emergencies
- Receive and register information related to crimes
- Initiate and investigate criminal cases
- Search for wanted and missing people and stolen property
- Secure public order on streets and in public places
- Provide protection services
- Conduct forensic evaluations
- Identify individuals and corpses
- Monitor fulfillment of residence and registration rules by Russian citizens and foreigners
- Administer the passport-visa and other authorization systems
- Enforce rules for the entry, exit, sojourn, and transit of foreign citizens or stateless persons through the territory of the Russian Federation
- Supervise freed detainees and monitor their behavior
- Conduct witness protection programs
- Secure the safety of judges
- Conduct mandatory state fingerprint registration

Police duties also include the issuance of licenses for engaging in private detective or personal security activity and permits for obtaining and possession of weapons. Police departments also are responsible for enforcing rules for traffic safety, registration of motor vehicles, and the issuance of driver's licenses. Police operations and searches are regulated by a specific law and may be conducted by plainclothes officers.

The law does not provide for an exhaustive list of responsibilities assigned to police; this continues the centuries-long tradition of the entity performing a range of functions, some of which have nothing to do with fighting crime. One of the major police responsibilities is patrolling the streets. In addition, the police force, which consists of 0.3 to 2 percent of a town's population, handles applications for driver's licenses, passports, and residential registrations as required by law. Each police district has units that conduct criminal investigations, handle public inquiries, and monitor known criminals residing in the district. As a rule, criminal investigation units focus on several of the city's most problematic crimes. Depending on regional specifics, these can be high-profile killings, residential burglaries, or drug trafficking. Criminal tracking units monitor criminals from the time of their release from prison, when they must register with their local police district. Ex-convicts must report monthly to the local police, although they frequently are visited between those times.

Every police department has a special group of officers assigned to a small geographic area (4,000–6,000 people). In big cities the officers may work in teams of two to three patrol officers, and sometimes these teams may include even an investigative officer. Most area officers police their territory on foot, monitoring sanitation conditions as well as criminal activity out of small offices or apartments in housing complexes. They work with volunteer auxiliary police who assist in patrolling neighborhood streets and developing local intelligence; these volunteers are generally the police's eyes and ears in the community. With the intention of maintaining good relations with local residents, area police officers can cover up minor crimes, chase off predatory criminals from outside the neighborhood, expedite paperwork, and choose to deal with infractions informally. The goal of police administrators is for their officers to be recognizable to people in their patrol area. Toward this end, a recent decree states that it is desirable for officers to reside in the neighborhoods for which they are responsible. The government's obligation to supply area officers with subsidized housing is often a major incentive for police officers to serve.

Area officers undertake efforts to engage citizens in crime prevention. Patrol officers work with local councils on crime prevention projects. Area officers cooperate with other police departments by assisting them to enforce laws in their areas and, according to recent research, by taking responsibility for approximately 140 tasks specified in ministerial instructions.

The law encourages the cooperation of police authorities with other state institutions, bodies of local self-government, and social and labor organizations. Police can encourage individuals to cooperate with other law enforcement authorities. They may issue awards to encourage citizens' assistance and cultivate a system of police informants. It is common for police to hold regular meetings with the public. District police stations usually designate two days each week for individuals to come and discuss neighborhood problems. A "hot-spot" approach to police work is adapted by the Internal Affairs Department in St. Petersburg. In this city, crime complaints are entered into a computer database from local precincts, and crimes are displayed on maps. Proactive steps are taken at locations that appear particularly active (Davis, Ortiz, & Gilinsky, 2004). This method exemplifies an effective approach toward registering crimes and was recommended by the MIA for implementation in other regions.

In their work, the police have the right to demand that citizens and officials stop activities that violate legislation or hinder the work of police or government authorities, check identification documents, search individuals and their belongings (if there is a reason to believe that they may have weapons, munitions, explosives, or narcotic substances), and review the validity of licenses to conduct certain activities. In 1998, the Arbitration Court of the Western Siberian Circuit ruled that it is proper for police to stop trade operations and detain persons involved in trade outside designated spaces or areas. The rights of police extend to summoning individuals and officials in relation to cases under police investigation and bringing them by force when those individuals refuse to answer official summonses. Police detain and keep under arrest suspects and those who avoid the execution of criminal punishment. Police may obtain necessary explanations, information, documents, and references and can conduct criminal procedures prescribed by the Code of Criminal Procedure. In order to secure this right, the law allows police to conduct operations and search activities, to enter residential premises, and to use means of transportation and connections belonging to citizens or organizations, if necessary. The Police Law does not specify limitations on police rights except for a general requirement that these rights be used to fulfill police duties. As the spectrum of police duties is incredibly broad, this provision does not affect daily police activities.

Methods of Operation

As long as police work complies with existing legislation, police are free to select methods of operation depending on the circumstances, the specifics of the crime, and the social status of the criminal. Police must collect evidence through photos and/or through video and audio recordings that signal preparation to commit crime or the conduct of criminal activity. The evidence may serve as a reason to initiate criminal proceedings when the information collected reveals features of a crime. Telephone reports on crimes are not enough to initiate a case, even though they are logged in by an on-duty officer, and the submission of a written personal statement by a person reporting a crime is required. The Code of Criminal Procedure, which entered into force July 1, 2002, obligates the public security police to conduct an inquiry even if they are not prepared to finish the investigation and formulate an accusatory statement. While the number of cases under investigation has tripled since the adoption of the code, the number of cases submitted to courts has decreased by 18.2 percent during the same period (Gavrilov, 2003).

The registration of crimes is performed by an officer on duty at a local internal affairs department, which is a component of the public security police. Written reports on crimes received by mail, fax, courier, or another service are directed to the heads of local police departments, who decide whether to register them after studying these statements. If the police station chief finds signs of a crime, the statement is referred to the officer on duty for registration. Because registration of a statement is based on the presence of criminal facts, the initiation of a criminal case is inevitable. However, the initial review of facts is not required when written statements personally are submitted by the applicant or the applicant's representative to the officer on duty. These claims are registered immediately.

Police officers perform the initial work of gathering evidence of a crime and conduct searches to apprehend culprits. They are granted unimpeded access to private property. According to the federal Police Operations Law, officers may enter homes and businesses to pursue suspects "if facts warrant the assumption that a crime has been committed or is being committed" (Section 14). This law gives officers the right to use vehicles belonging to citizens and private businesses to pursue suspects. The law does not compensate citizens for damage to property or physical harm inflicted during police operations and does not hold police officers responsible.

Procedural police functions can be divided into three groups—main activities, activities aimed at supporting criminal trials, and supplementary procedural activities, as shown in Table 6.1.

Table 6.1   Procedural Police Functions

Main activities	• Review and acceptance of statements on crimes • Conduct of inquiries and necessary operations and searches (inspection of the crime site; performance of searches and seizures; detention and interrogation of suspects, victims, and witnesses) • Compensation for damage inflicted by illegal activities • Undertaking of preventive and prophylactic measures • Direct participation in international legal assistance in criminal matters
Supporting activities	• Regular operational police actions (conduct of discoveries; search for criminals and evidence of crimes) • Completion of a prosecutor's or investigator's assignments • Summons and delivery of participants in trials • Delivery of correspondence between the court and the detainee • Seizures to secure property that is used to guarantee financial obligations of an accused person
Assisting activities	• Guarding, transporting, and escorting suspects and accused persons • Participation of the inspector for the affairs of minors in the interrogations of minors • Securing crime scenes

One of the traditional functions of the Russian police is to conduct investigations. In different times, this was performed by various police components. Even when the position of judicial investigator was created in 1864, police remained involved in investigations. After the 1917 Bolshevik Revolution, investigation in the form of inquiries was included in the police's responsibilities, and later, regardless of changes in legislation, police retained the right to conduct inquiries in a substantial number of cases and to perform preliminary investigations together with other law enforcement agencies, if a crime under investigation had fallen under their jurisdiction. Today, preliminary investigation is required in all cases involving severe crimes and crimes committed by government officials, but it is optional in all other cases. The goal of preliminary investigation is to determine all circumstances subject to proof before the trial. As the gravest crimes—crimes against life, sexual crimes, official crimes, crimes committed by or against judges and law enforcement officials—are included in the jurisdiction of the prosecution service (an office roughly comparable to that of attorney general in the United States), and crimes related to national security fall under the jurisdiction of the Federal Security Service (former KGB), police investigators are dealing with less grave crimes, including crimes against property, crimes affecting public security, crimes committed by minors, etc.

Police investigators are procedurally independent from other agencies. An independent institution with authority to initiate criminal proceedings and conduct investigations does not exist, although numerous proposals have been discussed by the legislature. The MIA Investigative Committee is one of the ministry's structural divisions. It supervises the investigative subdivisions of regional ministry branches and local police departments and oversees preliminary investigations in the most complex criminal cases. The head of the Investigative Committee is a deputy minister. An investigation conducted by a police department concludes with making a decision either for indictment or for terminating the proceedings. Police are entitled to support the state prosecution during the trial of cases where the investigation is included in their jurisdiction. The testimony of a police officer is equal to other evidence brought to the court's attention.

Police personnel and municipal units' officers under specifically issued orders have the right to carry weapons and apply force. The government of Russia regulates the procedure of receiving and carrying weapons. It is the responsibility of police officers to secure their weapons. Off-duty officers wearing their civilian clothes may not openly carry their weapons. Legislation prescribes situations in which the use of force, weapons, and special means is allowed and specifies the procedure for their utilization. Police officers are expected to attend periodical training and pass tests on the usage of force. For example, police are trained and required to issue a warning on the use of force whenever it is possible. Also, the law stipulates that the use of force be proportional to the threat and obligates police personnel to make all efforts to minimize the damage inflicted by the use of force.

The special means used by police include rubber batons, handcuffs, tear gas, paint dispensers, sound-and-light means of distraction, means to destroy barricades, shotguns, armored carriers, water throwing machines, and service dogs. Police in detention centers may use gas weapons in order to prevent escapes and suppress riots. The Law on Handling Prisoners provides an exhaustive list of rules for the use of firearms in prisons and detention centers, and the Police Law has a similar list for police officers, defining what kind of force may be used in a particular situation. However, the law lifts all restrictions in cases where a police officer defends individuals from an attack that threatens their lives or health. Special means and weapons may not be used against women with visible signs of pregnancy, minors, or handicapped people unless they conduct an armed resistance or attack, threatening the health and lives of other individuals. Also, firearms may not be used in crowds when strangers may suffer. Special means may not be used against peaceful assemblies, rallies, and demonstrations, if such assemblies do not disturb the work of Russia's transportation services, communication networks, and organizations. All cases involving the usage of special means or weapons are reported to the prosecutor, who must conduct an investigation and determine whether it was justifiable; however, the existing forms of public protection from indiscriminate use of weapons by police are not sufficient (Lukin, 2005).

Procedural Requirements and Police Abuses

Under the Soviet criminal justice system, criminal suspects and defendants were practically stripped of the rights granted to them in international law and standards. Fair trial standards were systematically violated, as an independent judiciary did not exist, and suspects and defendants were generally considered guilty before trial. Crime policy was based on a state plan, requiring police to solve specific numbers of crimes. The system did not allow for any form of public oversight over prisons or detention centers. The first serious attempts to reform the system were undertaken in the early 1990s. New laws were adopted that established a theoretically independent judiciary and provided due process rights, and crime policies were temporarily changed. However, the reforms came to a premature end several years later as they met great resistance from both the law enforcement institutions and political establishment.

Laws that dictate police behavior have not been brought into full accordance with the Constitution or the international standards to which the government purportedly adheres. The Police Law states that rights and freedoms of citizens are protected regardless of their gender, race, nationality, ethnicity, language, place of residence, religion, ideology, or other circumstances. The police are prohibited from using torture, violence, cruel punishments, and humiliation. Unfortunately, these rules rarely are implemented, because the militia still practices old methods of the Soviet system. Existing police legislation remains vague, and because there is no direct regulation of many procedural situations, it leaves resolution of disputed issues up to the discretion of a police officer. In a poll conducted among police officers in the Far East region of Russia, 44 percent of the respondents acknowledged regular use of illegal and unethical methods of inquiry and investigation, and 4 percent stated that they use these methods from time to time (Kolennikova, 2004).

One disputed issue is the requirement for a police officer to inform detainees of their rights. Russia does not have an equivalent of the U.S. Miranda rule, and the procedure for detention is not formalized. The violation of this procedure does not affect a case's procedural status and the legal rights of a detainee. There is no administrative or criminal procedure law that regulates procedures that occur between the time a person is apprehended by the police and the presentation of accusations by an investigator when the detention officially begins. Police officers are guided by the MIA *Manual on Policing and Patrolling*, which does not have the force of law and leaves a great amount of discretion to policemen.

Another unregulated issue is the legal obligation of police officers to inform a detainee's relatives of the detention upon the detainee's request. The provision stating this requirement is not elaborated. The Code of Criminal Procedural stipulates that information about the arrest shall be released within 12 hours of the detention's initiation, but the law does not specify a way of informing families. There is no obligation for police to inform the detainee's relatives by telephone, and a letter sent by regular mail is recognized as a sufficient method of informing, even though the normal time for mail delivery within a Russian locality is about seven days, and this fact may extend the period of informing substantially. The police officer who conducts the detention selects which relatives are informed. As a rule, these are relatives residing with the detained person; however, if the detained person insists on informing other relatives, his request may be taken into account. If police authorities believe that informing relatives about the arrest may harm further investigation, they may request the prosecutor's permission to withhold this information.

Another area of wide police abuse is a detainee's right to legal defense. The law states that this right starts at the beginning of detention; however, Russian practices exhibit violations of this right. For example, confidential meetings between detainees and their attorneys are often permitted only after the first interrogation (Ryzhakov, 2004).

Other police abuses in the form of brutality, harassment, and corruption constitute another serious problem. The lack of reliable data on the use of reasonable versus excessive force is partially attributable to the absence of a Russian equivalent of the U.S. Violent Crime Control and Law Enforcement Act of 1994. There are no government studies designed to obtain information on the prevalence and nature of citizens' encounters with the police. In 2003, more than 50 percent of residents in St. Petersburg, the second largest Russian city with 4.5 million persons, witnessed the use of excessive physical force and offensive language by police (Davis, Ortiz, & Gilinsky, 2004). Individuals who believe that a police officer's activities or failures to act violated their rights may complain to the officer's supervisors, a prosecutor, or a court; however, people are usually afraid to complain, because they have often heard warnings from victims of police abuse about repercussions should they lodge a complaint. In 2003 (the year from which the latest data are available), only 11 people in St. Petersburg filed appeals alleging police misconduct (Davis, Ortiz, & Gilinsky, 2004).

Police officers may be held responsible for their illegal actions according to existing legislation, and legislation requires that damage inflicted by a police officer shall be compensated. However, legal provisions for compensation for damages to crime victims largely remain a dead letter for victims of police abuse. It appears that there were only two cases of this kind during the last 15 years. Compensation for damages can also be awarded in civil cases; however, civil courts are unlikely to grant compensation for damages to torture victims, unless a criminal court has found the perpetrators guilty of such a crime.

The Internal Security Force, as established within the MIA's structure, inspects compliance of police work with legislation and observance of individuals' legal rights. Federal prosecutors handle cases where a police officer is suspected of having committed a crime or having acted inappropriately. According to MIA, about 100,000 officers were dismissed during the last 10 years. The number of crimes committed by police officers in 2004 increased by 4 percent. According to information reported by the Prosecutor General of the Russian Federation, in 2004, police officers committed 37 murders, 45 rapes, 138 acts of intentional causing of grave harm to health, 130 thefts, 75 plunders, and 41 robberies (Kots & Skoibeda, 2005). Reports of police wearing black ski masks, beating people with rifle butts, and taking victims' money and possessions during regular police raids are often made by the mass media in Moscow and St. Petersburg. In other cities, almost all incidents of police misconduct remain hidden from outsiders.

Sociological surveys demonstrate that age and gender are the strongest predictors of who is stopped by police, with younger male residents being more likely to be stopped than older male and female residents. Ethnic minorities have a higher chance of having involuntary encounters with the police than ethnic Russians. Fifty-two percent of those surveyed believed that the police stop people without a good reason. Human rights organizations have accused the Moscow police of racism in singling out non-Slavic individuals (especially immigrants from Russia's Caucasus republics), physical attacks, unjustified detentions, and other violations (Amnesty International, 2004). From time to time, the MIA leadership conducts a high-profile "Clean Hands Campaign" to purge the force of corrupt elements. In 2004, about 4,500 police officers were disciplined for misconduct, and about 2,000 were arrested for serious crimes.

Police leadership has explained that these abuses result from a low level of officer professionalism, insufficient financing, minimal equipment, and increased labor fluidity within the force. The inadequacy of the force became particularly apparent in the wave of organized crime that began sweeping Russia after the collapse of the Soviet Union. About 1 million qualified individuals have left the police for better paying jobs in the field of private security, which has expanded to meet the demand of companies needing protection from organized crime. Frequent bribe taking among the remaining members of the police has damaged the force's public credibility. Numerous revelations of police information peddling, tolerance of criminal acts, and participation in murders and prostitution rings have created a general public perception that all police are at least taking bribes (Curtis, 1998). According to experts, the main causes of corruption are insufficient funding to train and equip personnel, insufficient funding to pay adequate wages, poor work discipline, lack of accountability, and fear of reprisals from organized criminals (State Duma, 2005).

Policing Terrorism

Terrorism is a relatively new phenomenon in Russia. It is claimed that in post-Soviet Russia there have been over 500 contract murders, and terrorist acts during the 2002–2005 period have taken the lives of almost 2,000 Russians, most of them civilians, with no connection to the actual conflict in Chechnya. Since the first hijacking of an aircraft in the Soviet Union in 1958, there have been more than 110 hijacking attempts, half of which have occurred since the beginning of 1990s. The significance of fighting terrorism became especially important in the 1990s, when increasing Islamic militancy influenced developments in the Caucasus region, where 40,000 terrorists, apparently with considerable al-Quaeda links, formed a well-organized army able to conduct large-scale terrorist operations.

Russian counterterrorism strategy is focused on legal mechanisms to ensure public safety; this strategy views terrorism primarily as a problem of the criminal justice system. The legal framework for the fight against terrorism is defined by general criminal law regulations and a number of special legislative acts. The major role in the fight against terrorism historically belongs to the Federal Security Service, the former KGB. Its Antiterrorism Department was created in 1995, and in 1999, it merged with the reestablished secret police, the Constitutional Defense Department. The Ministry of Internal Affairs (regular police) also is involved actively in antiterrorist activities. In July 2003, management of the counterterrorist operation in the northern Caucasus, including the conduct of military operations in Chechnya, was transferred to police authorities. A federal antiterrorist "Center T" with subordinated departments in all constituent components of the Russian Federation was created as a supplemental service within the MIA. Officers of this center conducted most of the apprehensions of terrorist suspects. Functions of both services intermingled, and there was no effective coordination between them. Presently, federal legislation determines the duties of the responsible executive agencies as follows:

- *The Russian Federation Federal Security Service* fights terrorism by preventing, uncovering, and stopping terrorist crimes, including crimes pursuing political objectives, and also by preventing, uncovering, and stopping international terrorist activities. The Federal Security Service conducts preliminary investigations of criminal cases relating to such crimes.
- *The Russian Federation Ministry of Internal Affairs* engages in the fight against terrorism by preventing, uncovering, and stopping terrorist crimes in which criminals are pursuing mercenary objectives.

Authorized bodies have a wide range of preventive and repressive measures at their disposal. However, the responsibilities of law enforcement agencies and control mechanisms are not sufficiently specified. The combination of vague proscriptions with the broad powers of executive agencies creates potential threats to fundamental rights because of the lack of appropriate structures and procedures to control the implementation of antiterrorism legislation.

Detention and Interrogation of Suspected Terrorists

The rules and principles governing the criminal investigation and prosecution of terrorism-related offenses are generally the same as for any other "serious" or "especially serious" crime. Apart from the use of specialized investigation bodies of the Federal Security Service, there is, in general, no special procedure in such cases. Because of their classification as first or second degree felonies, most terrorism-related crimes can be investigated and prosecuted by use of early warning measures and urgent procedures, such as use of special means and extension of the maximum duration of pretrial detention up to 18 months. Among other terrorism-related exemptions from existing criminal procedure are the use of pretrial detention of juveniles in regard to terrorism investigations and the right of the police to disregard the mandatory requirement to notify a detainee's relatives or a corresponding consular body in case of an arrest of a foreigner in order to ensure the secrecy of the preventive arrest. However, the minimum standard of judicial guarantees, as set forth in the Constitution, is provided in proceedings against terrorists, i.e., effective judicial protection, a competent court as established by law, the right to legal assistance, and the right to the presumption of innocence.

Surveillance and Intelligence Gathering

Basic investigative measures are the following: searches of private residences, seizure of property, seizure of correspondence, telephone tapping, and interception of communications. Except in exceptional circumstances, there should be a preliminary court order for investigators to take these measures. In urgent cases, investigators can use these measures without a prior judicial order on the condition that within 24 hours the judge is informed and is able to evaluate the legal grounds for the use of such measures. If, according to the judge's assessment, the decision to use special means appears to be unlawful, evidence obtained through these measures would not be admissible in court. The criminal procedural legislation provides for limited judicial oversight and certain derogations in connection with criminal investigations relating to terrorist offenses, including the application of investigative techniques that are not prescribed by the Criminal Procedural Code. These techniques include observation, electronic surveillance, search of buildings and means of transportation, including secret search, and seizure. A court warrant is not required for use of these techniques if the investigation concerns a terrorism-related offense. The same test applies to the control of postal, telegraphic, and electronic correspondence. In addition, under federal legislation, requirements such as the prohibition against conducting investigative actions at night or to cease recording telephone conversations upon expiration of a six-month period do not apply to terrorism-related investigations.

Monitoring of Persons

In 1993 the old Soviet residence permit system, which had been established in 1927 to monitor movements of Russian citizens within the country by means of passport entries made by the police, was replaced by a new residence registration system; however, this did not change the essence of the institution. According to the law, all Russian citizens must be registered at their places of permanent residence. An individual who has changed his or her primary residence must register with local police authorities within seven days after arrival at a new place. Individuals who have arrived at a place of temporary stay for a period longer than ten days must apply for temporary registration within three days after their arrival.

The receipt of obligatory medical insurance, social services, and other benefits depends on the registration, because these services cannot be received outside the territory where an individual is registered. An employer has no obligation to hire only local people; however, an employer is held administratively responsible if an employee does not possess a residence registration. This system is best understood as a control function utilized by police that prevents Russian citizens from exercising their social rights outside of the constituent component of the Russian Federation where they are permanently registered. The existing registration procedure has more restrictions in certain localities, for instance, in the cities of Moscow and St. Petersburg and in some other regional administrative centers. Since March 1997, the application of the registration rules is extended to foreigners if their stay in Russia is longer than three days. Foreigners without registration caught during passport checks conducted by police, who are allowed to search apartments during passport control operations, can be deported from the country immediately.

Based on permanent residence registration, local police departments issue domestic passports, the main identification document for Russian nationals. All Russian citizens must obtain internal passports within three months of reaching the age of 14. Russian passports contain the bearer's photograph, information about his or her name, date and place of birth, marital status, minor children, religion, ethnicity, criminal and military service records, date of issuance, and name of the issuing authority. Passports have no expiration dates; however, when a bearer reaches ages 25 and 45, a new photograph must be placed in the passport. Even though this is not a formal renewal of the passport, passports are not valid without these new photographs. When photographs are replaced, a review of residence registration, military, and criminal records is conducted by the local police.

The Russian police have no restrictions against checking individuals' identification documents and detaining individuals without documents for identification purposes. Ethnic, religious, and racial profiling is often used for selecting people to be subject to random passport checks conducted by police on streets, public transportation, and in places of mass gatherings, and this practice is supported by local administrations and public opinion.

Recruitment, Training, and Employment

Officially, the MIA forces number around 2 million (Sweet, 2002). The Special Purpose Detachment has 50,000 officers, and the Internal Troops have 300,000. These figures are very rough because of high turnover and poor record keeping (Pustyntsev, 2002). MIA estimates require that there is one officer of inquiry for every 165 claims submitted to the police or for approximately every 50 cases brought before the court; yet, the real workload of a criminal investigator is about 200–220 cases per month. According to existing norms, police employ one juvenile delinquency inspector for every 4,000–5,000 persons under 16 years old residing in the territory of a police district and one inspector per every 3,000 vehicles in the automobile inspection unit. Police stations at airports and train stations usually consist of 8 to 12 officers (Thomas, 2000).

The share of women is slightly over 15 percent of the force. In 1994, women constituted 20 percent of the force, but this percentage has decreased, because women are fired first during a reduction in force. As a rule, women are employed in clerical positions, in passport and visa registration sections, and as inspectors for the affairs of the minors. Often, women in the police force work as researchers and forensic experts.

Since 1993, turnover within the force has ranged from 20 to 70 percent. Such a wide range can be explained by the specifics of service in different regions and police units. Some police departments renew their staff every 18 months, and in almost all departments, a complete turnover occurs every five years. This fluidity severely undermines the professionalism of the officers employed. The average understaffing of police units is 20 percent. The biggest shortage of officers is at the Moscow Subway Police Department, where this figure reaches 40 percent. The workload is distributed among the remaining officers, but their salaries remain unchanged. All these conditions make police employment unattractive. Kots and Skoibeda (2005) cited the following factors among reasons why officers have selected their profession: free or subsidized housing, business opportunities, employment while attending night study at law school, and gaining legal work experience necessary for future jobs in other fields of the legal profession.

Most patrol and low-ranking officers are recruited while serving their military duty. Commanding officers are trained at a network of the MIA's educational establishments. Graduates of police training schools receive an officer's rank. Officers who graduate from a four-year course of study at a police institution of higher education receive a law degree. A high school diploma is required to enroll in a police training course. Physical and other various aptitude tests also must be passed. However, recruits are being accepted without undergoing proper screening and are not being trained in up-to-date investigative techniques. Russian police training is dangerously weak. The curricula at the existing police education establishments do not emphasize individual rights, which is a new concept to most Russian police officers, and focus primarily on law enforcement issues. Average training for a patrol officer, who as a rule is a high school graduate as required, is about six months. Undertrained patrol officers are often recruited into the investigative forces.

After graduation from police training school, students are appointed to police stations, where they are required to obtain additional professional training. Basic professional training is conducted in regional MIA training centers during a probation period immediately after appointment to a police station. The probation period is from three to six months. Carrying firearms is not allowed during probation. All police officers take an oath within two months after beginning their service. The basic classes attended during training are the only form of professional education required for low-level police personnel.

Professional police staff are taught at the MIA's middle- and high-level educational institutions. Higher-ranking law enforcement personnel for commanding and specialized professional positions also are recruited from among graduates of civilian universities and law schools. Graduation from the MIA Academy, an institution aimed at retraining of higher-level police officers, is a requirement for being appointed to an executive-level position within the MIA system. In 1996, a reorganization plan was proposed for the MIA, with the aim of more effective crime prevention. The plan called for increasing the police force by as many as 90,000, but funding was not available for such expansion. Meanwhile, the MIA recruited several thousand former military personnel, whose experience reduced the need for police training. Hiring and low-level appointments are overseen by the heads of regional internal affairs departments. The minister of internal affairs appoints senior-level personnel and issues senior officers' ranks.

Prerevolutionary Russia did not have a nationwide education and training system for police personnel. A few short-term schools existed in several provinces. During the early Soviet period (1920–1940), police training remained sporadic. The network of police training establishments was created at the end of the 1950s. Presently, there are 21 graduate university-level and 11 college-level police schools (Kikot, 2004). In 2002, the government ordered the creation of the MIA University, which combined four other educational institutions in Moscow that were all subordinated to the Ministry of Internal Affairs. There are about 500 faculty members at the university, which has branches in Russia's eight largest regions. In addition to regular full time classes, the university conducts night, distance, and correspondence programs. The MIA Scientific Institute is a research arm of the police system. The institute conducts scholarly theoretical and applied studies in various areas of law relevant to the MIA. Among the most recent projects developed by the institute are a community policing pilot project, recommendations on new police performance evaluations, and recommendations on efforts to improve crime detection and recording. The projects are tested, not implemented, in several regional and local police departments and are viewed as scholarly exercises by MIA leadership.

The work week is 40 hours; however police personnel may be required to work longer if necessary. Annual paid vacation is 30 days, not including the time to travel to a vacation destination. Depending on their length of service, police officers are entitled to additional annual leave. There is an elaborate system of social benefits for police personnel, including eligibility for paid retirement upon 25 years of service regardless of age. All police personnel and their family members receive free health care provided by the MIA's medical establishments and are entitled to subsidized use of MIA-owned resorts. Police officers are entitled to mandatory life insurance paid by the MIA's budget. If a police officer loses the ability to work due to a disability received in the course of employment, he or she is entitled to lump sum payments in an amount equal to five to ten annual salaries, depending on the officer's seniority and the severity of the disability. The law guarantees some housing and other privileges for police officers, for example, a guaranteed telephone connection and subsidized child day care. Before January 1, 2005, police officers were allowed to use public transportation for free all throughout the Russian Federation. This privilege presently is cancelled.

Citizens of the Russian Federation with clean criminal records are eligible for police employment. The age bracket for entering the police service is 18–35, regardless of ethnicity, gender, origin, or religion. Police personnel are hired by contract, appointment, or open competition. Close relatives are not prohibited from work in the same police unit as long as they do not supervise each other. In tight rural communities, this rule often leads to the emergence of some families as dominant forces in their neighborhoods. Given that police officers are government employees, all existing norms that regulate government employment are applicable to them.

Russian law imposes two major restrictions on police officers. They are prohibited from being members of political parties. Creation of political organizations within the police force also is prohibited. This requirement was adopted to preserve political neutrality of law enforcement personnel and to increase social awareness that police officials serve only the law and the people. Even though this provision insulates the police from direct use by the dominant political party, the police force remains actively involved in promoting the agenda of the current administration and securing election results favored by governors. Professional organizations of police officers are allowed, but officers may not go on strike to resolve labor disputes.

Another restriction is the prohibition on police involvement in any entrepreneurial activity or supplemental employment, except for teaching or scientific work. MIA salaries generally are lower than those paid in other agencies of the criminal justice system and, as a result, this ban often is violated. It is common for police officers, mostly those of low and middle rank, to work as private guards or provide other security related services. An independent study conducted in 2003 showed that 50 percent of police personnel are involved in illegal economic activity during their spare time, and 18 percent are earning extra money while on duty (Kosals, 2003).

At the end of the 1990s, the MIA reported debts equal to US$717 million, including US$272 million in overdue wages. There were reports of police officers undertaking hunger strikes in order to receive their wages. The situation has improved recently. Since 2000, the budget of the MIA has increased by a factor of 2.5 (MIA, 2004). In 2005, the ministry received US$6 billion, which is 20 percent more than it received in 2004. However, there is no guarantee that all this money will be used for the purposes for which it was appropriated. In 2003, the police received only 87 percent of the amount that had been allocated to them in that year's budget, and a lot of the remaining money was embezzled. For example, the Accounting Chamber (Russia's counterpart to the U.S. General Accounting Office) has investigated the theft of one-third of the budget allocated to the Moscow Regional Internal Affairs Department, and the purchase of Mercedes Benz SUVs for the Ural Regional Police Department when funds were intended for implementation of new technologies (Kots & Skoibeda, 2005).

In addition to federal and regional budget financing, police departments are allowed to draw from nonbudget resources by offering their services in the fields of security, protection services, registration of foreigners, and traffic safety. According to some estimates, nonbudget funds may amount up to US$50 billion annually. There is strong opinion that most of this money is coming from illegal activities and close cooperation with criminal structures. Some Russian researchers conclude that local organized criminal structures are no longer the focus of the police's professional activity, but are really business partners (Kots & Skoibeda, 2005).

Close connections between police and criminals, lack of equipment to solve crimes (computers, weapons, cars), and a history of subjecting persons to sophisticated torture methods (perfected over the Soviet period) all affect the public's perception of the police as a corrupt institution. Russians are fully aware of the futility of working with the police, and it is estimated that 42 percent of crime victims do not approach the police for help (Galeotti, 2002). While it is becoming increasingly popular in the democratic society to think about the police as providing services and to think of the public as consumers of police services, most Russians do not turn to the police when crime or disorder arise. The most common reasons for an individual's contact with the police is to obtain a passport or drivers' license or to register an address.

Russian society has a long history of supplementing or even replacing minimally effective official police activities with self-policing. This tradition started with the prevalence of the mob law of village "self-judging" over often amateurish and overstretched policing in the previous centuries and continues today with people independently taking care of their own security. A willingness to accept the protection of organized crime rather than have no protection at all and the growth of the private security industry, which has expanded dramatically as people and enterprises seek their own "police," exemplify this process. There are about 10,000 private security agencies in Russia, employing more than 1 million people (Ustinov 2005). Largely underregulated, they range from street gangs to private armies of up to 3,000 armed security personnel run by former police and security chieftains.

Conclusion

Significant economic and political changes have had almost no positive effect on policing in Russia. Promises of building a law-governed state have had little effect, and although the new Russian Federation has given the police a wide array of powers and increased the size of the force to go along with the new powers, the daily experience of Russian citizens attests to the police's failure in combating petty and organized crime alike (Galeotti, 1997). The police did not get integrated into the multifunctional national security system, and their ability to be a first responder during an emergency situation is undermined by the ineffectiveness of command, lack of equipment, and lack of professionalism of the staff.

Scattered attempts for police reform have ended in failure. They seldom amounted to more than bringing in new commanders who ceremoniously would pledge to clean up the force and conduct some organizational changes, renaming and resubordinating departments within the MIA. Supporters of reforms have failed to take into consideration the inertia and sometimes even the open resistance of the political establishment and law enforcement bodies, which continue to perform their traditional role of protecting the interests of the elite (Pustyntsev, 2002). Even when crime and police misconduct rose steeply, the government did not introduce fundamental changes to the police force and the laws guiding this body. As a result, Russia's criminal justice system remains a hybrid of half-reformed and purely Soviet institutions and laws.

Public control over police activities is almost nonexistent in Russia today, although it is required under the Police Law. The police are largely controlled by all branches of government within their jurisdiction. The controlling institutions are not allowed to interfere in the procedural work of the police. The Prosecutor General supervises the legality of police activities and the uniform application of Russian laws all over the nation's territory. Recently published books on Russian policing suggest terminating the duality of prosecutorial control and dividing this function between two different institutions, where one would supervise police and the other would control actions of those who are the subjects of police activities. Other proposals recommend canceling the existing system of crime registration and police performance evaluations to stop the falsification of statistics and the hiding of crimes, amending the Criminal Code with harsher punishments for crimes committed by police personnel, and implementing measures of effective public control. Suggestions to produce a bill of rights, to end misleading detentions, and to introduce greater transparency and judicial and public control may lead to the improvement of the force. There is hope that implementing these measures with massive government investments will establish a modern and professional force ready to exhibit the democratic character of policing and to meet the challenges of booming crime, terrorist threats, public demands, and the rule of law.

Note

1. For the purposes of this paper, the term *militia* will be used as a synonym for *police* because of the nature of its operations.

References

Adrianov, S. (1902). *MVD 1802-1902. Istoricheskii ocherk [MVD 1802-1902. Historical survey]*. St. Petersburg: MVD Publishing House.

Amnesty International. (2004). *Concerns for Europe and Central Asia..* Retrieved June 24, 2006 from http://web.amnesty.org/library/index/ENGEUR010052004

Belskii, K. (2004). *Politseiskoe Pravo [Police Law]*. Moscow: Delo I Servis.

Butler, W. (2003). *Russian law*. Oxford, UK: Oxford University Press.

Curtis, G. (Ed.). (1998). *Russia: A country study*. Washington, DC: Federal Research Division, Library of Congress.

Davis, R., Ortiz, C., & Gilinsky, Y. (2004). A cross-national comparison of citizen perceptions of the police in New York City and St. Petersburg, Russia. *Policing, 27*(1), 37–64.

Galeotti, M. (1997). Cops, spies and private eyes: Changing patterns of Russian policing. *Europe-Asia Studies, 49*(1), 141–157.

Galeotti, M. (2002). *Russian and post-soviet organized crime*. Aldershot, UK; Brookfield, VT: Ashgate.

Gavrilov, B. (2003). Novelly ugolovnogo protsessa [Novelties of the criminal process]. *Rossiiskaia Iustitsiia, (10)*, 17–29.

Gerson, L. (1976). *The secret police in Lenin's Russia.* Philadephia: Temple University Press.

Jamestown Foundation. (1998). The interior ministry plans new special units. *Monitor,* 4(194) [Electronic version]. Retrieved August 15, 2007, from http://www .jamestown.org/publications_details.php?volume_id=21&issue_id=1405& article_id=14306

Khinstein, A. (2003, November 16). Vinovaty do suda (Guilty before trial). *Moskovskii Komsomolets,* p. 2.

Kikot, V. (2004). Mesto i rol organov MVD v politike Rossiiskogo gosudarstva (Place and role of the MIA authorities in the politics of the Russian state). *Gosudarstvo i Pravo, (1),* 11–32.

Kolennikova, O. (2004). *Pravoohranitelnye organy Rossiiskoi Federatsii (Law enforcement authorities of the Russian Federation).* Krasnoiarsk: Izdatelstvo KGU.

Kosals, Y. (2003). *Ekonomicheskaia aktivnost militsii v Rossii (Economic activity of police in Russia).* Moscow: Yurizdat.

Kots, A., & Skoibeda, U. (2005, June 7–10). Pochemu menty pytaiut i berut vziatki (Why policemen torture and take bribes). *Komsomolskaia Pravda,* pp. 2–3.

Lukin, V. (2005, April 16, May 27, 30, 31). On activities of the human rights commissioner in the Russian Federation in 2004: Report of the RF human rights commissioner. *Rossiiskaia Gazeta,* p. 3.

Ministry of Internal Affairs (MIA) of the Russian Federation. (2004). *Annual report.* Retrieved May 12, 2005, from http://www.mvdinform.ru/index.pxp?docid=3158

Peyser, M., & Vitsin, S. (2005). Russia. In M . Haberfeld (Ed.), *Encyclopedia of law enforcement* (Vol. 3, pp. 1273–1281). Thousand Oaks, CA: Sage.

Pustyntsev, B. (2002). Police reform in Russia: Obstacles and opportunities. *Policing and Society, 10*(1), pp. 54–72.

Putin, V. (2005, April 26). State of the nation address. *Rossiiskaia Gazeta,* pp. 1–2.

Rushailo, V. (2001). *Militsiia Rossii: Dokumenty I materially (Russia's militia: Documents and materials).* Moscow: Izdatelstvo MVD.

Ryzhakov, A. (2004). *Kommentarii k zakonu Rossiiskoi Federatsii o militsii [Commentaries on the Russian Federation law on militia].* Moscow: Norma.

Shelley, L. (1996). *Policing Soviet society.* New York: Routledge.

State Duma [legislature] of the Russian Federation, Committee on Civil, Criminal, and Procedural Legislation. (2005, March 11). Hearings on police tortures and abuses. *Dumskii Vestnik, (4),* p. 73.

Sweet, K. (2002). Russian law enforcement under President Putin. *Human Rights Review, 3*(4), 20–33.

Thomas, T. (2000). Restructuring and reform in Russia's MVD: Good idea, bad timing? in *Law Intensity Conflict & Law Enforcement, 9*(2), pp. 2–11.

Ustinov, V. (2005). O sostoyanii zakonnosti [State of justice]. Report to the state duma. *Rossiiskaia Iustitsiia, (4),* 3–8.

Weissman, N. (1985). Regular police in tsarist Russia, 1900–1914. *The Russian Review, 44*(1), 45–68.

Further Reading

Baker, P., & Glasser, S. (2005). *Kremlin Rising: Vladimir Putin's Russia and the End of Revolution*. New York: Scribner, 2005. (Examines the failure of democratic changes, including those aimed at reforming of the police.)

Butler, W. (2003). *Russian law*. Oxford, UK: Oxford University Press. (A study of new Russia's legal order, reflecting the demise of the Soviet Union and the transition to market-oriented legal rules and democratic institutions.)

Galeotti, M. (Ed.). (2002). *Russian and post-Soviet organized crime*. Dartmouth, UK: Ashgate. (Essays on the nature of criminality in Russia and specifics of the police response.)

Handelman, S. (1995). *Comrade criminal: Russia's new mafia*. New Haven, CT: Yale University Press. (Author treats the issue of organized crime as a political problem and reviews connections between criminal leaders and law enforcement institutions.)

Human Rights Watch. (1998). *Confessions at any cost*. New York: Author. (A detailed case study that introduces readers to the practice of police abuse in Russia and provides information on police techniques and the status of detainees.)

Knight, A. (1996). *Spies without cloaks: The KGB's successors*. Princeton, NJ: Princeton University Press. (Discusses the KGB role in the breakup of the Soviet Union and the unfolding development of the new Russia; analyzes how Soviet-era institutions have adapted to new conditions and became an integral part of the semidemocratic, semiauthoritarian new Russia.)

Liang, H.-H. (1992). *The rise of the modern police and the European state system from Metternich to the Second World War*. Cambridge, UK: Cambridge University Press. (A cross-cultural comparative study that explores the issue of integrating European police forces into the state structures, looking specifically at France, Prussia/Germany, and Russia/Soviet Union.)

Shelley, L. (1996). *Policing Soviet society*. New York: Routledge. (Examines the history, development, and daily activities of police institutions in the Soviet Union and their impact on the ongoing police reform in contemporary Russia.)

Zuckerman, F. (1996). *The tsarist secret police in Russian society, 1880–1917*. Basingstoke, UK: Macmillan. (Explores the activities of the political police in the wider context of policing and governing late tsarist Russia.)

Web Sites of Interest

http://eng.mvdrf.ru/: Official website of the Russian Ministry of Internal Affairs. Provides information on police legislation, structure, and activities of the law enforcement authorities.

http://www.hrw.org: Reports on police activities provided by Human Rights Watch.

http://www.hro.org/: Commentaries to legislation and analytical materials on law enforcement in Russia.

7 Emergence of Modern Indian Policing

From Mansabdari to Constabulary

Farrukh Hakeem

Introduction

Policing in India commenced as a military enterprise. It remained a military endeavor during the Aryan and Muslim periods. Early forms of policing were evident only in the big cities of medieval India. Prior to the tenth century CE, forms of policing during the Hindu period were fairly rudimentary (Rao, 1967; Sanghar, 1967). With the advent of the Muslim sultanates of northern India, a clearer structure of the policing apparatus emerged. Policing during this period followed a feudal military model that is referred to as the Mansabdari system. This structure continued to be employed throughout the Muslim period in India (1100 CE to 1700 CE). Even after the advent of the East India Company, this feudal model did not undergo any major changes. During the eighteenth century, the English colonists made a series of efforts to improve the policing apparatus. The initial efforts were feeble attempts to build on the old system of policing and did not lead to any tangible improvement. However, during the course of British rule this model came to be considered ineffective and was gradually replaced with a more civilian model of policing.

Colonial Policing

The reforms initiated by Robert Peel in 1829 in England led to important changes in policing. The directors of the East India Company advised that similar measures should be followed in India. A select committee was appointed in 1832 to look into problems leading to an increase in crime and oppression by the police agencies.

Three reports that were written during the 1830s provide some insight into the state of affairs of the police. These reports were instrumental in establishing the Indian police force. The first of these reports was by Frederick Shore, a seasoned district judge who wrote an insightful note regarding the duties and the problems of the police (*darogas* in Urdu) in 1837. Shore not only outlined the problems but also made some pragmatic suggestions to improve the functioning of the police apparatus. Some of the recommendations were the following:

- Provide respectable salaries for police personnel.
- Give promotions and rewards for good conduct.
- Give additional powers to the police in some petty cases.
- Vest authority in some of the upper-class landholders to persuade them to give their support, which was withheld under the system in place at the time of Shore's report.
- Have the magistrates exercise strict surveillance over all those who were connected to the colonial establishment of the East India Company.

A second report was made in 1838 by Thomas Metcalfe, who set up a committee to examine the problems related to policing. The committee pointed out that the reasons for the inefficiency of the police were as follows:

- The police received inadequate supervision from the magistrates, who were burdened with many other responsibilities.
- The union of the offices of magistrate and collector had a negative impact on the administration of the police force, because police officers had to pay more attention to the collection of revenue than to police duties.
- Due to lax oversight, the subordinate police staff was corrupt and negligent in the performance of their duties.

The committee recommended that the collector should stop exercising control over the police and that a magistrate in each of the districts should perform this task. It further suggested that the districts should be subdivided into subdivisions. In each subdivision, authority over the police would be vested in the deputy magistrate. It also recommended that the village police watch system be revamped.

The third report was by Frederick Halliday, who made some very detailed proposals for establishing a police force. He suggested that the entire police apparatus be placed under a superintendent general of police at headquarters. Under the superintendent general, there were to be 23 superintendents, 32 assistant superintendents, 888 *darogas*, 4,440 *jamadars,* and 66,600 *burkandazes* (see Table 7.1).

This proposal was implemented in part. A superintendent of police was appointed in every district with the superintendent general. A joint magistrate

Table 7.1 Police Structure Proposed by Halliday

Officer	Number
Superintendent General of Police	1
Superintendents of Police	23
Assistant Superintendents of Police	32
Darogas	888
Jamadars	4,440
Burkandazes	66,600

was also appointed in each district to perform the magisterial function. Except for these two changes the police functioned in the same lackadaisical manner that they had before.

The colonial police model originated in Ireland and followed the model of the Royal Irish Constabulary. As opposed to the metropolitan police model, which consisted of unarmed police, the Royal Irish Constabulary was a paramilitary force, a gendarmerie, which had the primary goal of maintaining law and order amongst a populace of which large elements actively or passively opposed the entire system of law that the force sought to uphold. The main purpose was to suppress disorder without the use of the military (Tobias, 1977).

In 1843 Charles Napier annexed the northwest province of Sindh to British India. To maintain order in this new province, Napier decided to implement the recommendations that had been made by Frederick Halliday in order to improve the efficiency of the police. Napier modeled his police on the lines of the Royal Irish Constabulary. This new system was a separate and self-contained police organization under which the officers had to perform only police duties. The system developed by Napier had its basis on two main principles:

1. The police should be completely separated from the military.

2. The police should be an independent body to assist the collectors in matters dealing with law and order, but they should have their own officers.

The main principle here was that the military forces and the civil police should be kept quite separate. This was a novel idea to solve the problem but it gradually came to be followed throughout India in phases.

Upon visiting Sindh in 1847, Sir George Clerk was very impressed by the efficiency of the Sindh police. He decided to organize the Bombay police on the model that Napier implemented. In 1853 a superintendent of police was appointed for each district in Bombay province.

The Indian Penal Code was passed in 1862. It defines basic crimes and punishments and is based mainly on English criminal law. Crimes are divided into nine categories (Hakeem, 1998). The three basic criminal statutes—the Indian Penal Code, the Criminal Procedure Code, and the Evidence Act were passed by the imperial parliament of Britain for its Indian colony during the tumultuous postmutiny era (Ramaswami, 1951).

The Police Commission drafted a police bill in 1860 (Bayley, 1969). The bill was enacted as the Police Act (V) of 1861. The last report of the Police Commission was made in 1862, after which the commission was dissolved (Saha, 1990).

The terms of reference for the commission can be gleaned from a dispatch by Charles Wood, secretary of state for India to the governor general. Some of the main provisions examined were as follows:

- There was to be a special emphasis on the predominance of civil elements for the proposed well-organized police force.
- The entire police force was to be put under the control of an officer who was in direct communication with the local government.
- Adequate measures were to be taken to improve the village watch, and it was to be placed under the control of a magistrate.
- In order to create a good police system, a fair pay scale was to be ensured to all ranks of the police.

The government concurred with the commission that the police organization in India should be placed under the exclusive control, superintendence, and responsibility of English officers only. The recommendations of the commission helped in abolishing the archaic police system and succeeded in ushering in a uniform system of policing under a unified command and established hierarchy throughout British India. The inspector general of police was to have overall control over the police in the provinces. The inspector general was to be assisted by the district superintendent of police in each district. The district superintendent in turn was assisted by a number of assistant district superintendents. These positions were meant for the English officers only, and Indians could not be appointed to these positions. The subordinate police ranks were categorized as inspectors, head constables, and constables. Indians could be appointed only to these subordinate police ranks. With respect to the village police, the commission recommended that they should be continued as an institution.

From an objective perspective, the police in the real sense of the term originated in India from the period when the East India Company got political control of eastern India in 1765 CE. The English authorities carried out a series of experiments over a span of 100 years in order to settle upon the present structure of police. The model of policing that evolved was one that had a definite structure and a robust command and control system.

Postindependence Period

The Police Act of 1861 established the main principles for the organization of the police forces in India. This organization has continued to the present with minor modifications. Though state police forces are separate and show some minor differences in detail, their pattern of organization and operation are very similar.

An inspector general of police who is answerable to the home minister of the state heads police forces in each state. For command and coordination purposes, the domain of an inspector general is divided into police ranges. A deputy inspector general, who in turn is responsible for three to six districts, heads each range. The superintendent of police is in charge of the district police headquarters and constitutes the fulcrum of the state police operations. District superintendents of police have much discretionary authority and are responsible for supervising subordinate police stations along with many specialty elements, which include the criminal investigation detachment, equipment storehouses/armories, and traffic police. The larger districts also have assistant district superintendents. Constables who are assigned to the police stations conduct much of the preventive police work. The number of stations in a district can range from less than 10 to over 50 in some cases. Stations are grouped into subdivisions and circles to facilitate supervision from district headquarters. Major metropolitan cities like New Delhi, Calcutta, Bombay, Madras, and Hyderabad have separate municipal forces that are headed by a commissioner of police (see Figure 7.1).

Within state police forces there is a distinction between armed and unarmed police. Unarmed police staff the police stations and departments of criminal investigation. Though they are uniformed, they are unarmed. They may carry a short bamboo staff called a *lathi*. They constitute the police with whom the public has contact during the normal course of affairs. Some of their typical tasks include searching for lost children, investigating crimes, patrolling streets, regulating traffic, interposing in village quarrels, and generally responding to the needs of the general populace for police assistance.

Armed police reside in cantonments concentrated at a few points across each state. They do not have daily contact with the masses. They do not respond to calls for assistance from individuals but to orders from superior officers. The armed police are recruited and trained separately from the unarmed police. There are two types of armed police: district armed police and special armed police. The district armed police force is composed of armed policemen quartered in each district headquarters under the control of the district superintendent. The special armed police are under the immediate command of the inspector general of police through a deputy inspector general and are concentrated at a couple of points in each state. They may have heavier armor than the district armed police and are often used for special kinds of enforcement actions.

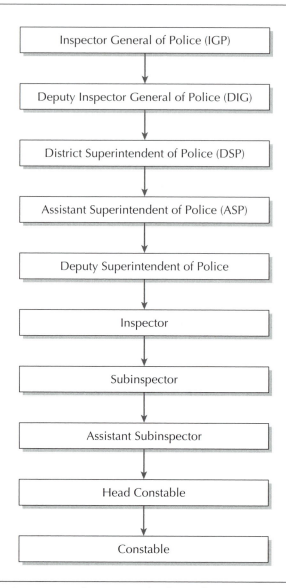

Figure 7.1   Organizational Structure of Indian Police

Structure of the Indian Police Force

The Indian police have three main features. The first feature is diversity and similarity. The police are organized, maintained, and directed by the states of the Indian Union. The federal government has some police agencies under its authority, like the Central Bureau of Investigation (CBI). There is diversity of operational control along with remarkable organizational similarity. India has avoided fragmentation of police under a system of local control (such as the system in the United States, with its 40,000 separate forces) but has the rigidity of a national police force controlled by a central government.

The second feature is horizontal stratification. The Indian police are horizontally stratified. They are organized into cadres based upon rank. The principle of horizontal stratification goes beyond the organization of ranks. It accounts for relations between the federal and state governments with respect to police administration and the distribution of police powers among the ranks. The officer cadre, known as the IPS, is recruited, organized, trained, and disciplined according to national legislation. Police power and authority differs with rank. This is different from the system in Great Britain, where a constable has all the authority any policeman can have. Horizontal stratification is reflected in rank structure, relations between levels of government regarding police personnel, and the distribution of legal authority among policemen.

The third feature is vertical division. The police in each state are divided vertically into an armed and an unarmed branch. This is a functional division. Unarmed police staff police stations, go on patrol duties, answer routine complaints, perform traffic duties, and prevent and investigate crime. The armed police perform those duties that require the presence of constituted physical force, such as guarding banks and quelling civil disturbances.

States that have armed police contingents use them as a reserve strike force in emergencies. These units are of two types: mobile-armed police under direct state control and district armed police that are less well equipped. The district armed police are controlled by the district superintendent of police and are normally used for riot control functions.

At all levels, the senior police officers are answerable to the police chain of command along with the general direction and control of designated civilian officials. In the municipal forces, the chain of command runs directly up to the state home minister. The dual hierarchy of accountability to civilian and police authorities has been the source of much confusion and disagreement. Though participation by political authorities can be regarded as a symbol of democracy and a safeguard for police accountability, it can also be considered to be problematic, because police have complained about political interference in police affairs. There are frequent charges that political parties have increasingly tried to influence police activities for their personal or partisan ends (Bayley, 1983; Verma, 1997).

Responsibility for policing is shared by the federal (central) and state government. The federal government elements include the Indian Police Service (IPS), various paramilitary units, and police in the union territories. In the 1970s new paramilitary forces were created under central government control to safeguard borders and provide for industrial security. In 1980 the state police forces were estimated to be about 765,000. These included regular as well as paramilitary forces.

In 1970 the federal government established the Bureau of Police Research and Development. This bureau was set up with the objective of modernizing the police forces. It has research and development divisions. Subsequently other divisions were added, including those for training (1973), forensics (1983), and correctional administration (1995).

Policing Under the Constitution

The responsibility for maintaining law and order rests on the states. Most of the routine policing, such as prevention and detection of crime, apprehension of criminals, and maintenance of public order is carried out by state police forces. The Constitution permits the federal government to participate in police operations and organization by authorizing the maintenance of the IPS. The IPS officers are recruited and trained by the federal government. Most of these recruits are assigned to senior positions in the state police forces, and they are under the operational control of the states.

The Constitution also permits the federal government to have other forces that are necessary to safeguard national security. Such paramilitary forces are legally created to assist the states only upon request of the state governments.

During the 1970s and 1980s, the police came under increasing public scrutiny due to their inability to deal with crime and public disorder. As an institution, the police were considered to be ineffective, corrupt, and unruly. This was a perennial problem with the Indian police. A 1902 report by the Police Commission surmised that the public did not have much confidence in the police. The public also considered the police to be corrupt and oppressive. The position is much the same today, if not worse; the police are considered to be highly corrupt, politicized, and dysfunctional (Dhillon, 2005).

Federal Level Forces

The federal Ministry of Home Affairs is in charge of law enforcement at the national level. It provides assistance and guidance to state governments to perform similar functions. The ministry deals with all matters that address maintenance of public peace and order, staffing and administration of public services, delineation of boundaries, and administration of union territories.

Officers from the IPS occupy most of the senior positions of all state and territorial police services. They are also deputed in national agencies that have responsibility for police and security matters. The Union Public Service Commission, through competitive examinations on a nationwide basis, recruits officers of the IPS. Upon completion of the basic course given to members of all national services, IPS officers attend the National Police Academy, Hyderabad. Upon completion of work at the academy, they are assigned to the state police forces, where they usually remain for the rest of their careers.

Police in the union territories are the responsibility of the Police Division, which also runs the National Police Academy, Hyderabad, and the Institute of Criminology and Forensic Science. The CBI investigates crimes that involve public officials and public undertakings.

The Ministry of Home Affairs also controls the paramilitary forces. These include the Central Reserve Police (CRP), which was established by the

British in 1939 and is one of the largest paramilitary forces. The CRP was established to help the military deal with the independence movement. Since independence, it has had the task of assisting the state police and the army. The CRP is used to quell internal disturbances. This force is called in when disorder escalates beyond the control of the local police. The CRP had a major role in assisting the army in checking insurgency in the Northeast. It is also used to protect the security of the Ministry of Defense and other federal government institutions. Another paramilitary force is the Border Security Force (BSF), which was created in 1965 to release the army from doing all the routine patrol duties on the border with Pakistan. It was organized by consolidating the state border units and had the additional responsibility of controlling smuggling, resisting infiltration, and assisting the army. It is also used for internal policing. The BSF is equipped with more advanced and sophisticated weapons than the other paramilitary forces. It has its own training facilities and has a factory at Tekanpur that produces tear gas and smoke grenades for all the police and paramilitary forces.

Other smaller paramilitary forces that are maintained include the following:

1. The Assam Rifles were established in 1866 as a frontier defense force for the Northeast. It is one of the oldest of the paramilitary forces and has its headquarters in Shillong. After independence, its main task has been to suppress uprisings among tribal people in the Northeast.

2. In 1962 the Indo-Tibetan Border Force was created to provide border security in the mountainous regions of the northern borders. It is mainly a mountaineering force.

3. The Railway Protective Force is assigned to protect and secure the national railroads.

4. The Central Industrial Security Force, which was set up in 1979, provides security for public sector enterprises and some government installations.

5. National Security Guards were established in 1984 as a paramilitary force. Members are used for internal security duties and combating terrorism.

Terrorism and Human Rights

Early instances of terrorism were experienced by the British in India during the nineteenth century. Politics and religious fanaticism combined briefly in the 1890s to create the problem of terrorism in British India. Located in the Sindh region, the Hur Brotherhood specifically resembled the earlier brotherhood of the assassins.

It is customary for Muslims to become followers (*murid*) of a spiritual leader who is known as *Pir*. One of the most important leaders in the nineteenth century was Pir Pagaro of Sindh. His followers were the fanatical sect of Hurs who were blindly devoted to his person. They committed violent crimes and maintained a close secret union within their brotherhood. The Hurs committed dacoities on such a scale that it can only be described as a war on society. This reign of terror could not be suppressed by all the normal methods. A novel method was employed to solve this problem.

The Hurs were proclaimed a criminal tribe, and their villages were constituted as settlements under the Criminal Tribes Act of 1871. The movements of the main inhabitants were restricted, and punitive police were permanently placed to supervise them and take roll call twice daily. There was a three-pronged approach—the incorrigible elders were segregated from the younger members of the tribe; the young were educated, and jobs were provided to the members of the tribe so that they could earn an honest living (Griffiths, 1971). During the 1940s and 1950s, a second Hur uprising occurred in Pakistan (Friedlander, 2004). The Hurs committed more than 200 violent crimes in six months and killed over 200 people in 1942. Martial law was imposed, and even aircraft were used to bring the situation under control. The problem was finally solved when the Hur leader was convicted and executed in 1943.

Current terrorism hotspots can be classified into two broad types: those of an extra-territorial nature and those that are indigenous. The Kashmir problem is one that goes back to the days of partition in 1947. This state was claimed by both India and Pakistan but is now practically occupied by both countries. The present insurgency in Indian-administered Jammu and Kashmir stems from the brutal, high-handed, and shortsighted policies of the Indian government. The other insurgencies are based on popular demands for social and economic justice by indigenous peoples. The federal government is viewed as being exploitative of the rights of local populations in, for example, Punjab, Assam, and Nagaland.

Most of these movements are handled by the federal government by means of special acts. The first in this series of acts was TADA (Terrorists and Disruptive Activities Prevention Act, 1985). When this act lapsed in 1995, it was replaced by POTA (Prevention of Terrorist Activities Act, 2002). There have been serious concerns voiced by human rights activists against these special acts. There are gross violations of human rights by the unfettered use of these acts against vulnerable and marginalized groups such as Sikhs, Muslims, and the Dalits. There have been many instances where the provisions of these acts have been abused by individuals or groups targeting political opponents and religious minorities (Das & Verma, 1998). Recently the state of Gujarat was admonished by the Supreme Court when Muslims were killed in riots all across that state and the provisions of the law were used to harass them (Dhillon, 2005).

Conclusion

The problems facing India today are similar to those faced during the early days of policing in the United States (Raghavan, 1999). In fact, India and the United States, in spite of the cultural and religious differences, have very similar problems: India, being a former British colony, is facing the problems faced by the United States during its political era of policing (1840–1930). During this era of the political spoils system, American policing was highly corrupt and politicized, and minorities were segregated and discriminated against. These problems are similar to some of those being faced by the Indian police, though some of the religious issues further complicate the problems. The Indian police are still operating under a legal and administrative apparatus that was designed to maintain order and hold on to the imperial possession that India was in 1850. The system is now being exposed for what it is and has become totally dysfunctional for a modern and democratic society. Local politicians have now replaced the British Raj as users of the police as an instrument for repressive control of the populace and to enrich themselves in all respects.

There have been recent rumblings against the established political elites, and the police apparatus is being mandated by the Supreme Court of India to be accountable to the people and not the politicians. It is also being asked to abide by the rule of law. In the case of *Prakash Singh v. Union of India* (2007), the court has now stepped into the arena of police reform. The court was highly critical of the police agencies and has begun to move in the direction of mandating certain minimum standards that the police have to meet. It calls for a courageous, fair minded, and farsighted leadership. As with the colonial police enterprise, it calls for solutions that address the core of the problems. Most of the problems facing the police are economic and political in nature. The modern police force of India is still operating under a colonial framework, where there was greater emphasis on order maintenance. A modern police force should be used to prevent and detect crime.

The Indian police were created after the Mutiny of 1857. Their main task was to maintain order and perpetuate the rule of the British over India (Das & Verma, 1998). The legal framework for policing was designed to protect the ruling elites and not to work for the benefit of the community (Dhillon, 2005). Some of the problems that are surfacing now are merely symptoms of a deeper malaise in the system. The goals and mission of the police will need to be reformulated in light of the enormous economic and social changes taking place in India. The reactive order maintenance model of policing needs to be replaced by one that is more proactive and preventive and has much more regard for citizens as customers and the police as service providers who have to treat the public with respect and dignity.

The solution may lie in experimenting with one of the other models that is employed in other parts of the world. India could borrow from one other former British colony—the United States—to solve some of the problems. The Indian system is midway between the political and the professional eras of American policing (Wrobleski & Hess, 2003). The Indian police could benefit from the community policing model so as to reduce the amount of political interference that presently hampers their potential. However, the police may need to move to a professional phase of policing so as to set up the necessary institutional framework and let it mature before a move toward community policing is made. Whether Indian police will move toward the professional or community era of policing is debatable; however it is certain that the present model is unsustainable.

References

Bayley, D. H. (1969). *The police and political development in India.* Princeton, NJ: Princeton University Press.

Bayley, D. H. (1983). The police and political order in India. *Asian Survey, 23*(4), 484–496.

Das, D., & Verma, A. (1998). The armed police in the British colonial tradition: The Indian perspective. *Policing: An International Journal of Police Strategies and Management, 21*(2,) 354–367.

Dhillon, K. S. (2005). *Police and politics in India—Colonial concepts, democratic compulsions: Indian police 1947–2002.* New Delhi: Manohar.

Friedlander, R. (2004). *Terrorism: Volume I. An historical overview.* Retrieved June 15, 2004, from http://web.syr.edu/~efbuitra/law%20school/Counter%20Terrorism/January%2020/historical_overview.pdf

Griffiths, P. (1971). *To guard my people. The history of the Indian police.* London: Ernest Benn.

Hakeem, F. (1998). From Sharia to mens rea: Legal transition to the Raj. *International Journal of Comparative and Applied Criminal Justice, 22*(2), 211–224.

Prakash Singh and others v. Union of India and others. Supreme Court of India. Writ Petition no. 310 of 1996 (Supreme Court of India, January 11, 2007).

Raghavan, R. K. (1999). *Policing a democracy: A comparative study of India and the U.S.* New Delhi: Manohar.

Ramaswami, P. N. (1951). *Magisterial and police guide* (Vol. I). Bombay: Ratanlal Dhirajlal and Thakore.

Rao, S. V. (1967). *Facets of crime in India.* New York: Allied.

Saha, B. P. (1990). *Indian police: Legacy and quest for formative role.* New York: Advent Books.

Sanghar, S. P. (1967). *Crime and punishment in Mughal India.* Delhi: Sterling.

Tobias, J. (1977). The British colonial police: An alternative police style. In P. J. Stead (Ed.), *Pioneers in policing, an anthology* (pp. 241–261). Montclair, NJ: Patterson Smith.

Verma, A. (1997). Maintaining law and order in India: An exercise in police discretion. *International Criminal Justice Review, 7*(1), 65–80.

Wrobleski, H. M., & Hess, K. M. (2003). *Introduction to law enforcement and criminal justice.* Belmont, CA: Wadsworth.

Further Reading

Anand, D. (2005). The violence of security: Hindu nationalism and the politics of representing 'the Muslim' as a danger. *The Round Table, 94*(379), 203–215.

Engineer, A. A. (2006). *Minorities and police in India.* Delhi: Eastern Book.

Mahajan, V. D. (1965). *Muslim rule in India.* Bombay: S. Chand.

Natarajan, M. (1996). Women police units in India: A new direction. *Police Studies: International Review of Police Development, 19*(2), 63–76.

Raghavan, R. K. (1989). *Indian police problems, planning and perspectives.* New Delhi: Manohar.

Raghavan, R. K. (2003). The Indian police: Problems and prospects. *Publius: The Journal of Federalism, 33*(4), 119–134.

Sarkar, J. (1967). *Mughal administration.* Calcutta: Orient.

Sharma, S. R. (1951). *Mughal government and administration.* Bombay: Hind Kitabs.

Thakur, R. (1993). Ayodhya and the politics of India's secularism: A double-standards discourse. *Asian Survey, 33*(7), 645–664.

Verma, A. (1999). Cultural roots of police corruption in India. *Policing: An International Journal of Police Strategies and Management, 22*(3), 264–279.

Verma, A. (2005). *The Indian police: A critical evaluation.* New Delhi: Regency.

Yasin, M. (1958). *A social history of Islamic India.* Lucknow: Upper India Publishing House.

8

Democratization of Policing

The Case of the Turkish Police

Ibrahim Cerrah

Turkey is a unitary state governed by the parliamentary democratic system. The Turkish Republic was founded on October 29, 1923, by Mustafa Kemal Atatürk. Its capital is Ankara. The citizens exercise their sovereignty directly by participating in elections and indirectly by means of authoritative structures. The structures that exercise the sovereignty are the legislative, executive, and judiciary branches of the Turkish government. The principle of separation of powers prevails among these three structures.

Turkey is divided into seven geographic regions. These are the Aegean Region, the Marmara Region, the Black Sea Region, the Eastern Anatolia Region, the Southeastern Anatolia Region, the Mediterranean Region, and Inner Anatolia Region. For administrative purposes, the country is divided into 81 provinces. Each province is also further divided into cities, towns, and municipalities. In the provinces, the central government is represented by a governor appointed by the central government. Each province has a capital city and a number of small towns. Towns are ruled by subgovernors. Subgovernors, who are under the authority of the respective provincial governor, are also appointed by the central government. Governors and subgovernors are all agents of central government and have little, if any, accountability to the local community. Ultimate power over officials belongs to the respective department at the central government. Finally, the respective ministers of these departments have the highest political control and authority over these institutions.

In addition to the officials appointed by the central government, the capital cities of provinces and towns all have elected municipal mayors and a local administration with very limited powers. Responsibility for maintenance of public services is divided between local and central government institutions. Local services, such as road maintenance, water supply, some public health services, and rubbish collection, are provided by local authorities. Other services, such as education, health care, and security are provided by the agents of central government. Unlike mayors who work under the democratic traditions seen in Western countries, elected mayors in Turkey have no formal authority over or participation in policing. Policing and security issues remain a central government task, as they are considered to be too important to be entrusted to local elected representatives.

Turkey's Ministry of Interior (MoI) has the formal mandate to guarantee "in practice" the full enjoyment of rights at the provincial and district levels through the powers and authority it vests in governors and district governors (Goldsmith & Cerrah, 2005). Governors and district governors, as MoI staff, are held responsible for the management and monitoring of the police and the Gendarmerie. Therefore, the police and the Gendarmerie do not fall under the elected mayor's authority. Mayors and other local elected representatives may develop informal relationships and cooperate with appointed police chiefs and the Gendarmerie, but there is no formal hierarchy between them.

Security services are also categorized into two groups: the civilian police for urban policing and the Gendarmerie for rural law enforcement. The civilian police are responsible only for policing urban areas, such as within the municipal boundaries of cities and towns. The Gendarmerie, which is part of the army, is legally responsible only for policing rural areas and villages. However, the Gendarmerie in recent years has maintained its jurisdiction at the expense of violating existing legislation. The Gendarmerie is still serving in some towns and cities, which in the past were small villages, but which have since grown and acquired town status. According to existing laws, these new towns should now fall under police jurisdiction. Furthermore, despite the fact that the Gendarmerie's jurisdiction is by existing law limited to rural areas, it has stations, military posts, military installations, and barracks in cities and towns all over the country. Today, Gendarmerie vehicles with armed soldiers patrol many of Turkey's cities.

Modern Turkey has been ruled by a parliamentary democracy since 1946. It is a multiparty system with a unicameral legislative parliament. However, despite this experience of democracy, Turkey has a highly centralized and authoritarian administration system. The administrative system is overly centralized and lacks essential community participation at a local level. The prominent role of the military in political and public life in Turkey is a well-known phenomenon. Since the establishment of modern Turkey, the military has seized power on three occasions and has exerted influence on the democratic life of the country. Some have described this as a case of "militarized democracy," drawing an analogy to some Latin American states. However, the European Union (EU) has defined a number of political, social, and economic criteria as part of its requirements for Turkey to join the union. In particular, the EU has demanded a number of political reforms from Turkey.

One critical and problematic issue within this context is the role and place of the military in Turkish political, social, and even economic life. As part of this reform process, the structure and functioning of the National Security Council (NSC) has recently been amended (2003), and there have been other legislative and administrative reforms. All of these are expected to have positive impacts on the democratization of the country.

But, the influence of the military is not limited to the NSC, although it exerts power over the day-to-day running of the government and civic life in Turkey. The power legally held—or in some cases de facto assumed—by the Gendarmerie, in terms of providing internal security services, is much more important. Although the current legislation was intended to allow the Gendarmerie to provide security services in rural areas only, it extends its power to urban areas. This is partly due to ambiguities in the law with respect to definitions of the boundaries of rural and urban areas and partly because of the army's deliberate insistence on maintaining a prominent role in the country. Currently, the Gendarmerie is deployed in the centers of cities, which are outside its legally and legitimately defined jurisdiction. This practice is also in contradiction with principles of internal security services of modern countries. The current behavior of the Gendarmerie, which operates under the authority of the military command without any political accountability or community participation, cannot be reconciled with the principles of the rule of law or with those of democratic accountability.

The police and the military (Gendarmerie) are two different and separate professions, and it is difficult for one to perform the other's functions and duties adequately. The entire Gendarmerie personnel are members of the military. However, an overwhelming majority of them are noncommissioned soldiers performing military services with no professionalism. The training and militarized mentality of Gendarmerie personnel is neither sufficient nor suitable for providing internal security services in a democratic society.

Community participation on a local level is a crucial element in democratic policing in Turkey. The central issues with the present policing system and the Gendarmerie should be about bringing accountability and community participation into policing. It is apparent that, with its highly centralized organizational structure, the so-called civilian Turkish police force lacks community participation and is far from being democratic. The Gendarmerie as a military institution will be a major concern regarding the democratization of the policing services in Turkey. Judging from the army's interference with democratically elected governments in Turkey in the form of a military coup and military interventions, the army has historically had problematic relations with politicians. The army sees itself as above the elected government and is not comfortable being controlled by central and local officials. Army officers, who are not at ease with being controlled by the central government, will certainly not be comfortable with being under the control of locally elected officials. Therefore, the Gendarmerie, as an agent of the army, serving as an internal security service, clearly raises more questions about the legitimacy of the regime.

History of Military Intervention in Government

Turkey's experience with democracy dates back to 1946. However, since then Turkish democracy has been interrupted by frequent military interventions. Between 1946 and 1997, Turkey experienced several military interventions in different forms, and democratically elected governments were either overthrown or forced to resign from power.

The level and degree of civilian control over the military has turned into an important aspect of the definition of contemporary democracy. Civilian-military relations have been one of the problems of democratic governance in Turkey (Cizre, 2004). The Turkish armed forces have enjoyed wide-ranging political autonomy, especially since the 1960s. "The political autonomy of the military is defined as the ability of the military to go above and beyond the constitutional authority of democratically elected government on matters pertaining to its institutional properties, political goals and influences" (David Pion-Berlin, 1992, cited in Cizre, 2000). The Turkish armed forces with "its self-identified role as the ultimate custodian of the western, secular and modern parameters of the regime and of the unity and integrity of the nation itself" (Cizre, 2000, p. 3) have historically been keen to maintain their above-politics position. As a result, military-civilian relations have always been a subject that raises tensions in the Turkish democracy. Turkey has been struggling with the EU requirements on reducing the political role of the military. The armed forces still retain a de facto and de jure veto power over a wide range of domestic and international issues, which in western democracies would be considered purely political not military issues, but the process of undermining their role in the political realm on issues that should be delegated to constitutionally elected civilian bodies is also making some headway.

The first military coup took place in 1960, 14 years after Turkey's first democratic elections. Following intensive antigovernment student protests, the military overthrew the very popular government from power. The prime minister of that time and two other very popular ministers were put on trial and sentenced to death. The second military intervention took place in 1971. This time, the democratically elected government was forced to resign by the military. Turkey's third experience with military intervention was another military coup in 1980. This time there was a coalition government in power. The prime minister and his deputies were first imprisoned and later released. However, they were banned from politics for some time after this. The last military intervention, the so-called postmodern coup, took place in 1997 when a democratically elected coalition government was again forced to resign by the military.

After the 1960 and 1980 military coups, the army not only overthrew the democratically elected governments but also took power into its hands. The military, who accused governments of violating the constitution, changed the constitution and banned the overthrown political parties from politics. Generals played a key role in the preparation of a new constitution.

They were also very active in establishing the new political parties, and some of them even got involved in politics. However, in the first free elections held after each military coup and intervention, the people chose and indeed brought back to power almost the same people who were overthrown by the army.

For instance, after the execution of the Adnan Menderes, who was prime minister in the years between 1950 and 1960, Süleyman Demirel, who has the same political roots, came to power in 1961 as the successor of Menderes. Demirel was also removed from power twice, first in 1971 by a military intervention and second in 1980 by a military coup. After the 1980 military coup, Demirel and his deputies were banned from politics, but the ban was lifted by a referendum held by the first elected government after the coup. Later Demirel became prime minister and was finally elected by the Turkish Grand National Assembly (TGNA) as the president of Turkey, a position he held for seven years.

The most recent example is the latest military intervention, which took place in 1997 and removed the elected government from power. The second election after this intervention was held in 2002, and it resulted in the overwhelming victory of R. T. Erdoğan, who was also earlier banned from politics and even served a prison sentence for reading a poem. The poem, which was considered to be provocative, was read in a public meeting almost 10 years before his conviction. As a victim of military intervention, Erdoğan, who is presently serving as prime minister of Turkey, and his government have enacted a number of laws and made revolutionary changes in the field of human rights and civil liberties.

_____ Corruption History: Major Scandals and Incidents

Turkey has a very corrupt political past. The credibility of politicians has over the years been damaged by numerous political scandals. This is one of the factors that the army uses as a pretext for their military interventions. Politicians are relentlessly blamed and criticized by the media and each other. Army generals, who enjoy a military immunity, also criticize the politicians in general and the ruling government in particular for corruption. Although the army interferes with a number of nonmilitary services such as education and the economy, it enjoys an integrity based on unquestionable immunity. Politicians have had to be very cautious about their relations with the army. A number of writers and journalists have served prison sentences for criticizing the army. Because of its extensive immunity, the army remains the only "perfect" institution in Turkey. Army members believe that, because they constitute the only uncorrupt institution in Turkey, their job, even their duty, is to put things right when corrupt politicians mess things up.

There was a big rise in corruption and scandals following the economic growth experienced under the Ozal government in the 1980s. Scandals surrounded politicians, businessmen, and high-level bureaucrats. Political scandals have sometimes involved senior police officials in some cities such as Istanbul, Ankara, Izmir, and Bursa. A number of senior police officers were fired from the force for their corrupt practices. Sometimes there have been instances of police officers forming gangs and acting together. In recent years, high-tech surveillance technology has been abused by some intelligence officers working for their own personal benefit. Some politicians' and bureaucrats' telephone conversations were tapped and recorded and later used against them to obtain promotions and economic benefits for the intelligence officers. For instance, a scandal called "tele-ear" (*tele-kulak* in Turkish) took place in Ankara in the late 1990s. The police commissioner of Ankara and a number of police chiefs were interrogated and later removed from their positions.

Crime Trends and Rates

The generally held belief is that crime rates in Turkey have always been low compared to those in Western countries. However, as crime figures are not systematically collected, it is difficult, if not impossible, to identify crime rates and trends in Turkey. Crime statistics are not kept on a national basis, and in some years no systematic data have been collected for comparison with other years. It has also been believed that this lower crime rate was partly due to the influence of religion and Turkish family life on the community. However, this argument seems to be an illusion, as it is not supported by any sound statistics collected in this field.

The Department of Public Order collects statistics about crimes, including those against people and property (see Figure 8.1). In general, there has been a significant increase in almost all crime categories between 1994 and 2004. A noticeable increase recorded after 1995 is believed to have been the result of a domestic migration from the east to the western parts of Turkey, due to the significant economic effects of the First Gulf War. However, it is again difficult to rely on these statistics because of the frequent changes in the ways in which the figures are reported and recorded.

Influence and History of Organized Crime

Since the 1970s, Turkey has experienced an increase in internal immigration from rural areas to big cities. Immigrant communities have had to cope with social and economic hardships and have faced difficulties in urban life. They have tried to overcome these problems and survive by maintaining their close family and community ties. In rural life communal and familial solidarity often required the use of violence against outsiders. This type of solidarity has served as a catalyst for early organized criminal groups. Communal gangs, which were not directly antiestablishment, were at first not seen as a

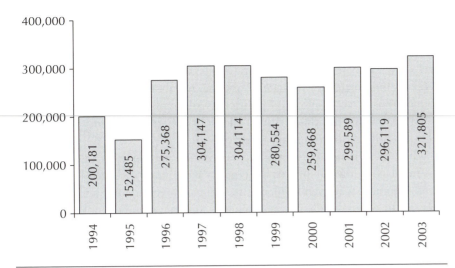

Figure 8.1   Crimes Committed Against People, Excluding Terrorism, 1994–2004

major threat to the establishment. Some of these groups, who had proestablishment political elements, even enjoyed governmental and communal tolerance, if not support, at a time when antiestablishment Marxist terrorist activities were increasing. Some members of these groups, it is argued, were illegally deployed by the state security forces in fighting against subversive terrorist groups such as the Armenian Secret Army for the Liberation of Armenia (ASALA) and Partiya Karkaren Kurdistan (PKK, or Kurdistan Workers Party). (See the section on terrorism at the end of this chapter.)

The dramatic increase in organized crime also has a correlation with the expansion of the free market economy in the 1980s. The free market economy brought a number of legitimate and illegitimate opportunities. Turkey, being a bridge between the East and the Western world, offered illegitimate business opportunities to organized crime gangs, whose activities including human trafficking and trade in illegal weapons and drugs. The tourism sector also experienced rapid growth, and a number of casinos were built. Gambling became a social issue. While the economy was flourishing, some businesses were experiencing financial hardship and difficulties in paying their bills. An illegal sector emerged at the same time as legal businesses. Illegally earned money has to be legalized, so money laundering developed.

On the other hand, as a transit country for illegal smuggling and bidirectional drug trafficking, Turkey has always been subject to massive money laundering schemes. In 1996, when the amount of money laundered in Turkey peaked to 5 percent of the total amount laundered globally, the Turkish parliament enacted an Anti–Money Laundering Law (law number 4208). Although this law was recently written, it has some huge gaps. Instead of generalizing criminal activities, as legislation in Western nations does, this law lists those specific crimes considered to be money-laundering activities. Because of such definitions, many organized criminals simply improved their political connections and acquired political protection and immunity. As a result, traditional organized crime was promoted to the level of white collar crime. Politicians involved in this white collar crime have included prime ministers and a number of cabinet ministers. Connections of very high-level politicians and mafia leaders exposed by the media have eroded public trust in the political structure, and people have begun to talk about a military intervention.

While these major corruption cases were taking place, the Turkish army was involved in the running of the country at an unprecedented level. In fact, the government was even formed at the army's direction after a military intervention. In other words, all these major economic scandals took place at an unprecedented level while the army was involved in running the country. Corruption scandals directly discredited the politicians, while the army, despite its involvement in every aspect of civic life in Turkey, enjoyed an unquestionable immunity. The amount of money involved in white collar crime while the army took a dominant role in government reached tens of billions of dollars and brought the country to the point of bankruptcy. A new term, "bank hosing" was coined to explain the extent of the economic corruption.

For instance, some white collar criminals bought private banks or established new ones and collected money from the people. The capital was then "hosed," or used illegally, and the banks were then declared bankrupt. The money hosed by corrupt private bank owners had to be compensated by the state, as all capital was under state guarantee. Between the years of 1997 and 2002, a number of private and public banks went bankrupt, and the loss had to be covered by the state and the people.

These corruption cases, coupled with a major earthquake in 1999, caused the biggest economic crisis in the history of the Republic of Turkey. An Anti–Organized Crime Law (4422) was enacted in 1999 in order to neutralize such criminal organizations and their threatening links among politicians and government officials. However the strong connections with politicians and the army made the law inefficient and not applicable to white collar criminals. As a result, the public lost trust and confidence in politicians, and the 2002 general election caused a total cleansing of the four traditional political parties (three of which were running the government in a coalition and one of which was the opposition party). In the election, two brand new political parties shared almost 70 percent of all votes, and a new cabinet was established by a single party, the Justice and Development Party, for the first time in 15 years. As soon as this government took power, the U.S.-Iraq war crisis started, and the new government has had to struggle to alleviate the problem for Turkey.

Organized crime in Turkey usually has two major sources: one is the residue of the ideological movements that were involved in the military coup of 1980, and the other is groups with ethnic or communal connections. The first type of organized crime activities can be traced back to the right wing (Ülkücü) and left wing movements. Members of the Ülkücü movement claim that they defended the country against rebellious assaults before the 1980 military coup. A number of them have spent considerable time in prison. After they were released from prison, the majority of them chose to lead decent lives and became businessmen or politicians. However, a large number, who also have criminal records, have been exploited by existing mafia groups, while others have gone on to establish their own organizations and become mafia bosses.

In the second type of organized crime, there are strong ethnic and communal ties. Under this category two different groups can be seen. On the one hand there are mafia groups and families who are called *Laz* or *Karadenizli* (people of the Black Sea region), as they originally come from the part of Turkey near the Black Sea. Members of these groups mainly deal with political and economic corruption. They threaten people and cover checks that might otherwise go unpaid, for a fee. They also deal with real-property crimes, prostitution, gambling, money laundering, and trafficking in drugs and firearms.

On the other hand, there are youth gangs who commit crimes that reflect their community solidarity. In the late 1970s, Turkey experienced a severe economic decline. This gave rise to a black market and created so-called small "father" (*baba*) figures on a local basis. These modern Robin Hoods would deliver social justice by taking from the rich and powerful and giving to the poor and the weak. As the country's economy began flourishing in the 1980s, the babas and their men evolved into big mafia bosses and organized crime on a national level. Youth living in violent inner city areas of Istanbul, such as Kasımpaşa and Karagümrük, formed youth gangs around the local babas.

This type of organized crime was not entirely free from communal and ideological ties. While some babas' organizations had communal and ethnic ingredients, others had right wing or left wing ideological motives. Kurdish mafia groups were an example of the former. The Kurdish community, which has relatively strong communal ties in rural areas, carried these ties with them to big cities. The Kurds migrated to big cities because of economic decline and the PKK terror, and they live mainly in inner city areas where proper housing and job opportunities are minimal. Some of these Kurdish populations engaged in organized crime as a form of maintaining continuity of communal ties. Communal bonds, which can be a source of cooperation and solidarity, sometimes turn out to be a source of cooperation in committing crime.

The Turkish Deep State

Although the issue of organized crime has a very long history in Turkey, a road accident on November 3, 1996, in Susurluk, a small township in northwestern Turkey, revealed very complex mafia relations and sparked a series of fruitless investigations. The car involved in the accident belonged to a member of parliament. Among the passengers were a member of parliament, a young woman model, a well-known police chief, and a fugitive. All the passengers, except the member of parliament, died in the accident. Some automatic rifles were also found in the car. The fugitive in question was involved in right wing student movements before the 1980 military coup. His name was involved in some murder cases. He had been missing for 16 years, since the 1980 military coup. He had a fake identity and a green passport, which is only given to public servants with a very high status.

This accident was instrumental in awakening the public's consciousness to the reality of a criminal triangle of mafia bosses, politicians, and some members of the security forces. This accident played an important role in drawing attention to complex organized crime activities that reached right up to ministers and prime ministers and generals in the army. A joint parliamentary commission was established to investigate the case, but there was no satisfactory result. A number of retired and serving generals, enjoying military immunity, did not even bother to come to the commission's hearings to give testimony. This was only the tip of the iceberg. A number of politicians and state officials were involved in this case. The term "deep state" (*derin devlet*) was coined, referring to an illegal state within the state using state authority and its resources to its own ends. A proper investigation could not be conducted, and the extent of this illegal deep state within the state could not be identified. A number of officials, whose names were linked with this scandal, were later cleared, and some of them even became involved in politics. Police operations carried out against organized crime have proved that all of these groups have some insiders and collaborators within state institutions, mainly political institutions, the army, and the police.

Following the notorious Susurluk accident in 1996, the deep state became the center of debate. A Parliamentary Investigation Committee was established to investigate the issue. The committee contacted certain political figures, civilian and military bureaucrats, who were considered to be knowledgeable about, if not having connections within, the deep state. They were not very cooperative, and nothing important came out of this parliamentary investigation. The deep state remained anonymous and untouched. While some individuals kept writing about the deep state in the mass media, its existence was not officially acknowledged.

Yet, everything suddenly changed after a well-known journalist, Yavuz Donat, conducted a series of interviews with Kenan Evren and Süleyman Demirel, two former presidents, and Bülent Ecevit, a former prime minister (Donat, 2005). All parties acknowledged that a deep state, an unidentified state within the legitimate state structure, was functioning in Turkey. However, interestingly enough, Demirel, in his interview, purposefully stated that the deep state was the military. On the one hand, while his insistence created an impression that he was trying to deflect attention from the real deep state, he was, on the other hand, trying to legitimize an illegal power structure by associating it with the very powerful Turkish armed forces.

The Turkish army neither denied nor confirmed Demirel's claims. It was, however, widely believed that the Gendarmerie, which is a part of the Turkish army, had established, without legislation, an operational unit called the Gendarmerie Intelligence and Antiterrorism (JITEM) to fight against terrorism and other unspecified threats. Confusing and conflicting arguments were made regarding the existence of the JITEM. Some Gendarmerie generals claimed that it was once established at a crucial time but disbanded after completing its mission. Others argued that such an organization never existed ("Varligi tartişilan," 2004; "Veli Küçük," 2004). Some claim that JITEM, as an illegal organ within the army, was used as a subcontractor by the deep state to commit assassinations. A number of unsolved murder cases, including the ones committed by the PKK against its members, were claimed to be the work of the JITEM. Subsequently, JITEM, which allegedly is responsible for many illegal acts, has not been officially endorsed or mandated by the criminal justice system. Finally, the chief public prosecutor for Diyarbakir province, where some unsolved murder cases took place, stated that "JITEM is an illegal organization allegedly operating on behalf of the state" ("İşte JITEM'in," n.d.).

Finally, the so-called deep state is also mentioned in the European parliament's progress report on Turkey. The report states, "In Turkey there are powerful forces at work in the bureaucracy, the army and the judiciary (the 'deep state') which resist reforms and their implementation" (European Parliament, 2003, p. 13).

Public Support for Government and Law Enforcement

Despite its highly centralized and authoritarian administrative system, the Turkish government enjoys an inherited deference from its subjects. However, public support enjoyed by the government in general and security forces in particular seems to be reminiscent of traditionally held deference to the state rather than a benefit that has been earned by the ruling governments. A low level of participation on the part of the people may also be a factor for the people's support of the government. The people have traditionally been used to accepting whatever is offered by the state. For the people, the state always knows what is best for them.

The army and the police are among the most popular institutions in Turkey. Public support for the police also bears the traces of this inherited obedience. Despite the fact that the people do not approve of military interventions, the army is the most respected and popular institution in Turkey. This is partly because the Turkish people, whose religion is overwhelmingly

Muslim, see the army as a holy institution above criticism. The second factor is that, because it is risky to criticize the army explicitly or implicitly, the army is able to maintain credibility.

Use of Force by the Turkish Police

The Turkish police force has, since its inception, been a fully armed paramilitary force (Aydin, 1997). All police officers receive basic firearms training during their preservice training. They also receive refreshment training once or twice a year in order to maintain and develop their shooting skills. Every single police officer, including the ones who are working at desk duties, is issued a personal weapon, usually a handgun. Until the mid-1980s, the Turkish police were armed only with traditional weapons. However, the incidence of coercive policing in Turkey is currently increasing in the form of heavily armed police units. There is also an increase in the number of powerful weapons and armored vehicles available to the police. As a response to an increase in PKK terror campaigns, starting in the mid-1980s, the police have been given more extended powers and weapons. Old handguns have been replaced with new and more powerful ones, and a new, military-style police department, Special Operations, has been set up (Aydin, 2003). The Special Operations department includes Special Operation Teams (SOT), similar to the Special Weapons and Tactics (SWAT) teams in the United States and the Special Air Services (SAS) in the UK. SOTs are equipped with more powerful weapons and armored vehicles than other polices forces, and they also receive very sophisticated antiterrorist training.

The use of force in traditional police tasks is an individual decision left to the discretion of an individual officer in violent crowd events. The officer in charge of the riot police team decides, depending on the circumstances, the level of force to be used. In situations where the use of force is not clearly defined by the law or regulations, the officer on duty has to ask for a decision from the commander in charge and act according to the order given.

Legal Context for Search and Seizure

The police have the power to stop and search any individual in cases where they have reasonable grounds for suspecting that the individual has illegal articles or something made or adapted for use in connection with an offense against the police officer in question or against his vehicle. In addition, the police have the power to enter premises and conduct searches, although a police officer cannot perform a search without written authority from a supervisory body.

The police have the authority to search premises and individuals under different levels of supervision. Under the existing law, searches can be conducted for judicial and administrative purposes. For judicial searches, in principle, the supervising authority is a justice of the peace, and this judge must issue a search warrant. But in cases of great urgency, where there is reason to believe that the evidence or person suspected will disappear during the time application is made to the judge, the authority for a search can be given by a senior police officer or a public prosecutor. For administrative searches and in urgent cases, a judge still has the authority to issue a search warrant, but the police officer may instead go to the head of the police of the province or county to authorize a search. In any case, the written order of the person who authorizes the search must be submitted to a judge within 24 hours after the search. In cases where the search order is not approved by the judge, the search is declared null and void (Eryılmaz, 2003).

Where the police inquiries are being made under the Anti-Terror Act, an application for a warrant has to be made to the State Security Court judge. An application to the judge must indicate how the evidence or person in question is related to the inquiry. An order may be made by a judge, public prosecutor, or senior police officer, but he or she has to be satisfied that there are reasonable grounds for thinking that the items or individuals named in the search warrant will be found at the premises indicated. An order may be given to obtain evidence that is expected to be of substantial value in identifying those responsible or in finding the individuals responsible for the crime committed. Such an order requires the person to whom it was directed to allow the police to look at the items covered by the order. In cases where the person in question refuses to comply with the order, the police have the right to use force to conduct the search.

The order should state (1) the name of the person suspected or the item to be found (2), the nature of the offense to which the evidence is thought to relate, (3) the grounds for suspecting that the evidence is on the premises or on the individual, and (4) the address of the premises. A search must not go beyond what is reasonably required to discover the evidence in question. No general search is permitted. The police have the power to enter and search premises to execute a warrant of arrest in connection with or arising out of criminal proceedings or to recapture someone unlawfully at large that the police are pursuing. Without judicial authority, the police may not search the home of a person taken into custody for evidence connected with the crime for which the person has been arrested. On the other hand, a search of the arrested person's premises is permitted in cases where the arrest is conducted at the premises of the suspect and where there are reasonable grounds for suspicion that relevant evidence might be found there.

The police may seize anything they find that is or that they reasonably believe to be covered by the warrant. The police are also permitted to seize items found incidentally if they provide evidence of any other offense. Persons who have illegal items or evidence on their bodies, in their vehicles, or on their premises may be arrested and detained for interrogation.

Protections for Arrested Persons

The police may arrest anyone without a warrant if the person in question is in the act of committing an offense or anyone about whom they have reasonable grounds to suspect (high degree of probability) of committing an offense. Persons who have been arrested may be searched to find out if there are articles on them that are a danger to themselves or others or that provide evidence of a suspected crime.

Arrested suspects must be informed about their rights as soon as possible. They have the right (1) to learn the grounds for their arrest, (2) to have a relative informed of the arrest and detention without delay, (3) to have the benefit of free advice of a lawyer before and during interrogation, and (4) to remain silent. However, during detention, arrested individuals have no right to demand to have visits, to make phone calls, or to send letters. Arrested individuals must be taken to a police station promptly after their arrest unless their presence is needed elsewhere in the interests of the investigation. Suspects may not be detained for more than 24 hours after they are arrested. In cases where the number of suspects is more than two for the crime under investigation, and the difficulties of the investigation require the collection of further evidence, the public prosecutor may extend the detention to up to 96 hours. The detention may not be authorized for more than 96 hours, after which time the suspect must be brought before a judge for charging.

During detention, fingerprints of suspects may be taken, and they may also be photographed, if photographs and fingerprints will prove or disprove their involvement in a criminal offense and will be necessary to ascertain the identity of the suspect. In any 24-hour period, suspects must have a reasonable period of rest during which they are free from questioning or travel. There is no rule as to the maximum length of an interview, but it is accepted that there must be breaks for meals and refreshments. No one may be subjected to penalty or treatment incompatible with human dignity. The freedom of suspects to determine and exercise their will may not be impaired by ill treatment, fatigue, physical interference or force, the administration of medicines, torture, deception, hypnosis, or different devices. The threat of consequences or the promise of an advantage not permitted or provided by law are prohibited. The prohibitions apply even if the accused person consents to them. Statements that are obtained in violation of these provisions may not be used as evidence, even if the suspect agrees to their use.

Organizational Structure and Issues _____

Although no single and universally accepted classification of the police has been developed, police organizations can broadly be classified as coercive or consensus. While terms such as *military*, *para-military*, and *quasi-military* policing are interchangeably used as different versions of coercive policing, democratic policing and its derivative community policing can be seen as the reflection of consensus policing. The Turkish National Police (TNP), as a national force having a highly centralized organizational structure, falls within the category of military policing and the philosophy of policing as force rather than service.

Turkey has a highly centralized administrative system. Institutions are organized nationally and have their headquarters in the capital, Ankara. Every organization, including the police, also has provincial subheadquarters. The head of police in a province is called director of security or police chief and is appointed by the interior minister as the representative of the central government. The police chief is accountable to the interior minister through its local representative, the governor.

The General Directorate of Security

The General Directorate of Security has several departments and subunits that are directly controlled by the general director. These include the following:

- General Directorate
- Inspection Board
- Division of Press, Protocol, and Public Relations
- Police Academy
- Department of Intelligence
- Expert Chiefs of Police for Research, Planning, and Coordination
- Department of Special Operations
- Department of Legal Counsel
- Civil Defense Experts Office

The general director is the only police chief in the country holding a five-star badge. Five deputies who have the second-highest position—four-star police chief—assist the general director with the administration of 24 departments operating within the boundaries of their fields of interest. The departments include the following:

1. Research, Planning, and Coordination

2. Administrative and Financial Affairs

3. Maintenance and Supply

4. Construction and Real Estate

5. Archive and Documentation

6. Communication

7. Aviation

8. Counter Smuggling and Organized Crime

9. Public Order

10. Road Traffic

11. Information Technologies

12. Central Command and Control

13. Foreigners

14. Border and Immigration

15. Training

16. Security

17. Health Services

18. Personnel Affairs

19. Counter Terrorism and Operation

20. Criminal Police Laboratories

21. Interpol

22. Safeguard

23. Foreign Relations

24. Social Services

A four-star police chief also heads each department. They are responsible for administering the services within their department and coordinating the services in the provinces operating in their respective fields.

Provincial Police Forces

Each province has its own provincial police headquarters. However, from the chief to the line officers, all of the appointments are made by the central government. The national headquarters in Ankara determines all issues pertaining to personnel, pay, training, appointments, inspection, and promotion. Local governments have no say or control over policing policies or practices. The mayor of a city or a town does not have any authority or formal involvement with police services. Hence, the highly centralized Turkish administrative system does not allow any formal local participation or involvement in policing.

The provincial forces have copied the departmental structure of the national police headquarters. However, a unit that has the status of a department at the national level is reduced to a branch in the provinces. For instance, the provincial counterpart to the national Department of Personnel is called the Branch of Personnel. Each branch of the provincial police force functions in coordination with its counterpart or corresponding department within the national headquarters.

Civilian Oversight

Presently there are no systematic civilian oversight mechanisms on policing policy and practices in Turkey. The quality of police performance is monitored only by senior police officers at different levels of supervisory positions, and it is they to whom any accusations about the violation of police powers are taken. If the allegations are very serious, inspectors are appointed from the Inspection Board of national police headquarters to conduct an investigation. If the accusations involve senior police officers, some civilian inspectors are appointed from the Ministry of the Interior to conduct an investigation. These oversight and inspection mechanisms are all governmental and do not include any NGO element. There is no NGO type of civilian oversight institution on a local or national level (Goldsmith & Cerrah, 2005). Members of the public are not allowed to visit and monitor police stations and cells as lay visitors. Only the close relatives of the detainees are allowed to visit the people who are detained or are under arrest. Conditions of the police cells and the detainees are not monitored by a lay visitor, a member of the civilian board, or a member of an NGO. The only civilians who are allowed to see the detainees, besides their relatives, are their defense lawyers and the public prosecutor who is in charge of the investigations.

The civilian oversight of the police and Gendarmerie is limited to governors in cities and subgovernors in towns. Yet, the capacity of governors and subgovernors to control the security personnel is limited by institutional capacity shortcomings; they have limited access to decision-making support or the knowledge required for sound decision making. Good governance mechanisms that should underpin this process of decision making in critical security issues are limited as well. The provincial units within and outside each governor's headquarters are not equipped to support the governor and district governor in security sector oversight. Therefore there is a need for Turkey to adopt sector approaches to civilian oversight of the security sector. Turkey's administrative system at the provincial and district levels must also build the appropriate systems of accountability within the context of good governance (Goldsmith & Cerrah, 2005).

The existing administrative system is not at ease with civilian oversight and public scrutiny. The nature of the relationships between the state and members of the public is not based on mutual trust. Despite the so-called democratic system, the highly centralized administrative structure is not transparent enough and open to public scrutiny. Although existing legislation acknowledges universal principles of the rule of law and innocence until guilt is proven, there are some common practices that contradict these principles. For instance, a background check is a standard procedure for every job application in the civil service. However, in addition to the background check carried out by the respective institutions, individuals themselves are also required to produce a "criminal record paper" as a part of their standard application documents. Not only ordinary citizens, but even members of the security forces are sometimes required by law to obtain and produce such a paper as a standard document when they apply to obtain a driver's license, to enroll at a university, and so forth. In other words, citizens are required to prove that they are innocent by submitting a criminal record document. This implies that all citizens are assumed to be criminals or potential criminals until they prove their innocence. This can be seen as a direct and total violation of the principle of assumed innocence.

Complaint Procedures

Civil servants enjoy a traditionally high degree of trust by the state, and hence a de facto exemption when they are challenged or accused by members of a civilian population. They are always right until they are proven to be wrong. With this approach it is usually difficult, if not impossible, to prove that a civil servant is or can be wrong. Again, this discrimination is not based on any written legislation but rather on de facto practices.

A civilian who is not happy with police practices has a choice of complaint procedures. Technically a complaint can be made to a police station, to provincial or national police headquarters, or to the offices of provincial governors or subgovernors, the public prosecutor, or even the minister of the interior. The most commonly used procedure is to make such complaints to the public prosecutor. A public prosecutor is a civilian lawyer and a member of the Ministry of Justice, not the Ministry of Interior. However, he or she is in charge of the police when conducting investigations. Regardless of the agency, any complaints against the police end up with the public prosecutor where a mindset of civil servant solidarity prevails. The public prosecutor, who is also in charge of the police and to some extent a working partner, decides whether to start an investigation or to drop the case. So a public servant is investigated by another public servant without any public involvement in the complaint and evaluation procedure.

In 2001 the Human Rights Presidency was established within the Prime Minister's office "to monitor the implementation of regulations related to human rights," and "to examine and investigate human rights violation claims" (Prime Ministry, Human Rights Presidency, 2004), mainly those committed by law enforcement personnel as well as other civil servants. The human rights presidency has human rights province boards in 81 provinces and human rights district boards in 850 townships. Provincial governors and subgovernors, who are also in charge of the law enforcement agencies such as the police and the Gendarmerie, serve as the chairpersons of the human right boards.

Internal Accountability Mechanisms

Inspectors of the MoI and police inspectors who are members of the Inspection Board investigate criminal and disciplinary cases and handle complaints against police officers. Decisions are made by the provincial or central disciplinary boards, which are composed of police chiefs and some civilian officials. Administrative functions of the police are monitored by the governors and subgovernors, whereas the judicial functions are controlled and monitored by the public prosecutors. Police officials can be dismissed from their organizations owing to disciplinary, corruption, or criminal causes by the decisions of the disciplinary boards. Appeals can be made to the administrative courts.

Turkish police are not usually prepared to acknowledge the existence of systematic police malpractice and abuse of power. Police misconduct and violations are seen only as a personal deviation of officers involved rather than being an organizational responsibility to be dealt with. The lack of a systematic anticorruption policy and mechanisms encourage the corrupt officers to carry on their corrupt practices. In some cases police corruption and malpractices are handled with unofficial disciplinary punishments such as verbal reprimands or the transfer of an officer to a lower and less popular position. If a case of police corruption or abuse of police power is too visible or is covered by the media, a disciplinary and criminal investigation is inevitable, depending on the seriousness of the violation. Police organizations, like many other civil service organizations in Turkey, tend to cover up and overlook minor and less serious police malpractices. The idea that lies behind this state of affairs is that the police already have too many enemies, so "we should shield our own."

Recruitment, Selection, Ranks, and Training of Police Officers

As a highly centralized national police force, the TNP also has a centralized police selection and training system. The selection is made by ad hoc committees formed mainly by police chiefs, a medical doctor, and a physical fitness instructor. Training was revised and major changes were introduced at the end of 2001. Currently, there are four different levels of pre-service police training institutions in Turkey. These include the Police College (of which there is only one in the country), 20 Police Schools at the two-year college level, the Faculty of Security Sciences (a four-year, university-level training program), and the Institute for Security Sciences (at the graduate-school level). There are slightly different application procedures for each institution. However, the basic and common criterion is that police applicants must be Turkish citizens.

All these institutions, with the exception of the Police College, operate under the National Police Academy. (Because the Police College is not a university-level educational institution, it operates under the national headquarters of the TNP.) The Police Academy is a university operating as an umbrella institution. Either a police chief with at least a master's degree or a civilian faculty professor can be appointed as the president of the academy.

Police Training Institutions

Police College: Training at the High School Level

The Police College is a four-year high school–level training institution. There is only one Police College, located in Ankara. Students of the college are between the ages of 13 and 17 and must pass a national entry exam to gain admittance. The Police College is a boarding school, and the curriculum is delivered by correspondence from other public high schools and does not include any police-oriented instruction. Police-related training is limited to "occupational spirit and marching" training provided by staff officers. Students wear a student uniform and obey strict rules. They are familiarized with the hierarchical structure of policing, as they are required to respect their civilian teachers and senior students. Concurrently the Police High School provides a very early occupational socialization. Students who graduate from this school are directly enrolled in an undergraduate program of the Faculty of Security Science. If they earn a place, they can attend a civilian university with the support of the police, which is in the interest of the police organization.

Police Schools: Two-Year College Level

The second level of police training institutions is Police Schools. Only civilian high school graduates are admitted to the Police Schools. There are 20 Police Schools in Turkey, and they are located on a regional basis. Recruits are admitted based on the grades they receive on a general university entry exam. Once accepted, the cadets receive a two-year, mostly classroom-based, theoretical education in a boarding school environment. This initial education and training period is also an essential part of police occupational socialization and an introduction to police culture. Cadets undertake one month of supervised field experience during the summer. Students who successfully complete their studies at a Police School serve as rank and file officers throughout their careers, unless they pass promotional examinations.

Faculty of Security Sciences: University Level

The third provider of training is the Faculty of Security Sciences, which functions under the umbrella of the Police Academy. There are two different sources for students who attend this training; one is the Police College, and the other is civilian high schools. Students who originate from the Police College are directly admitted, whereas cadets from a civilian high school background need to achieve a very high grade in the general university entry exam to be accepted.

Like the Police College and Police Schools, the Faculty of Security Sciences is a boarding training institution. Cadets from both the Police College and civilian high school background receive a four-year university education. Cadets who complete their studies at the Faculty undertake two months of supervised field experience during the summer. After graduation, they are appointed to the TNP with the rank of sergeant. They have the opportunity of promotion through all the ranks up to police chief.

Institute for Security Sciences: Graduate School Level

The Institute for Security Sciences is a graduate school offering MA and PhD programs in policing and associated fields such as criminology, international policing, police management, comparative policing, and criminal justice administration. The minimum educational requirement for admittance is a four-year university degree from the Faculty of Security Sciences or any other civilian university in Turkey. Civilian applicants who have backgrounds in social sciences such as law, politics, and sociology tend to have a better chance of being admitted than those from other disciplines. Students who receive advanced degrees from this institute are likely to become eminent senior police officers.

Probation Period for New Recruits

Recruits who graduate from the Faculty of Security Science and Police Schools all technically begin their careers as probationary officers. This period varies between one and one-half and two years. However, no specific or special training is given in this period. Probationary officers are not systematically monitored and evaluated by seasoned and tutor police officers. Officers who complete this so-called probationary period without fault automatically become commissioned officers without any formal test or evaluation process. The only further requirement of every probationary officer is to submit a medical report after going through a medical check-up.

Police Ranks

The above mentioned national training institutions offer preservice training for the TNP, while the Department of Training of the national headquarters offers in-service training courses for the whole organization. Some of the departments have their own in-service training centers. For instance, the Department of Counter Smuggling and Organized Crime facilitates the Turkish International Academy against Drugs and Organized Crime

(TADOC), and the Department of Public Order facilitates the Training Centre for Crime Research and Investigation.

The TNP maintains nine operational ranks, which can be categorized as upper management, middle management, and line supervision ranks. The upper management ranks include police chief (police commissioner for metropolitan cities), four-star police chief (commissioner for small cities), and three-star police chief (deputy commissioner). Middle management includes two-star police chief, one-star police chief, and superintendent (major). Line supervision ranks include chief inspector (captain), inspector (lieutenant), sergeant, and police or line officer. Police personnel within each category receive automatic promotion once the rank of sergeant is achieved. Promotional examinations are conducted in the presence of individuals with the rank of superintendent or three-star police chief. The examinations are paper-based written exams and are evaluated and ranked by a computerized system. Individuals who pass the exams then take two-week promotional courses designed by the Institute for Security Sciences.

In-Service Training

The Department of Training, under the Turkish National Police organizes in-service courses for police personnel throughout the country. This department is the only training institution operating outside the umbrella of the Police Academy. Its sole task is to organize and offer in-service courses for the entire force. This department offers a number of basic in-service courses in traditional police tasks. Usually, the Department of Training organizes in-service courses in conjunction with other departments tailored to their specific needs. However departments that need very special training organize their own programs. These departments sometimes receive academic and technical support from outside, such as from the Police Academy and civilian universities.

Some specialist departments such as Intelligence, Counter Smuggling and Organized Crime, and Counter Terrorism and Operation organize their own in-service courses. Once officers are assigned to one of these special departments, they have to go through a number of basic and follow-up courses. Some of these departments, such as TADOC and SASEM (another in-service training organization), even work in collaboration with international police organizations. Their training facilities and the quality of their training have an international reputation and recognition. These training institutions also offer in-service courses, not only to their own staff, but also to officers from neighboring or overseas countries.

The Racial and Ethnic Context of Turkish Policing

Demographic Figures

Turkey is situated between 36 and 42 degrees north latitude and between 26 and 45 degrees east longitude at the intersection of the continents of

Europe and Asia. Its neighbors are Georgia, Armenia, Nakhichevan (Azerbaijan), Iran, Iraq, Syria, Greece, and Bulgaria. Turkey's area is 779,452 square kilometers as projected on a flat map, and the real area as measured on the ground is 814,578 square kilometers. Approximately 97 percent of this area is in the continent of Asia, and 3 percent is in Europe. The population of the country in 2003 was 70.5 million; 40.6 million (65 percent) live in provincial and district centers, and 22.2 million (35 percent) live in rural villages. The largest three cities, in terms of population, are Istanbul with 10 million people, Ankara with 3.6 million, and Izmir with 3.1 million ("Mahalli İdareler," 2003).

Turkey is a predominantly Muslim country. Over 98 percent of the country's population is Muslim. The two main religious minority groups are Christian Armenians and Jews. The relationship between Turks and the religious-ethnic minorities in Turkey has usually been harmonious. Despite an Armenian genocide claim, the Turks and Armenians have peacefully lived together for well over a millennium. The Jews, who were saved from the Spanish Inquisition in 1492 by the Ottoman Turks, were brought to Turkey by Muslim Turks during the Ottoman era and have been living in Turkey peacefully for well over 500 years. Turkey is one of the few countries in the world where Jews have not had atrocities committed against them.

Ethnic Group Breakdown

Turkey has historically been a multiethnic and multicultural land (Ayata, 1997). Because of its geographical location, it has been a stage for many invasions and emigrational waves such as those of the Mongols from the East and the Crusades from the West. It was a meeting place between Asia and Europe, as well as between Islam and Christianity. Cultural, ethnic, and religious heterogeneity was the norm rather than the exception in Turkey. Despite the fact that Anatolia has always been a land of different cultures and ethnic groups, the Islamic-Turkish culture has always been dominant compared to other cultures. For this reason, *mosaic* may not be the best term to describe the ethnic and cultural fabric of Anatolia.

The word *minority* does not have an ethnic connotation but a religious one in Turkey, and only religious groups such as Christians (Armenians and Arabs) and Jews are defined as ethnic minorities. Other groups such as Abkhazians, Albanians, Bosnians, Caucasians, Chechens, Georgians, Kurds, and Laz (people of the Black Sea region) have always been regarded as integral parts of mainstream Turkish identity. The word *Turk* is more of a national umbrella identity rather than a purely ethnic term. What is more, Muslim ethnic groups such as Abkhazians, Albanians, Bosnians, Caucasians, Chechens, Georgians, Kurds, and Laz have preferred to identify themselves as integral parts of Ottoman or modern Turkish society rather than as separate and independent minority groups living under an alien dominant culture. Even the Kurds, who now claim to be an ethnic minority group, chose to be defined as Turks when they had an option during the writing of the

Lausanne Treaty in 1923. One of the most important factors, if not the only one, that made these groups, including the Kurds, identify themselves with dominant Turkish culture and identity is religion, which is Islam.

Languages Spoken

The official and most commonly used language of the country is Turkish. An overwhelming majority of the Turkish vocabulary comes from Arabic, Persian, and some Latin languages. The Latin alphabet was chosen for the written language after the establishment of modern Turkey in 1928. Arabic, Armenian, and Hebrew are also used by very tiny minorities. Other languages—such as different versions of the Kurdish language and dialects, Bosnian, Albanian, and Laz—are also used as spoken languages. However, as these groups are all Muslims, they are not considered to be ethnic minorities just on the basis of language difference.

Trends in Immigration

Turkey has been a country of emigration as well as immigration, and it has been subject to internal migration on a great scale since the postwar period (IOM, 1996). Turkey connects the Asian and European continents like a bridge. Because of its strategic geographic location, Turkey has received a large number of immigrants both as a target and as a transit country. In the early 1960s, Western European countries, mainly Germany, asked for legal immigrant workers from Turkey (Çiçekli, 1998). The number of immigrant workers working and living in Europe today has reached 3.5 million. Over 1 million have now acquired the citizenship of their respective countries. However, the total number of legal and illegal Turkish immigrant workers living in foreign countries today is more than 4.5 million (Ministry of Labor and Social Security, 2002).

Almost in the same time period, Turkey also experienced internal migration from rural areas of the eastern, southeastern, and Black Sea regions to the western, Marmara, Aegean, and Mediterranean regions. A number of cities such as Istanbul, Izmit, Bursa, Izmir, Denizli, Manisa, Antalya, Adana, and Mersin, in their respective regions, were target cities. Ankara has turned into a metropolitan city, while it was only a small town before it became the capital city of Turkey. Economic and social factors played a major role in the internal migration from east to west. However, a dramatic increase in PKK terror in the late 1980s also was an important contributing factor. Many of the occupants of small hamlets in southeastern parts of Turkey were evacuated to the cities, and their houses were razed by government forces to prevent the PKK from using them (Cerrah & Moore, 1997). During the last decade, over 2 million people have moved from rural areas to big cities such as Izmir, Ankara, and Istanbul as well as to regional cities such as Diyarbakir, Adana, and Mersin. However, the PKK has sometimes turned this strategy to its own ends, claiming that Turkish security forces not only razed the houses but also killed the occupants.

Between the years of 1980 and 1990, Turkey had to accommodate an influx of refugees from Iraq, a neighboring country (Kirişçi, 1995). Several times, Kurdish immigrants living in northern Iraq were forced to escape from Saddam Hussein's atrocities and seek refuge in Turkey. Turkey also was a transit country for illegal immigrants from countries such as Iran, Afghanistan, Pakistan, and India (IOM, 2003). Iranian political dissidents used Turkey as a transit and target country. Another external immigration wave came from the Central Asian Turkic republics and other former Soviet bloc countries such as Ukraine, Georgia, and even Russia itself. Turkey again served as a transit and target country for the influx of people coming through the Black Sea region to Turkey. Following the disintegration of the old Soviet bloc, a number of legal and illegal immigrants arrived in Turkey; some were seeking legitimate jobs, while others were involved in illegal activities such as prostitution, drug trafficking, and weapons smuggling. Finally, Turkey is a recipient of immigrants from Europe, mainly from Germany. A large number of retired German citizens have chosen to live in the coastal towns of the Mediterranean region. The number of foreigners migrating to Turkey for work or marriage purposes has also been increasing steadily for the last decade and is estimated to be at around 1 million.

Inter- and Intragroup Conflicts

The disintegration of the Ottoman state and caliphate, which was a binding factor among the Muslim residents, contributed to the rise of Turkish nationalism and the potential for intergroup conflicts. Interesting enough, the frequency of internal conflicts in Turkey has been especially strong since its experience with democracy in the 1950s. All this internal turmoil was followed by a number of military coups or interventions.

In the last three decades, Turkey has had a number of potential intergroup conflicts. Motives for these conflicts were right- and left-wing political ideologies, religious differences such as those between Aleviates and Sunni Muslims, or ethnic concerns such as those between Turkish and Kurdish people, but they have always been coupled with a political affiliation.

In the first period of such conflict, violent student protests began in the late 1950s after Turkey's first experience with democracy began in 1946. The Democratic Party successfully took power and ruled Turkey for 10 years until it was removed from power by a military coup in 1960. The coup took place after the political climate was destabilized by widespread and violent student demonstrations.

In the second period, Marxist-Leninist student protests and early terror activities began in the 1960s after another conservative political party, the Justice Party, came to power after the election that was held two years after the military coup. This party's rule coincided with the student demonstrations all over the world. Again, this government was brought to an end by a military interception in 1971. This period was again marked by violent student demonstrations and Marxist terrorism.

In the third period, armed conflict between left wing and right wing students began in the early 1970s and was brought to an end by another military coup in 1980. Although some sectarian violence occurred between Aleviates and Sunnis in cities such as Çorum and Maraş, this period was principally known for the armed conflicts that took place between right-wing and left-wing students and between unions and workers.

In the fourth period, conflict between government forces and people of ethnic Kurdish origin began in the mid-1980s. The first election that took place after the 1980 military coup yielded the Motherland Party, another conservative party that took power. This party ruled Turkey very successfully for almost 10 years. Following political stabilization, the economy, which was at the point of collapse before the military coup, began flourishing. The PKK, which was established in the late 1970s, began its armed assaults in the 1980s while this government was successfully ruling Turkey.

The final period is known as the 28 Subat Sureci (which translates to 28 February period or process), as the army once again expressed its displeasure and forced the ruling Welfare Party to step down on February 28, 1997. This political party was accused of taking Islamic actions rather than ruling in a secular manner. This political party did not officially identify itself as Islamic, but it was known for its religious sensitivities and priorities. Between the years of 1994 and 2000, religious conflicts were seen to rise between Sunnis and Alleviates. There were some activities that could be seen to be religiously provocative for both sides. Some Sunni villages were attacked and almost completely destroyed.

Some sections of Turkish society, including a number of intellectuals, believe that the above-mentioned religious and ethnic groups and others are manipulated by outsiders. This implies that some neighboring and Western countries have internal collaborators in Turkey. Although this brings to mind often-denied conspiracy theories, the fact that regular and continuous presence of intergroup conflicts started with Turkey's experience of democracy would seem to give some credit to this claim. However, the lack of institutionalized democracy can also be seen as a major factor. Rural parts of Turkey, especially the eastern and southern regions, still maintain traces of feudal social structure. Additionally, the army's self-appointed position as the so-called guardian of democracy has caused frequent military coups and interventions. Turkey's experience with democracy has been limited to the election of deputies to the Grand National Assembly in certain periods. Existing political systems lack local representation and participation and therefore do not represent the diversities of Turkish social structure.

Relationship Between Police and Diverse Populations

The relationship between the police and Turkey's diverse populations is not problematic in the ethnic sense. The two main sections of Turkish society that are officially defined as ethnic minorities are the Armenians and the Jews. The majority of these two religious minority groups live in big cities, mainly in Istanbul, İzmir, Bursa, Adana, and Ankara. They are economically and politically the most powerful groups in Turkey. Because of their prestigious positions and the areas in which they live, they do not very often have adversarial relations with the police.

However, the Kurdish people who immigrated to big cities have tended to have problems with the police. Kurdish immigrants in big cities are mainly concentrated in shantytown areas, and some of these areas are almost seen as "no go" areas for the police. The districts of Armutlu in Istanbul and of Kadifekale in İzmir can be given as two examples. The relationship between the Kurdish people and the police is not a racial discrimination issue; rather it is politically motivated with a hint of ethnic influence.

Representation of Diverse Populations in Government and the Police

All citizens of Turkey are regarded as Turkish, not purely in an ethnic sense but in terms of national identity; therefore no official records are kept about the representation of any ethnic groups in any institution in Turkey. Members of every ethnic group are eligible to join the police through official exams based on merit. Despite this legal position, however, there is a commonly held belief that those who are officially accepted as minorities are excluded from certain positions. However, the issue of discrimination is not limited to ethnic minorities. For example, a number of army officers have been fired from the army because of their religious beliefs.

Secularism is considered to be of utmost importance in Turkey. The Turkish army, as the sole guardian of the regime, puts an extraordinary premium on practices seen to be violations of the secular governing system. As a result of this overemphasis, women are deprived of a number of civil liberties that they could enjoy if they were living in a Western democratic society. For example, women who wear head scarves for religious reasons are not allowed to work in public services. Some in the private sector institutions also, partly for fear of a state reprimand or by their own policy, do not employ women who wear head scarves. For instance, a female who wore a head scarf who was elected to parliament in 1999 was not allowed to take her oath of office by other members of parliament. Wearing a head scarf is considered to be a violation of secularism. What is more, the board of higher education has also strictly imposed a ban on female students wearing head scarves. Female students who wear head scarves are not allowed to attend universities, and thousands of students are prevented by the police from attending. This practice continues even though it is not illegal for women to wear head scarves in Turkey.

There is no evidence to show that there is systematic discrimination on the basis of race, color, or ethnic origin. The Kurdish issue in particular is quite different from the discrimination seen against the blacks for example in the Western world. The Kurdish issue in Turkey is not similar to the racial conflicts that occur in countries such as Germany, the United States, or South Africa. Turkish Kurds are the host, not the guest, in Turkey and enjoy full citizenship. They participate in all aspects of political, economic, and social life. Almost one in three members of the Grand National Assembly is of Kurdish origin. A number of leading officials in Turkey have also been of Kurdish origin. There have been presidents, prime ministers, cabinet ministers, generals in the armed forces, numerous police chiefs, and the general director of the Turkish police among the citizens of Kurdish origin.

Community Policing

Community policing is seen as a dramatic move from traditional policing. It is defined simply as an attempt to reconnect the police with the community they are supposed to be serving. The overall aim is that the police, in an ideal society, should have not only the support of the community but also its consent. Community participation is a vital factor in obtaining the consent of the community. Community policing activities that are not based on community participation will not yield the consent of the community. Such practices are viewed by the critics of community policing as penetration practices into the community.

Factors That Make Community Policing Difficult

Community policing activities can be developed in three stages: policy, program, and structure. Turkish police presently are at the first of these three stages. There are no systematic community policing programs, and the present organizational structure of the police is not conducive to community policing.

Community support, which is a vital element to successful policing, can be achieved by systematic community participation. Yet, the Turkish police lack community participation and institutionalized police-community relations, which are instrumental in creating a climate conducive to community policing. No systematic meetings with members of the local community take place, and there is no community participation in policing on a systematic and regular basis. The majority of senior police officers who are in a position to create a suitable climate are not even conscious of the difference between traditional and community policing styles. Some senior police officials even confuse community policing with public relations. Some efforts toward community policing seen in recent years are not a result of policy change made by the top management. Rather, they are the result of the efforts by some midmanagement police officers who, individually and independently, strive to develop good relations with their communities.

Factors affecting community policing activities in Turkey can be summarized as a resistance stemming from the traditional police culture and police organizational structure. The first major resistance to community policing activities stems from the traditional Turkish police culture. According to this culture, the police force is strong enough to fight against crime. There is no need to involve the community with policing or to ask what their views are in fighting crimes. The police organization, like any other government institution, always knows what is best for the people. Members of the community should come forward and provide the necessary support. There is no need to develop systematic and regular community involvement with policing issues. Policing is a national security issue. The state and its appointed officials always know what is right and best for the people.

The second major factor affecting community policing is the organizational structure of the TNP. A highly centralized general Turkish administrative system naturally creates an authoritarian state and policing system in the country. Turkish police, as a part of a social structure and establishment, persistently maintain the authoritarian government structure. This seems to be more of a "force" than a "service." A highly centralized and authoritarian administrative system is not conducive to systematic and legitimate community participation. Therefore, in Turkey, community policing activities find it hard to flourish.

The Turkish police can be defined as being a highly centralized and militarist force. The policy of the organization can be summarized as being a force rather than a public service, although it is often said in ceremonies and public statements that the Turkish police is there to serve its public. This argument is not supported by systematic community participation and remains only as rhetoric. The present organizational structure is not conducive to community policing.

Turkish police practices fall within the category of traditional policing. In other words, community policing activities, as an alternative to traditional policing, have no chance of survival because the present organizational structure is not conducive to community policing (Kavgacı, 1995). Police officers are deliberately removed from day-to-day contact with citizens. This is considered a preventive measure against police corruption. Frequent interpersonal contacts with members of the community by police officers are considered to be a source of corrupt relations. Therefore, typical police officers are expected to be out in their cars patrolling, responding to radio calls after a crime has been committed, and dealing more with the criminals and less with the victims. The police spend most of their time and resources responding to calls. They are not expected, on their own initiative, to deal with either the crime problem or the public safety needs of citizens living and working in their unsafe neighborhoods.

Community policing is an aspect of democratic policing and can only be applied to police practices in democratic societies. As long as the Turkish administration system and the police remain highly centralized in nature, community policing efforts are doomed to fail. In other words, resistance to community policing in Turkey is the natural result of a highly centralized organizational structure rather than the result of deliberate resistance to community policing.

In Turkey, policing policies can be determined only by the central government via the general director of the police. Police chiefs in provinces have no room to maneuver. However, some police practices that can be seen as community policing efforts have unconstructive effects, as they are not considered and applied carefully. For example, in the late 1990s, the Istanbul police and some other police departments organized "peace meetings" with people in different parts of the city on a regular basis. However, rather than listening to what the people had to say and taking into consideration the communities' needs and expectations, the police used these meetings to instruct people about what they should do. Police-community relations are usually seen, on the part of the police, as a way of coaxing people to come forward and help with the gathering of information about a particular crime.

Turkish police are not familiar with the idea of involving civilians in policing practices. The community has traditionally accepted whatever the state offers them. The state and its institutions are presumed always to know what is best for its people. This approach summarizes the nature of state-community relations in general. However, senior police officers occasionally make public statements urging people to help the police in fighting crimes. But, community support is perceived as people coming forward with information and helping the police to solve a particular crime. Systematic community involvement in policing policies exercised locally is not an issue that is generally considered. Other types of police-community relations are usually of an adversarial nature, such as people contacting the police when they are victims of a crime or suspects of a crime. The second most common police-community interaction is an individual serving as an informant.

Community policing, as a derivation of democratic policing, is meaningful as long as it is based on civilian participation in policing policies and in practices on both a national and local level. Civil and local participation should be based on systematic communication with regular and planned meetings between the police and the community. Accountability and responsibility are the two key concepts in democratic policing. Police accountability is of pivotal importance, not only to the national government, but also to the local governments and communities. In Turkey, there is a lack of civil involvement in local police practices, and this raises questions of legitimacy in the system in general and in the police in particular.

Systematic civil participation, which is an essential element of participatory democracies, will not only contribute to the legitimacy of the police in Turkey but also to the legitimacy of the police force in general. However, the TNP does not see the concept of legitimacy as an issue to be maintained. Official state perception on legitimacy is that the Turkish state has the inherited consent of its people and there is no need to maintain or encourage this inherited consensus. In other words, consensus of the people and the legitimacy of the TNP are taken for granted. In modern democracies, however, consensus and legitimacy are not static concepts but dynamic ones. Legitimacy of a police force or consent of the society toward a government in general or an institution such as the police may fluctuate up or down depending on its practices and relations with the community.

In short, Turkish police do not have any systematic civil involvement and participation in policing on a local basis. Individually initiated community policing activities, such as police officers visiting schools and meeting students, or a police officer establishing good relations with unofficial community leaders, fall short, because they are not systematic enough to be effective community policing practices. On the other hand, some contacts between civilians and police that have been intended to build good relations between the police and the community have been used by police for nothing more than advising people on what to do at best or instructing people on how to help the police. The peace meetings in Istanbul were an example of this. Instead of seriously trying to involve local people in solving or fighting crime, the police were selling their so-called services or trying to persuade people to help them more. In some of these meetings, the person who was police commissioner for Istanbul at the time had very controversial discussions with the people.

Crime Prevention Programs

In order to implement community policing, a variety of innovative organizational and procedural models and programs need to be initiated. Presently, there are no systematic crime prevention programs such as Neighborhood Watch, nor is any formal community participation embedded into policing. Neither NGOs nor any other civilian institution has any say about policing policy and practices. Crime prevention activities are based mostly on harsh policing methods. Policing policies are designed by senior police officers without consulting civilian boards or NGOs. It is believed that traditional harsh policing practices will deter crime, if not prevent it completely.

Community Outreach

Community outreach, like community policing, is not a familiar concept in Turkish policing. It is assumed that the police, as an agent of the state, are always within reach of all sections of the community. It is true, to some extent, that the police do not have a particular communication problem with society based on ethnic divisions. Police malpractice or corruption is not focused on any ethnic minority or other group. Police malpractice is evenly distributed and there is no discrimination in improper police practices. Members of the two officially acknowledged ethnic minority groups, the Jews and Christians, have economically and socially high standards of living in Turkey and therefore do not have serious adversarial contacts with the police.

However, particularly in big cities, the police frequently have problematic relations with people based on their economic and social status rather than their race or ethnic group. Like many other developed or developing countries, increased urbanization and inner-city deprivation in Turkey has led to societal turbulence. As stated earlier, some inner-city areas are now seen as no go areas for the police, because, within these areas, the police face difficulty in enforcing the law and have little support from the local community. These locations are usually, but not exclusively, populated by people who migrated from rural areas of the country, mainly from eastern Turkey. The police find it hard to reach these locations.

To conclude, police practices that are attuned with the community's needs and expectations will result in improved community and police relations. They will further contribute to the legitimacy of the police force in general. In other words, a lack of systematic and democratic participation in policing will erode legitimacy of the force. Resistance to community policing in Turkey stems partly from the centralized Turkish administration system and the police organizational structure. However, despite the present negative atmosphere for community policing, there is reason to be optimistic about the future. First, an overwhelming majority of current police middle managers and the new generation of police officers are familiar with the ideas of community policing, and they hold positive views about it. So resistance stemming from the traditional police culture seems to be gradually fading away. Second, Turkey is near to joining the European Union, and in recent years a number of legislative changes have been made by the central government to facilitate Turkey's EU membership. These legislative changes will improve the quality of democracy in Turkey and are likely to create a favorable environment for community policing.

Terrorism

Turkey's experience with terrorism began in the late 1960s. Since then, Turkey has suffered from various forms of terrorist activities, including domestic and international terrorism. Having common borders with Syria, Iraq, Iran, and Greece, Turkey has had to fight against a number of terrorist organizations, most of which have had political and logistical support from these neighboring countries. These terrorist organizations could be categorized broadly as either domestic or international terrorist organizations. The following organizations are the most notorious organizations.

Sources of Terrorist Threats

The most infamous international terrorist organization in Turkey is the Armenian Secret Army for the Liberation of Armenia (ASALA), which is of Lebanese origin (Aktan & Köknar, 2002; Cerrah & Peel, 1997). In 1973, in order to achieve autonomy for provinces of northeastern Turkey that had formerly been populated by Armenians, Armenian terrorist groups ran a terror campaign for 13 years that involved the systematic assassination of Turkish diplomats. By 1982, two groups, known as the ASALA and the Justice Commandos of the Armenians, had killed 22 Turkish diplomats, members of their families, and Turkish embassy staff.

Domestic terrorist organizations can be divided into several subcategories, including organizations based on ethnicity, ideology, and religion. Some of the terrorist organizations may well fit into more than one category.

The Partiya Karkaren Kurdistan or PKK

By far the largest and most active ethnically and ideologically motivated terrorist organization operating in Turkey today is the Kurdistan Workers Party (Partiya Karkaren Kurdistan or PKK). The PKK was formed on November 27, 1978, in the province of Diyarbakir. Although they have occasionally ventured outside this area, the PKK generally confines its activities to the mountains of southeastern Turkey.

The PKK is motivated mostly by Kurdish nationalism, but at the same time it is ideologically a Marxist terrorist organization. Seeking independence or at least autonomy for the Kurds, the PKK has been involved in terrorist activities since 1984 and has caused the deaths of over 30,000 people, including Kurdish civilians, members of the security forces, and terrorists (Bal, 1999).

For the first six years of its existence, the PKK was engaged in recruiting people for its organization, building teams, acquiring weapons, and undergoing training. Then it launched a violent terrorist campaign in August 1984, which has now lasted more than 20 years. Initially, its aim was to establish an independent socialist state in southeastern Turkey and then to extend the state into Kurdish areas in Syria, Iraq, and Iran. However, it now has a more limited aim—a degree of autonomy over southeastern Turkey.

Operating in an area that covers tens of thousands of square miles of rugged terrain, the strategy of PKK is first to take over the rural areas and then to move into the cities. In order to achieve this aim, this terrorist organization has attempted to unite workers in the cities with those living in the many small villages dotted all over the area. The poor educational standards in southeastern Turkey have made it easier for the PKK to recruit new members.

Estimates of the number of active members of the PKK vary from 5,000 to 10,000, which includes those based in Syria, Iraq, and Iran, as well as in Turkey. They are organized in teams of between 7 and 11 people. Their tactics are based on those used by the Viet Cong in the Vietnam War—they identify a target, hit it, and run. For some of the larger operations, teams come together to form groups (three teams) and units (six teams). The PKK is in touch with various terrorist groups, and operators have been trained in Syria and in Lebanon.

Unlike other well-known terrorist groups, such as the Irish Republican Army (IRA) in the UK and the Euskadi Ta Askatasuna (ETA or Basque Fatherland and Liberty) group in Spain, who tend to target what they regard as military and economic targets, the PKK is totally indiscriminate when mounting its operations. Bombs are placed in public places with total disregard for who might be affected by the explosions. Men, women, and children have been systematically killed in raids on villages. Because state education is delivered only in Turkish and not Kurdish, the PKK has deliberately targeted teachers and killed at least 90. Despite a claim by the PKK in August 1994 that the organization was committed to Article 3 of the Geneva Convention, which states that people taking no active part in hostilities must be treated humanely and should not be ill-treated or killed, the PKK has continued to kill civilians totally unconnected with the conflict. In late 1994, 19 teachers were abducted and killed in a single raid.

Like the IRA, the PKK acts in a decisive manner to kill its own members in order to maintain discipline and also exercise authority over the Kurds by killing those believed to be traitors or unwilling to cooperate with the organization. Abdullah Öcalan, the so-called general secretary of the PKK, lived in Damascus under the protection of the Syrian government until he was forced to flea the country by the Turkish government in 1998. He went first to Russia and then to Greece seeking protection, and he finally took refuge in Italy. Then the Italian government was forced to surrender Öcalan. He was finally captured by Turkish security forces in Kenya in 1999 and brought back to Turkey, where he was sentenced to life in prison.

Since the terrorist attacks on the World Trade Center in New York in 2001, the international approach to terrorism has dramatically changed, and antiterrorist pressures have reached a peak. As a result, the PKK could not resist the pressure coming from the Western world and decided to transform itself. It changed its name to Kurdistan Freedom and Democracy Congress (Kongreya Azadi-u Demokrasi-a Kurdistan or KADEK) and made a fresh start, aiming both to cover up its violent past and to adapt its infamous reputation into political capital. In 2004, it changed its name again to The People's Congress of Kurdistan (KONGRA-GEL) and claimed to be the legitimate representative of the Kurdish people. However, despite these name changes, it remains known as the PKK, and despite its claim that it is able to solve existing conflicts among the peoples of the Middle East—including the Kurdish issue—by democratic and peaceful means, the residue of armed PKK/KONGRA-GEL terrorists still engage in terrorist activities in northern Iraq. They frequently declare ceasefires and then mount terrorist attacks similar to those that they used to mount.

Politically and Religiously Motivated Terrorist Organizations

Several well-known Marxist terrorist organizations are currently active in Turkey. They usually engage in terrorist activities in urban areas. The Revolutionary People's Liberation Party/Front–Revolutionary Left (DHKP/C–DEVSOL) is a Marxist-Leninist nonethnic terrorist organization. It is principally based in big cities such as Istanbul and Ankara. Originally known as Revolutionary Left, it began its operations in late 1975 and changed its name in 1994. As its name implies, it is a left-wing organization that grew out of the student movements of the late 1960s. DHKP/C operates on a cell structure similar to that of the IRA and ETA. The group tends to target members of the security forces, prosecutors, and politicians.

The Turkish Communist Party/Marxist-Leninist–Turkish Workers and Peasants Liberation Army (TKP/ML-TIKKO) is a Maoist organization with a sectarian element. Although most members of the organization are Alawite, which is an Islamic sect, the second recruiting source is the Kurdish population. The Marxist-Leninist Communist Party/Foundation (MLKP/K) is another Marxist and nonethnic terrorist organization (Aktan & Köknar, 2002).

Terrorist Organizations Motivated Primarily by Religion

Despite the fact that Islamic teachings and tradition have always been against terrorism and the indiscriminate use of violence, some terrorist groups define themselves as Islamic. An overwhelming majority of the Turkish population resent the fact that these organizations are called Islamic. The so-called Islamic terrorist organizations have always been marginal groups and have failed to receive support from the public.

The major religiously motivated terrorist organizations are the Party of God (Hizbullah), Islamic Great Orient Raiders Front (IBDA/C) and Islamic Movement. The most active and the largest in size is the Hizbullah. Although its Lebanese namesake Shieti Hizbullah was a Shiite, the Turkish version of Hizbullah is an exclusively Sunni organization. Despite the fact that Turkish security forces have mounted successful operations against Hizbullah in recent years, the organization still has considerable public support in eastern and southeastern Turkey, where most Kurds live. The other two so-called Islamic terrorist groups, IBDA/C and Islamic Movement, have had to cease their activities as almost all of their members have been captured by the Turkish police.

On November 15–20, 2003, Turkey experienced a wave of terrorist attacks that targeted two synagogues, a British bank, and the British consulate in Istanbul. A total of 61 Turkish citizens lost their lives, as well as

2 British citizens and 6 Turkish Jews. Police identified the suicide attackers within a couple of days. They had ties with a domestic terrorist organization that is seen as a derivation of the al-Quaeda terror organization. However, despite the apparent links with al-Quaeda, some questions have been raised about the real mastermind of these attacks. Because Jews have not been subject to attack in Turkey for many centuries, terrorist attacks apparently targeted against Jewish minorities are believed to reflect some ideology that comes from outside the country. This has raised questions about the true origin behind the attacks. Some commentators have argued that these attacks, which seem to be organized by a so-called Islamic terrorist organization, are manipulated by those who want to destabilize the democratic system of the country and prevent it from becoming a part of the Western world.

It is true that a very small minority of the Turkish population in Turkey does not want the country to be a part of Europe. In addition, there are those in the Western world who argue that Turkey cannot belong to the West and that there will, in the future, be a clash between Christians and Jews on the one side and the Muslim world on the other. Therefore, such terrorist attacks have seemed to serve not only the cause of the so-called Islamic terrorist organizations but also the cause of those who argue that the future will witness a clash between civilizations.

Terrorist organizations acquire funds from a variety of sources. Contributions for the PKK are collected from Kurdish businesses operating in Germany, France, and the United Kingdom in the same way that terrorist groups from Northern Ireland have raised funds for the IRA from Irish Americans living in the United States. One of the other sources of funds for the PKK is smuggling of humans, weapons, and drugs. It has been very involved in trafficking between the Eastern world and Western Europe. In particular, it has smuggled drugs into European countries, which are the source of the majority of its funding.

Counterterrorism Training

Because the PKK terror activities were mainly concentrated in the eastern and southeastern parts of Turkey, which is a very mountainous rural area, traditional urban antiterror methods were not successful. Therefore army units were deployed at the early stages of the PKK terror surge. During these early stages, the Turkish government's military response to terror was handicapped. Despite the continuous presence of terrorism in Turkey since 1984, both the police and the army have lacked the necessary skills and expertise to launch effective counterterrorist operations. On a number of occasions, this has led to armed conflict between security forces and terrorists in which innocent people have been killed. However, while fighting against terrorism, Turkish security forces, both the civilian police and the military, gained a great deal of experience by trial and error.

Later the police established a Special Operations department for counterterror activities. Now both the military and the police have special units that are trained in fighting against terrorism. These units have been very successful using rural guerrilla tactics. However, fighting terrorism with paramilitary methods has always had its disadvantages. The issue has gradually turned into a war between the terrorists and the armed forces. This was a situation the PKK deliberately wanted to create. The PKK has always argued that the eastern and southeastern parts of Turkey were Kurdish lands occupied by the Turks. The Turkish government's use of the army to fight terrorism instead of the civilian police has enhanced the PKK's claims that it was not a domestic security issue but a war between two different and separate peoples.

Weapons of mass destruction (WMDs) have so far not been used by any terrorist group in Turkey, and therefore training against biological attacks and WMDs has not yet been adopted. However, because of its geographic location, Turkey has been used as a transport route for terror related drug trafficking. Following the demolition of the Soviet Union, nuclear materials stolen from former Soviet countries were smuggled into Turkey and were transported between the Eastern and the Western world. The only preparation that the Turkish armed forces have made to counter WMD attacks is the purchase, in 2005, of protective clothing for its personnel that will shield them in nuclear-biological and chemical (NBC) attacks ("Ordu'da nükleer hazırlık," n.d.).

Counterterrorism Policy and Strategy

The Turkish government has adopted a number of strategies in its fight against the PKK. In 1984, it imposed martial law in the nine provinces that were immediately affected by PKK terrorism. By July 1987, this had been replaced by a "state of emergency," which gave the security forces wide-ranging powers. Eastern and southeastern provinces were ruled under this state of emergency from late 1980 until 2002.

Many villages in the region were annihilated by the PKK attacks. A number of villages were encouraged, if not forced, to evacuate because of the inability of the security forces to protect them. The government also encouraged the formation of the civil defense corps of village guards in the mid-1980s. Now numbering about 55,000, village guards mount roadblocks in the affected areas and assist the security forces in mounting operations against the PKK. But the villagers are in a dilemma. Many are reluctant to serve as village guards because they fear being killed by the PKK. But, if they refuse to join, they can be accused by those who have joined the civil defense corps and the security forces of being PKK sympathizers.

To conclude, the Turkish government's strategy to eliminate the PKK has largely been to mount a military offensive. The cost of fighting the PKK with military strength exceeds several billion dollars a year, crippling an economy that might otherwise be blossoming. However a solution that depends solely on a military response has so far showed that it is unlikely to succeed. This is what the British government found in Northern Ireland, the Spanish government experienced in the Basque region, and Israel is currently facing in Palestine. Furthermore, the use of force as the only strategy against the PKK or other terrorist organizations has also raised human rights questions and legitimacy concerns.

Terrorism is a domestic security problem. It has a number of contributing factors such as social, political, economic, and historical influences. Terror as a multidimensional social problem cannot simply be solved by force. The other factors contributing to terror must be taken into consideration and addressed in fighting against terror in general and against the PKK in particular.

References

Aktan, G. S., & Köknar, A. M. (2002). Turkey. In Y. Alexander (Ed.), *Combating terrorism: Strategies of ten countries* (pp. 210–420). Ann Arbor, MI: University of Michigan Press.

Ayata, A. (1997, Fall). The emergency of identity politics in Turkey. *New Perspectives on Turkey, 22,* 59–73.

Aydın, A. H. (1997). *Police organization and legitimacy: Case studies of England, Wales and Turkey.* Aldershot, UK: Avebury.

Aydın, A. H. (2003, October). *Policing system in Turkey: A critical analysis.* Paper presented to the International Police Executive Symposium, 10th Annual Meeting: Policing and Community, Manama, Bahrain.

Bal, I. (1999). *Prevention of terrorism in liberal democracies: A case study of Turkey.* Unpublished doctoral thesis, University of Leicester, UK.

Cerrah , I., & Moore, T. (1997). Public order policing in Turkey: The need for command training. *Turkish Public Administration Annual, 22–23,* 19–22.

Cerrah, I., & Peel, R. (1997). Terrorism in Turkey. *Intersec: The Journal of International Security, 7*(1), 19–22.

Çiçekli, B. (1998). *The legal position of Turkish immigrants in the European Union.* Ankara: Karmap.

Cizre, U. (2000). *Politics and military in Turkey into the 21st century.* Robert Schuman Centre For Advanced Studies, European University Institute, Florence, EUI Working Paper RSC No. 2000/24: Badia Fiesolan, San Domenico.

Cizre, U. (2004). Problems of democratic governance of civil-military relations in Turkey and the European Union enlargement zone. *European Journal of Political Research, 43,* 107–125.

Donat, Y. (2005, April 2). Interviews with Kenan Evren and Süleyman Demirel. *Sabah* [Electronic version]. Retrieved April 2, 2005, from http://www.zaman.com.tr/webapp-tr

Eryılmaz, M. B. (2003). *Türk ve ingiliz hukukuna ve uygulamasında durdurma ve arama.* Ankara: Seçkin.

European Parliament, Committee on Foreign Affairs, Human Rights, Common Security, and Defence Policy. (2003). *Regular report of the commission on Turkey's progress towards accession.* Brussels: Commission of the European Communities.

Goldsmith, A., & Cerrah, I. (2005). *Civilian oversight of the security sector in Turkey.* Unpublished project report. Ankara: United Nations Development Program.

International Organization for Migration (IOM). (1996). *Transit migration in Turkey.* Budapest: IOM Information Programme.

International Organization for Migration (IOM). (2003). *Irregular migration in Turkey.* IOM Migration Research Series, No. 12. Budapest: IOM Information Programme.

İşte JİTEM'in resmi tanımı. (n.d.). *Aktif Haber* [Electronic version]. Retrieved April 17, 2005, from http://www.aktifhaber.com

Kavgacı (Bahar), H. İ. (1995). *The development of police/community relations initiatives in England & Wales post Scarman and their relevance to policing policy in Turkey.* Unpublished doctoral thesis, University of Leicester, UK.

Kirişçi, K. (1995). *Refugee movements and Turkey in the post second world war era.* Research paper, ISS/POLS 95-01, Boğazici University, Istanbul.

Mahalli ıdareler. (2003). Retrieved August 15, 2007, from http://www.mahalli idareler.gov.tr/Home/Home.aspx

Ministry of Labor and Social Security (Çalışma ve Sosyal Güvenlik Bakanlığı). (2002). *2000–2001 Raporu: Yurtdışındaki vatandaşlarmiza ilişkin gelişme ve say?sal veriler.* Publication no. 110, pp. 31–34. Ankara: Author.

Ordu'da nükleer hazırlık. (n.d.). *Aktif Haber* [Electronic version]. Retrieved August 28, 2005, from http://www.aktifhaber.com

Prime Ministry, Human Rights Presidency. (2004). *Document files.* Ankara, Author.

Varlığı tartışılan JİTEM yargıda. (2004, December 11). *Zaman,* p. 3.

Veli küçük: JİTEM yok, devletin verdiği emirleri yaptim. (2004, December 26). *Zaman,* p. 3.

Further Reading

Aydın, A. (1992). *Kürtler, PKK ve A. Öcalan.* Ankara: Kiyap.

Çermeli, A. (2002). *Jandarma genel komutanlığı tarihi: Asayiş ve kolluk tarihi içersinde Türk jandarma teşkilatı.* Ankara: Jandarma Genel Komutanlığı Yayınları.

Cerrah, İ. (2002). Ethnic identity versus national identity: An analysis of PKK terror in relation to identity conflict. In J. D. Freilich, G. Newman, S. G. Shoham, & M. Addad (Eds.), *Migration, culture conflict and crime* (pp. 223–232). Aldershot, UK: Ashgate-Dartmouth.

Cerrah, İ. (2003, March). *Teaching ethics to the police: Turkish case.* Paper presented to the Academy of Criminal Justice Sciences 40th Annual Meeting, Boston, MA.

Eryılmaz, M. B. (1999). *Arrest and detention powers in English and Turkish law and practice in the light of the European Convention on Human Rights.* The Hague: Martinus Nijhoff.

Günes-Ayata, A., (1996). *Türkiye'de etnik kimlik ve etnik gruplur.* Toplum ve Göç: II Ulusul Sosyoloji Kongresi, Başbakanlik Devlet Istatistik Enstitüsü, Ankara.

Günes-Ayata, A. (1996). Ethnic identity and ethnic groups in Turkey. *II. National Conference on Society and Migration.* Ankara: Prime Minister's Office.

Haberfeld, M., Cerrah, I., & Grant, H. (2005). *Terrorism, legitimacy, and human rights within a comparative international context.* Unpublished final report of the Fulbright Alumni Initiatives Awards Program, June 1, 2003–June 1, 2005. John Jay College of Criminal Justice, New York.

Türkdoğan, O. (1996). *Sosyal siddet ve Türkiye gerçe*g. Istanbul: Timaş.

9 Traditional Policing in an Era of Increasing Homeland Concerns

The Case of the Israeli Police

Lior Gideon, Ruth Geva, and Sergio Herzog

Police studies are very much like field experiments in an ever-changing society, as they correspond to social change and may be seen as an indicator of such change. Being the primary formal social control agency in a democratic society, the police do not operate in a vacuum and thus must be responsive to social change and society needs. Generally, it is argued that law enforcement agencies reflect the priorities, divisions, and social and economic conditions of the societies in which they exist. Therefore, police characteristics and innovations, such as organizational and functional changes, should be viewed from a broader perspective, that is, as an attempt by police forces to adapt to the changing needs and character of the society in which they operate and from which its officers are being recruited (Herzog, 2001).

Such is the case with the Israeli Police (IP), which, since its inception as a national police in 1948 (parallel with the establishment of Israel as an independent state), has been challenged by variety of tasks aimed at order maintenance as well as maintaining the security and quality of life of its citizens. Facing extreme ongoing security threats has demanded that Israeli police officers and the Israeli Border Guard Police (BGP) deal with responsibilities that are somewhat different from the traditional and classical policing duties as manifested in other democratic societies. To a large extent, the IP nowadays is concerned with homeland security and preventing and responding to terrorist threats and attacks as well as preventing and reacting to crime. As such, the IP is usually found in the hub of the most painful conflicts of Israeli society. (For a detailed discussion of such conflicts, see Smooha, 1988, and Smooha & Hanf, 1992.)

The aim of this chapter is to present an overview of the Israeli Police in a fairly young society that is constantly facing new challenges as well as the challenge of mass in-migration and terror attacks.

Israel in a Nutshell

Bordered by Lebanon in the north, Syria in the northeast, Jordan in the east, Egypt in the south, and the Mediterranean Sea on the west, Israel's population at yearend 2005 is about 6.99 million, with approximately 1.37 million Arab Israelis (Israeli Central Bureau of Statistics, 2006). This number does not include about 3 million Arab residents in the recently established Palestinian Authority and in the Administered Territories (i.e., East Jerusalem, the West Bank of the River Jordan, and the Gaza Strip; henceforth *territories*) controlled by the Israeli army since the 1967 Six Day War (Israeli Central Bureau of Statistics, 2006).

Consequent to the widespread immigration from Europe following World War II and the Holocaust, in November of 1947 the United Nations approved a partition of the area that was called "Palestine," then under British Mandate, into two states—Jewish and Arab. As a result Israel declared its independence and statehood on May 14, 1948. Following this, the surrounding Arab countries, which did not agree with this resolution, declared war on Israel (i.e., the War of Independence), but failed to defeat the new state. Since that time Israel has constantly struggled to maintain its independence while experiencing waves of armed conflicts with its Arab neighbors, as well as with Arab residents in the territories.

As noted by Geva, Herzog, and Haberfeld (2005), terrorist activity has been part of daily life in Israel for decades. This activity has been carried out mainly by Palestinian armed groups, escalating during the first *intifada* (the Palestinian uprising against Israel's military control of the territories), between 1988 and 1993, and again in the second intifada, which has been going on continuously since October 2000. This last uprising has resulted in almost constant fighting between the Palestinians in the West Bank and Gaza Strip and the Israeli security forces (including the IP, the BGP, and the Israeli Defense Forces, or IDF), with Palestinian armed groups using terrorist tactics against primarily civilian Israeli targets (Geva, Herzog, & Haberfeld, 2005) killing about 680 Israeli civilians in the years 2000–2004 (Israeli Defense Force, 2004).

Demographic Figures

According to the Israeli Central Bureau of Statistics report of 2004, the Jewish population in Israel is about 5.16 million, and there are about 1.07 million Moslems, 142,400 Christians (Arabs and non-Arabs), and 110,800 Druze.

(In Israel, Druze are granted Israeli citizenship and are distinct from other Arabic-speaking populations; they are expected to serve in the Israeli army.) During the first years of statehood, 1948–1951, massive migration (about 687,624 immigrants) from Asia and Africa as well as from Europe, entered the country as a result of World War II. Such migration waves were observed again during the 1950s and early 1960s, and another huge group of more than 1 million new immigrants arrived during the first half of the 1990s, mostly from the former Soviet Union and Ethiopia (a significant majority was from the Soviet Union). In addition, during the 1990s, and as a result of the escalating terrorist attacks and the drastic reduction in the employment of Palestinian workers by Israeli employers (see Herzog, 2005), Israel opened its gates to foreign workers from Romania and the Far East (especially to Thailand and China). Consequently, the variety of spoken languages in Israel is enormous, with Hebrew being the primary language, although Arabic and Russian are spoken by a large number of the residents as their first language. In such a social climate, conflicts are inevitable, not only due to the difference in language but also due to the differences in culture and values. Such a diversity also demands more police attention in maintaining public order as well as in dealing with new and unfamiliar issues such as alcohol-related problems and human smuggling (in particular female smuggling for prostitution purposes) to name just a few.

In order to reflect this population growth and cultural diversity, the Israeli Police have begun recruiting officers that have a profound knowledge of Arabic, Russian, and Amharic (the Ethiopian language). Also, in areas where there is a high concentration of Arabs, such as in Jerusalem and in the Galilee, Arab Israelis are represented in the force and in particular by members of the Druze community. On another level, in the second half of the 1990s the IP initiated a recruitment project known as "Police 2000." Because of this massive recruitment effort, many university graduates joined the force, thus elevating the educational level of the officers as well as their professionalism and ability to deal with various situations.

Israeli Police: Historical Development and Policing in a Political Context[1]

Since its inception in 1948, the IP has been a national, highly centralized force that has been the responsibility of the Minister of Public Security, formerly called the Ministry of Police (Sebba, Horovitz, & Geva, 2003). However, the first roots of the IP may be observed as early as 1909, when a force called *H'Shomer* (Hebrew for *the guard*) was formed to protect Jewish immigrants to Israel, who faced massive attacks by hostile neighbors. This necessitated the establishment of an organized body to maintain order and protect their lives and property when the Turkish Mandate—which then controlled the Palestine area—failed to do so.

Eight years later, in 1917, after World War I ended, when Palestine was conquered by the British, General Allenby ordered the establishment of police stations within important population concentrations and the formation of a gendarmerie (a military body charged with general police duties) from local police officers. This force was called the Superb Police. Officially it was known by the British as the Palestinian Gendarmerie, and its primary goal was to deal with public order in those concentration areas. Participating in the police force under the British Mandate gave the Jewish population in Israel an opportunity to train and carry firearms, which was later an advantage to the Jewish settlement in Israel, especially during the Arab pogroms of 1936, when the British Mandate government could not protect the life and property of Jewish citizens. Subsequently, a Jewish reactive force was formed that was called the Hebrew Settlement Police; this force later became known as the *Hagana* (Hebrew for *defense*). In its first stages, the Hagana had 1200 men who joined 700 Jewish police officers who already served under the British Mandate. This organization later developed into what is now known as the Israeli Defense Force (IDF).

About six months before the establishment of the Israeli state, strategic plans for the formation of an Israeli police were made under the leadership of Yechezkel Sahar, who later became the first commissioner of police (with the rank of inspector general). The birth of the IP in 1948 was attended by severe wartime conditions (the War of Independence). As a result, traditional police work was very low on the list of priorities of Israel's first government, in contrast to the need for an army, the labor shortage (able-bodied youth had been sent to fight the war), and the very limited budget. Under these difficult conditions, the new police administration chose to adopt the existing militaristic model of the British Mandatory Police, which had operated under the British Mandate in Palestine between 1922 and 1948, for its primary organizational, administrative, and operational structure.

Apart from being the most convenient model to adopt at that time, the choice was also based on the knowledge that British rule had introduced advanced police-work patterns and a professional approach in several areas, including police administration, discipline, and organization. The new IP adopted from the British police its legal basis, conventional policing techniques and tools (uniforms, rank structure, orders, training systems, discipline norms, organizational outlook, buildings, and even their military-style ceremonies), and in particular its centralized administration and structure.

However it should be noted that as a colonial police force, the main role of the Mandatory Police was to assist the British government to rule the colony, with its Jewish and Arab residents, by means of a paramilitary centralized force. Thus, its primary tasks were combat- and security-oriented missions to deal with serious mass disturbances, riots, and terrorism (Herzog, 2001). As a result, training of new officers was done in a military manner. Nevertheless, a sense of mission along with a strong motivation to serve the public characterized the new police officers, who also were engaged in other community services. Taking into consideration a severe shortage of manpower during this era, the IP had to deal with infiltration of terrorists, maintaining public order, dealing with demonstrations, a rising crime rate, preventing black market activity, and even providing social services to new immigrants.

In its second decade of independence, the new state's infrastructure was more established, and other problems began to emerge. Tension from bordering Arab countries increased, and an economic depression resulted in social turmoil. It was during this period that the IP renounced the British Mandatory Police heritage, making room for training in police studies and for the increasing demand for police services. According to Ross (1998), one can argue that the IP chose the liberal reformist approach,[2] as it was constantly trying to improve its ability while increasing its efficiency. Indeed, IP history reveals that between 1958 and 1966, an accelerated process of professionalism and specialization began to emerge in all aspects of police work (IP, 2004).

In 1958, a reorganization of the police separated the role of headquarter units from the operational units. The number of geographical jurisdictions decreased from five to three (i.e., north, south, and Tel-Aviv, which is in the center of Israel). In addition, a police force of full- time officers was formulated, and the Investigation Department was transformed into the proactive Investigations and Crime Fighting Department (the change in name mirrors the change in emphasis—from a merely reactive investigative one to a proactive preventive one). Beat cops were mobilized, and women were integrated into the operational units as well. Juvenile divisions were also established, and in Tel-Aviv all regional investigative units were integrated under one centralized unit. Also during this time, an Academy for Senior Officers was established, and in 1966 the Cadet School for police officers was established in Haifa. Databases were computerized, and forensic labs were improved with an addition of a mobile forensic lab to serve the needs of field investigations.

During the Six Day War (1967), Israel captured territory in the Sinai Peninsula, the Golan Heights, and the territories, expanding the geographical area under its control. Afterward, the Israeli economy came out of an economic depression, though with this recovery, the social cleavage among Israel's diverse residents went deeper, finding its expression in social unrest and the establishment of activist groups that demonstrated and created much civil disorder. Additionally, terrorist activity escalated, reaching new peaks while also targeting Israeli targets abroad. Consequently, the IP reorganized its authority to include the territories, the Sinai Peninsula, and the Golan Heights. In addition there were other organizational adjustments in the structure of the BGP (see below). In the territories new police jurisdictions were formed under the supervision of military governors to address issues of law enforcement and to provide police services to the population. The municipal jurisdictions were turned into regional jurisdictions subordinate to the Jerusalem IP headquarters. More emphasis was directed toward specialization and professionalism; more university graduates and former military officers were hired and received commissioned officers' ranks immediately, and specific activity became more and more dependent on computerized data sets. Research and development were expanded, and information and knowledge were exchanged with countries abroad.

When the Yom Kippur War broke out on October 6, 1973, the IP commissioner declared a mandatory recruitment of all police personnel to military duties. After the war ended, Israeli society was unstable politically until the election of 1977, which later resulted in the peace agreement with Egypt. During the entire period, Arab terrorist activity did not cease, and the northern part of Israel was constantly attacked by terrorist groups infiltrating from Lebanon. As a result, in 1974, following a government decision, additional responsibility for maintaining "internal security" (i.e., providing proactive and reactive functions to fight terrorism within the borders of the country) was transferred from the IDF to the IP (Herzog, 2001; Sebba, Horovitz, & Geva, 2003). Following this, a Civil Guard Department was formed and joined together tens of thousands of civilians that volunteered to guard their neighborhoods. The BGP began securing the air and sea ports, and in 1975 a new department was established—the Operational Department—to coordinate the activities of the various operational units (i.e., patrol, traffic, bomb-disposal, etc.) and increase their efficiency. A special Antiterrorist Unit was formed as well as a Bomb Disposal Division. Additionally, and in order to respond to a steep increase in white collar crime and other sophisticated crimes, the IP revised its ranks. All investigative units, detective work, intelligence, forensic, and juvenile units were united under one special unit—the Investigation and Crime Fighting Department. The 1978 *Shimron Report* (a report prepared by a parliament-appointed investigative committee), dealing with crime in Israel, contributed to this change with its recommendations to formulate guidelines and establish new units to investigate and tackle serious crime. These included the National Serious Crimes Investigation Unit, the National Fraud Unit, the Internal Investigations Unit, the Tel-Aviv District's Central Unit, and others.

After the Lebanon War was over (a period known by its Hebrew term, *Shalom HaGalill*) and throughout the 1980s, the IP faced new challenges. It began this period by drawing up a five-year plan known as the Tirosh Plan. This was the first time in its history that the IP had conducted a formal analysis of its society's need for police services, drawn up forecasts, and laid down clearly drawn policies for each section of its operations. The tasks and objectives for each succeeding year were derived from this long-term plan. In 1981, the IP set up its fourth police district, the Central District. New units were created—among them the Community Relations Unit—as part of the attempt to further prevent crime while providing more support to victims of crime, and the Zvulun Unit for policing the sea and air ports was formed (IP, 2004).

In this regard, it should be added that

> one of the serious challenges that confronted the IP during that time
> was riotous demonstrations by Ultra-Orthodox Jews [against Sabbath
> desecration and archeological excavation of Jewish graves], in addition
> to riots by Arabs, and by a range of political movements. The evacua-
> tion of protesting residents from the town of Yamit [part of the Sinai
> Peninsula returned to Egypt under the Israeli-Egyptian peace agree-
> ment] and the new problem of crime motivated by nationalistic ideolo-
> gies consumed much police time and resources. (IP, 2004)

From the second half of the 1980s up until the first half of the 1990s, the
rate of Jewish immigration to Israel began to pick up sharply, especially from
the former Soviet Union and Ethiopia, resulting in a demand for new police
recruits who could speak the language spoken by these immigrants to be able
to communicate with them and serve their needs. Such immigration also
brought many new problems that Israel had not witnessed before (e.g., organized crime, higher rates of alcohol consumption, and drunkenness accompanied by violent behavior, to name just a few). At the same time public disorder
and disturbances by Palestinian Arabs erupted in the territories and became
routine. After a while, this unrest began to spread, although on a smaller scale,
into Israeli Arab towns. Arab terrorist attacks became more frequent and took
many forms—open attacks in town centers launched for their shock effect, con-
cealed explosive devices placed in markets and on the streets, arson, attacks on
individual soldiers and civilians, infiltration attempts from the sea, and the like.

As a result of the economic depression and the 1985 economic emergency
plan that was put into place at that time, recruitment to the IP was frozen, and
because the demand for policing kept increasing, prioritizing had to be done.
The first three priorities were dealing with drug abuse while tackling drug trafficking, combating the high accident rate on the roads, and increasing public
order in Jerusalem. During this period the IP continued to search for useful technological and scientific advances to be introduced to its daily activities, while
promoting the professionalism and specialization of its personnel (especially in
the area of forensics, bomb disposal, and intelligence), who could benefit
greatly from use of new advances in technology. The IP also decided to invest
in education for values and professional ethics within the service itself. The aim
was to instill into every officer that any lapse of integrity and improper behavior would not be tolerated. Because of pressure from the public regarding the
need for transparency in the investigation of complaints submitted against
police officers, the IP's Internal Investigations Unit (called *Yahash*—the Hebrew
acronym for the unit) was transferred to the Ministry of Justice, and in 1992
Israel's new civilian board for the investigation of suspect police officers was
established. (For a review of this topic, see Herzog, 2000.) In addition, in 1997,

> the IP's new Code of Ethics was officially introduced. The aim of the
> Code was to make precisely clear to every serving officer the standards

of professionalism and integrity and public service he or she was required to attain and maintain. (IP, 2004)

The second half of the 1980s was also characterized by the first intifada, in which daily violent rioting became reality. Arab terrorism rose to new levels. Once more the IP priorities had to be changed. The police forces in Jerusalem and other areas of disturbance (i.e., in the north—the Galilee and Northern Valleys—and in parts of the Central and Southern Districts) were heavily reinforced with police officers to maintain order. Such rearrangements resulted in mobilization of officers from all other areas of traditional policing responsibilities, which inevitably suffered more and more from this change in the order of priorities. Such was the case at the beginning of the 1990s, when the intifada intensified, and terrorist attacks also became more frequent. Again the IP had to reallocate its resources, transferring officers from its conventional anticrime policing functions to the maintenance of internal public order and public security. Some effort was made to compensate by using the BGP and the Civil Guard volunteers for regular police work in addition to their internal security duties. Restoring law and order demanded a militaristic approach and in many cases use of force, which sometimes was deemed excessive and also resulted many times in the escalation of the conflict.

Along with the gradual development of an Israeli civil society at the macro level, the demand for more police services had raised the emphasis on the police officer as a public servant who needs to provide the public with efficient and reliable service . (For a review of such social changes, see Herzog, 2001). Accordingly, attention was given to increasing collaboration between the public and the police, resulted in the implementation of the community policing philosophy, which began in 1995. The idea was to make police work more responsive to the needs of the ordinary citizen and to integrate the resources and goals of the police with those of local government authorities and community agencies (Herzog, 2001; Weisburd, Shalev, & Amir, 2002).

Another important organizational modification during this period was the creation of two new departments—the Traffic Department and the Intelligence Department (which was taken out of the Investigation Department and set up as a separate entity). The purpose of the change was to coordinate widespread operations and to upgrade the methods and technologies employed—the one in the battle against the heavy toll of road accidents and the other in the battle against crime.

Additional resources were also allocated to deal with serious crimes, while the war on drugs was reinforced by creating an Anti-Drugs Unit in the Southern District. This kind of unit had been operating successfully for some years on the northern Lebanese border. This unit was designed specifically to prevent drug trafficking across the Egyptian border.

It was also during the second half of the 1990s that the IP made good on its long-term intention to improve officers' working conditions, wages, and welfare. It further upgraded and refined its in-service training system. Recruitment efforts were expanded with the specific purpose of raising the quality of candidates for police work. Within the context of bringing the IP to up-to-date levels of organization and logistics, the computerization of the service was extended, particularly into the Manpower Division, and a massive equipment procurement drive was set in motion. Sophisticated, high-performance antiterrorist and anticrime equipment and technologies were bought, and relevant officers were carefully and thoroughly trained in their use (IP, 2004).

From this review, it may be seen that the development of the IP is intertwined with the historical development of the Israeli society and state of Israel. From its inception, the IP has adapted continually to serve the constantly changing needs of its citizens. Thus, as argued before, the IP can be reviewed as an organization that adopted the liberal reformist approach to policing; that is, the IP regularly adapted its operation and organizational structure to the changing needs of its society. From its inception in 1948 and up until today, the IP strives to enforce the law in the spirit of the basic values of a democratic state, while aiming to ensure the security of both individuals and society as a whole and enhancing the quality of life of its citizens. Especially when taking into account the complexity of combining two major tasks—the traditional enforcement and crime prevention role of police with the task of preventing terrorist activity—this has not always been easily accomplished.

Organizational Structure and Issues[3]

Structure and Organization

The IP is commanded and directed, operationally and organizationally, by its commissioner, who is appointed by the government on the recommendation of the minister of public security and who is responsible for the police and prison services. Seven departments constitute the IP's national headquarters located in Jerusalem, Israel's capital: Investigations and Crime Fighting (incorporating the intelligence function, which for the past few years was a separate department), Patrol and Security, Traffic, Logistics, Personnel, Planning, and the Community and Civil Guard Department.

In 2003, the IP employed 25,700 policemen and women, including soldiers doing their mandatory military service in the IP, a ratio of one for every 293 citizens. Twenty percent of police officers are women. Nearly all staff are sworn members of the force. Since 1999 the IP has employed civilians, primarily in secretarial and logistical support jobs.

As of 1994, the IP was organized into six district commands. The district commanders report directly to the police commissioner; they and the department heads at police headquarters all hold the rank of major general and compose the senior command staff of the force. The commander of the BGP also reports directly to the commissioner. These districts are divided again into subdistricts, each of which is under the direction of a police commander. The subdistricts are, in turn, divided into large regional police stations or smaller police stations and police substations. The commanding officers in each of these police units are all selected by national and regional headquarters.

In 2003 there were 10 large regional stations (mostly in the metropolitan centers), 53 stations, and about 100 substations. In addition, there were approximately 350 community policing centers—usually these are one-person police centers in neighborhoods or rural villages, but sometimes a mobile or temporary center is set up in a specific area to deal with specific problems— and about 400 neighborhood Civil Guard bases, some of them within or attached to the community policing center.

Each district and subdistrict is managed by an administrative and operational headquarters that parallels the organization of the central IP headquarters in Jerusalem. Since 1997, reorganization has attempted to flatten out the organizational structure and do away with the middle management (subdistrict) levels, and there has been some success.

Personnel: Selection, Training, and Promotion

Between 1995 and 2000, an average of more than 1,000 men and women were recruited to the IP each year, the majority for core duties such as patrol work, investigations, intelligence, traffic control, bomb disposal, and service in the Community and Civil Guard Department. Some were recruited to the BGP or other branches of the police as part of their compulsory military training after completing their high-school studies at the age of 18. (Mandatory service has a duration of three years for males and two years for females.) However, it is possible that some of these will later pursue careers as regular police officers in the BGP or in other units within the police. Other than that, the minimum age for regular police recruitment in Israel is 21 years, and the minimum educational requirement is a high school diploma.

Candidates are examined for general suitability and for suitability to a particular area of activity of the IP. They must pass a security clearance and assessments of their psychological and physical health as well as educational and intelligence testing. Although candidates are obligated to have at least completed high school (which requires 12 years of schooling) and taken their matriculation exams, many times the Israeli police will seek to recruit candidates with more then just a high school diploma, as they did during the second half of the 1990s when recruitment targeted former military officers and people with an associate's, bachelor's, and in some case higher academic degrees.

A new police officer, once recruited, participates in a basic 25-week training course. New officers become eligible for promotion after three years, subject to performance on a proficiency test in their area of work. After another year on the job, they can be recommended by their commanders to go to the advanced police officers' course, which consists of four to six weeks of specialized training in a particular field of work. Also, during their fifth year in the service, officers are eligible to attend a five- to ten-week senior police officers' training for those who will become noncommissioned commanders. Only after this second training course can a police officer become eligible to be recommended for promotion to commissioned officer status.

The commissioned officer course lasts 30 weeks, and during this training, the officers also take part in academic studies for one semester at Haifa University (for those who do not have academic degrees). Commanders then receive further specialized training.

Promotion from rank to rank is achieved by seniority, completion of training courses, and individual evaluation by both commanders and peers. The IP has the following ranks:

1. For noncommissioned officers: constable, lance corporal, sergeant, sergeant major, staff sergeant major, advanced staff sergeant major, senior staff sergeant major.

2. For commissioned officers: subinspector, inspector, chief inspector, superintendent, chief superintendent, commander, brigadier general, major general, and the commissioner's rank—inspector general.

Today, unlike in the 1970s and 1980s, potential police officers holding academic degrees are also recruited to the lowest noncommissioned rank, but they can advance to commissioned officer after approximately one year of service if they pass the assessment exams and complete the commissioned officer's training course.

The Border Guard Police

Rooted in the early days of the Israeli state, the purpose for the formation of the BGP was to deal with security and guard tasks in areas that are located outside the main cities and on the borders of the country. This paramilitary gendarmerie within the IP was established at first by recruiting senior Jewish officers of the British Mandate Police. It was determined that this force would remain small and highly professional. The force was also designed to protect and assist the regular police in maintaining order and as an "iron fist" force for suppressing civil disorders. With its own independent organization and structure, it was determined that this unit would act under the direction of the district commands. The BGP has separate bases and training centers from those of the districts' regular police personnel, and accordingly those who serve in it are called "soldiers." The BGP has existed in its current form, as known today, since April 1953. Since its establishment, it has had a crucial role in protecting the country's borders against infiltration while also protecting the life and property of its citizens in rural areas.

In 2003 there were some 8,000 soldiers serving in the BGP. Its tasks are to deal with security and antiterrorist activities, to guard and patrol the Israel-Palestinian Autonomous[4] Area border, to deal with disruptions to public order, and to prevent agricultural theft. In addition, the BGP serves as a highly mobile, rapid response and reinforcement force—both in criminal and civil order matters—and is available to the IP districts as well as to the IDF upon request. From the time of the Oslo accords in 1993 until October 2000, when the second intifada broke out, the BGP's police officers conducted joint patrols with the newly established Palestinian Police Force in areas where there was joint Israeli-Palestinian responsibility.

Major Functions of the Israeli Police

Criminal Investigations

There are approximately 2,500 investigators and police prosecutors in the IP. Police prosecutors present misdemeanors and some felonies to the magistrate courts.[5] The Investigations and Crime Fighting Department also is responsible for dealing with juveniles—both as suspects and as victims—from age 12 (the lowest age of criminal responsibility) to age 18 in coordination with the agencies responsible for child and youth welfare, juvenile delinquency, and juvenile parole as well as with other organizations assisting in victim support. A Victim Support Unit (VSU) provides professional input on all policy and its implementation regarding the support given to victims of crime—especially regarding special groups of victims, such as those of domestic abuse, sexual abuse, "helpless" victims (such as the mentally retarded), or the aged. Special domestic violence investigators have been trained and deployed since 2001 to deal with and investigate both the victims and the perpetrators of domestic violence.

The Division of Identification and Forensic Sciences, also in the Investigations and Crime Fighting Department, analyzes evidence with an entire range of tests (DNA, fingerprints, drugs, explosives and flammable materials, ballistics, etc.) in specialized laboratories at IP headquarters in Jerusalem. Each regional subdivision has its own crime-scene technicians who gather evidence from crime scenes and send it to the IP's centralized laboratories, or if possible, make initial tests *in situ* or at the regional station. An automatic fingerprint identification system (AFIS) helps compare latent fingerprints found at the scenes of crimes with a centralized database of known criminals and is used to authenticate identification of suspects with the help of their fingerprints. A mobile crime lab from the headquarters is often mobilized to gather evidence in complex crime scenes or those involving murder or terrorist activities.

There are two national investigation units: one for serious and international crimes, (such as the operation of car theft rings, money laundering, and drug trafficking) and the second for dealing with white collar crime, fraud, and computer crime. All these units are considered understaffed and are constantly inundated with cases. A system of prioritization of investigation cases, using standardized guidelines, has recently been established in order to assist officers in dealing with their caseload.

Intelligence

The Intelligence Division coordinates and directs the intelligence and undercover work undertaken throughout the country at all levels. Efforts are concentrated upon serious target criminals in accordance with an evaluation that is made at the various levels of the police hierarchy. In addition to the above functions, the division is responsible for all drug-related enforcement work, as well as for international cooperation with foreign police forces. At the district level, there are some centralized intelligence units whose tasks are to gather evidence and perform undercover work.

Since 1949, Israel has been a member of the INTERPOL, and extensive operational cooperation takes place on a regular basis via this organization. Several police representatives are stationed abroad (e.g., in the United States, Germany, France, the Netherlands, Russia, Ukraine, and Thailand) in order to facilitate international investigations.

Patrol and Operations

The IP's central and largest force is the patrol unit, whose main responsibility is responding to public calls for assistance, usually received by the Emergency Calls Center. (A "100" telephone number allows the caller quick connection to these centers.) The patrol officer is also the first line of response to an emergency, whether road accident, natural disaster, or terrorist attack. In events and gatherings requiring a massive police presence (e.g., mass-attendance events, events of particular political and public significance, protest marches, big sporting events), patrol units maintain public order and safety.

Special patrol units have been established to give the IP a highly skilled and rapid response capacity for incidents of particular severity or danger. Together with the BGP's special units (such as its Anti-Terrorist Special Combat Unit), they are the first to respond to any life-endangering security incident or mass-casualty disaster. They are routinely deployed against particularly dangerous criminal targets or where there are geographical concentrations of criminal activity. Any unit within the IP can request the assistance of such a unit for immediate reinforcement, and backup.

In the context of its direct responsibility for antiterrorist activity, the government placed responsibility for school perimeter security on the IP in 1995 and for public transport security in 1997. For these assignments, the IP allocated a fleet of motorized patrol units that were briefed to patrol the perimeters and vicinity of schools and other educational institutions and of bus, train, and taxi stations to detect and prevent terrorist or criminal activity.

As one of the methods to assist in proactive crime prevention, the Patrol and Security Department is also responsible for providing input regarding the security standards needed to enable the local licensing of high-risk businesses. [6] Other units under the direct supervision of the Patrol and Security Department include the Helicopter Unit, the National Vehicle Theft Prevention Unit, and a National Negotiation Team, which is used when hostage situations arise.

The Civil Guard Department[7] and Community Policing

In order to prevent terrorist and criminal activity in residential areas, the Civil Guard maintains a network of neighborhood Civil Guard bases (some 400 in 2004). The Civil Guard recruits volunteer citizens for armed mobile and foot patrols. It also runs training programs and organizes rapid response teams for emergency duty.

In 2004, Civil Guard volunteers, ages 17 to 90, numbered approximately 50,000. While on duty—guard members have four hours of compulsory duty per month—Civil Guard volunteers have police authority (i.e., they may search cars and suspects, detain suspects, ask for identification papers, etc.) and are usually armed with police rifles and provided with portable radio transmitters and identification vests. The regular volunteers patrol in groups of two to three on foot or by car (using private or police vehicles) in their own neighborhood, providing for a crime and terrorist prevention patrolling function. The Civil Guard also includes special units that provide volunteer aid to regular police units in a range of activities: traffic control and enforcement of traffic regulations, patrol functions, emergency rescue units, and agricultural theft prevention (mainly as volunteers with the BGP), to name a few. These uniformed volunteer auxiliaries undergo specialized training and usually volunteer for many more hours than the compulsory minimum—about four to six hours per week.

In 1994 the IP command adopted a community policing strategy and began to implement its ideas on a large scale in January of 1995. The essence of this approach is that local police forces should work in partnership with the Civil Guard, local government (municipalities and local authorities), and community agencies, all pooling their resources to minimize crime, social problems that lead to crime, and incivilities that decrease the quality of life (Geva, 2003; Herzog, 2001). The implementation process was initially led by the Community Policing Unit, which was directly responsible to the commissioner. Since 1999 the unit has been merged with the Civil Guard Department, thus joining the two functions of mobilizing volunteers and working with the community on crime prevention and enforcement activities. This department has since been called the Community and Civil Guard Department.

In 1999 a system to make the police commanders more accountable to their communities and for achieving their measurable objectives was implemented based on the COMPSTAT (COMPuter STATistics or COMParative STATistics) method used by the New York City Police Department. The IP commissioner holds biweekly meetings with each area commander and uses statistical information to pinpoint areas and patterns of crime that need to be addressed. The computerization of most policing activities and the linking of the stations to the central computer at head-quarters via an intranet allows local commanders as well as management to keep track of changing crime and traffic accident patterns and to provide appropriate responses—both proactive and reactive.[8]

When community policing was conceived and planned in Israel, it was seen as part of a total reformation of the Israeli police in structure, philosophy, and action (Geva, 2003). However Weisburd, Shalev, and Amir (2002) suggest that "this broad idea of community policing was not implemented in Israel, and indeed the program of community policing was found to lose ground. . . . While community policing did have specific impacts on the Israeli police, it did not fundamentally change the perspectives and activities of street level police officers" (p. 102). According to Weisburd and his colleagues (2002; see also Herzog, 2001), one of the possible explanations for the failure of implementation is due to "the resistance of traditional military style organizational culture within the Israeli police to the demands of community policing models" (p. 80). However, they argue that "such barriers to successful community policing are not unique to the Israel case, and are indeed likely to be encountered in the development of community policing in many other countries" (p. 105).

In recent years, although it has been pushed aside by security matters, there has been a renewed increase in the formation of community policing centers around the country and especially in the Arab towns and villages in the northern part of the country. Community policing officers have been trained to implement interagency models of crime prevention in dealing with various common crime problems. Implementation of this model is initiated mainly by the police officer. However, these officers rarely use "problem-oriented policing" strategies to analyze problems and encourage communities to form their own original crime prevention strategies, as was suggested by the original community policing strategy. (For a review of the difficulties with implementation, see Herzog, 2002.) Furthermore, these police officers are usually taken off their beats to participate in security-related activities together with the other officers in their area, thus affecting their ability to respond to their assigned communities.

Other Departments

Traffic: The IP's Traffic Department enforces road traffic laws, keeps traffic moving smoothly, investigates road accidents, brings offenders to justice, provides for research and development in the traffic enforcement areas, and educates and informs the public in road discipline.

Management and Logistics Departments: Other departments include the Logistics Department, charged with the management and care of the IP's material supplies and equipment, and the Planning Department, which manages all IP resources and its budget, staff, and computerized databanks as well as research and development of technology within the force.

Personnel/Human Resources Department: Israeli Police human resources (HR) management is designed to develop the organization's human resources by providing each officer with high-quality services and support. The department constantly develops its training track and programs according to changes and needs within the organization and in its changing environment. While doing so, the department looks after the personal welfare and work conditions of employees, and it organizes in-service training courses and study days. The department constantly encourages its officers to continue their education. Recruitment and promotion decisions are done on objective and professional grounds, with equal opportunity given to both genders and all ethnic groups.

Accountability

Complaints against police officers about the unlawful use of force or about criminal matters punishable by over one year of imprisonment are dealt with by the recently established external civilian Unit for Investigation of Police Officers (known in Hebrew as *Machash*), which is headed by an attorney and is under the supervision of the Ministry of Justice. According to Herzog (2001), about 1,000 police officers are investigated each year, which is less then 4 percent of all uniformed police officers. The main innovations of the newly established civilian board include the following (Herzog, 2000):

1. *The investigation of suspicions against police officers:* All the investigators are former police officers; the board's criteria for membership include experience in police investigations, knowledge of police work in the field, and a high level of professional discretion. As noted, the function of the investigators is to investigate police officers suspected of committing offenses (on or off duty) involving the illegal use of force as well as criminal offenses punishable by over one year of imprisonment. Less serious cases that do not meet these criteria continue to be dealt with by the (police) department's internal investigations unit.

2. *The recommendation to continue treatment of a complaint:* This specific recommendation, made after the external investigation, is made by the board's attorneys, headed by a district prosecutor. Recommendations range from a disciplinary trial (in a one-official trial or a disciplinary court) to trial in a

criminal court to the closing of the case. In offenses involving the use of force (as opposed to other criminal offenses, in which the board can only make a suggestion), this recommendation becomes a formal decision for the police force.

According to Machash's internal regulations, complaints against police officers may be submitted to Machash in person, in writing, or by fax, in different languages, at any police installation, including police stations and Machash's offices, in any part of the country. If the complaint is submitted at a police installation, the duty officer is required to receive it immediately, and there is a strict prohibition against advising a complainant otherwise. After receipt of the complaint, an investigative file is opened if, on the one hand, it is suspected that a criminal or a use of force offense has been committed, and if on the other, there is public interest in the investigation as defined by the head of the unit.

Files are distributed among the board's investigators according to the geographic location of the offense. Upon completion of the investigation, the file together with the recommendations of both the investigator and the head of the team (who has the authority to demand further investigation) is scrutinized by the head of Machash. Only the head of Machash and its attorneys are entitled to decide on continued treatment of a file. At the end of the process, notification has to be sent to the complainant, the suspect police officer(s), and relevant police bodies (personnel department, direct commander, etc.). If the case is sustained, it is transferred to the state prosecutor (for criminal cases) or to the police attorney (for disciplinary cases) (Herzog, 2000).

However, less serious cases (disciplinary in essence) continue to be dealt with by the internal investigations unit within the IP, usually following a complaint from the public brought to the public complaints officer at the district or headquarters level, or to the Ministry of Public Security's ombudsman or complaints' unit. At each district, a public complaints officer receives these less serious complaints from the public and investigates them. Alternatively, the public can send such complaints either to the police headquarters ombudsperson or to the Ministry of Public Security ombudsperson. The Discipline Division draws up indictments for the IP's disciplinary court, where hearings are heard before the police judge, two additional officers who act as judges, and usually a public representative, who is a lawyer from another agency. There is also an appellate court. This internal unit also decides on whether a complaint is sustained or not. If it is, then a disciplinary board hears the case and provides judgment. All verdicts are subject to appeal and are then passed on to the disciplinary appeals board for further decision.

Terrorism[9]

As noted above, the early seeds of the IP can be found in the establishment of the *H'Shomer* organization in 1909 that declared itself as the first Hebrew police and a Hebrew gendarmerie in the land of Israel. Its purpose was to guard and protect Jewish settlers from Arab attacks. Israel has suffered repeatedly from infiltrations and terrorist attacks on civilian targets since it became a state in May 1948, and as stated in 1974 the IP was given the additional responsibility of maintaining internal security. It is under these historical and developmental conditions that Israel has one national centralized police force that is geared toward mobilization of its forces from crime fighting to homeland security upon demand.

Following the 1974 decision, two special units were established: The Civil Guard and the Bomb Disposal Division.

The Civil Guard

The Civil Guard has already been described above as a department of the IP. But the establishment of this department was a result of the escalating infiltration and terror attacks on Israeli citizens, mainly in the northern part of the country, in Jerusalem, and in the surrounding area. At first it was decided that the Civil Guard would operate as an auxiliary to the IP and not as a unit within it. This voluntary organization's preliminary aims were to assist the BGP and a military Civil Defense Unit (known as HAGA, a Hebrew acronym for *civilian protection,* this is different from the previously mentioned Hagana). Six months after its establishment, the Civil Guard had about 60,000 volunteers, of which a tenth were senior high school students, trained to patrol their neighborhoods with police cars and to use police weapons—all with the intention of detecting and preventing terrorist activity. During 1975, and as a result of the steep increase in terror attacks in Jerusalem and other parts of the country, the number of volunteers reached 110,000. In its first years of operation, the activities of the Civil Guard focused mainly on patrolling the streets during the night. In many ways it can be seen as a paramilitary organization with former military commanders acting as commanders of the local Civil Guard stations and operations. Also, in its first stages, this organization received its support from the IDF, the BGP, and HAGA.

It is only a decade later that the Civil Guard was incorporated into the police and began to provide auxiliary policing services as well, as discussed briefly above.

Bomb Disposal

Established in 1975, the Bomb Disposal Division (under the Patrol and Security Department) operates in the realm of both criminal and terrorist sabotage activities. The division's teams, at the local level, handle about 100,000 calls per year to check suspicious objects, parcels, and cars, and lately also to check persons suspected of carrying on their person bombs in the form of bomb belts or vests. On average, less than 1 percent of these calls actually involve incendiary or explosive devices.

An important aspect of the Bomb Disposal Unit's work is its prevention program, which includes surveillance of crowded public areas and facilities and educational programs in the schools. Police headquarters has its own research and development unit to develop specialized equipment and techniques to address bomb threats as well as a separate laboratory to provide analysis of explosive devices and modes of operating. The Israel Bomb Disposal Information Center gathers, analyzes, and disseminates information to police sappers and to other security organizations in the country and worldwide.

In addition to the above, the IP's Anti-Terrorist Special Combat Unit (which organizationally belongs to the BGP) deals with terrorist activities within the borders of the country, operates in hostage-taking situations—both terrorist and criminal in nature—and sometimes assists in the handling of serious public disturbances. To comply with these emerging problems, specialized equipment and techniques—some of which are developed in-house—allow for quick deployment throughout the country.

Although they are geared toward fighting terrorism, these organizational entities are not the sole players in the IP war on terrorism. Each of the other departments may at any given time allocate resources to such activity.

Between September 2000 and the end of July 2004, there were 22,406 terror attacks on Israeli targets both in the territories (against Jewish settlers living in the vicinity or driving through) and inside Israeli borders, resulting in the death of 677 Israeli civilians and about 300 members of the security forces (Israeli Defense Force, 2004). As a result all the IP units work in close collaboration with the IDF and with the National General Security Service (indicated by the Hebrew acronym SHABAK), placing the war on terrorism and the security of the Israeli citizens as their top priority.

Figure 9.1 shows the never-ending challenge of this struggle. Starting in the beginning of 2002 there has been a steep escalation in the number of terror attacks, both successful and unsuccessful. The successful prevention of planned attacks is due mainly to thorough intelligence work as well as to collaboration among the above mentioned bodies. One can also see that from February 2002 until the end of November 2004, a higher percentage of attacks were successfully prevented. This goal could not have been achieved if Israeli forces had used the model known as "due process"[10] by many Americans and had operated with local and municipal police forces, because the challenges of terror attacks threaten public safety rather then civil rights. In other words, operating under the assumptions of due process while using municipal police forces will limit the ability of law enforcement agencies and the other organizations they collaborate with, and this may result in the loss of critical reaction time that is highly important to the prevention of terror attacks.

For this reason, a national centralized police force has merits, as it can work more efficiently under such constant emergency and stressful

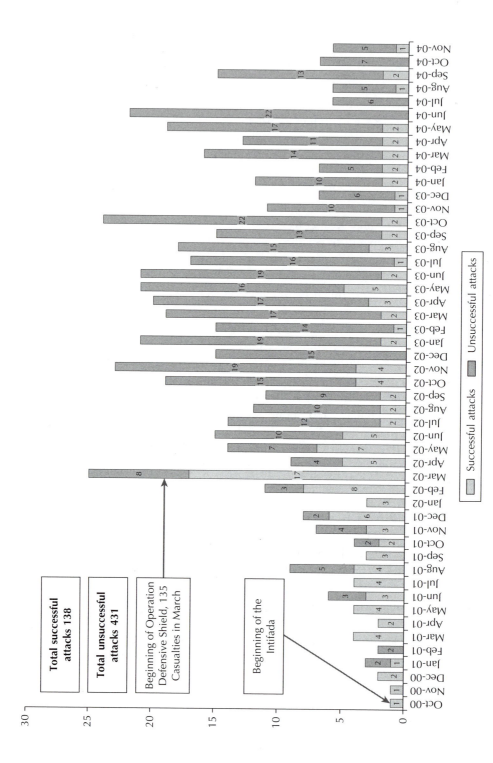

Figure 9.1 Successful Versus Unsuccessful (Thwarted) Terrorist Attacks

SOURCE: IDF official Web site (http://www1.idf.il/dover/site/mainpage.asp?sl=EN&id=22&docid=16703).

242

conditions than a local police force, which is decentralized in authority and mobilization potential and has fewer resources as its command. A centralized national police force can provide massive and quick deployment of emergency forces where needed, throughout the country. Furthermore, a national agency allows for centralized intelligence gathering and investigating processes, as well as for analyzing complex national data. This makes easier the task of detecting, identifying, deterring, and preventing potential terror attacks.

Summary

The Israel Police (IP) is trying to deal simultaneously with maintaining public order, preventing crime, and performing classical and traditional law enforcement duties while also providing a public service and security to the public it serves. Taking into account the dearth of resources available to the force, the IP is constantly trying to adapt to the changing social environment as well as to the macro-level needs of homeland security. These last needs often demand the IP's almost exclusive attention, causing it to reallocate, reorganize, and reassign its crime-fighting, traffic, and other operational units according to immediate, midrange, and long-range needs.

As a result many times harsh public criticism is directed toward the IP way of doing its job and regarding its competence to prevent crime. Gideon and Mesch (2003), describe the image of the police in Israel and the Israeli police officer in particular as "not especially good; nor is the image of the level of service given by the police. . . . Usually they [Israeli police officers are] perceived as slow, violent . . . and impolite" (p. 115). One must keep in mind that the police are under high pressure as a result of constantly feeling as though they are taking part in a combat situation, as is the case when they are dealing with high-risk terror attacks, and this causes police officers to burn out (Herzog, 2001). On the other hand, about 13 percent of Israeli citizens who have been victimized and did not report their victimization to the police rationalized their failure to report by saying they "did not want to bother the police" (Gideon & Mesch, 2003, p. 110). This suggests that the public is somewhat aware of the national priorities and makes a rational decision in regard to the damage done by their victimization and their expectations for service. Nevertheless, fighting terrorism also brings other outcomes—some positive—as described by Herzog (2003), who found that motor vehicles stolen from Israel and smuggled into Palestinian Authority areas decreased when counterterror activities of the police and security forces brought about a strict closure of the borders or increased surveillance of traffic crossing roadblocks.

Being under constant terror threats, both external and internal to the state, the IP is challenged to maintain public safety. In such a milieu, it is often hard to follow a due process model and to maintain civil rights and liberty—in particular those aspects of this model that pertain to search and seizure. For this reason, a policing style that is other than national will not be suitable. Using a militaristic organizational culture and approach under such conditions corresponds well to current national security needs, allowing the IP to operate countrywide while responding to the rising demands of the public. It is for this reason, we believe, that community policing in Israel did not manage to become entrenched as an all-embracing operational philosophy in its first years of implementation and up to the present, as described by Weisburd and his colleagues (2002). This is also the reason why the idea of municipal or local policing—as it is practiced in the United States and in most European countries—will encounter difficulties in Israel, where police are seeking to respond to growing national demands (Weisburd, Shoham, & Gideon, 2001).

Notes

1. The majority of the material presented in this section is taken from IP (2004).

2. According to the liberal reformist approach, police activity is constantly being evaluated in order to improve its efficacy and efficiency. Advocates of this approach propose recruitment of higher-quality personnel while improving and prolonging training and introducing more women to the police force as well as recruiting members of minority groups to serve as police officers. In addition, they argue for academic studies as a supplement to police training. Usually, advocates of this approach are academic scholars, policy makers, and other police executives that emphasize the need to modernize police work to meet the needs of today's changing environment.

3. The majority of the material in this section is taken from Geva, Herzog, and Haberfeld (2005) with permission from the authors and the editor.

4. These are territories that were transferred to Palestinian authority after the Oslo agreement signed by Israel and PLO in early September 1993. The agreement involved autonomy for parts of the Gaza Strip and the West Bank with Jericho as the first territory to achieve autonomy.

5. Other categories of offenses are presented to the court by civilian prosecutors.

6. For an in-depth survey of the development of the crime prevention function and community policing implementation within the Israeli Police, see Geva, 1998 and 2003.

7. Further discussion of the Civil Guard in regard to homeland security is presented in the section on terrorism.

8. The setting of measurable objectives by each police unit in their yearly plans started in 1998, and in January 2005 it was put on hold while new proposals for setting objectives and measuring success at achieving them were being considered.

9. See Geva, 1995.

10. Unlike the United States, Israel does not have a constitution; therefore "due process" as known by U.S. criminal justice practitioners is not a valid concept.

References

Geva, R. (1995, April-May). Effective national and international action against terrorism: The Israeli Experience. In R. Geva (Ed.), *The prevention of crime and the treatment of offenders in Israel.* Paper presented at the Ninth UN Congress on the Prevention of Crime and the Treatment of Offenders, Cairo, Egypt.

Geva, R. (1998). Crime prevention strategies: Twenty-year summary. *Innovation Exchange,* 7, 228–237. Jerusalem: Ministry of Public Security.

Geva, R. (2003). Crime prevention: A community policing approach. In S. P. Lab & D. K. Das (Eds.), *International perspectives on community policing and crime prevention* (pp. 95–112). Upper Saddle River, NJ: Prentice-Hall.

Geva, R., Herzog, S., & Haberfeld, M. (2005). Israel (State of Israel): The Israeli Police. In L. E. Sullivan & M. Haberfeld (Eds.), *Encyclopedia of law enforcement: international* (Vol. 3, pp. 1130–1134). Thousand Oaks, CA: Sage.

Gideon, L., & Mesch, G. (2003). Reporting property victimization to the police in Israel. *Police Practice and Research,* 4(2), 105–117.

Herzog, S. (2000). Treatment of illegal-use-of-force complaints against police officers in Israel: The beleaguered path to civilian involvement. *Police Quarterly,* 2(4), 477–501.

Herzog, S. (2001a). Militarization and demilitarization processes in the Israeli and American police forces: Organizational and social aspects. *Policing and Society,* 11(2), 181–208.

Herzog, S. (2001b). Suspect *police* officers investigated by former *police* officers: Good idea, bad idea? *Law and Policy,* 23(4), 441–467.

Herzog, S. (2002). Does proactive policing make a difference in crime? An implementation of problem-solving policing in Israel. *International Journal of Comparative and Applied Criminal Justice,* 26(1), 29–52.

Herzog, S. (2003). Border closures as a reliable method for the measurement of Palestinian involvement in crime in Israel: A quasi-experimental analysis. *International Journal of Comparative Criminology,* 3(1), 18–41.

Herzog, S. (2005). The relationship between economic hardship and crime: The case of Israel and the Palestinians. *Sociological Perspectives,* 48(1), 77–104.

Israeli Central Bureau of Statistics. (2006). *Selected demographic data from the annual statistic report.* Publication Number 57. Retrieved August 6, 2007, from http://www1.cbs.gov.il/reader/newhodaot/hodaa_template.html?hodaa=200601204.

Israeli Defense Force. (2004). *Successful vs. unsuccessful terrorist attacks.* Retrieved December 27, 2004, from http://www1.idf.il/dover/site/mainpage.asp?sl=EN&id=22&docid=16703

Israeli Police (IP). (2004). *Welcome to the Israel police website!* Retrieved December 27, 2004, from http://www.police.gov.il/english/default.asp

Ross, J. I. (1998). Radical and critical criminology's treatment of municipal policing. In J. I. Ross (Ed.), *Cutting the edge: Current perspectives in radical/critical criminology and criminal justice* (pp. 95–106). Westport, CT: Praeger.

Sebba, L., Horovitz, M., & Geva, R. (2003). Israel: *Criminal justice system in Europe and North America* (pp. 14–19). Helsinki, Finland: The European Institute for Crime Prevention and Control, affiliated with the United Nations (HEUNI).

Smooha, S. (1988). Internal divisions in Israel at forty. *Middle East Review, 20*(4), 26–36.

Smooha, S., & Hanf, T. (1992). The diverse modes of conflict-resolution in deeply divided societies. *International Journal of Comparative Sociology, 33*(1–2), 26–47.

Sullivan, L. E., & Haberfeld, M. (Eds.). (2005). Israel (State of Israel). *Encyclopedia of law enforcement* (Vol. 3). Thousand Oaks, CA: Sage.

Weisburd, D., Shalev, O., & Amir M. (2002). Community policing in Israel: Resistance and change. *Policing: An International Journal of Police Strategies and Management, 25*(1), 80–109.

Weisburd, D., Shoham, E., & Gideon, L. (2001). Municipal policing in Israel—Problems of efficiency, community, equality and integrity [in Hebrew]. *Police and Society, 5*, 5–25.

10

The French Police System

Caught Between a Rock and a Hard Place—The Tension of Serving Both the State and the Public

Benoît Dupont

The French model of policing is often presented in English-language histories of policing as an exact opposite of the Anglo-Saxon model. This symmetrical and elegant antagonism has more than theoretical or academic implications. It also conveys a rhetorical and normative message, which asserts the democratic superiority of one system over the other. This posture dates back to the parliamentary debates that led to the creation of the London Metropolitan Police in 1829, where the idea of a new structure modeled on the French centralized and professional system was strongly opposed, the terms "odious" and "repulsive" being used by some politicians to describe it (Critchley, 1967; Emsley, 1996). On the issue of effectiveness, it also seems that Anglo-Saxon popular culture has assigned to the French police an image associated with pompous, ridiculous, and inadequate practices, fuelled in part by the fictional character of Inspector Clouseau, brilliantly interpreted by Peter Sellers in the *Pink Panther* movies. If those representations are of little consequences beyond their immediate purposes—political reform and entertainment—they must nonetheless be gently pushed aside in the context of a more rigorous comparative policing approach.

These opening comments are particularly important in the case of the French policing system because of the scarcity of texts available in English on this topic. This situation can partly be attributed to the anemia of French criminology and police studies, the language barrier, and the lack of linkages between the Anglo-Saxon and French academic communities (Ferret, 2004). For those reasons, most accounts of French policing written in English so far tend to be the work of outsiders (Mawby, 1990), an arrangement whose potential for omissions and misinterpretations has been highlighted by Bayley (1999). Furthermore, most of those texts are outdated and are more interesting for their historical value than for their contemporary accuracy. Hence, a majority of the references used in this chapter will be taken from the expanding French literature. Until the early 1980s, very little research had been done on policing, which was considered a "dirty research object" by academics (Brodeur & Monjardet, 2003), essentially for ideological reasons. The creation of a research committee by the Ministry of the Interior in 1982, followed in 1989 by the foundation of a National Institute for the Study of Homeland Security (IHESI) and the availability of research funding facilitated the development of a scientific knowledge on the work of the police and its organization (Loubet del Bayle, 1999a).

The aim of this chapter is to offer a contemporary overview of the organization and latest policing reforms in France. In line with the approach taken in this book, I will follow a structure that will facilitate implicit cross-country comparisons. First, I will examine the history of the French police and its current political context. In the second section, immigration trends and their impact on the delivery of policing services will be described, with a particular emphasis on the problems faced by poor North African families in public housing neighborhoods. The third section will delineate the dual organizational structure of the police system and assess some of the recent efforts made to rationalize it and make it more accountable. The fourth section will be dedicated to the implementation of community policing strategies and their impact. Finally, the last section will briefly examine the various forms of terrorism experienced in France over the past 20 years and the antiterrorist capabilities developed by the French police. Whereas it would be an insurmountable task to provide a comprehensive outline of a policing system that comprises so many bureaucratic and cultural layers sedimented over centuries, in the following pages the writer hopes to provide the reader with a window on the evolution of democratic policing in a country that has often placed the interests of the state above those of the public.

The Police of the Republic: A Monarchical Creation

The history of policing in France can be characterized by the predominance of political influences, from the first edicts passed by monarchs in the seventeenth century to the early dualism of its structure and the constant tension between national and local political authorities. The far-reaching legal powers conferred to police officers derive from this role of instruments of the state.

Early Police Structures

If the birth of the English model of policing coincides with the creation of the London Metropolitan Police in 1829 by Sir Robert Peel, the French model is generally said to have appeared in 1667, with the proclamation of a royal edict that created the office of general lieutenant of the police for the city of Paris. In 1699, this arrangement was extended to the rest of the country. A fragmented night watch system had nevertheless existed since the year 580, and criminal investigation officers had been appointed for the first time in 1306 by King Philippe le Bel, but the reform implemented between 1667 and 1699 asserted the authority of the king over policing and was accompanied by a centralization of other public services such as the administration of justice and revenue collection (Gleizal, Gatti-Domenach, & Journès, 1993). A number of years before the establishment of permanent professional police officers in urban centers, a constabulary force or Gendarmerie had also been established to patrol the roads and protect isolated settlements from looters and mercenaries. This force was geographically reorganized in 1720, when five-man stations (or *brigades*) were built at strategic locations all across the kingdom.

The Revolution of 1789 caused the fall of the monarchy, and most of its symbols, such as the centralized police, were abolished. Policing became for a short period of time a municipal responsibility: Elected mayors took over from general lieutenants and appointed national guards—armed citizens— to patrol the streets and other public places. However, this local form of policing soon became too impractical to administer for the various undemocratic regimes that seized power after the Revolution. Most of the nineteenth century and the first half of the twentieth century can then be characterized by the efforts of central governments to reassert control over the police while legally maintaining the fiction of some form of local responsibility. This was accomplished by defining police powers as "delegated" by the state to municipal governments, and by regulating the appointment of police chiefs and constables, while letting local authorities pay for their salaries.

This strategy encountered strong resistance from local politicians, who argued in favor of more democratic and direct arrangements (Gleizal et al., 1993). As a result, reforms were implemented gradually—and sometimes temporarily halted or withdrawn—to avoid open conflict, particularly in large cities. This less-than-linear process remained nevertheless a high priority for successive central governments, mainly because of the rapid industrialization and urbanization of the country, leading to social and political unrest that municipal police forces could not handle adequately. The centralization and unification of the French police were finally completed in 1941 by the Vichy régime, under German occupation. All police forces in municipalities with more than 10,000 people were brought under state control to form one single entity, the Sûreté. Only Paris kept a separate force until 1966, when the Paris police and the Sûreté were amalgamated to become the modern National Police.

The history of the Gendarmerie, a rural police force operating under military command, has not been affected to the same extent by the debate on centralization and unification. It was originally known as the *Maréchaussée;* its current name was adopted in 1791, during the Revolution, in order to sever the ties of the organization with its royal origins. The law of 1798 and the reign of Napoleon gave the Gendarmerie its modern structure and its military character. The institution's subsequent evolution and multiple reforms never altered the founding features of the Gendarmerie. This dual civil-military police system, which was "exported" to other European countries and African colonies, is the result of a tension among the social and political agitation that threatened governments, the limited capacities of local police forces in the field of public order maintenance, and the reluctance of the state to use the military to suppress revolts. The creation and maintenance of the Gendarmerie, a police force made up of soldiers, which is also primarily responsible for civil police duties in rural areas and can conduct criminal investigations on its own initiative, must be understood as a compromise between democratic values and the fear of political disorders. To borrow the words of Emsley (1999, p. 2.), the Gendarmerie was "providing the first line of defense against insurrection in [the] capital" and was regarded "as a valuable prophylactic against economic and social disorder." This historical dualism and the duplication of resources associated with it are nevertheless questioned in the face of increasing crime rates.

The Crime "Inflation"

The past 30 years have seen a sharp increase in criminal activity, particularly in the areas of property crime and assaults. However, the data available to us are not as detailed or complete as we would expect, since crime statistics are collected in France by the two main police organizations and by the justice ministry. As a result, they mainly reflect police activity, which can vary with the adoption of new practices or strategies. Furthermore, in the absence of independent and transparent protocols for their collection and presentation, they are not subject to the same amount of scrutiny found in other countries and must be analyzed with caution (Mucchielli, 2001). Of course, annual victimization surveys have been conducted by the National Statistics Institute since 1996, but they are merely an add-on to the more general household survey (Aubusson, Lalam, Padieu, & Zamora, 2002).

The data available from the 1970s show that property offenses represent two-thirds of all crimes recorded in France. Among them, breaking-and-entry and car thefts are especially problematic. If official statistics show a decrease for those crimes since the beginning of the 1990s, victimization surveys indicate that they are now underdeclared by their victims, despite the incentive to obtain a police report for insurance purposes (Robert & Pottier, 2002), and that they are evenly distributed across urban and rural areas, while they were previously mainly experienced in large cities (Mucchielli, 2001). The levels of interpersonal violence have also increased significantly over the past 25 years. If murders and homicides are stable (1.6 per 100,000 population in 2003), assaults have multiplied by a factor of three since 1972 to reach 220 per 100,000 population in 2003, generating strong feelings of insecurity among the public.

Other interesting categories include drug-related crimes and destruction and damage to property, which accounted respectively for 3 percent and 13.6 percent of all recorded crimes in 2003. The later category of crimes, which has seen a 10-fold increase since the early 1970s, has constituted a sore point for governments and police forces for many years, signaling to the public the slow decay of the social fabric. It includes the vandalism and arson of public buildings such as schools, police stations, and community centers; the frequent plunder of popular clothing and music stores during public protests; and more routine acts such as the burning of public transport buses, phone booths, and private cars. This category of crimes is usually concentrated in or around public housing neighborhoods, where a majority of the tenants are poor first- or second-generation immigrants. This has led some observers to conclude that this phenomenon, which very often directly targets the police or any symbol of authority, reflects the despair and anger of an entire generation of young people of foreign origin who have little or no prospect of social and economic integration (Duprez & Hedli, 1992; Mucchielli, 2001).

An Evolving Legal Context

The legal system distinguishes two main police functions: administrative policing and judicial policing. This distinction is linked to the dissociation of public and private law and to the historical development of the idea of policing. Prior to the Revolution, the notion of policing encompassed all areas of government intervention (Napoli, 2003), and it is only in more recent times that it acquired its contemporary meaning, which is defined by the detection and control of crime (L'Heuillet, 2001). Hence, administrative policing refers to the remnants of this earlier era, designating all ancillary tasks and regulatory activities conducive to the maintenance of public order in its most general definition. By contrast, judicial policing is confined to the detection and repression of specific offenses that administrative policing is unable to prevent. This dual legal framework does not mean that different units or forces are exclusively responsible for one form of policing or the other, but instead helps determine which judges and courts (administrative or judicial) should oversee particular policing activities. Administrative jurisdictions are hence more concerned with the defense of civil rights on a general level, while judicial courts deal with the integrity of criminal procedures.

The inquisitorial nature of the French criminal justice system creates a particular set of constraints on the work of police investigators. A judge is involved from the early stages in the collection and preparation of evidence by the police, directing the investigation. It also entails a secret, written, and noncontradictory procedure in the discovery of truth, where the judge acts on behalf of all parties. When a crime or a grave offense is detected, the district attorney opens a file and assigns the investigation to a specialized magistrate: the investigating judge. Investigating judges exercise their authority over criminal investigators, and the criminal procedure code specifically states that they can choose to assign a case either to the National Police or the Gendarmerie investigative units. This entails a constant monitoring of the effectiveness and professionalism of investigators by magistrates. If they are dissatisfied with the performance of one agency, they are at liberty to transfer the case to the other. A result of this prerogative is the development of a fierce competition between the National Police and the Gendarmerie to secure and retain the most prestigious investigations and a certain reluctance to cooperate and exchange information. The term *police war* is frequently used when this competition reaches extremes.

Investigators from the National Police and the Gendarmerie are divided in two groups with different legal powers. Judicial police officers (OPJs) are granted full investigative powers after having passed a legal exam, while judicial police agents (APJs) include all rank and file police officers, who may undertake only basic investigative activities. Both judicial police officers and judicial police agents need a delegation of power from the judge to undertake tasks such as detaining and interrogating suspects, entering and searching premises, seizing assets, or intercepting telecommunications. It must be noted that police officers may detain suspects for up to 24 hours, the limit being extended to 96 hours in cases of terrorism and drug trafficking. However, certain tasks, such as interrogating suspects and confronting them with witnesses, are often carried out by the judges in person.

The Code of Criminal Procedure also states that all police officers have the power to check the identity and address of individuals in public places who are suspected of having committed a crime, suspected of preparing to commit a crime, able to assist the police in its investigations, or wanted by the police. Such a "control of identity" may also be carried out in order to prevent a breach of public order, particularly when the safety of persons or goods is threatened. This very vague wording allows police officers to check people's identity at the officer's discretion, and numerous cases have been reported of officers using this power to harass young people of North African origin (Garcia, 2002).

These traditional powers have been extended in the wake of the terrorist attacks of September 11 by the socialist government through the Daily Security Act of 2001. Violently opposed by civil rights organizations, the act grants more extensive stop-and-search powers to police officers and private security guards, extends the surveillance of Internet communications, and criminalizes meetings held in the corridors of public housing residences. This last measure seeks to forbid loud gatherings of young people, mainly of North African origin, but it has been ridiculed, the link between the fight against terrorism and this mild form of incivility appearing tenuous at best (Monjardet, 2003). More recently, the Chirac administration, elected on a law and order platform, pushed through parliament another law, the Homeland Security Act of 2003, which effectively removed the sunset clause of the Daily Security Act of 2001 and made most of the new police powers permanent. It also created new offenses such as aggressive begging or "passive solicitation for prostitution" in public places and made it easier to incriminate suspects in cases of assaults or threats against police officers and their families. These new measures have certainly increased the legal arsenal of the police, but they have also strained police relations with ethnic minorities, and these relations were already of poor quality.

Racial and Ethnic Context

Immigration Trends

According to the latest census data, France has a population of 59 million people. The number of immigrants was estimated at 4,310,000 in 1999, or 7.4 percent of the mainland population. They originated mainly from other European countries (45 percent) and from Africa (40 percent), with a minority coming from Asia (9 percent) (Boëldieu & Borrel, 2000). Other data, from the Ministry of the Interior, placed the number of legal immigrants at 4.5 million in 1990. The main countries of origin are immediate European neighbors such as Portugal (17 percent), Italy (6.2 percent), and Spain (5 percent). The majority of immigrants from Africa come from former North African colonies such as Algeria (18 percent), Morocco (16.2 percent), and Tunisia (6.5 percent). Officially, permanent work visas have not been issued since 1974, except to European Union nationals, but family reunion programs and regularization initiatives account for a yearly intake of 60,000 people.

In 1990, the Ministry of the Interior believed that there were a million illegal immigrants in France, but recent estimates are more conservative and oscillate between 300,000 and 500,000 people. The impact of illegal immigration on crime and delinquency has been used as a recurring political theme by the far-right National Front Party since its inception. However, the geographical features of the country and its involvement in the construction of the European Union make border control very difficult. In 2002, for example, approximately 40,000 illegal immigrants were ordered by the courts to leave the country, and 7,500 of them were effectively deported. Simultaneously, 68,000 asylum seekers who had entered the country were refused permanent residency, making them de facto illegal immigrants (Sarkozy, 2003).

The cultural and ethnic diversity of a country is also reflected by citizens of foreign origins. According to statistics compiled by the National Institute for Demographic Studies, immigrants and citizens of foreign origins (either through naturalization[1] or by right of birth) account for approximately 20 percent of the overall population. There is very little information available on spoken languages, but a 1992 survey by the National Institute for Statistics and Economic Studies showed that 68 percent of French children (all origins included) spoke French at home with their parents. The second most spoken language in the survey was Arabic, with 11.5 percent, and the third Portuguese (6 percent).

An Exhausted Model of Integration

The statistics enumerated above describe a diversified racial and ethnic fabric, but mean very little in terms of social integration. The French sociopolitical system is based on a secular and universalistic idea of citizenship, which is encapsulated by the "Liberty, Equality, Fraternity" motto. As a consequence, immigrants of various ethnic and religious backgrounds are denied any minority status and are summoned to embrace a Frenchness that acts as the cement of the Republic. Unfortunately, this republican model of integration is not working as well as it ought to or has been, particularly in the case of immigrants from former North African colonies, a majority of whom are Muslims who suffer from discrimination and poverty, and as a result, violently question the legitimacy of the republican principles. Disproportionate numbers of young people from this background are experiencing learning difficulties in school, leave school without any diploma or formal qualifications, and are unemployed or underemployed (HCI, 2004). These social challenges are compounded by a phenomenon of spatial segregation: A large majority of North African families live in high-rise public housing neighborhoods that lack basic public services, are remote from economic and cultural hubs, and are poorly served by public transportation. The disintegration of parental supervision mechanisms and the development of illegal underground markets are two additional problems that afflict poor immigrant communities and strengthen their disaffection, despite attempts by central and local governments to design and implement mitigating policies.

It is therefore hardly surprising to find that public housing neighborhoods, whose number is estimated to be close to 1,500 (HCI, 2004), experience higher levels of crime and insecurity (Peyrat, 2001) than the rest of the country. More surprising maybe is the fact that they have been consistently blamed by a number of politicians and social commentators for being responsible for the general increase in crime and disorder over the past 20 years (Mucchielli, 2001, 2003), segregating their inhabitants even more.

This convergence of factors has led to systematic conflictual relations between young unemployed immigrants, who spend most of their days congregating in public places,[2] and the police, who are perceived as a force of occupation in those spaces. So entrenched is the level of antagonism between the two groups that the National Police has developed over the years an "urban violence scale" that contains eight degrees, the most extreme representing "urban riots and massive destructions for more than three nights by more than 50 youths" (Bui Trong, 1998). As we have noted above, this violence is randomly directed against all public services and symbols representing the authority of the state, and in 2003, more than 44,000 incidents of destruction and vandalism against public property were recorded (Ministry of the Interior, 2004). Social and health workers as well as firefighters are not spared and are also frequently attacked (Peyrat, 2001).

The tensions between immigrants of African origin and the police culminated in November 2005 following the accidental death in a Paris suburb of two teenagers who were fleeing a police patrol. Urban riots quickly erupted and spread from the capital to the rest of the country. For more than 21 nights, young people attacked public buildings and burned 10,000 cars in hundreds of cities in defiance of a state that had abandoned them. The unprecedented levels of violence and the poor police response overwhelmed the government, which proclaimed a state of emergency on November 8. The police arrested more than 4,700 rioters, and considering the number of belligerents on each side, very few casualties were recorded (Cazelles, Morel, & Roché, 2007). It is nevertheless telling than a couple of years after these critical events, no public inquiry has been held, and very little empirical research has been published on the subject, as if ignoring the symptoms could magically cure the disease.

Organizational Structure and Issues

The history of the French police has produced two national forces with discrete geographical responsibilities: the National Police in urban areas (towns and cities with more than 10,000 people) and the Gendarmerie in rural areas. Both enforce the same laws with the same legal powers, over different geographical jurisdictions, but while the former is a civilian organization located within the interior ministry, the latter is a military force placed under the authority of the defense ministry. This dual structure has led to criticism related to the lack of coordination and the episodic emergence of turf wars in sensitive domains, such as counterterrorism or international police cooperation. As we will show in a subsequent paragraph, attempts have been made in recent years to better integrate the operational activities of the two forces.

A third group of small municipal forces must also be mentioned. There were 3,143 of them in 2001, serving municipalities ranging from small resort towns on the Riviera to large cities such as Paris, Marseille, and

Toulouse. Despite these statistics, only a minority of the 36,000 municipalities maintains municipal forces, and most of them employ fewer than 10 officers. The number of municipal forces expanded significantly between the 1980s and the 1990s in response to the rise of the fear of crime, with a geographical concentration in the south and around the capital. Sixty-two percent of municipal police officers carry firearms, but they do not have any powers of arrest or investigation and do not compete with the law enforcement and order maintenance activities of the two major police forces. The main responsibility of municipal police officers is to provide a visible uniformed presence in the streets, enforce local bylaws, and deal with quality of life issues. They represent a second tier of policing, and they have little training, low pay, and reduced prestige. Table 10.1 represents the size of these police as well as the National Police and National Gendarmerie.

Table 10.1   Police Strength

Police Division	2002
National Police	132,000
National Gendarmerie	98,000
Municipal Police	15,400
Total	245,400

National Police

The French system is probably one of the most centralized administrative systems in the world, particularly in terms of policing (Bayley, 1985; Brodeur, 2003). In the case of the National Police, for example, a director general answers directly to the minister of the interior. The director general supervises and coordinates the work of the various directorates, which reflect the high degree of specialization of the institution. Each directorate is subdivided into central and local services, the latter being characterized by important variations in terms of geographical jurisdiction. The annual budget of the National Police was US$5.7 billion in 2002.

The Administration Directorate of the National Police (DAPN) is in charge of human resources, logistics, general administration, and finances, as well as procurements. The Training Directorate (DFPN) manages 33 police academies and training centers all over the country. The Central Directorate of the Judicial Police (DCPJ) handles most criminal investigations. It deals mainly with murders, drug trafficking, organized crime, white collar crime, human trafficking, terrorism, and art theft. Other units of the National Police can be called to investigate in less serious cases. This directorate also houses forensic units and the National Central Bureau of the International Criminal Police Organization (ICPO)—Interpol—which dispatches all requests for information and assistance, including those emanating from the Gendarmerie.

The Central Directorate of Public Security (DCSP) is in charge of maintaining public order in urban areas. It staffs and coordinates the work of police stations all over the country. Its tasks include patrols; answering calls for assistance from the public (17 is the French equivalent of 911); crime prevention and detection; road safety and traffic management; organizing the security of large political, cultural, and sports events; and supporting the judicial process. The Central Directorate manages local directorates at the department level, which are themselves subdivided into public security districts. A security district is usually covered by a large police station. There are 463 of them in 1,606 municipalities, providing security to 30 million people. It must be noted that separate arrangements exist for Paris, where the police prefecture brings together the judicial and public security functions. The Paris prefect is directly responsible to the minister and manages a structure that parallels that of the national organization. It constitutes more than a quarter of the National Police's strength.

The General Intelligence Directorate (DCRG) collects political, economic, and social intelligence in order to inform the government's decision-making process. It is also responsible for monitoring casinos and racetracks. The surveillance of political parties' internal activities was discontinued in 1995 following a number of scandals. This directorate now focuses its activities on terrorist organizations, sects, extremist religious and political groups, organized crime, and urban violence phenomena.

The Central Directorate for Border Policing (DCPAF) protects the integrity of French borders and combats illegal immigration in close cooperation with its European counterparts. It also assists French consular offices all over the world. The International Technical Police Cooperation Service (SCTIP) is placed under the direct authority of the director general. It arranges bilateral and multilateral cooperation initiatives, manages the careers of police attachés and liaison officers posted in 52 permanent delegations and 40 hosting police organizations abroad, and participates in the work of European and United Nations institutions in the field of security. Other units directly attached to the director general include an antiterrorist and hostage-rescue unit (RAID), an antidrug coordination unit (MILAD), a counterterrorism coordination unit (UCLAT) and an antimafia coordination unit (UCRAM).

The Central Service of the Companies for Republican Security (SCCRS) constitutes the permanent mobile reserve of the National Police. The 61 companies for republican security were created at the end of World War II and can be dispatched nationally on short notice for antiriot and emergency situations.

National Gendarmerie

Just like its police counterpart, the Gendarmerie is centralized to the extreme. A director general heads the Gendarmerie. He must be a civilian, but he answers to the minister of defense. For administrative policing functions (53 percent of its activities), the Gendarmerie obeys to the highest-ranking public servant in each department, the prefect. For judicial policing functions (35 percent of its activities), it is placed under the authority of the district attorney and/or investigating judges. Moreover, the Gendarmerie institutes proceedings in a number of cases on behalf of the Ministry of the Economy and Finance and other ministries and administrations. The Gendarmerie is geographically divided into seven regions that match the army defense zones, a legacy of its military origins and current missions. The Gendarmerie consists of two major forces that reflect the division of labor within the organization and an array of miscellaneous specialist units. The annual budget of the Gendarmerie was US$4.5 billion in 2002.

The Departmental Gendarmerie is the generalist component of the Gendarmerie, with more than 63,500 officers in its ranks (2002). It operates 3,600 police stations in rural and suburban areas and is in charge of public security, highway policing, police investigations, mountain rescue, criminal intelligence, river patrol, and youth crime prevention. It also runs air wings in each region. The Mobile Gendarmerie, which employs 17,000 officers, is a force dedicated to policing public protests and dealing with riots. The GIGN (National Gendarmerie Intervention Group), a unit specialized in antiterrorist and hostage rescue operations, and the GSPR (Security Group of the Republic's Presidency), a team assigned to the protection of the president, are also attached to the Mobile Gendarmerie.

The most famous of the specialized units is the Republican Guard, a mounted corps of 3,000 that provides security and honor guards to state institutions and during foreign dignitaries' visits. There are other arms of the Gendarmerie dedicated to air transport safety and to the protection of air force and navy bases. The Gendarmerie's Institute of Criminal Research develops new scientific and forensic capabilities to support the work of investigators. As a result of its military status, the Gendarmerie also assumes responsibility for certain aspects of national security, such as the recall of the reserves or the protection of military nuclear capabilities. Furthermore, it regularly sends officers to civilian police operations coordinated by the United Nations or NATO in Lebanon, Albania, Haiti, Kosovo, East Timor, etc.

Toward the End of Dualism?

In 2002, the newly elected government placed the coordination and redeployment of the two police forces at the top of its reform agenda. In order to minimize the duplication of resources and efforts, a presidential decree (Number 2002-889) transferred operational control of the Gendarmerie from the minister of defense to the minister of the interior. This new authority allowed the president to end the long-standing rivalry between the two forces and facilitated the implementation of the Homeland Security

(Orientation and Programming) Act, promulgated in August 2002. This special appropriation act, among many other measures, provided a financial and administrative framework for the reshuffle of National Police and Gendarmerie resources in order to better reflect the demographic makeup of the country and the spatial distribution of crime. Also, the planning and implementation of policies is now made by a single ministry, offering more homogeneity in service delivery.

In addition, Regional Intervention Groups (GIR) have been formed to investigate the underground economy's hidden financial transactions and bring down the criminal networks that operate in public housing neighborhoods. These 29 permanent task forces bring together investigators from various National Police directorates, the Gendarmerie, customs and revenue agencies, and labor and fraud inspectors as well as prosecutors. It is still too early to determine whether they will have a lasting impact on crime levels, but one of their major achievements has been the cultural change they have brought about, replacing an entrenched animosity between competing agencies with a culture of cooperation and information sharing (Le Fur, 2003).

Weak External Oversight and Opaque Internal Accountability Mechanisms

The recent changes in homeland security policies have not been exclusively concerned with effectiveness but have also addressed the issues of accountability and oversight. Up until the implementation of the National Security Ethics Commission Act of 2000, the internal affairs departments of various police units provided the only means of monitoring the accountability of the police, creating a situation where the independence of oversight mechanisms could not be guaranteed. The new law created an independent administrative authority, the National Security Ethics Commission,[3] that is responsible for investigating ethical misconduct by both public and private security providers such as the police, corrections and customs officers, and private security guards. It is perhaps the most original aspect of this law that it confers on a single organization oversight powers over the fragmented world of security producers. Unfortunately, the commission faces many challenges and does not seem at the moment to be able to realize this ambitious mandate.

There are several reasons for this inability. First, it does not have any regulatory, injunction, or disciplinary powers, and its sole means of pressure is the yearly public report outlining the cases addressed and the actions taken by the organizations implicated (Le Roux, 2001). Second, the procedure for complaining to the commission is cumbersome: Citizens must lodge their complaint through a member of parliament (either a representative—*député*—or a senator) or through the prime minister, who then decides whether it falls within the jurisdiction of the commission. This procedure creates a political filter between the commission and the citizens and makes it difficult, if not impossible, for people from minority or hard-to-reach groups to signal unethical conducts. This is particularly true when law and order politics dominate the agenda and politicians do not wish to be seen as weakening the authority of the police. The low number of complaints reported by the commission confirms this: Nineteen were recorded and investigated the first year (CNDS, 2002), while 33 were lodged the second year (CNDS, 2003), none of them related to the private security industry.

Such low numbers of complaints, considering that the public and private security sectors employ altogether more than 340,000 people (Simula, 1999), can also be attributed to the inadequate infrastructure of the commission, which employs only three full time clerical staff and received in 2001 a budget of US$510,000. The eight members of the commission are appointed for six years on a nonrenewable basis, but their main professional activities do not allow them to investigate the complaints they have to examine.[4] Under those constraints, it is not surprising that many consider the commission to be a paper tiger and that the public makes very little use of it to call public or private security organizations to account. Furthermore, the commission does not maintain any ties with existing internal accountability mechanisms, which also receive complaints from the public (Labrousse, 2001).

As a result, police deviance remains essentially investigated and dealt with internally by two units: the IGPN (General Inspectorate of the National Police) for all officers posted outside Paris and the IGS (General Inspectorate of Services) for the Paris region. The latter was formed in 1854, while the former appeared in 1884. Statistics are not released every year, but in 2000, the IGPN investigated 300 cases of police violence, misconduct, and corruption[5] (Razafindranaly, 2001). The same year, the IGS opened 932 new files, either at the request of investigating judges or because of complaints lodged by members of the public or police officers (Labrousse, 2001). The police's use-of-force policies have proved contentious, particularly in cases of shootings involving young fleeing suspects—often of North African origin—which have led to urban riots through the 1980s and 1990s. However, the fragmentary data available show a low frequency in the area of firearms discharge by French police officers, with an average of 0.3 annual firings per 1,000 officers between 1990 and 1996 (Jobard, 2002).[6] There appears to be no overrepresentation of one group of victims over another. Other forms of police violence are not measured, and it should certainly be a future priority of police researchers to fill this void. In line with the inquisitorial model, internal affair units are placed under the authority and control of the judiciary when criminal investigations are launched against police officers, which might explain the more aggressive stance taken by investigators and the relative underdevelopment of external oversight mechanisms.

Lateral Entry Recruitment and Training

The recruitment and training of French police officers is based on a lateral entry model that mirrors the human resources practices found in the military and in most other public services and in the private sector: Recruits join the police at a rank commensurate with their level of education, their skills, and their career aspirations. Of course, a promotion system based on merit and seniority also allows officers to climb the hierarchical ladder, ensuring the diffusion of frontline experience among administrators and managers. The recruitment and training system is centralized, with the exception of the system for municipal police officers, whose recruitment and training is left to the mayors.

In the National Police, applicants can join at the level of constable, lieutenant, or commissioner. There is no diploma required to take the constable entry exam, but a high school diploma is the norm. At the middle management level, two years of college are required. For applicants who want to take the commissioned officers' exam, a minimum of four years in university with higher-than-average marks is essential. These tests are very competitive and attract a lot of candidates vying for permanent positions. However, their emphasis on legal knowledge and rote learning is being questioned, in favor of more modern assessment techniques based on cognitive and leadership skills. Depending on the level of entry, an additional period of training ranging from 12 months (for constables) to 24 months (for commissioners) is undertaken. In 2001, the makeup of the National Police was 20 percent women and 80 percent men.

The Gendarmerie's lateral entry program operates under a two-tiered system. Noncommissioned officers must hold French citizenship, be at least 18 years of age, and pass a number of physical and written exams. The usual education level of recruits is at least a high school diploma. Commissioned officers must either have completed an officer's course in one of the three military academies or have successfully completed four years of university education. They must also pass physical and written exams. The length of training for commissioned officers is 24 months; for noncommissioned officers it is 9 months.

Like all other military personnel, Gendarmes are denied the right to unionize, but nevertheless they voice their demands for better working conditions through retired Gendarmes' associations and spouses' associations. It must be noted that the obligation of the Gendarmes to live in barracks with their families was at the origin of some tensions during the 1990s (Mouhanna, 2001).

National Police officers won the right to unionize in 1946, but they are barred from going on strike. More than three-quarters of officers, all ranks included, are members of a police association. Police unions are fragmented and represent narrow interests, such as those of uniformed or plainclothes police officers, constables, middle managers, or commissioners. Political and ideological divergences are also at the origin of a multiplication of police associations (Loubet del Bayle, 1999b). The main police unions are the SNOP, Synergie, Alliance, UNSA, and the SCHFPN (commissioners).

Community Policing

In the early 1990s, it became obvious to the population, the media, and politicians that the police no longer provided a level of service that could be called satisfactory. As the author has shown, property crime has grown exponentially over the past 30 years, and this has been accompanied by a symmetrical collapse of the clearance rates—down from 36.8 percent to 26.8 percent in 2000 (Courtois, 2001). Violent crime has also increased sharply, and the fear of crime is prevalent in France; 40 percent of the total population fears victimization in the very near future (ENA, 2000). Over this same period, one of the main criticisms voiced against the French police has focused on its isolation, its incapacity to listen to the public's demands, and its failure to deal with the types of crimes that affect citizens most. If the expertise of the French police in the fields of order maintenance and other specialist areas such as criminal investigations and intelligence is widely recognized, uniformed street-level policing has never enjoyed the same level of attention or resources. However, the pressure of spiraling crime rates and frequent public outcries over the impunity of young delinquents has become unbearable for the government and the police organization. The result has been community policing reform, inspired by American and British programs.

In line with its centralized tradition, in 1995 the French government passed the Orientation and Programming Security Act (LOPS). This law articulated officially the new concept of "security coproduction," in which the centralized state shares its responsibility for security provision with local and private actors. The outcomes of this law remained mostly a rhetorical statement until June 1999, when the government and the Ministry of the Interior finally implemented police reform under the label of *police de proximité*, or "proximity policing." It is important here to explain why this term was preferred to the more traditional *community policing*: This very deliberate choice was made to emphasize the universal aspiration of the French integration model and its refusal to see various communities treated differently or receive special benefits from state agencies. As a result, proximity policing does not entail outreach or liaison programs directed at specific minorities, such as can be found in other countries. This new strategy was implemented gradually: It was initially implemented in five pilot sites, then was extended to 62 districts, and was finally rolled out to all police districts in three waves between 2000 and 2002.

This community policing program is designed around five major operational principles (Ocqueteau, 2003):

1. A new territorial organization that increases the visibility of police patrols at the local level and that lets police stations decide how to allocate their personnel in order to meet local needs

2. Individual officers at all levels given more responsibility

3. Recruitment and training of police officers for multiple skills; they must be able to undertake a broad range of patrol, preventive, and investigative tasks

4. Frequent interactions with local stakeholders in order to build strong partnerships

5. A "privileged relationship with the population," implying better service to the public (especially victims of crime), better identification of its needs, and better information about the outcomes achieved

The reform was not limited to a redefinition of the roles and tasks of police officers. A significant budgetary effort was made initially to accompany the change, with a net increase of 5.7 percent in the National Police budget in 2000. However, this effort was not sustained in 2001 and 2002.

Most of the new resources were allocated to the recruitment of new police officers and special constables. These special constables, or more precisely police auxiliaries, are young people, recruited under five-year contracts, whose tasks put them in direct contact with the public. The training they receive is considerably shorter than that given to their full-fledged colleagues (2 months instead of 12). They wear a police uniform adorned with distinctive features, but they are not granted any of the legal powers required to conduct investigations or even make an arrest. Some cynical commentators compare them to "bodies in uniform" that free well-paid and better-qualified police officers from their most mundane tasks. If such harsh criticisms are somewhat warranted, these new jobs have nevertheless allowed young people from ethnic minorities to gain employment with the police, making the institution more diverse and bridging the gap between the police and a group in the community characterized by its confrontational relationship with the police. These police auxiliaries numbered 28,000 at the end of 2002,[7] representing a significant addition to the 233,000 police officers and Gendarmes already active.

However, this centrally planned reform has faced a number of challenges. Some of these challenges are intrinsic to the resistance experienced during any change process undergone by large bureaucracies. Others are more specific to the centralized character of the French police, and it is this particular group on which I want to focus here.

Concerted Action and External Partnerships:
The Local Security Contracts

The external challenges are probably the first that come to mind in a centralized police environment such as the one outlined in this chapter. By "external challenges," I mean the reluctance of other institutional actors to support the police. It is one of the central tenets of community policing that police organizations must rely on institutional and civil society partners in order to resolve the complex social problems that produce or at least have an effect on crime. However, when all the potential partners share the same high level of centralization, they derive from it the strength to resist any form of partnership that they do not see as useful or at least beneficial to their own institutional interests. In short, the larger and the more complex an organization, the more inertia it develops to resist external stimuli that do not threaten its existence or offer immediate rewards. By definition, the kind of partnerships involved in community policing strategies do not fit either of these two conditions.

In order to overcome this inertia and to integrate the diverse dimensions of community policing and crime prevention, a new administrative framework was implemented at the end of 1997 at the initiative of the central government. Its aim was to facilitate the development of interinstitutional partnerships that would also be able to integrate major civil-society stakeholders. This new tool follows contractual principles, which explains the name it was given: Local Security Contract or *Contrat Locaux de Sécurité* (CLS). The aims of the CLS are to encourage the coproduction of security by offering to a range of state and nonstate actors a common platform to identify, discuss, and negotiate a joint response to the problems of all kinds that negatively affect communities and the quality of life in their immediate environment.

One of the strengths of the CLS is that it acknowledges for the first time the fact that crime problems and incivilities[8] cannot be systematically delimited along administrative boundaries, whether these are geographical or functional. The centralized state is attempting an exercise in partial devolution, encouraging its crime control agents to organize themselves at the local level and collaborate with local political, business, and social actors in order to create a collective intelligence in the response to crime problems (Tiévant, 2002). To this day, more than 637 CLSes have been signed. They involve the police and their rural counterparts, the Gendarmes, but also judges and prosecutors, corrections officials, educators, health and social services managers, mayors and town councilors, community groups, housing authorities, public transport operators, etc.

Once a territory and the parties to the contract have been identified by the representative of the state (the prefect), a local security audit (or diagnosis) is commissioned. It must be noted that the territory in question varies from one district to another and can consist of a town or an entire county or can be limited to a transport network. Sometimes, it can even be a number of adjacent neighborhoods, if the problems they experience are specific. The diagnosis provides an overview of the situation prior to the implementation of the contract, addressing issues such as crime rates, incivilities, school attendance levels, urban decay, and fear of crime. The effectiveness and efficiency of existing strategies are assessed in order to detect opportunities for improvement and to determine priorities. At this stage, the local actors that should be involved in the CLS are identified and consulted in order to secure their participation early on. At the end of the diagnosis, all the actors meet and negotiate together a set of objectives, strategies, and deadlines that are best suited to the local environment. The contract represents this mutually agreed-upon action plan and the formal engagement of each participating institution to channel its resources and pool them with others toward its completion. Tools that will allow the evaluation of each institution's and the collaborative strategy's performances are also designed at this stage of the contract, so that all parties can monitor the progress made.

The link between the CLS and proximity policing is not obvious, and in centralized states, two such policies can easily be implemented at the same time without any sort of coordination, if they happen to be placed under the responsibility of two different ministries. In France, for example, such a situation occurred in the 1980s, when the National Police attempted to reform its operational philosophy within the portfolio of the Minister of the Interior, while a national crime prevention strategy inspired by the Bonnemaison report was established under the umbrella of the Minister for Urban Development (Dieu, 1999). These two efforts to provide better security to the French people were less than successful, partly because their fragmented administrative approach exacerbated differences between the two bureaucracies and duplicated services that had to be paid for with the same sparse resources instead of encouraging the emergence of a synergy. Hence, in order to avoid a repeat of this policy failure of the 1980s, the government decided to provide a financial incentive to the districts that had demonstrated a firm commitment to the CLS, facilitating the early move to community policing and allowing the recruitment of police auxiliaries. However, this was not sufficient to avoid some of the pitfalls that can be attributed to a long established tradition of centralization. Even though the policy placed the emphasis on partnership, some partners remained more equal than others.

Unsurprisingly, institutional heavyweights such as the local police authority and the justice ministries are overbearing and have a tendency to talk more than they listen, ensuring that their interests take precedence over their partners' interests. Episodically, there is also a blur between the primary objective of the CLS, which is to target local crime priorities and to bring the police closer to the community, and the tendency of all participants to see this process as a political game that could negatively impact their organization's standing and future resources if not played well, placing the interests of the institutional structure to which they belong ahead of the needs of the citizens (Ocqueteau, 2004). When this is the case, the CLS and the notion of partnership become an empty shell with few practical implications for the public. For example, the community policing reform was at the origin of some misunderstandings between the centralized police hierarchy and the centralized judicial hierarchy, which was not kept informed of all the details of the reform and its implications for the workload of prosecutors and other judicial officers, and which therefore undermined the implementation of the reform (Mouhanna, 2002).

The implications for each institution in terms of reputation and image are high, and none of them wants to be seen failing in the eyes of the public. For example, research shows that this reform generated high expectations among the public. However, the reforms were rarely followed by any visible effect, leading the population to feel even more frustrated and dissatisfied. The outcomes were contrary to the ones desired, and the public came to trust the police even less (Ferret, 2001). Additionally, some partners had a lot of difficulty entering into collaborative arrangements with the police, mostly for ideological reasons: Social workers or teachers, for example, tend to perceive responses to crime problems through a black-and-white repression/prevention dichotomy. For some of them, who see the police as the oppressor of young people and ethnic minorities, entering into a partnership with law enforcement representatives would be unethical. Prejudices also run high among police officers, who sometimes see social workers more as enemies than as potential partners.

However, when formal institutional partnerships were complemented by informal interpersonal relationships, evaluations showed that the CLSes achieved their objectives and that the partnerships became productive and sustainable (Tiévant, 2002). The consequences of a positive individual experience also created a transfer-and-diffusion effect, whereby public servants who had participated in a successful partnership at the functional and personal level were eager to promote the model when transferred to a new district.

Promoting Community Policing Competencies and Police Training

The transition to community policing has been accompanied by a huge effort in terms of recruitment and training in order to equip police officers with the toolbox required to translate the community policing philosophy into reality. Redesigned training curricula were offered to new recruits and to experienced police officers in order to make them more aware of the diversity of the population they serve. In this regard, recruitment strategies have an important role to play in shaping police organizations that reflect more accurately the ethnic composition of the French society. However, the number of young officers recruited from ethnic minorities and delinquent-prone neighborhoods remains very small because of these young people's academic scores, which are low compared to those of their middle-class counterparts who join with university diplomas. As we have seen above, many have been recruited as police auxiliaries, but their salaries are close to the minimum wage, and their career prospects are limited by the short duration of their contracts, making them second-rate police officers. This also results in very low retention rates. Special preparatory classes have been established in a few high schools located in socially disadvantaged neighborhoods, and the constable exam has been simplified in order to increase the number of young recruits from ethnic minorities who join the National Police,[9] but it is still too early to assess the outcomes of these measures. This lack of minority representation is amplified by the national and centralized nature of the recruitment and promotion systems, which make local adjustments almost impossible.

In the area of police training, courses in communication, conflict resolution, sociology of delinquency, and ethics have gradually been added to drilling exercises, weapons training, and the traditional courses covering criminal law and procedure. External consultants and community members are also invited on a more regular basis to share a different perspective with the students on a range of issues. More than 10 percent of National Police instructors must for example come from other organizations, but finding and keeping them is not always easy. Changing and updating training programs almost overnight has also been problematic for an organization that trains thousands of recruits each year. Trainers who have taught the same police doctrine for many years must learn, understand, and teach new procedures and practices.

Moreover, the training challenge is not limited to new recruits, as all operational officers must also be exposed to the new ways of policing. The continuing education program that supports community policing reform is costly, both financially and in terms of human resources taken off the streets to attend training. Too often, it has been apparent that training is not regarded as a high priority, leaving it to those on the street to work out on a case-by-case basis how to improve their skills, if they wish to do so (Mouhanna, 2002).

At the organizational level, the engagement of middle management officers or the lack thereof proved to be a crucial element. For example, the French police included some middle managers who were true believers or missionaries that had advocated closer relationships with the community for years and who acted accordingly, almost in a clandestine manner (Ferret, 2001). When these police officers took the lead and showed their reluctant colleagues how they could benefit from the reform, a favorable environment was created, facilitating the implementation of the new strategies more than any central directive could have. By contrast, when no positive role model was available in their midst, police officers proved a lot more hesitant to adopt the new strategies and often ended up discarding them as a fad that would eventually go away, when the central bureaucracy would come up with a new reform.

In retrospect, this strategy reflected a detailed understanding of the cyclical nature of police reform, and the 2002 presidential election announced a shift in the policing strategies promoted by the Ministry of the Interior. Without formally abandoning proximity policing, a new emphasis was placed on aggressive crime reduction, performance indicators, a more intensive use of criminal intelligence, and the creation of regional integrated task forces. What will remain of community policing in a few years is relatively hard to predict.

Terrorism

Over the past 30 years, four different types of groups have been at the origin of terrorist acts against the French government or French citizens. Regional independence movements (also called separatists), secret organizations, revolutionary organizations, and transnational terrorist organizations have been active and at times successful in reaching their targets. This section will provide a brief overview of the four categories, followed by an examination of the antiterrorist structures that have been put in place to respond to these threats.

Resistance to the centralist form of government found in France has led to the creation of the most active terrorist organizations and the most resilient to police intervention, mainly because of the strong support they enjoy among some segments of the population. Their form of political violence is concentrated in two regions: Corsica and the Basque country. A third region, Brittany, was the scene of marginal terrorist activity between the 1960s and the 1980s, but the levels of violence never reached the heights seen in Corsica or the Basque country (Crettiez, 1993). The reasons for the development of this particular form of terrorism are complex and interrelated, but the existence of a common local language and culture, the successes of the wars of independence and the ensuing decolonization process in Africa (especially in Algeria), and the popularity of leftist ideals are important factors.

In Corsica, terrorism appeared in 1975 with the creation of the FLNC or National Front for the Liberation of Corsica. The FLNC is responsible for a large number of small-scale bombings against government buildings and similar state symbols, but it has always voluntarily limited its casualties (Crettiez, 1993, 1998). In 1990, ideological disagreements within the FLNC led to a split and the creation of three entities: *FLNC–canal historique, FLNC–canal habituel,* and *Resistenza* (resistance). The old tradition of interpersonal violence rooted in the honor code or vendetta created an environment that explains the widespread support enjoyed by the FLNC and its offshoots. The only detailed study of Corsican terrorism depicts a core of 100 operational terrorists trained in combat and sabotage techniques, a second circle of 200 people in charge of logistics, and a third group of 1,000 active sympathizers. This three-tiered structure committed an average of 500 bombings a year on the island in the 1980s and early 1990s (Crettiez, 1998). At the end of the 1990s, the violence in Corsica reached a peak with the assassination of the highest representative of the central government on the island, Prefect Erignac (in 1998), but it now seems that this action was carried out by a rogue cell loosely operating at the periphery of the main terrorist organizations.

Terrorist violence emerged in the Basque country in 1959 with the creation in Spain of ETA (*Euskadi Ta Azkatasuna* or *Basque Country and Freedom*) by a group of students opposed to the Franco dictatorship and asking for the independence of the Basque provinces on both sides of the border. This organization is one of the most violent in Europe: Since 1968, ETA has been responsible for the death of more than 800 people.[10] Its military and support structures are complex and very compartmentalized and are often compared to the ones developed by the IRA. ETA maintains many links with terrorist and guerilla organizations all around the world.[11] For many years, with the tacit knowledge of the French government, it used France as a logistical base, establishing infrastructures such as weapons caches, bomb factories, safe houses for operational members, etc. The fact that it restricted its attacks to Spanish targets might explain the lack of interest of the French government at the time. The fight for the independence of the Basque country crossed the Pyrénées in 1973 with the creation of Iparretarak ("those from the North"), the sister organization of ETA (Crettiez, 1993). However, Iparretarak never reached the levels of violence of ETA and ceased to operate after the arrest of its leader, Philippe Bidart, in 1988.

It was the activity of a new antiterrorist terrorist organization, the GAL, in 1983 that precipitated the involvement of French police authorities alongside the Spanish government to fight ETA. For five years, the GAL, or Antiterrorist Liberation Group, killed Basque refugees (suspected ETA members living in France) each time ETA struck, forcing the French government to acknowledge the role of sanctuary played by France and to take action. Recent judicial developments have implicated the highest spheres of the Spanish government in the creation and financing of GAL (Amnesty International, 2000, 2001). The GAL represents the perfect example of a secret or front terrorist organization acting on behalf of hidden interests.

Besides separatist groups and secret or front organizations, a revolutionary movement inspired by the German Red Army Faction and Italian Red Brigades emerged under the name of *Action Directe*. Grounded in radical leftist ideals and believing in the need to destabilize capitalist governments, this group was active during the first half of the 1980s and carried out a number of assassinations against high-ranking public servants and CEOs before being dismantled by the police.

Islamic terrorism is certainly the most prominent form of transnational terrorism to have targeted the French government. Over the past 20 years, it has caused the death of 900 people, 300 of them on French soil (Conrad,

2002). In the early 1980s, the Lebanese conflict fuelled a number of attacks, such as the bombing of a French military compound in Beirut in 1983, which killed 54 paratroopers who had been sent on a peacekeeping mission.[12] Thirteen French hostages were also detained by Iranian-backed Hizbullah during the conflict. Between December 1985 and September 1986, a terrorist cell closely connected to Hizbullah and calling itself the CSPPA (Support Committee for Arab Political Prisoners) planted 15 bombs in various Paris department stores, killing 13 and wounding 325 (Conrad, 2002). Iran's motivation in supporting this terrorist violence was to put pressure on France in order to obtain the delivery of enriched uranium under an agreement signed with the shah's regime and to halt the support provided to Saddam Hussein's armed forces.

In the 1990s, the main "exporter" of Islamic terrorism to France proved to be Algeria, where the cancellation of elections won by Islamic parties led to the installation of a military dictatorship and a bloody civil war between the two forces. As Algeria's former colonial power and its main creditor, France is considered to be the main supporter of the military regime. As a result, the GIA (Armed Islamic Group), known for its gruesome civilian massacres in Algeria, became very active in France between 1993 and 1996.[13] It committed a number of assassinations and bombings, the most spectacular being the hijacking of an Air France plane on December 24, 1994, which ended with a successful assault by the National Police's antiterrorist unit. It is assumed that the hijackers intended to crash the plane over Paris, in an ominous sign of things to come (Wilkinson, 2002). In stark contrast with the terrorist wave of the 1980s sponsored by countries such as Iran, Syria, and Libya, the GIA depended heavily on local cells implanted in Muslim disaffected neighborhoods, enrolling young second-generation immigrants and even native-born French converted to a radical brand of Islamism.

This new phenomenon raised concerns about the emergence of direct links between low-level delinquency, drug trafficking, and terrorist activities in "difficult" neighborhoods and about the development of a new form of homegrown terrorism, directly linked to the al-Quaeda terror network. However, it appears that young Muslims have not embraced political violence, contrary to what some pessimist politicians predicted, and according to recent data released by the Minister of the Interior, no more than 200 young people from Muslim backgrounds have traveled to Al Qaeda's training camps (Sarkozy, 2004).

Counterterrorist Capabilities

A number of police units are engaged in the fight against terrorism and enforce the provisions of section 15 of the Code of Criminal Procedure, which defines the objective and subjective elements of terrorist acts. This section was added by the Fight Against Terrorism Act of 1986, which deals specifically with terrorism and grants specialized investigating judges with exceptional powers, such as extended periods of detention. Pursuant to this law, a pool of four investigating judges was created within the Paris district attorney's office and granted national jurisdiction over terrorist activities. The magistrates work closely with the various police units in charge of terrorism and have accumulated over the years an impressive expertise in this field, but some hasty decisions and procedures have also annoyed their own hierarchy and colleagues, and human rights organizations have called for greater accountability on their part (Courtois & Garrec, 1999).

Most specialized police units have been assigned leadership over specific forms of terrorism. The General Intelligence Directorate (*Renseignements Généraux* or DCRG) of the National Police is in charge of internal terrorist groups such as ETA or FLNC. This unit mobilizes more than 750 agents in counterterrorism related activities. Since general intelligence officers do not have powers of arrest, they must work closely with their criminal investigation colleagues to initiate an arrest. They must deal with the National Antiterrorist Division (DNAT), a specialist section of the Judicial Police Directorate, which can mobilize more than 150 agents. The DST, or Directorate for the Surveillance of the Territory, is in charge of international and transnational terrorism. This responsibility derives from the broader counterespionage mandate given to this arm of the National Police, and its expertise is in the area of foreign intelligence. A little less than half of all DST's agents are assigned to antiterrorism tasks (Sarkozy, 2004). The Gendarmerie also collects intelligence related to terrorist activity, particularly in rural areas, which have been used extensively by members of the ETA and FLNC to evade surveillance. In the field of intervention, both the National Police and the Gendarmerie have formed their own tactical and hostage rescue teams (RAID for the police and GIGN for the Gendarmerie). In times of crisis or heightened alert, the *Vigipirate* plan allows the prime minister to mobilize the army in a support capacity to protect government buildings and critical infrastructure such as airports, public transport systems, nuclear power plants, etc. Since 1978, it has been activated four times.

The diversified terrorist threat and the allocation of responsibilities to various units on an *ad hoc* basis has impeded coordination of the counterterrorism effort. The work of the antiterrorist magistrates somehow compensated for this trend, but significant overlaps persisted between services that maintained their own set of practices, informants, and databases and were engaged in an unproductive competition in order to benefit from the prestige associated with successful operations. Sources were also seen as an asset to protect at all costs, including protecting them from other agencies that might need their information. In order to remedy this situation, UCLAT, the Antiterrorism Coordination Unit, was created in 1984. UCLAT is staffed by liaison officers detached from the various antiterrorist units and intelligence services. Its mandate is to "improve processes related to the allocation of responsibilities, the assessment of threats and to advise, manage and permit a more effective information and intelligence sharing between services."[14] It is however important to note that UCLAT does not have any power over those services and that it must rely on persuasion rather than coercion.

Conclusion

Most texts on French policing available in English emphasize the differences between the French system and the more familiar North American or British systems. This approach allows their authors to rely on the assumed knowledge of the readers. I have voluntarily refused to follow this path in order to provide a more neutral view of the elements and forces at work in this complex assemblage. Instead, I have highlighted the dualist structure of the French police, inherited from the royal era, and the adaptations required in the face of exploding crime statistics, public demands, and the pressures of globalization. In contrast to the bipolar situation depicted in certain academic texts, this chapter and the other contributions in this book have confirmed the relevance of a conceptual framework based on the idea of a continuum that can accommodate local variations and evolutions.

We are witnessing for example an interest among French police managers and politicians in strategies developed in the U.S. or the UK: the national proximity policing reform, largely inspired by the community policing philosophy; the temptation of zero-tolerance and "get-tough" policies; and the new culture of performance indicators all attest to the intensity of policy transfers at work (Jones & Newburn, 2002). Similarly, the acknowledgment by foreign observers of the French police's expertise in combating terrorism (Shapiro & Suzan, 2003) and running a large centralized and professionalized system must be highlighted. In this regard, the concept of *policy convergence* seems much more appropriate to describe the relationship between French and Anglo-Saxon policing. Obviously, police organizations respond and their reforms are responses to contextual stimuli, and it is highly unlikely that the French system will ever resemble its American or British counterparts. However, as ideas, practices, technologies, and officers travel from one system to another with increased frequency, exaggerated statements such as the ones cited in the first paragraph of this chapter are likely to fade away and be replaced by more objective assessments.

Notes

1. In 1999, 4 percent of the population was naturalized.

2. As noted previously, a section in the Daily Security Act of 2001 criminalized meetings in social housing stairwells.

3. This organization has a Web site: http://www.cnds.fr.

4. Current members include a senator, a congressman, an administrative judge, a high court judge, a general accounting office counselor, a professor of forensic medicine, and a writer.

5. Excessive use of force by the police represents 40 percent of the cases, and more minor forms of police misconduct represent 30 percent.

6. Interestingly, the rate in the Paris area is double (0.6 per 1,000 officers) the national average.

7. Auxiliaries numbered 14,200 in the National Police and 13,800 in the Gendarmerie.

8. I will define *incivilities* as behaviors and incidents that are not strictly unlawful but that are disturbing enough to elicit among those who experience them a feeling of insecurity.

9. This lowering of exam requirements has occurred to the dismay of police associations, which feel that this will result in lower standards and affect the professional image of the police.

10. Most victims have been police officers and military personnel.

11. These included links to individuals and organizations in Cuba, Algeria, San Salvador, Peru, Nicaragua, and Yemen in the past, and more recently, in Colombia.

12. The same day, 241 U.S. Marines were killed in the same fashion by a car bomb.

13. For a more detailed chronology of those events, as well as the wave of bombings in 1986, see Shapiro and Suzan (2003).

14. This is the mandate according to a high-ranking antiterrorism official quoted in Crettiez (1993, p. 46).

References

Amnesty International. (2000). *Annual report 2000*. London: Author.

Amnesty International. (2001). *Annual report 2001*. London: Author.

Aubusson, B., Lalam, N., Padieu, R., & Zamora, P. (2002). Les statistiques de la délinquance. In *France: Portrait social 2002-2003* (pp. 141–158). Paris: National Institute for Statistics and Economic Studies.

Bayley, D. H. (1985). *Patterns of policing: a comparative international analysis*. New Brunswick, NJ: Rutgers University Press.

Bayley, D. H. (1999). Policing: the world stage. In R. I. Mawby (Ed.), *Policing across the world: Issues for the twenty-first century* (pp. 3–12). London: University College London Press.

Boëldieu, J., & Borrel, C. (2000). Recensement de la population 1999: La proportion d'immigrés est stable depuis 25 ans. *INSEE Première*, (748), 4.

Brodeur, J.-P. (2003). *Les visages de la police*. Montréal: Presses de l'Université de Montréal.

Brodeur, J.-P. & Monjardet, D. (2003). En guise de conclusion. In J.-P. Brodeur & D. Monjardet (Eds.), *Connaître la police* (pp. 417–425). Paris: La Documentation Française.

Bui Trong, L. (1998). Les violences urbaines à l'échelle des renseignements généraux: un état des lieux pour 1998. *Les Cahiers de la Sécurité Intérieure*, 33, 215–224.

Cazelles, C., Morel, B., & Roché, S. (2007). *Les violences urbaines de l'automne 2005, événements, acteur: Dynamiques et interactions*. Paris: Centre d'Analyse Stratégique.

Commission Nationale de Déontologie de la Sécurité (CNDS). (2002). *Annual report for 2001*. Paris: Author.

Commission Nationale de Déontologie de la Sécurité (CNDS). (2003). *Annual report for 2002*. Paris: Author.

Conrad, J.-P. (2002). Origines et réalités de l'islamisme activiste. In G. Chaliand (Ed.), *Les stratégies du terrorisme* (pp. 19–71). Paris: Desclée de Brouwer.

Courtois, J.-P. (2001). *Projet de loi de finances pour 2002—Tome II—Intérieur: Police et sécurité*. Paris: Assemblée Nationale.

Courtois, J.-P., & Garrec, R. (1999). *Rapport de la commission d'enquête sur la conduite de la politique de sécurité mené par l'État en Corse*. Paris: Sénat.

Crettiez, X. (1993). *Terrorisme indépendantiste et anti-terrorisme en France*, Paris: National Institute for the Study of Homeland Security.

Crettiez, X. (1998). Lire la violence politique en Corse. *Les Cahiers de la Sécurité Intérieure, 33*, 195–214.

Critchley, T. A. (1967). *A history of the police in England and Wales 900–1966*. London: Constable.

Dieu, F. (1999). *Politiques publiques de sécurité*. Paris: L'Harmattan.

Duprez, D., & Hedli, M. (1992). *Le mal des banlieues? Sentiment d'insécurité et crise identitaire*. Paris: L'Harmattan.

École Nationale d'Administration (ENA). (2000). *La police de proximité: Une révolution culturelle?* Paris: Author.

Emsley, C. (1996). *The English police: a political and social history* (2nd ed.). London: Longman.

Emsley, C. (1999). *Gendarmes and the State in Nineteenth-Century Europe*. Oxford, UK: Oxford University Press.

Ferret, J. (2001). Police de proximité en France: Une expérience de recherche institutionnelle à l'IHESI (1998–2001). *Les Cahiers de la Sécurité Intérieure, 46*, 97–117.

Ferret, J. (2004). The state, policing and "old continental Europe": Managing the local/national tension. *Policing & Society, 14*(1), 49–65.

Garcia, A. (2002, April 20). Les contrôles d'identité abusifs aggravent les tensions dans les cités. *Le Monde*, p. 11.

Gleizal, J.-J., Gatti-Domenach, J., & Journès, C. (1993). *La police: Le cas des démocraties occidentales*. Paris: Presses Universitaires de France.

Haut Conseil de l'Intégration (HCI). (2004). *Le contrat et l'intégration: Annual report 2003*. Paris: HCI.

Jobard, F. (2002). *Bavures policières? La force publique et ses usages*. Paris: La Découverte.

Jones, T., & Newburn, T. (2002). Learning from Uncle Sam? Exploring U.S. influences on British crime control policies. *Governance: An International Journal of Policy, Administration, and Institutions, 15*(1), 97–119.

L'Heuillet, H. (2001). *Basse politique, haute police*. Paris: Fayard.

Labrousse, F. (2001). L'inspection générale des services, la légitimité d'un service de contrôle interne et judiciaire. *Les Cahiers de la Sécurité Intérieure, 44*, 171–188.

Le Fur, M. (2003). *Rapport d'information sur les Groupes d'Intervention Régionaux*. Paris: National Assembly Committee on Finance, the General Economy and the Plan.

Le Roux, B. (2001). Sécurité et déontologie, la création d'une autorité administrative indépendante. *Les Cahiers de la Sécurité Intérieure, 44,* 143–151.

Loubet del Bayle, J.-L. (1999a). Jalons pour une histoire de la recherche française sur les institutions et les pratiques policières. *Les Cahiers de la Sécurité Intérieure, 37,* 55–71.

Loubet del Bayle, J.-L. (1999b). L'état du syndicalisme policier. *Revue Française d'Administration Publique, 91,* 435–445.

Mawby, R. (1990). *Comparative policing issues: The British and American experience in international perspective.* London: Unwin Hyman.

Ministry of the Interior. (2004, January 14). *Annual press release on homeland security.* Paris: Author.

Monjardet, D. (2003, February). *International terrorism and the stairwell.* Paper delivered at the International Conference on Policing and Security, Montreal, Quebec.

Mouhanna, C. (2001). Faire le gendarme: De la souplesse informelle à la rigueur bureaucratique. *Revue Française de Sociologie, 42*(1), 31–55.

Mouhanna, C. (2002). Une police de proximité judiciarisée. *Déviance et Société, 26*(2), 163–182.

Mucchielli, L. (2001). *Violences et insécurité.* Paris: La Découverte.

Mucchielli, L. (2003). Délinquance et immigration en France: Un regard sociologique. *Criminologie, 36*(2), 27–55.

Napoli, P. (2003). *Naissance de la police moderne: Pouvoirs, normes, société.* Paris: La Découverte.

Ocqueteau, F. (2003). Comment évaluer l'impact du travail des policiers de proximité. *Criminologie, 36*(1), 121–141.

Ocqueteau, F. (2004). Public security as "everyone's concern"? Beginnings and developments of a useful misunderstanding. *Policing & Society, 14*(1), 66–75.

Peyrat, P. (2001). *Habiter et cohabiter: La sécurité dans le logement social.* Paris: Secrétariat d'État au Logement.

Razafindranaly, J. R. V. (2001). L'inspection générale de la Police Nationale (IGPN): Entre discipline et prévention. *Les Cahiers de la Sécurité Intérieure, 44,* 153–170.

Robert, P., & M.-L. Pottier (2002). Les grandes tendances de l'évolution des délinquances. In L. Mucchielli & P. Robert (Eds.), *Crime et sécurité: L'état des savoirs* (pp. 13–24). Paris: La Découverte.

Sarkozy, N. (Minister of the Interior). (2003, July 3). *Introductory comments on a bill dealing with immigration controls and the stay of foreigners in France.* Address to the National Assembly, Paris.

Sarkozy, N. (Minister of the Interior). (2004, February 11). *The results of international cooperation in the fight against terrorism.* Presentation to a hearing of the National Assembly Foreign Affairs Committee, Paris.

Shapiro, J., & Suzan, B. (2003). The French experience of counter-terrorism. *Survival, 41*(1), 67–98.

Simula, P. (1999). Offre de sécurité et forces publiques régaliennes. *Les Cahiers de la Sécurité Intérieure, 37,* 135–159.

Tiévant, S. (2002). Partenariat et police de proximité: Dilution ou consolidation des spécificités professionnelles? *Les Cahiers de la Sécurité Intérieure, 48,* 149–170.

Wilkinson, P. (2002). Comment répondre à la menace terroriste. In G. Chaliand (Ed.), *Les stratégies du terrorisme* (pp. 195–218). Paris: Desclée de Brouwer.

Further Reading

Body-Gendrot, S. (2004). Police race relations in England and in France: Policy and practices. In G. Mesko, M. Pagon, & B. Dobovsek (Eds.), *Policing in central and eastern Europe: Dilemmas of contemporary criminal justice* (pp. 134–145). Maribor, Slovenia: Faculty of Criminal Justice, University of Maribor.

Filleule, O., & Jobard, F. (1998). The policing of protest in France: Toward a model of protest policing. In D. Della Porta & H. Reiter (Eds.), *Policing protest, the control of mass demonstrations in Western democracies* (pp. 70–90). Minneapolis: University of Minnesota Press.

Hodgson, J. (2001). Police, the prosecutor and the juge d'instruction: Judicial supervision in France, theory and practice. *British Journal of Criminology, 41*(2), 342–361.

Horton, C. (1995). *Policing policy in France.* London: Policy Studies Institute.

Liang, H.-H. (1992). *The rise of modern police and the European state system from Metternich to the Second World War.* Cambridge, UK: Cambridge University Press.

Monjardet, D. (1995). The French model of policing. In J.-P. Brodeur (Ed.), *Comparisons on policing: an international perspective* (pp 49–68). Aldershot, UK: Avebury.

Monjardet, D. (2000). Police and the public. *European Journal of Criminal Policy and Research, 8*(3), 353–378.

Roché, S. (2002). Towards a new governance of crime and insecurity in France. In A. Crawford (Ed.), *Crime and insecurity: The governance of safety in Europe* (pp. 213–233). Cullompton, UK: Willan.

Stead, P. J. (1983). *The police of France.* New York: Macmillan.

Williams, A. (1979). *The police of Paris: 1718-1789.* Baton Rouge: Louisiana State University Press.

Zauberman, R., & Levy, R. (2003). Police, minorities and the French republican ideal. *Criminology, 41*(4), 1065–1100.

11

United Kingdom

Democratic Policing—
Global Change From
a Comparative Perspective

Matt Long and Stuart Cullen

In historical terms, although the United Kingdom is one of the world's oldest democracies, policing is a comparatively modern phenomenon. Following the founding of the London Metropolitan Police by Sir Robert Peel in 1829, the formation of other police forces throughout the country was an incremental process, with each newly created local police force operating according to the needs of the individual communities they served. Hence, policing was part of the democratic process insofar as it was intended to reflect the needs of the people. This chapter will provide an overview of the history of modern policing in the United Kingdom, examining events that either threatened or helped to reinforce the principles of policing within a liberal democratic society. Further, an examination will be made of how, both operationally and organizationally, policing in the United Kingdom has been able to prepare to respond to the effects and consequences of globalization that threaten the security of the state and its citizens.

History and Political Context of Policing

During the eighteenth century, civil power was insufficient to deal with dire emergencies of public disorder. Local constables were unable to deal effectively with major outbreaks of disorder, and the government deployed the military in a public order role. For example, during the Gordon Riots of 1780, the government deployed the military, which used disproportionate force by firing on and killing hundreds of anti-Catholic rioters (Stead, 1985).

Despite there being a constitutional power allowing the police to call upon the military, there is in practice nowadays a distinct separation of powers between the military and the police. In Britain, according to Wright, "There had never been a strong military influence on policing" (2002, p. 62). As policing became more systematic and bureaucratized, government felt that civil disorder could be dealt with without having to call on the military. The relationship between the police and government is however more intertwined and complicated.

Henry and John Fielding were progressive thinkers who advocated reform, and in many ways their London-based Bow Street Runners were a precursor to Sir Robert Peel's Metropolitan Police. Peel was an advocate of preventive policing, and that is precisely why members of the force wore visible and readily identifiable uniforms. Officers were both unarmed and equipped with minimal powers in order to reinforce the philosophy that policing should be with the people in terms of gaining their consent, rather than a force against the people to be used in a coercive way. It was intended that the Metropolitan force serve as a model for other county-based forces throughout the country. Following attempts to encourage local areas to establish their own forces throughout the 1830s, police forces were made compulsory through legislation in 1856 (the County and Borough Police Act), which ensured that forces would be at least partly funded by the Home Office (see Rawlings, 2002).

What is referred to as the tripartite system of policing was established by the Police Act of 1964. This is basically a power-sharing relationship between the following three bodies: (1) central government (via the home secretary), (2) chief constables of individual forces, and (3) police authorities. The exercise of powers through government circulars and regulations was something that the home secretary could effect under the 1964 act. Such regulations, for example, related to pay and conditions of service, the approval of certain equipment for police use, and the endorsement of chief officers selected by their local police authorities. In financial terms, the 1964 act meant that policing was funded by both central and local government (51 percent central versus 49 percent local).

The number of police forces rapidly expanded throughout the late nineteenth century due to the existence of both county-based forces and more locally based, smaller borough forces. Forty-three individual county-based police forces currently exist in England and Wales, and this more localized structure is distinct from other European countries such as France and Finland, which are characterized by far more centralized policing systems. Although there is no national force, there are in existence mutual aid procedures that allow for a more centrally coordinated response to crisis situations that require assistance above and beyond that available through the county-based policing arrangements (see Long, 2005).

Following the 1964 Police Act, each police force in England and Wales had a police authority. These authorities consisted of two-thirds members who were elected councilors and one-third appointed magistrates.[1] The defining purpose of these police authorities was and still is to secure the maintenance of an adequate and efficient police force for its local area. Police authorities had the specific duty of appointing senior officers and receiving an annual written report with regard to force performance from the chief constable. The act made chief constables responsible for the "direction and control" of forces in operational terms. This latter point has come to be referred to as the "doctrine of constabulary independence" in that theoretically, the home secretary should not get too heavily involved in operational matters, because it would be deemed to be detrimental to the professional judgment and impartiality of chief officers (see Reiner, 2000).

The National Policing Plan 2005–2008 outlines five key priorities that the police should focus on. These are the following (Home Office, 2005):

1. Reducing overall crime (including violent and drug-related offenses)

2. Being citizen focused and responsive to local communities, in order to inspire confidence especially amongst minority ethnic communities

3. Taking action along with partner agencies to target prolific or repeat offenders

4. Reducing community concerns and fears about crime and antisocial behavior

5. Combating more serious and organized crime

Serving police officers themselves are either uniformed or nonuniformed. While uniformed officers tend to conduct routine patrol work, nonuniformed officers are ordinarily associated with the criminal investigation department (CID) within particular forces. After serving a number of years in uniform, many officers attempt to develop their careers either by gaining promotion to the supervisory or managerial ranks or through lateral career development. Specialist departments may include child protection, fraud investigation, firearms, public order, media relations, and corporate development.

Upon completion of their two-year probationary period, officers are allowed to undertake an examination that qualifies them for the rank of sergeant, which is a first-level supervisor. Further promotion to the middle management ranks of inspector and chief inspector is then a future option. Ranks from constable to chief inspector are referred to as the federated ranks. These ranks are represented by a staff association (rather than a union, because police officers are not allowed to strike) known as the Police Federation. Above these ranks, the Superintendents Association represents the interests of both superintendents and chief superintendents, who are responsible for policing in local divisions (now called basic command units) within force areas. The ranks of assistant chief and chief are found above the superintending ranks, and these officers lead the force and work with the Home Office and its police authorities in order to formulate policy and strategy. These most senior officers are represented by the Association of Chief Police Officers (ACPO).

Corruption History: Major Scandals and Incidents

The United Kingdom ranks as the eleventh-least corrupt nation on the planet (Transparency International, 2006). In light of this finding, it would be safe to suggest that the UK police are not institutionally or routinely corrupt. However, periodically, a minority negative subculture emerges within any police organization when a small element of police officials becomes involved in crime, dishonesty, corruption, or other malpractices (see Zander, 1994).

The term *police corruption* most commonly tends to refer to violence and brutality, bribery, and the fabrication and destruction of evidence. Whilst we have argued that in comparative terms the UK police should not be seen as institutionally corrupt, nevertheless corruption was something that seems to have been present prior to the birth of modern public policing in the mid-nineteenth century. According to Reiner (2000, p. 17), "Those members of the old constabulary who were not ineffective were represented as corrupt, milking their offices for rewards and fees. Thief-takers became thief makers." Periodically, corruption scandals have dogged the "modern" police in Britain as well. As early as 1902, a Metropolitan Police constable was sentenced to five years in prison for planting a hammer on a man and then arresting him. After the wrongful arrest of a woman charged with street prostitution, a Royal Commission upon the Duties of the Metropolitan Police in Relation to Cases of Drunkenness, Disorder, and Solicitation in the Streets was established in 1906. Despite this, allegations against and convictions of serving police officers continued. In 1928, for instance, the head of the vice squad at Vine Street, in London's West End, was exposed as having taken bribes from nightclub owners for whom he had a policing responsibility (see Rawlings, 2002).

More recently, in the 1960s, Detective Sergeant Harry Challenor's squad of detectives appeared in court charged with corruption, including the brutalization of prisoners to gain confessions. Throughout the 1960s and 1970s, detectives from the Metropolitan Police were found to be involved with fabrication and destruction of evidence. According to Cox, Shirley, and Short (1977), the spotlight focused heavily on both the force's Drugs Squad and its Obscene Publications Squad. Corruption was not confined to London, however, as there was also concern over the illegal activities of the West Midlands Serious Crimes Squad in England's second city of Birmingham. In 1972, Sir Robert Mark was appointed Metropolitan Police commissioner. Having set up a department to proactively investigate complaints and corruption, he pressed on to further reform that force's criminal investigation department by introducing greater interchange between the CID and uniformed ranks (Mark, 1979).

In 1981, a Royal Commission on Criminal Procedure was established to investigate, inter alia, what is commonly referred to as noble cause corruption. This is where the police basically claim that the end justifies the means in terms of the manner in which suspects are detained and interrogated. The overwhelming majority of cases were in the context of Irish Republican terrorism. Throughout the 1980s and 1990s, high-profile miscarriages of justice saw the release of the so-called Guildford Four, Birmingham Six, Tottenham Three, and the Maguires. The Royal Commission made recommendations for significant reform of police powers in order to attempt to prevent further abuse of human rights (see the section below on the legal context for police powers).

It would be fair to say that despite legal and procedural reforms, however, allegations of corruption still occur. Indeed, Reiner spoke of "a repeated cycle of scandal and reform" (2000, p. 62). The inquiry into the murder of the young black teenager Stephen Lawrence as recently as 1999 brought criticism of the Metropolitan Police, who were found to have failed to properly investigate the murder of an innocent minority ethnic young man by white racists (MacPherson, 1999). The lack of an efficient investigation by police was attributed to institutional racism within the force. This issue is discussed further below in the section on the racial context in which policing occurs in the United Kingdom.

Despite these events, and particularly since the Stephen Lawrence inquiry, the British police service has attempted to make progress to ensure that ethical standards are met through more effective leadership, more stringent management and supervision procedures, increasing levels of accountability, and the delivery of training for awareness of diversity and community and race relations issues to all ranks (see Marlow & Loveday, 2000).

Crime Trends

Since 1995, when a total of almost 19 million crimes were estimated to have been committed, recorded crime has been falling ("Crime Statistics," 2007). According to British Crime Survey data, it is estimated that just over 11 million crimes were committed in the 12 months between December 2005 and December 2006. On average, one in four people is likely to be the victim of a crime within this 12-month period (Lovbakke, Taylor, & Budd, 2007). As well as focusing on crimes such as burglary, robbery, and theft, the police and various partner agencies have in recent years been keenly encouraged by the government to focus on tackling antisocial behavior. This may include such social problems as noisy neighbors, teenagers hanging around on street corners, and littering (Squires & Stephen, 2005).

According to official statistics, the United Kingdom is one of the least violent societies in the world. Compared to a world average of 8.8 homicides per 100,000 citizens (World Health Organization, 2002) the homicide rates for England and Wales are 1.3 per 100,000 citizens (Home Office, 2007) and 1.8 per 100,000 citizens in Scotland ("Homicide in Scotland," 2006).

It is because of the most stringent firearms laws that historically gun crime, including homicides, has been rare. However, the effects of leakages of firearms from Balkan conflicts and the trafficking of firearms by organized crime groups has led to their increased availability and use by criminals in some of the major cities—notably London, Manchester, and Nottingham. The carrying and use of firearms and knives by young members of street gangs and their readiness to use extreme violence in the course of street robberies has become a worrying crime trend in some cities. In an unpublished 2007 Metropolitan Police report, 169 separate gangs were identified throughout London, with more than a quarter involved in murders ("Police Identify 169," 2007). The gangs are based largely on ethnicity, with Afro-Caribbean youths constituting almost half of them. Disturbingly, there was empirical evidence that the most violent of young gang members—those who were likely to commit multiple homicides or other acts of violence—were from immigrant groups seeking refuge from countries engaged in violence and armed conflict, including the committing of atrocities by armed groups (for example, Somalia).

Black on black homicides, primarily shootings over drug-selling territories and gang rivalries, have resulted in the Metropolitan Police forming Operation Trident. Over 300 police officers are dedicated to Trident and operate closely with London's black communities in targeting known criminals, preventing and investigating gun crime, arresting and prosecuting anyone involved in shootings within the black community, supporting witnesses and victims of crime, and reducing the fear of crime in London's black communities (Metropolitan Police Authority, n.d.).

The emergence of street gang cultures in the United Kingdom is beginning to present special problems requiring a multipronged strategy from government, education, police, and other agencies. Most challenging will be resolving how alienated youth, particularly from increasing numbers of immigrant groups, can be encouraged to share a sense of national identity and be provided with opportunities to become equal and valued members of mainstream society.

History and Influence of Organized Crime

According to Levi,

"Organized crime" used to be a phenomenon that was central only to American and Italian crime discourses about "the Mafia," but—stimulated by the growth of international drugs and people migration trades and by the freeing up of borders since the collapse of the USSR— the debate about it and specific national and transnational powers to deal with "it" has extended to Britain and other parts of Europe and beyond in the course of the 1990's. (2003)

The debate about international organized crime has also spread because specific crimes that pose a "new" threat, such as human trafficking and identity theft, are on the increase. It is impossible to examine organized crime without appreciating the truly international context in which it has to be policed. Mechanisms are in place to facilitate exchanges of intelligence between nation-states. At the national level in the United Kingdom, specialist force squads have been established to concentrate on specific crimes. Commonly these may include vice squads, fraud squads, and drug squads. In 1996, The Phillips Report (see Levi, 2003) was authorized by the Association of Chief Police officers in order to look at how police effectiveness in dealing with cross-border criminality could be improved. The report found that almost half of "serious" crime crossed traditional police borders.

In 2006, UK national law enforcement agencies and the National Criminal Intelligence Service were amalgamated to form the Serious Organized Crime Agency (SOCA). SOCA describes itself as "an intelligence-led agency with law enforcement powers and harm reduction responsibilities. Harm in this context is the damage caused to people and communities by serious organized crime" (SOCA, 2006). A major strategic target of SOCA is organized immigration crime. The United Kingdom is a destination nation for the smuggling of Eastern Europeans and Chinese into the agriculture and fisheries sectors and the human trafficking of females from Eastern Europe, the Balkans, and the Far East for exploitation in prostitution and the sex industry ("The Scale and," 2006).

Postconflict societies are especially vulnerable to the activities of organized criminal groups who seek to exploit the misery of those attempting to escape economic deprivation. Globalization is likely to increase the scale of these crimes. It is estimated that worldwide trafficking in persons (essentially a modern form of slavery) and migrant smuggling is generating income of US$30–35 billion per year to organized criminal groups. Yet currently, these crimes remain a low priority for the majority of most law-enforcement agencies around the world, certainly much lower than drug trafficking.

Additionally, SOCA seeks to enhance intelligence through covert methods and to target identified organized crime activities including drug trafficking, individual and private-sector fraud, money laundering, and other organized crime (SOCA, 2006).

Public Support for Government and Law Enforcement

It would appear to be the case that white people are more likely than those from minority ethnic backgrounds to publicly support the police. The British Crime Survey conducted in 2000 found that 38 percent of blacks had been "really annoyed" by police actions, compared to 23 percent of Asians and only 19 percent of white respondents. The same survey found that more than half (54 percent) of white respondents thought the police were doing a good job, compared to only 42 percent of Asian respondents and 40 percent of black respondents (Bowling & Phillips, 2003). This may well be due to the fact that historically, the police have tended to recruit white males into the organization. Due to the requirements of positive action, more black people, women, and members of other minority groups are being targeted for recruitment (see Chan, 1997). As the police force itself becomes more and more diverse in terms of its composition, so one may expect the police institution to be perceived to be more legitimate by minority groups who have traditionally been underrepresented (see Walklate, 2000).

History of the Use of Force

The modern UK police force is unarmed and is underpinned by what is often referred to as the doctrine of minimal force. It was believed by Sir Robert Peel that to have routinely armed the police would have compromised the notion of policing by consent. Since the creation of modern policing in 1845, the UK police have tried to present themselves as mere citizens in uniform, using no more power than is absolutely necessary in order to carry out their duties. For police use of force to be legitimate, it is expected to be used as a last resort and that no more force is used than is needed in order to prevent anticipated harm. According to Mawby, "Recent years have seen considerable pressure from within the ranks to issue firearms on a routine basis" (2003, p. 18). This is mainly due to the fact that some perceive that it is almost impossible to police an increasingly violent world without recourse to arms.

Every single force in the UK has trained officers who are qualified to use firearms, and armed response teams can be deployed where it is deemed necessary. These response teams tend to be deployed alongside police issued with riot gear in public order situations. Police officers routinely carry truncheons and also in recent years have become more likely to be armed with counter-strike sprays in order to temporarily incapacitate citizens who may be becoming increasingly violent or who are resisting arrest vigorously.

Legal Context for Search and Seizure, Detention, and Interview

Historically, it would be fair to say that the police have had considerable powers to stop and search people whom they suspect of criminal activity. Throughout the 1970s, for example, what became known as the "sus" (*suspected* person) laws allowed the police to arrest people who were deemed to be loitering with intent to commit a crime in a public place, by recourse to the Vagrancy Act of 1824. In the late twentieth century, the Police and Criminals Evidence Act of 1984 (PACE) and its five accompanying Codes of Practice introduced greater legal controls over police powers, which had previously been the subject of common law only. Under this key legislation, in order to carry out most arrest and stop-and-search powers, the police need to have "reasonable suspicion" or "reasonable grounds" to believe a crime has been or is about to be committed. These suspicions or grounds must have some objective basis and cannot rely purely on the subjectivity and discretion of the individual officer. Despite this introduction of bureaucracy designed to prevent corruption and abuse of power, in reality, officers still have to exercise their discretion in making decisions as to whether to stop and search (Sanders & Young, 2003). One of the positive requirements of PACE was its introduction of the requirement that police officers make written records of each search, in order to prevent misuse of power.

Suspects may be detained and questioned under PACE and are taken directly to a police station upon their arrest for these processes to occur. It is the decision of the custody sergeant (first-level supervisor) as to whether a suspect is to be detained or not. Under PACE, free legal advice can be given to suspects who request this, although civil libertarians often point out that in practice many do not do so, because they are persuaded it could be counterproductive. Suspects may be detained in order to be charged or held while extra evidence is collected. The normal period of detention lasts 24 hours, but in serious cases the police may apply to the courts for a 36-hour extension, which can be ultimately further extended up to 96 hours.

Over half of suspects who are detained at police stations under PACE are interviewed (Bucke & Brown, 1997). Basic standards for interviews, in terms of access to legal advice and comfort breaks, are provided by the 1995 PACE Code of Practice for the Detention, Treatment and Questioning of Persons by Police Officers. Interviews, which were previously written up by police officers, now have to be tape-recorded to safeguard the rights of the suspect, and over the last few years many custody suits have been covered by the use of CCTV. This is designed both to protect suspects from maltreatment and to protect police officers against malicious allegations. Under section 76 of PACE, confessions can be excluded as constituting legitimate evidence if it is determined that they were obtained by the police through oppressive means, be they physical or psychological. In addition to the relatively long-standing PACE legislation, the more recent Human Rights Act of 1998 has had an even greater impact on the attempt to safeguard the rights of suspects and to prevent inhuman and degrading treatment. This has had a big impact in terms of ensuring that the police treat suspects as citizens who have rights.

In the context of search and seizure, police most commonly use powers granted to them under section 18 of PACE, which allows them to search the homes of arrested persons. According to Sanders and Young, "Over the last 20 years or so the police have been given increasingly extensive powers of entry, search and seizure, consistent with the growing crime control orientation of the system" (2003, p. 244). Currently, due to the West's war on terror, many of the provisions to search and seize under PACE can be used together with provisions from antiterrorist legislation such as the Regulation of Investigatory Powers Act of 2000 and the Anti-terrorism, Crime and Security Act of 2001 (see Matassa & Newburn, 2003).

Racial and Ethnic Context of Policing

The United Kingdom has a population of 60 million. Its capital city, London, is considered to be one of the three main financial capitals of the world, alongside New York in the United States and Tokyo in Japan. The United Kingdom's inhabitants are predominantly of European ethnic origin (90 percent). Significant minority ethnic groups are Afro-Caribbeans and Africans, Indians, Pakistanis, Bangladeshis, and Chinese. The United Kingdom is predominantly Christian in religious terms, with large communities of Muslims, Hindus, Jews, and Sikhs also being in existence. English is the main language spoken throughout the United Kingdom. Many Welsh people can speak English as well as their native Welsh. Urdu is the language spoken by members of the Pakistani community.

Trends in Immigration

After World War II, in the late 1950s and 1960s, immigration from the Commonwealth countries increased. Black Afro-Caribbean people were invited to come to Britain by the government, which was keen for them to fill available jobs and to boost the growing economy at that time. In terms of monitoring immigration, a decade or so later, the Immigration Act of 1971 gave police increased powers to detain and question persons suspected of violating the law by entering the country illegally or overstaying their terms of entry (Gordon, 1984). Since the September 11 attacks on New York and Washington, immigration cannot be separated from issues of national security, terrorism, and civil liberties (see section on terrorism later in this chapter). Some commentators have questioned whether more recent legislation such as the Immigration and Asylum Act of 1999 and the Antiterrorism Act of 2001 may be discriminatory against minority ethnic groups (see, for example, Bourne, 2001, and Fenwick, 2002).

Inter/Intragroup Conflicts

Race was an important factor in accounting for much of the urban, inner-city unrest and rioting that occurred in the early and mid-1980s. A police tactic known as *Operation Swamp,* whereby large numbers of young black males were stopped and searched on suspicion of possessing illegal drugs, was perceived by many blacks to be overly aggressive and an infringement on their civil liberties. In his report on one of these riots, Lord

Scarman (1981) found that this tactic was a contributory factor in leading to the riots in Brixton. Similar riots occurred in Toxteth in Liverpool and Handsworth in Birmingham in the 1980s, and relations between police and minority ethnic communities reached a low point in 1985 following the brutal murder of Police Constable Keith Blakelock on the Broadwater Farm estate in London.

In the summer of 2001, similar outbreaks of disorder occurred in several cities and towns in the north of England, most notably Bradford, Burnley, and Oldham (Ousley, 2001; Ritchie, 2001). Waddington notes however that "this time they were more closely associated with Asian youth rather than Afro-Caribbeans and appeared to have been sparked by opposition to far-right political activity in conditions of increased racial tension" (2003, p. 397). More recently interracial conflict occurred in 2005 in Britain's second city, Birmingham. This followed an apparently false rumor that a young black girl had been raped by a group of Pakistani youths. While there was no evidence brought forward to suggest rape and apparently no victim, two people lost their lives as a result of the riots (Vulliamy, 2005).

Relationship Between the Police and Diverse Populations

At the time of the urban unrest in the early 1980s, the Scarman report (Scarman, 1981) recognized the often strained relationship between the police and minority ethnic communities and made a number of recommendations in order to attempt to improve this relationship. Such recommendations included attempting to recruit more ethnic minority police officers, making racially prejudiced language and practices a sackable offense for police officers, requiring police units to consult more with communities, and introducing lay visitors to scrutinize police detention facilities.

Despite these recommendations and the appearance of a genuine commitment to reform by the police, allegations concerning excessive force and police violence and brutality against members of minority ethnic groups persisted (Inquest, 1996). Additionally, in the context of stop and search, Bowling and Phillips point to the continued "extremely heavy use of these powers against people from ethnic minority communities, particularly young black people" (2003, p. 534). Statistics have showed that black people are eight times more likely to be stopped and searched by the police than whites, while Asians are three times more likely (Bowling & Phillips, 2003). According to the Home Office (2003), in 2001–2002, blacks were five times more likely to be arrested than whites, while Asians were twice as likely as their white counterparts to be arrested.

Representation of Diverse Populations in the Department

Despite recent attempts at recruitment, minority ethnic individuals continue to be underrepresented in police forces relative to their representation in the wider population. There is good news, however, in that the proportion of serving police officers from minority ethnic backgrounds has risen from less than 1 percent in 1986 to 3 percent in 2001–2002 (Home Office, 2003). Retention rates are also lower amongst minority ethnic officers than white officers, with minority ethnic recruits leaving the job for a variety of reasons more often than their white colleagues (Bowling & Phillips, 2003). Empirical evidence also demonstrates how minority ethnic officers have been less likely to be promoted than white colleagues (Home Office, 2003). In order to attempt to counter this, local and national targets for the increased recruitment, retention, and promotion of police officers were set by the home secretary in the late 1990s (Home Office, 1999). This process, referred to as *positive action,* also includes initiatives like attempting to persuade so-called hard-to-reach groups to consider joining the police.

The stimulus for much of this kind of change came from the murder of Stephen Lawrence back in 1993. Lawrence was murdered in an unprovoked attack by five white youths. The flawed police investigation into this murder led the subsequent MacPherson report to cite professional incompetence, institutional racism, and a failure of police leadership (MacPherson, 1999) as reasons for the failure of this police investigation. In all, the report made some 70 recommendations for police reform, including improvements in the monitoring and investigation of racist incidents, police training on issues of diversity, and the regulation of stop-and-search powers. In addition to the MacPherson report, the Race Relations (Amendment) Act of 2000 made both direct and indirect or unconscious discrimination on the part of the police unlawful.

Organizational Structure and Issues

As was mentioned earlier, there is no national police force in the United Kingdom. The delivery of policing in England and Wales continues to be divided among 43 semiautonomous individual county and metropolitan area forces,[2] all of which operate under the same national laws and legal standards. Some specific policing functions are provided nationally; an example is the National Policing and Improvement Agency described later in this chapter.

Centralization and Decentralization: Overview of Organizational Structure

Periodically, a debate arises as to whether the police forces of England and Wales should be centralized into a national police force or larger regional units. During 2006, the home secretary proposed such mergers, deeming them necessary to make policing more effective against the threat of organized and transnational crime and terrorism. The proposals were shelved after concerted opposition by local and national politicians, who typically claimed they were excessively expensive to implement. There was an additional sensitivity to their potential to erode the local accountability of police (*Police Amalgamations*, 2006).

There is no national force in Scotland, but rather eight forces were created by the (Scottish) Government Act of 1973. Scotland has a tripartite system of policing not unlike that of England and Wales, with responsibility for policing delivery being shared among respective force chief officers, joint police boards, and the justice department of the Scottish Executive (Donnelly & Scott, 2002a). As in England and Wales, chief officers are expected to be nonpolitical in terms of their independent management of police operations. Resource and budgeting issues are made by locally elected councilors who sit on joint police boards. Overall policing policy is directed by ministers who sit in the Scottish Executive. Since the Scotland Act of 1998 and the creation of a devolved Scottish Parliament and Scottish Executive, more control over policing has been exerted from within Scotland rather than from the English Parliament in Westminster (Donnelly & Scott, 2002b).

The Province of Northern Ireland is served by a single police organization, the Police Service of Northern Ireland (PSNI). The majority of Protestants in Northern Ireland are Unionists in that they see themselves as British rather than Irish, hence their reference to maintaining "the Union." The majority of Catholics on the other hand are Nationalists or Republicans. Some believe that Britain colonized Ireland without their consent, and they have long wished for the North to unite with Southern Ireland, Eire. After much violence in the twentieth century (particularly between the 1970s and 1990) and prolonged negotiations, the signing of a multiparty peace agreement between the UK and Irish governments took place on April 10, 1998. This fundamental part of the peace process has become known as The Good Friday Agreement (Mulcahy, 2000). The creation of a power-sharing executive to include all major political parties was made possible through conditions allowing for the release of paramilitary prisoners plus a commitment to the decommissioning of weapons.

As a product of the Good Friday Agreement, an independent commission on policing was established with the intention of attracting support from both Catholics and Protestants within the community. The Royal Ulster Constabulary has existed since 1922 and was composed of mainly Protestant and Unionist officers, and it thus became associated with English colonial rule according to some Catholics. Precisely because of the underrepresentation of Catholics in the force, the commission felt that reform was necessary in order to achieve policing by consent. The commission was chaired by the Right Honourable Christopher Patten (formerly governor of Hong Kong), and by late 1999 it had produced 175 recommendations for reform. Better representation of both Protestant and Catholic sections of the community was to be achieved through the creation of a new policing board.

Positive discrimination measures were put in place for recruitment, in that equal numbers of Protestants and Catholics were to be selected and drafted into the force. (A target was set of reaching 30 percent Catholic representation in the force over the next 10 years.) The Policing (Northern Ireland) Bill of 2000 ensured that the Royal Ulster Constabulary was renamed the Police Service of Northern Ireland (PSNI) with new badges and symbols designed to avoid overt association with either Britain or Ireland (Independent Commission on Policing in Northern Ireland, 1999).

Civilianization

Since the 1980s, police forces have recruited civilian staff into specialist posts. This occurred for two reasons. First, there was a conviction that there were some specialist skills that police officers did not normally possess and that needed to be filled by outsiders to the organization. Second, there was a drive in the 1980s toward cost cutting, and civilians tend to be cheaper to employ than police officers. Civilians are typically employed in posts such as crime and forensic analysis, training, and performance management. Since the 1990s, civilian staff have been recruited into equivalent chief officer rankings alongside their uniformed colleagues, and it is an ongoing debate as to whether we are likely to witness a chief constable who is a civilian rather than a uniformed officer in the near future. At the other end of the spectrum, The Police Reform Act of 2002 was a precursor to the creation of community support officers, whose work is designed to complement that of uniformed patrol officers. In addition to this, the Police Act of 1964 established what is known as the Special Constabulary. These are volunteer officers who work a number of hours every week supporting the regular work of full-time officers.

The current government has been keen to endorse what could be referred to as a mixed-economy approach. In the south of England, Surrey Police have led the way on this issue by means of the introduction of mixed-economy teams as part of their Wider Workforce Modernisation Programme. Under this scheme, relatively well-skilled and well-rewarded constables have been made responsible for the management of teams consisting of both trained police staff and civilian administrative assistants (Loveday, 2006).

Complaints Procedures

Great care needs to be taken in interpreting figures of complaints against the police. If any police complaints system is easily accessible, coherent, and transparent, then, paradoxically, citizens seeking redress are more likely to complain because they have confidence in the system. Hence, complaints may rise and will be higher than in societies where citizens fear the police and complaints are ignored or discouraged.

Citizens in the UK can make a formal complaint about police misconduct through the Independent Police Complaints Commission, which was established by the Home Office in 2000. Despite the existence of this relatively new body, there are still occasional allegations of policing cover-ups and what is often referred to as the "blue wall of silence" (Bowling & Phillips, 2003). Increasingly however, official complaints procedures are being overlooked in favor of attempting redress through civil litigation. We live in a society of ever-increasing litigiousness, and to demonstrate this, the Metropolitan Police had to pay out £3.9 million in damage payments between 1999 and 2000, compared to just over £1 million five years earlier (Metropolitan Police, 2001).

Internal Accountability Mechanisms: Policies and Procedures

Police forces in the United Kingdom are made up of a headquarters and a varying number of basic command units (BCUs), depending on force size. There are some 318 BCUs in England and Wales (Mawby & Wright, 2003). Strategy and policy are set by force headquarters. Headquarters also has the job of controlling the overall budget set by the police authority and allocating resources accordingly (Audit Commission, 2001). The pressure to devolve more and more resources and decision-making power to local BCUs has greatly increased in recent years, and since 2001, the Police Standards Unit (an inspectorate body along with Her Majesty's Inspectorate of Constabulary and the Audit Commission) has focused heavily on BCU performance rather than force performance (Home Office, 2001). Since the late 1990s, as well as demonstrating transparency in the way in which they perform, forces have had a legal obligation, under the Crime and Disorder Act of 1998, to work in partnership with other agencies in other to deliver better social outcomes. These are referred to as Crime and Disorder Reduction Partnerships.

Recruitment and Selection: Strategies and Standards

Eighteen and a half years is the minimum age for a constable, there no longer being an upper age limit for applying to join the service.[3] As with age, due to equal opportunities legislation, there is no longer a minimum height requirement to join the service, although good eyesight is normally a precondition for entry. In theory, recruitment is not formally dependent upon achieving specified educational levels, but due to the nature of a postindustrial economy, more and more graduates are entering the service. While applicants are recruited by specific forces that do retain the right to set their own standards and conditions of entry, in practice there is little variation in recruitment and selection procedures across the United Kingdom.

The first stage of recruitment typically involves all applicants being required to pass two written tests, which are designed to make sure potential recruits have a sound grasp of the English language. These written tests alongside a numeracy test and an examination of observational skills together form what is collectively referred to as the Police Initial Recruitment Test. The second stage in the process involves a fitness-related physical test in a gymnasium. The third stage typically involves an assessment center where candidates face a number of role-playing scenarios designed to test their suitability for a public service role. The fourth and final stage involves interview by a panel consisting both of senior police officers and equivalent civilian personnel officers. At this stage, acceptance into the police is still conditional and is dependent upon a positive outcome being obtained from criminal conviction checks and national security clearance.

Policy and Discretion

Each force may determine its own policy after consultation with its local police authority. Policies are however not simply determined from the bottom up and based on local needs, concerns, and expectations. Rather, each force's annual policing plan has to take account of the centrally driven objectives and targets set out by the home secretary. This is often why police managers feel a tension between the pursuit of central targets on the one hand and the attempt to take into consideration local perceptions of what constitutes crime or social problems on the other.

Recruit and In-Service Training

New recruits have to undertake an extensive period of training as probationer constables. In Scotland and Northern Ireland, core policing skills are developed during a residential phase of training at the Scottish Police College and Northern Ireland Police College respectively. In England and Wales, training of probationer constables is now localized and delivered at in-force facilities according to a common curriculum and agreed-upon national standards of competence. Probationer training also involves spending time with an experienced tutor constable so the new recruit can gain invaluable practical operational experience to equip him or her for the demands of policing the streets. It is intended that this combination of classroom-based learning with on-the-street policing will enable the probationary constable to develop sufficient confidence to be able to perform patrol duties independently.

Strategic Training and Change

To be successful, any organization has to be in a constant state of change. Change is especially problematic for police leaders. Elected governments and police organizations are accountable to society. Only governments have the mandate to change or introduce laws. The mandate does not extend to the police, who are the servants of both government and people. The police must operate only within the law and enforce it with fairness and discretion (Crawshaw, Cullen, & Williamson, 2007).

The police should also be tolerant of diverse radical and alternative causes and lifestyles that challenge the values of the majority of mainstream society. As society and its values and laws change, the police must respond accordingly. In management terms, this puts the police at a disadvantage: They are not directing society but responding to it. They are always a step behind. As a consequence, it is difficult to keep pace with training needs to meet the ever-changing demands of society. Additionally, training is expensive, and resources are finite. Therefore, critical choices have to be made in the prioritization of training content and delivery. As a general principle, police training in the United Kingdom is utilitarian: It is delivered only to specific personnel identified as requiring the training at a specific time on an absolute training needs basis in accordance with operational and organizational demands. Significant emphasis is placed on training in response to quality of service issues and matters that are of greatest concern to citizens. Such matters are often raised at meetings with community forums and in other interactions with the citizenry and their representatives. Thus, the people have a democratic voice in training.

Since the early 1990s, there has been a succession of training change and reform programs in England and Wales in an endeavor to match training and development with local, regional, and national priorities and to enhance professional competence. In April 2007, the National Policing Improvement Act (NPIA) was launched. In addition to providing national training and development programs for police officers of all ranks, the body will also be responsible for national information systems such as the Police National Computer (PNC), the DNA database, and the national fingerprint and palm print system. Additionally, the NPIA provides round-the-clock specialist operational policing advice to police forces for murder investigations, public order events, major incidents, and searches. (For further information, see the National Police Improvement Agency Web site at http://www.npia.police.uk.)

Higher-level training for those officers in managerial ranks continues to take place at the former Police College at Bramshill in the south of England. Rank-based courses have traditionally equipped police officers from the inspecting ranks and above with the skills to perform as middle managers in the organization. The Strategic Commanders Programme, for example, must be negotiated by middle managers who wish to progress to membership in the Association of Chief Police Officers and become assistant chiefs and perhaps chief constables eventually. The High Potential Development Scheme (formerly the "special" course) has been in existence since the 1960s and aims to take those recruits with the most ability and develop them into the police leaders of tomorrow.

There has been a restructuring of leadership and management training at Bramshill over the past few years due to the belief that leadership should increasingly be a role-based rather than a rank-based activity. It was noted, for instance, that many chief inspectors had to assume more of the roles and responsibilities of superintendents, who were their superior officers, due to the pressures of increased workload (Long, 2003). Recent years have seen the rise of facilitative learning taking the place of traditional didactic or "front-loaded" learning. Learning is now expected to be experiential and tends to be based on case-study exercises or simulations.

Training of international officers through the international leadership programs and other customized courses is also delivered at the International Faculty, Bramshill, to senior and middle ranking officers from around the world identified as likely to become the most senior leaders of their nations' police organizations. These courses are designed to equip them with the strategic awareness, knowledge, skills, and attitude necessary to operate effectively in the ever-changing global policing environment and to encourage adherence to the principles of progressive service.

Community Policing

It has become a maxim that community policing is democratic policing. Moreover, if their practices are to be truly defined as community policing, police leaders should have a high degree of public accountability for effective operational performance and use of policing resources.

Police and community collaboration, particularly with respect to relations between police minority ethnic communities, has traditionally been poor, as evidenced in an earlier section of this chapter. That section mentioned how the Scarman report (Scarman, 1981) on the riots in Brixton at the start of the 1980s focused attention on the need for the police to develop closer engagements with members of the communities that they served. This was because the police had lost the confidence of large sections of the community, particularly young, black males in this case. This led to a feeling that the police were detached from the community and that therefore they lacked the legitimacy required to police by consent. Indeed Bennett describes community policing at its simplest as "a greater working partnership between the police and the public" (1994, p. 224). A key advocate of community policing in the United Kingdom, back in the late 1970s and 1980s, was the former chief constable of Devon and Cornwall police, John Alderson. Alderson (1979) stressed the need to police with and for the community rather than to police against the community in a more authoritarian manner.

For community policing to take place there needs to be a significant degree of decentralization to local policing areas, which is only now being encouraged (see section above describing this process). Authority has to be devolved from the center in order for local responsiveness and two-way dialogue between police and community to occur. According to Tilley (2003), community policing involves the following:

- Defining what constitutes problems or policing needs
- Shaping forms of local policing by the police service
- Involving the community in taking responsibility and working along-side the police service in identifying local problems
- Determining responses to identified issues
- Implementing responses to issues as participants in community policing
- Working with the community to address community-defined problems
- Informing or supplementing the operational work of police officers

It would seem to be the case that community policing works best in more affluent and middle-class areas where police-community relations are already relatively good. The evidence suggests that alternatively, the poorest and most deprived areas, where there is distrust of the police, tend to be the very areas that are resistant to the implementation of community policing schemes (Hancock, 2001). Sustainability of community policing schemes also appears to be a problem.

Crime Prevention Programs

We have seen that modern policing has existed since the nineteenth century, yet it was not until the latter part of the twentieth century that crime prevention was accorded specific attention in the United Kingdom. The Cornish Committee on the Prevention and Detection of Crime (Home Office, 1965) was a precursor to some forces establishing crime prevention sections within their preexisting criminal investigation departments. It was recommended that each force have a designated crime prevention officer and that this job should be carried out by a police middle manager. The work of the Cornish committee was complemented two years later with the establishment of the Home Office Standing Committee on Crime Prevention in 1967, which recommended the creation of crime prevention panels in all towns and cities in the United Kingdom (Byrne & Pease, 2003).

In 1995, the Crime Prevention College in Easingwold in the north of England was established. What became known as the Morgan Report (Standing Conference on Crime Prevention, 1991) made recommendations that were given statutory backing via the Crime and Disorder Act of 1998. The act required the police and local authorities to work together in partnership rather than independently of each other. After consulting local citizens and designing local strategies, partnerships have to satisfy central government by producing crime audits every three years. Critically, section 17 of the act makes it essential that local authorities give due consideration to issues of crime in all of their decision-making processes. Despite the establishment of a crime prevention college and the more recent legislation, according to Byrne and Pease, "crime prevention has never fully permeated police thinking and practise" (2003, p. 287). According to the Audit Commission (1999) crime prevention is not something that the overwhelming majority of police officers are concerned with in their day-to-day duties. This is probably due to the fact that police performance continues to be judged around indicators of detection, such as burglary, car crime, and theft. It is in fact notoriously difficult to establish indicators of performance around crime prevention. Byrne and Pease (2003) further note that the Home Office seems to be keen to allocate much of its funding to closed circuit TV monitoring systems, which is only one small aspect of what should be a much bigger picture in crime prevention terms.

On a more positive note, the police are now more aware of criminal hotspots and the phenomenon of repeat victimization than they ever were before, and future attempts at taking crime prevention seriously will be assisted by rapid developments in crime analysis and mapping (Byrne & Pease, 2003).

Community Outreach

Examples of specific community crime prevention programs in the United Kingdom include such things as conducting crime prevention seminars and creating neighborhood watch programs (Laycock & Tilley, 1995). Additionally, drug education projects became very popular from the mid-1980s onward (Collison, 1995).

Terrorism

Until the peace settlement was signed in Northern Ireland at the end of the last century, the policing of terrorism in the United Kingdom had been dominated by the "troubles" in Northern Ireland, which began in 1969 (Ellison & Smyth, 2000). The dispute over the issue of a united Ireland meant that the policing of Republican paramilitary groups such as the provisional Irish Republican Army (IRA) and Loyalist paramilitary groups such as the Ulster Volunteer Force took precedence over other issues. From the point of view of the British government and policing, it was the IRA bombing campaigns throughout the 1970s, 1980s, and 1990s, targeted at pubs, hotels and shops predominantly in Northern Ireland's capital Belfast and London in England, which were perceived to present the most dangerous threat (O'Leary & McGarry, 1993). Since the troubles ended with the ceasefire by Republican and Loyalist paramilitaries, the decommission of terrorist weapons, and the final power-sharing agreement by all political groups to work together in the devolved Northern Ireland Assembly, police attention has tended to

withdraw from Irish terrorism and focused on the more potent and dangerous threat of the global terrorism of Islamist extremists.

Counterterrorism

Until al-Quaeda's September 11 attacks were made, it would be fair to
say that counterterrorism training was not a policing priority. It has traditionally been seen as something that is undertaken by specialist departments
and individuals and something that is divorced from the realities of day-to-
day operational policing. This attitude has had to change fast. On March 11,
2004, Islamist terrorists carried out the Madrid train bombings that killed
191 people. On July 7, 2005, British Islamist suicide bombers caused explosions on the London transport system resulting in the deaths of 52 people
and the injury of 700. On September 1, 2005, al-Quaeda officially claimed
responsibility for the London bombings on the Al Jazeera news network.

The need to fund additional resources for counterterrorism, intelligence
gathering, and associated training has been given added impetus by the perception, since the bombings occurred, that Britain is an inevitable target due
to her foreign policy and political alignment with the United States over the
Iraq war and the military presence in Afghanistan. All forces are now taking
the training of designated officers very seriously with regard to preparing for
the possibility of chemical, biological, radioactive, and nuclear attacks. (For
more information on this subject, see the Web site of the National Counter
Terrorism Security Office, http://www.nactso.gov.uk/index.php.)

Counterterrorism Policy and Strategy

The Metropolitan Bomb Squad was formed in 1971 largely as a response
to the sectarian killings that were associated with the struggle over the
future of Northern Ireland. This bomb squad became known as the Anti-
Terrorist Branch from 1976 onwards. The police were given the statutory
backing of the Prevention of Terrorism (Temporary Provisions) Act of 1974
in order to arrest, search, and detain without warrant those suspected of
terrorist activities. London's Metropolitan Police are also supported by
agencies like Special Branch, the Diplomatic Protection Group, and the
Royalty Protection Group (Matassa & Newburn, 2003). Special Branch
has departments within every force in the United Kingdom. The metropolitan force's antiterrorist squad is expected to work closely with Special
Branch and the Security Services (M15 and MI6), whose role it is to protect
national security.

Due to the changing nature of globalization, in recent years the UK
police have had to work in greater cooperation with Europol, which was
established via the Maastricht Treaty in 1992. When terrorist activities go

beyond European boundaries, then the UK police will work in collaboration with Interpol (Matassa & Newburn, 2003).

Section 1 of the Terrorism Act of 2000 defines terrorism as an actual or threatened act of violence against people or property effected to try to influence the course of government for political, religious, or ideological reasons. This act, along with the Regulation of Investigatory Powers Act of 2000 and the Anti-terrorism, Crime and Security Act of 2001, has greatly extended police powers with regard to those people and organizations suspected of terrorist activity. This legislation cannot be divorced from the outrage at the September 11 attacks in New York and Washington launched by al-Quaeda. In an attempt to counter the argument that the policing activities of the Security Services are largely unaccountable, the Regulation of Investigatory Powers Act of 2000 attempts to police the police by establishing a tribunal, founded on human rights principles, which can deal with complaints.

Terrorism and Its Threat to Democracy

During 2007, a number of young British Muslim male citizens of Pakistani descent have been convicted of conspiring to plant bombs in public places with the intent of causing maximum fatalities of innocent citizens. Other such young British Muslim Asians residing in various cities in the United Kingdom are awaiting trial for similar alleged crimes. All are alleged to be connected to the al-Quaeda network or similar organizations. Disturbingly, many are alleged to have received training at terror camps in Pakistan and Afghanistan. It is of the gravest concern to British society, government, security services, and police that a minority of young Muslims who have been born, brought up, and educated in Britain feel so alienated from British society that they feel compelled to vent their frustrations through extreme radical violence. The situation begs questions about allegiance to citizenship in a democratic society and about how society can respond to prevent such young people from falling prey to the inflammatory and extreme rhetoric of resident radical mullahs and other Islamist exhortations to attack the West. The police will have an important part to play, not only in enforcing laws but also in fostering harmonious community relations. They will need to be seen to be operating equitably, not as operating a witch hunt and marginalizing the great majority of the 1.6 million UK citizens who are law-abiding Muslims ("Religion in Britain," 2003).

Looking to the future, the threat of terrorism from extreme Islamist groups is a long-term potential threat to democracy and freedom. Terrorists seek to provoke governments and law enforcement agencies into disproportionate responses to their acts. They seek to undermine democracy. Thus, the terrorist can claim the moral high ground (Marighella, 1969). Following the London suicide bombings, government, police, and security services sought additional powers to detain terrorist suspects for up to 60 days without trial in order to complete effective investigations. A public and political debate ensued: Sixty days was considered by many to be an excessive period, and there was concern that allowing such a lengthy detention period would set a precedent that undermined fundamental principles of the freedom of the individual and the detention of suspects without charge. In November 2006, Parliament rejected the period of 60 days and reduced the legal period of detention of terrorist suspects without charge to 28 days ("Terrorism Bill," 2006).

The above exemplifies a special challenge to lawmakers and law enforcement officials: namely, the question of how to effectively deal with acts of terror while maintaining freedom and harmony between communities within the democratic framework of the United Kingdom. It seems likely that this challenge will remain for many years to come.

Notes

1. This was with the exception of London's Metropolitan force, which had a police committee rather than a police authority.

2. This number does not include forces with a special jurisdiction throughout the United Kingdom, such as the Ministry of Defense Police and the British Transport Police.

3. Ordinarily retirement is at age 55 years however.

References

Alderson, J. (1979). *Policing freedom*. Plymouth, UK: Macdonald and Evans.

Audit Commission. (1999). *Safety in numbers—Promoting community safety*. London: Author.

Audit Commission. (2001). *Best foot forward: Headquarters' support for police basic command units*. London: Her Majesty's Stationery Office.

Bennett, T. (1994). Community policing on the ground: Developments in Britain. In D. Rosenbaum (Ed.), *The challenge of community policing* (pp. 224–246). Thousand Oaks, CA: Sage.

Bourne, J. (2001). The life and times of institutional racism. *Race and Class, 43*(2), 7–22.

Bowling, B., & Phillips, C. (2003). Policing ethnic minority communities. In T. Newburn (Ed.), *Handbook of policing* (pp. 528–555). Devon, UK: Willan.

Bucke, T., & Brown, D. (1997). *In police custody: Police powers and suspects. Rights under the revised PACE Codes of Practise*, Home Office Research Study 174. London: Home Office.

Byrne, S., & Pease, K. (2003). Crime reduction and community safety. In T. Newburn (Ed.), *Handbook of policing* (pp. 286–310). Devon, UK: Willan.

Chan, J. (1997). *Changing police culture: Policing in a multicultural society*. Cambridge, UK: Cambridge University Press.

Collison, M. (1995). *Police, drugs and community*. London: Free Association Books.

Cox, B., Shirley, J., & Short, M. (1977). *The fall of Scotland Yard*. Harmondsworth, UK: Penguin.

Crawshaw, R., Cullen, S., & Williamson, T. (2007). *Human rights and policing: The Raoul Wallenberg Institute professional guide to human rights*. Leiden, the Netherlands: Martinus Nijhoff.

Crime statistics for England and Wales. (2007). British Crime Survey data. Retrieved June 8, 2007, from http://www.crimestatistics.org.uk/output/page54.asp

Donnelly, D., & Scott, K. (2002a). Police accountability in Scotland: (1) The "new" tripartite system. *The Police Journal, 75,* 3–14.

Donnelly, D., & Scott, K. (2002b). Police accountability in Scotland: (2) "New" accountabilities. *The Police Journal, 75,* 56–66.

Ellison, G., & Smyth, J. (2000). *The crowned harp: Policing Northern Ireland*. London: Pluto Press.

Fenwick, H. (2002). The Anti-terrorism, Crime and Security Act 2001: A proportionate response to 11 September? *Modern Law Review, 65*(5), 724–762.

Gordon, P. (1984). *White law*. London. Pluto Press.

Hancock, L. (2001). *Community, crime and disorder: Safety and regeneration in urban neighbourhoods*. Basingstoke, UK: Palgrave.

Home Office. (1965). *Report of the Committee on the Prevention and Detection of Crime* (Cornish Committee). London: Author.

Home Office. (1999). *Staff targets for the Home Office, the prison, the police, the fire and the probation services*. London: Author.

Home Office. (2001). *Policing a new century: A blueprint for reform*. (Cm 5326). London: Author.

Home Office. (2003). *Statistics on race and the criminal justice system 2002: A Home Office publication under Section 95 of the Criminal Justice Act 1991*. London: Author.

Home Office. (2005). *National policing plan. 2005–2008. Safer, stronger communities*. London: Author.

Home Office. (2007). *Criminal statistics. 2007*. Retrieved May 14, 2007, from http://www.homeoffice.gov.uk/rds/

Homicide in Scotland, 2005/06—Statistics Published. (2006). Retrieved May 14, 2007, from http://www.scotland.gov.uk/Publications/2006/11/17112458/1

Independent Commission on Policing in Northern Ireland. (1999). *A new beginning: Policing in Northern Ireland—the Report of the Independent Commission on Policing in Northern Ireland*. (Patten Report). Belfast, UK: Independent Commission on Policing in Northern Ireland.

Inquest. (1996). *Lobbying from below: INQUEST in defence of civil liberties*. London: University College London Press.

Laycock, G., & Tilley, N. (1995). *Policing and neighbourhood watch: Strategic issues*. Crime Detection and Prevention Series Paper 60. London: Home Office.

Levi, M. (2003). Organized and financial crime. In T. Newburn (Ed.), *Handbook of policing* (pp. 444–466). Devon, UK: Willan.

Long, M. (2003). "Leadership and performance management," in T. Newburn (Ed.), *Handbook of policing* (pp. 628–654). Devon, UK: Willan.

Long, M. (2005). United Kingdom. In L. E. Sullivan & M. R. Haberfeld (Eds.), *Encyclopedia of law enforcement* (pp. 1358–1364). London: Sage.

Lovbakke, J., Taylor, P., & Budd, S. (2007). *Crime in England and Wales: Quarterly update to December 2006*. London: Home Office.

Loveday, B. (2006). Workforce modernisation: Implications for the police service in England and Wales. [Special issue: Evaluating HMIC, 2004 Thematic: Modernising the Police Service]. *The Police Journal, 79,* 105–124.

MacPherson, W. (1999.) *The Stephen Lawrence inquiry*. Report of an Inquiry by Sir William MacPherson of Cluny. Advised by Tom Cook, The Right Reverend Dr. John Sentamu, and Dr. Richard Stone (Cm 4262-1). London: Her Majesty's Stationery Office.

Marighella, C. (1969). *Minimanual of the urban guerrilla*. Retrieved May 17, 2007, from www.marxists.org/archive/marighella-carlos/1969/06/minimanual-urban-guerrilla

Mark, R. (1979). *In the office of constable*. London: Fontana.

Marlow, A., & Loveday, B. (Eds.). (2000). *After MacPherson: Policing after the Stephen Lawrence inquiry*. Lyme Regis, UK: Russell House.

Matassa, M., & Newburn, T. (2003). Policing and terrorism. In T. Newburn (Ed.), *Handbook of policing* (pp. 467–500). Devon, UK: Willan.

Mawby, R. (2003). Models of policing. In T. Newburn (Ed.), *Handbook of policing* (pp. 15–40). Devon, UK: Willan.

Mawby, R., & Wright, A. (2003). The police organisation. In T. Newburn (Ed.), *Handbook of policing* (pp. 169–195). Devon, UK: Willan

Metropolitan Police Service. (2001). *Annual report*. London: Author.

Metropolitan Police Authority. (n.d.). *What is Trident?* Retrieved May 16, 2007, from http://www.stoptheguns.org/whatistrident/index.php

Mulcahy, A. (2000). Policing history: The official discourse and organisational memory of the Royal Ulster Constabulary. *British Journal of Criminology, 40*(1), 68–87.

NaCTSO: National Counter Terrorism Security Office. (2007). Home page. Retrieved October 25, 2007, from http://www.nactso.gov.uk/index.php

O'Leary, B., & McGarry, J. (1993). *The politics of antagonism: Understanding Northern Ireland*. London: Athlone Press.

Ousley, H. (2001). *Community pride not prejudice: Making diversity work in Bradford*. Bradford, UK: Bradford Vision 2001.

Police amalgamations forced through. (2006). Retrieved May 16, 2007, from http://conservatives.com/popups/print/cfm?obj_id=127690&t

Police identify 169 London gangs. (2007). Retrieved on May 19 from http://news.bbc.co.uk/2/hi/uk_news/england/london/6383933.stm

Rawlings, P. (2002). *Policing. A short history*. Devon, UK: Willan.

Reiner, R. (2000). *The politics of the police* (3rd ed.). Oxford, UK: Oxford University Press.

Religion in Britain. (2003). UK National Statistics Online. Retrieved June 15, 2007, from http://www.statistics.gov.uk/cci/nugget.asp?id=293

Ritchie, D. (2001). *Panel Report, 11ᵗʰ December 2001: One Oldham, One Future*. Manchester, UK: Government Office for the North West.

Sanders, A., & Young, R. (2003). Police powers. In T. Newburn (Ed.), *Handbook of policing* (pp. 228–258). Devon, UK: Willan.

The scale and nature of human trafficking in the UK. (2006). Retrieved May 14, 2007, from http://www.publications.parliament.uk/pa/jt200506/jtselect/jtrights/245/24507.htm

Scarman, L. (1981). *The Brixton disorders 10-12 April 1981: Report of an inquiry by the Rt. Hon. The Lord Scarman, O.B.E.* London: Her Majesty's Stationery Office.

Serious Organized Crime Agency (SOCA). (2006). *About us*. Retrieved May 14, 2007, from http://www.soca.gov.uk/aboutUs/index.html

Squires, P., & Stephen, D. (2005). *Rougher justice: Anti-social behaviour and young people.* Cullompton, UK: Willan.

Standing Conference on Crime Prevention. (1991). *Safer communities: The local delivery of crime prevention through the partnership approach* (Morgan Report). London: Home Office.

Stead, J. P. (1985). *The police of Britain.* London: Macmillan.

Terrorism Bill—Extension Of Period Of Detention to 60 Days—25 Jan 2006 at 18:38—Lords Division No. 2. (2006). Retrieved May 14, 2007, from http://www.publicwhip.org.uk/division.php?date=2006-01-25&number=2&house=lords

Tilley, N. (2003). *Community policing, problem-oriented policing and intelligence-led policing.* In T. Newburn (Ed.), *Handbook of policing* (pp. 311–339). Devon, UK: Willan.

Transparency International. (2006). *Corruption perceptions index.* Retrieved May 16, 2007, from http://www.transparency.org/policy_research/surveys_indices/global/cpi

Vulliamy, E. (2005, November 29). Rumours of a riot. *The Guardian* [Electronic version]. Retrieved August 17, 2007, from http://www.guardian.co.uk/race/story/0,11374,1653120,00.html

Waddington, P. A. J. (2003). Policing public order and political contention. In T. Newburn (Ed.), *Handbook of policing* (pp. 394–421). Devon, UK: Willan.

Walklate, S. (2000). Equal opportunities and the future of policing. In F. Leishman et al. (Eds.), *Core issues in policing* (2nd ed., pp. 232–248). Harlow, UK: Longman Pearson Education.

World Health Organization. (2002). *World report on health and violence.* Geneva: Author.

Wright, A. (2002). *Policing: An introduction to concepts and practise.* Devon, UK: Willan.

Zander, M. (1994). Ethics and crime investigation. *Policing, 10*(1), 39–48.

12 Democratic Policing

The Canadian Experience

Curtis Clarke

As occurs in many jurisdictions, the perspectives of Canadian policy makers and police leaders have and will continue to shift over time. In the context of Canadian policing, policy analysts currently emphasize the need to reorganize police administration and operational strategies so that they may reflect practices and language drawn from private-sector management. Pat O'Malley states that policing has begun to reflect "the ascendance of neo-liberal political rationalities and related social technology of new managerialism" (1996, p. 10). Others suggest that the previously insular culture of Canadian policing "is being increasingly colonized by business concepts, values and terminology. In this context police services are encouraged to see themselves in the 'business' of supplying policing services to clients, customers and consumers" (Murphy, 1998).

And yet, this recent critique offers us a limited analysis of the contemporary reality of Canadian policing, a pursuit that has been shaped by a range of political, economic, and social factors. Notable among these are the 1982 enactment of the Canadian Charter of Rights and Freedoms, federal and provincial government fiscal policies, extensive budget reductions, specific commissions of Inquiry, transnational policing responsibilities, and growing competition from the private security sector. These elements, while consistent across the country, have not always been addressed in a similar fashion, and as such have created an interesting array of policy and operational responses. In order to illustrate both the diversity and similarity of these responses, it will be necessary to place these outcomes into a contextual framework that captures the political and historical reality of Canadian policing.

Historical and Political Context

Prior to Canada's confederation in 1867, it would have been difficult to characterize Canadian policing as a blend of any two models. The nature of preconfederation policing may be best captured in comparing it to the diverse Canadian geography. The early expansion of settlements and increased commerce presented particular pressures for the Atlantic region of Canada, Lower Canada (now the province of Quebec) and Upper Canada (now the province of Ontario) to adequately provide law and order. It was not until the mid 1800s that communities began to replace the night watch system with full-time police forces. Between 1835 and 1847, the cities of Toronto, Hamilton, Ottawa, Quebec, and Montreal all instituted systems whereby chief constables were appointed and a varied number of full-time and special constables were employed. In 1858, the government of Upper Canada enacted the Municipal Institutions of Upper Canada Act, enabling communities to form police forces and institute boards of commissioners to oversee the governance of these newly formed police agencies. One of the first organized police forces was created by an order in council in 1864 for the Upper Canada county of Essex. The goal of this service was to serve as a frontier police force, a trend that was to be repeated in numerous regions throughout Canada.

While the Constitution Act of 1867 delegated to the provinces the responsibility for enforcing the criminal law and authority to make laws in relation to the administration of justice, it also ensured that upon entry into confederation the provinces would create provincial police services. The creation of provincial police services began with Manitoba and Quebec in 1870; they were followed by British Columbia (1871), Ontario (1909), New Brunswick (1927), Nova Scotia (1928), Prince Edward Island (1930), and Newfoundland (1935). The provinces of Alberta and Saskatchewan broke from this trend by contracting with the federal government to police their regions using the Royal North West Mounted Police (RNWMP). This negotiated agreement was in effect until 1916, at which time both Alberta and Saskatchewan withdrew from the federal/provincial agreement in order to create their own provincial police forces.

While a number of these provincial forces would evolve into viable and current police organizations, others would eventually be disbanded. For reasons including fiscal concerns, lack of qualified personnel, and inappropriate facilities, many provincial police services could no longer offer the required levels of policing. The first service to disband was the Saskatchewan Provincial Police (SPP) in 1928; the services of Alberta, New Brunswick, Nova Scotia, and Prince Edward Island would follow in 1932 and British Columbia's in 1950. The policing void left by their dissolution would be filled by the Royal Canadian Mounted Police (RCMP). Currently, there are three remaining provincial police services: the Ontario Provincial

Police, the Sûreté du Quebec, and the Royal Newfoundland Constabulary.

As various forms of municipal and provincial policing were taking shape, so too was federal policing developing in its unique way. The concept of a federal police service had evolved, in part, from the Canadian government's need to assert its sovereignty in the face of American frontier expansion. In 1873, by way of an act of Parliament, the North West Mounted Police (NWMP) was founded and modeled after the Royal Irish Constabulary. In its early incarnation, the NWMP was tasked with the imposition of civil law in Canada's western territories. It was a role that would contrast with the violent and anarchistic nature of the American frontier. The NWMP presence in the western territories ensured the orderly settlement of the region and guarded against the American annexation of the Canadian west.

In 1904 the North West Mounted Police (NWMP) would undergo a name change and become the Royal North West Mounted Police (RNWMP). In parallel to the evolution of the RNWMP, another federal police service was created by the enactment of the Police of Canada Act of 1868. This newly formed Dominion Police Force was responsible for protecting the parliament buildings and enforcing a range of federal and criminal laws. The force's region of operation was predominantly within the Atlantic provinces and Ontario. These two federal police services would exist separately until 1920, when the Royal North West Mounted Police Amendment Act would create the Royal Canadian Mounted Police (RCMP) by amalgamating the RNWMP and the Dominion Police Force.

Equal Protection, Accountability, and Reform Mechanisms

The above historical review indicates that over the past two centuries Canadian policing has been shaped by both regional and political factors. Yet a more detailed historical analysis offers us the opportunity to examine how Canadian police services can stray from their legal and political function, how these actions undermine Canadian citizens' trust in the justice system, and how these concerns are also remedied. While officer misconduct and disreputable actions have profound implications for police credibility, it is perhaps the process by which such officers are held accountable that is most interesting for this analysis. It is these mechanisms of accountability that both assist in recapturing a community's faith in their police service and bring about procedural and operational change.

One prominent mechanism for change and redress has been the use of commissions of inquiry. Depending upon the severity of police misconduct and the need for public accountability, various levels of government have through orders in council mandated commissions of inquiry to investigate the conduct of police services and individuals and to make recommendations for change intended to prevent further miscarriages of justice. Notable examples of these commissions are the following:

- McDonald Commission (Royal Commission of Inquiry into Certain Activities of the RCMP, 1977)
- Keable Report (Quebec, 1981)
- Royal Commission on the Donald Marshall Jr. Prosecution (Nova Scotia, 1989),
- Ontario Race Relations and Policing Task Force (1992)
- Report of the Saskatchewan Indian Justice Review Committee (1992)
- Policing in British Columbia Commission of Inquiry (1994)
- Commission on Proceedings Involving Guy Paul Morin (Ontario, 1998)

Commissions of inquiry traditionally focus their attention upon the "behaviour of an organization, taken as a whole" (Brodeur & Viau, 1994, p. 246), and thus the resulting recommendations are tailored to address problematic organizational practices. This is not to suggest that the activities of individual or groups of officers are not scrutinized, but they are critiqued in terms of how organizational culture, structure, and practices may support disreputable conduct, etc. One might argue that at this level of inquiry proceedings are guided by the questions: What proportion of an organization facilitates or supports elements of wrongdoing, and how might these organizational/operational characteristics be remedied? Commissions of inquiry have throughout Canadian history been valued mechanisms of accountability and procedural change. And yet they are but one mechanism for accountability and change.

The Charter of Rights and Freedoms (1982), as many would argue, has had the most profound influence upon police powers and practices. Sections 7 through 14 of the charter set out the guiding principles whereby police activity and authority are framed and ultimately governed. Section 7 articulates the broad provisions of legal rights by stating, "Everyone has the right to life liberty and security of the person and the right not to be deprived thereof except in accordance with the principles of fundamental justice." More directly, sections 8 to 10 reference the principles of fundamental justice applied in the context of police powers:

- Everyone has the right to be secure against unreasonable search or seizure (§ 8)
- Everyone has the right not to be arbitrarily detained or imprisoned (§ 9)
- Everyone has certain rights on arrest or detention including the right to retain and instruct counsel without delay (§ 10)

Furthermore, under section 24 anyone whose rights and freedoms have been infringed upon or denied may apply for a remedy to a court of competent jurisdiction. It is in the context of these remedies, more specifically Supreme Court decisions, that police powers and practices have been challenged and reformed.

The following are selected examples of Supreme Court of Canada decisions corresponding to challenges under sections 8, 9, and 10 of the charter. What is most important about these examples is the manner in which they have set clear parameters for future police actions and distinct boundaries of police powers.

Court Decisions Affecting Police

In *Hunter* (1984), the Supreme Court decided that section 8 required that unjustified searches be prevented. The court asserted three constitutional standards. It first established basic requirements for a search warrant and then declared charter standards for such warrants:

1. Where feasible, prior authorization is a precondition for a valid search and seizure.

2. The person authorizing the breach of privacy must assess the need for the breach in an entirely neutral and impartial manner.

3. There have to be reasonable and probable grounds, established upon oath, to believe that an offence has been committed or that evidence will be found at the place of the search.

In *Collins* (1987), the Supreme Court outlined the following dictum:

A search will be reasonable if it is authorized by law, if the law itself is reasonable and if the manner in which the search was carried out is reasonable.

In *Simpson* (1993), the Ontario Court of Appeals held "that, where an individual is detained by the police in the course of efforts to determine whether that individual is involved in criminal activity, detention can be justified under common law ancillary powers doctrine if the detaining officer has some articulable cause for detention" (Stuart, 1996, p. 246). In this case, "articulable cause" was clearly contrasted to the broad understanding of a "hunch," which is based on intuition and subjective assessments.

With respect to the right to retain and instruct counsel, in *Bartle* (1994), the Supreme Court held that

the purpose of the right to counsel guaranteed by section 10 (b) of the Charter is to provide detainees with an opportunity to be informed of their rights and obligations under the law and, most importantly, to attain advice on how to exercise those rights and fulfill those obligations. This opportunity is made available because, when an individual is detained by state authorities, he or she is put in a position of disadvantage relative to the state. Not only has this person suffered of a deprivation of liberty, but also this person may be at risk of incriminating him or herself . . . Under section 10 (b), the detainee is entitled as a right to seek such legal advice without delay and upon request.

Here, the court sought to ensure that detained individuals were not merely read a statement but had to be afforded the opportunity to retain and instruct counsel without delay. This placed an onus on police officers to not treat the process as merely a programmatic statement without any requirement to implement.

While these are specific examples, they do emphasize the direction and role of the courts. Moreover, they are a representation of how police services have been held accountable for actions and policy as they pertain to the preservation of rights and freedoms. As these cases suggest, the Charter of Rights and Freedoms has and will continue to guide Canadian policing, but more important, the Charter will continue to offer a remedy for miscarriages of justice attributed to police activity. The ongoing importance of this redress mechanism cannot be underscored enough, particularly within the current context of antiterrorism initiatives and legislative guidance set out by the federal government's Bill C-36 (the Anti-Terrorism Act). Bill C-36 gives new investigative tools to law enforcement agencies to ensure "that the prosecution of terrorist offences can be undertaken efficiently and effectively" (Department of Justice, 2001, p. 3). Some of the measures referred to here are powers that make it easier to utilize electronic surveillance against terrorist organizations. A more contentious component is the creation of the "preventive arrest" power that will allow a "peace officer to arrest and bring a person before a judge to impose reasonable supervisory conditions if there are reasonable grounds to suspect that the person is about to commit a terrorism activity" (Department of Justice, 2001, p. 3). The premise supporting these and other powers is the need to protect Canadian citizens with respect to the new reality of risk, and yet, there remains the need to be vigilant in terms of potential abuses. As the current realm of antiterrorism activity is uncharted, it will be necessary for Canadian policing to be held accountable to the principles of justice, and therefore the role of the courts will continue to shape the future of policing.

Further Layers of Accountability and Governance

As indicated previously the constitutional responsibility for policing is shared between the federal and provincial/territorial governments. The Constitution Act of 1867 confers authority on the federal government to legislate in relation to criminal law and procedure as well as the power to legislate in respect to peace, order, and good government. The act empowers the provincial governments to make laws in relation to the administration of justice, of which policing is one facet (Ministry of Human Resources Development, 2000). The result of this is that police services are accountable to a range of governing bodies inclusive of local and regional oversight bodies, provincial authorities, and with respect to the RCMP, the federal solicitor general. In most instances the responsibility for policing falls to the attorney general or solicitor general in each province. The exceptions to this are Quebec, where this responsibility is held by the director of public security, and Ontario, where this responsibility is in fact shared between the attorney general and the solicitor general. The governance of municipal police services is generally set out by provincial legislation, which outlines the requirements of local authorities, such as municipal councils and municipal boards of commissioners as well as provincial police commissions.

Municipal oversight plays a critical role in the assurance of police accountability. These oversight bodies undertake the task of ensuring fiscal and legal accountability as well as providing policy direction. Municipal oversight bodies also have the important task of representing citizen concerns and priorities in relation to pertinent public security issues. There are two models of municipal oversight used in Canada. Within the provinces of Quebec and Manitoba, the responsibility for police oversight is assumed by the municipal council. With respect to the remaining provinces, police oversight is the responsibility of either a police board or commission. These particular oversight bodies are made up of civilians appointed either by the province or by the municipal council. In most instances there is representation from the municipal council. In 1989, the Canadian Association of Police Boards was founded with the goal of providing support and direction to municipal boards and communities in order to ensure they achieve effective representation for their police oversight bodies. There are also provincial associations mandated with similar support functions.

While municipal oversight bodies are a key component in the governance of policing, it is also important to ensure that a healthy regulatory environment is maintained. In order to accomplish this task, provincial and federal governments have established legislation and policy that regulate standards and policing authority. Most provinces have set (or are in the process of defining) formal police standards throughout their jurisdiction. The common objectives are as follows (Ministry of Human Resources Development, 2000):

- Promote consistent service delivery.
- Establish clear expectations for procedures and operations.
- Guide human resource practices and ensure particular standards of administration.

A specific example of these standards can be found in Ontario's Police Services Act Regulation 3/99, "Adequacy and Effectiveness of Police Services." The objective of these adequacy standards is to articulate and ensure the delivery of the six core policing functions prescribed by the Police Services Act. Moreover, these core functions are understood as the foundation of adequate and effective police services. The six core functions are crime prevention, law enforcement, victims' assistance, public order maintenance, emergency response services, and administration and infrastructure. To ensure police services could achieve these core functions, the Ontario Policing Standards Manual was revamped to contain guidelines and sample board policies designed to assist police services in understanding and implementing the Police Services Act and its regulations, including the *Adequacy Standards Regulation*. The Manual, to-date, has included 70 separate guidelines, establishing a framework to provide consistent police service delivery in the province of Ontario. All police services were to be compliant with the *Adequacy Standards Regulation* by January 1, 2001. (Blandford, 2003, p. 1)

The assurance of governance and accountability is aided by the establishment of provincial police commissions. To assist these agencies in holding police services accountable, most commissions have the authority to conduct inquiries into police activity and practices. This authority of inquiry can include the review of municipal police boards and internal police discipline decisions. A complementary layer of accountability is achieved through the establishment of formal complaint bodies such as public complaint boards, law enforcement review boards, etc. The task of these oversight bodies is to field and investigate civilian complaints about individual officers or police services. In many jurisdictions the concept of a civilian oversight and complaints process has been viewed with some disdain by police services. And yet, the option of allowing only the police to investigate themselves is considered problematic by many citizens. In response to these concerns and the perceived bias of internal police oversight, there are provisions for investigation and review established by provincial police acts and, in the case of the RCMP, under the RCMP Act.

Essential to the success of these oversight mechanisms is the requirement of civilian review and the assurance that the process is open and transparent. For example, in Manitoba all complaints against police are investigated by the Law Enforcement Review Agency. In British Columbia, public complaints proceedings are chaired by an independent commissioner, and in Ontario the special investigations unit, "which operates under the jurisdiction of the Attorney General, investigates all cases involving serious injury or death" (Griffiths, Whitelaw, & Parent, 1999, p. 438). The following are further examples of provincial police conduct review agencies:

- Ontario Civilian Commission on Police Services
- Alberta Law Enforcement Review Board
- Quebec Police Ethics Commissioner
- British Columbia Office of the Complaints Commissioner
- Commission for Public Complaints Against the RCMP

While these various agencies have been tasked with oversight authority, they have tended to respond to a traditional understanding of police core functions. In a post–September 11 environment, there is little argument that these functions are changing. This is particularly true with respect to the RCMP and its renewed national security responsibilities. The concern over whether or not appropriate oversight exists was thrust to the foreground with a complaint filed on October 23, 2003, by the Chair of the Commission for Public Complaints Against the RCMP, Ms. Shirley Heafey, This complaint centered upon RCMP conduct in relation to the deportation and detention of Mr. Maher Arar. The thrust of this complaint

> requires the RCMP to report on whether members of the RCMP improperly encouraged U.S. authorities to deport a Canadian citizen, Mr. Maher Arar, from U.S. territory to Syria. Similarly, it requires the RCMP to report on the allegation that members of the RCMP failed to discourage U.S. authorities from deporting a Canadian citizen, Mr. Maher Arar, from U.S. territory to Syria. The RCMP must also report on whether members of the RCMP improperly divulged information and/or conveyed inaccurate or incomplete information about Mr. Maher Arar to U.S. and/or Syrian authorities. Finally, the RCMP must report on allegations that members of the RCMP improperly impeded the efforts of the Canadian government and others to secure the release of Mr. Maher Arar. (Commission for Public Complaints Against the RCMP, 2003)

Under the new antiterrorism legislation (Bill C-36), the RCMP has been granted new powers that will enable it to combat terrorism. And yet, an underlying concern of the commission chair is that the "new security legislation did not provide the Commission for Public Complaints Against the RCMP with similar new oversight powers to review the RCMP's antiterrorism activities" (Commission for Public Complaints Against the RCMP, 2004). The tone of recent commission statements suggests a profound concern for the lack of effective civilian oversight with respect to the national security activities being performed by the RCMP (Commission for Public Complaints Against the RCMP, 2004).

In summary, Canadian police services are held accountable through a range of mechanisms. These fall into five categories (Law Commission of Canada, 2006, p. 88):

1. Political accountability to governing authorities and beyond, through normal political processes

2. Legal accountability or accountability to the law through the courts and judiciary

3. Accountability to administrative agencies such as complaints commissions, human rights commissions and tribunals, government departments, provincial police commissions, treasury boards, auditors general, or ombudsmen

4. Direct public accountability through such mechanisms as freedom of information legislation

5. Special ad hoc accountability mechanisms such as royal commissions and other public inquiries

Racial and Ethnic Context

Philip Stenning (2003) aptly captures the challenges of policing Canada's increasingly culturally, racially, and ethnically diverse society by suggesting it is a task of policing a cultural kaleidoscope. Over the past four decades the cultural and racial composition of Canada has undergone dramatic shifts. In 1961, 97 percent of the Canadian population were identified as being of European extraction, with the largest percentage having British ancestry. Between 1961 and 2001, 5.5 million immigrants entered Canada. The greatest number of these arrived from Asia, with Europe as the second prominent geographic region of origin. The 2001 national census indicates that visible minorities represent 13.4 percent of the Canadian population; this represents an increase of 24.6 percent since the 1996 census. Not included in the above percentages are aboriginal peoples, who make up 3.3 percent of the Canadian population. The growing trend of immigration will continue to shape the cultural landscape, as it is estimated that in order to meet projected labor market needs Canada must accept a minimum of 250,000 immigrants per year.

The importance of diversity and support of a multicultural society was given legislative direction when the Canadian Parliament enacted the Canadian Multiculturalism Act of 1988. The thrust of this act was to proclaim that the policy of the Canadian government was to ensure "that all individuals receive equal treatment and equal protection under law, while respecting and valuing their diversity" (paragraph 3.1.e); moreover; it would ensure that all federal government institutions would operate in a manner consistent with these objectives. Thus the RCMP and other federal law enforcement agencies must operate in accordance to these objectives. Legislative support for a multicultural society is further supported by section 15 of the Charter of Rights and Freedoms, which includes the following: "Every individual is equal before and under the law and has the right to equal protection and equal benefit of the law without discrimination based on race, national or ethnic origin, colour, religion, sex, age or mental or physical disability."

Although these legislative guidelines are in place, this does not necessarily suggest that the adoption of these principles has been an easy process for Canadian policing. One hurdle that police services have needed to confront is that of equal representation within police services. In a report entitled *Strategic Human Resources Analysis of Public Policing in Canada* (Ministry of Human Resources Development, 2000), 1996 statistics highlight the status in the labor force of various designated groups, comparing minority representation in policing to that in other sectors. For example, aboriginals make up 3.1 percent of all police officers, and other visible minorities represent 2.9 percent. This is compared to all Canadian industries, which aboriginals make up 1.7 percent of the labor force and visible minorities make up 9.9 percent of it. As one can tell by these statistics, police services do not accurately reflect the multicultural makeup of Canadian society.

Yet, this does not suggest that police services have not actively engaged in attempts to recruit members of visible minorities. In fact, as Stenning (2003) notes,

> Despite genuine and often quite vigorous attempts by many police leaders to change the faces of their organizations to better reflect the cultural makeup of the communities they policed, and despite some formal statutory employment equity requirements introduced in the 1990s, the ethnic and cultural composition of police services in Canada has remained stubbornly out of alignment with that of many of the communities they police. (p. 19)

The policing needs of Canada's multicultural communities cannot be dealt with by simply attempting to meet employment equity criteria. In fact, police services have required wholesale reviews of their internal cultures in an effort to encourage an understanding between police officers and members of the diverse cultural communities they interact with. The premise for this assertion is influenced by the belief that if police services are to effectively offer equitable service to ever-changing communities, then officers must both understand and recognize the diverse values, beliefs, and customs of those communities. In an effort to address existing shortcomings of cross-cultural understanding, police services and training academies have been tasked with the development and delivery of cultural diversity programs. And while this level of program development had received legislative support, there has been little ongoing research into the effectiveness of these programs in altering the attitudes and practices of police officers.

Unfortunately, recent cases of police officer misconduct, such as the September 1995 shooting of aboriginal protestor Dudley George by the Ontario Provincial Police and the 2002 conviction of two Saskatoon Police officers for apprehending and abandoning an aboriginal male in subzero temperatures, have undermined the various police services' relationships with aboriginal communities.[1] More important, these incidents have refocused the debate on whether or not existing cultural programming is indeed effective. And while these events have brought increased attention to the need for greater cultural sensitivity, they do not represent any systemic rot within policing (Barry Leighton, cited in Quigley, 2004). Moreover, a British Columbia provincial poll undertaken in the fall of 2003 and cited in the same article indicates that "89 percent of respondents" agreed that the police were doing a good job (Quigley, 2004).

Other efforts to bridge cultural divides have manifested themselves in the efforts of police service liaison committees. Stenning (2003) suggests that while these committees had proven successful in facilitating dialogue between community and police, they were fraught with problems. These concerns have evolved from legitimate queries as to whether or not the liaison committees were truly representative of the community to whether or not they were effective forums for community consultation. RCMP findings suggest that the failure of these committees was due to "lack of genuine consultation, lack of response by police and dissipating interest" (Topp, 2003). In review of both legislative and operational initiatives, one can readily argue that efforts have been undertaken with the purpose of addressing the ever-shifting cultural mosaic of Canada. And yet, from a policing perspective little has been done to capture the effectiveness of these initiatives or examine best practices. As several scholars have suggested, if we are to ensure that policing effectively protects and embraces the principles of diversity, we must at some level engage in proactive analysis of police initiatives (Jain, 1995; Stenning, 2003; Topp, 2003). We cannot merely wait for incidents of conflict and misconduct to be the gauge of success or failure.

Organizational Structure and Issues

Like many postmodern organizations, Canadian police forces are adapting to an increasingly multicultural society, economic constraints, changing international/domestic crime patterns, and shifting governance paradigms. Response to this changing environment is made more difficult by the fact that Canadian policing is carried out at three levels (municipal, provincial, and federal). In this context consistent and coordinated adaptation is further complicated by the existence of differing provincial and federal police acts, criss-crossing jurisdictional boundaries, and a history of disparate national and provincial standards. From a statistical point of reference, contemporary Canadian police forces consist of 62,458 police officers (Canadian Centre for Justice Statistics, 2007) providing for a national citizen per officer ratio of 520/1, an annual expenditure on policing of $8.8 billion (Canadian Centre for Justice Statistics, 2007), 579 municipal police services, 3 provincial police services, and one federal police agency. (All dollar amounts in this chapter are in Canadian dollars.)

And yet, to understand Canadian policing one must move beyond the thumbnail sketch that these broad statistical snapshots offer. A more thorough statistical analysis indicates the existence of disparate levels of policing from province to province. Some of these differences are aptly noted in a comparison of provincial population per police ratios. In 2002 the range varied from 237.5/1 in the Yukon Territory to 682.4/1 in the province of Newfoundland and Labrador, with Canada's most populous provinces of Ontario (533.4/1) and Quebec (516.7/1) representing the mean. These differences are further articulated when one examines the differential in per capita spending on municipal and provincial policing by province. Once more the range varied from $97 per capita in Prince Edward Island to $179 in the province of Quebec, with the province of Alberta representing the median of $132 (Canadian Centre for Justice Statistics, 2007).

A further understanding of Canada's policing arena can be accomplished by examining the different jurisdictional responsibilities, mandates, and organizational structures inherent to municipal, provincial, contract, and federal policing.

Municipal Policing

Communities with a population of 10,000 or more are required under legislation to have a police service operated by the municipality or under contract to either the RCMP or a provincial police service. There are no requirements placed upon municipalities under this population threshold. Conversely, there are no restrictions preventing these smaller communities from developing their own police service. Municipalities in all regions have the option of providing their own service as long as they meet relevant legislative guidelines and standards. This legislated framework and a community's desire for public safety and law enforcement has created a national patchwork of police services ranging in size from one or two officers to those with over 7,000 officers (e.g., in Toronto and Montreal).

With respect to enforcement responsibilities, municipal officers are tasked with the enforcement of municipal and provincial statutes, the criminal code, and specific federal statutes, e.g. the Controlled Drugs and Substances Act. The authority of municipal police officers is limited by the jurisdictional boundary of the municipality they are employed by. (There are exceptions to this restriction when, for example, RCMP or Ontario Provincial Police officers are policing communities under contract. This exception is due to the broader enforcement mandates and authority these officers are granted via provincial and federal legislation.)

Municipal policing is an integral component of Canadian policing, and any change in the structure or practices of municipal policing has a direct impact on the nature of Canadian policing. For example, recent provincial requirements for increased regionalization of municipalities and the resulting amalgamation of existing police services has had a direct impact on the governance, size, and enforcement tasks of municipal police services. Furthermore, these initiatives reflect an increased desire by provincial governments to assert greater control and impose particular legislative guidelines upon police services.

Contract Policing

Contract policing is an interesting feature of Canadian policing, a practice that traces its history to frontier policing undertaken by the NWMP. Today it accurately refers to cost-sharing agreements that exist between large police services and provinces or municipalities to undertake policing operations. In Canada there are two police services that are characteristically associated with contract policing, the Ontario Provincial Police (OPP) and the RCMP. The OPP is limited to the provincial jurisdictional boundary of Ontario, and as they are in fact Ontario's provincial police service, the extent of contract policing is limited to municipalities that, for a range of reasons, have not developed their own municipal service. The RCMP on the other hand is involved in contract policing nationwide and undertakes provincial and municipal policing in all but two Canadian provinces (Ontario and Quebec). The RCMP commits 57 percent of its budget and 47 percent of its members to contract policing. Current contract agreements are governed by a cost-sharing formula wherein the province pays 70 percent and the RCMP (federal government) covers the remaining 30 percent. This contract formula changes when the RCMP polices municipalities with a population greater than 15,000; here the municipality is responsible for 90 percent of the cost and the RCMP the remaining 10 percent. These agreements incorporate a review mechanism whereby the cost-sharing formula can be renegotiated every five years. (As of the winter of 2007, the RCMP and provincial governments have begun preliminary negotiations regarding the upcoming 2012 contracts.)

Provincial Policing

The Constitution Act of 1867 granted the provincial and territorial governments responsibility for the administration of justice and with it the responsibility for overseeing the operation and development of policing within their jurisdictional boundaries. Provincial police services are charged with enforcing the criminal code and provincial statutes in areas not policed by municipal police services, usually rural areas and small communities. These police services are traditionally under the purview of the provincial attorney general or solicitor general. As noted previously there are three independent provincial police services in Canada: the OPP, the Sûreté du Quebec (SQ), and the Royal Newfoundland Constabulary (NRC). The NRC is unique in that it does not police rural areas of the province but is limited to the municipalities of Corner Brook, Churchill Falls, Labrador City, and St. John's. (The RCMP polices the remaining sections of the province.) While both the OPP and NRC police municipalities, there is no provision under Quebec law for the Sûreté du Quebec to provide municipal policing.

Aboriginal Policing

In 1991 the federal government introduced the First Nations Policing Policy, which set out the foundation for future developments in aboriginal policing. At the core of this initiative was the need to negotiate the development of cost-sharing agreements between the First Nations communities, provincial governments, and the federal government. But more important, this policy enabled First Nations communities to articulate the type of policing best suited for the needs of their reserve communities. Within the context of this policy, communities could continue to utilize the services of the RCMP or OPP under the realm of contract policing, or they could develop their own autonomous police services. Examples of these autonomous police services are the Six Nations Tribal Police in Ontario, the Amerindian Police in Quebec, and the Blood Tribal Police in Alberta. The number of First Nations communities that are adopting autonomous police services continues to increase, as communities are now embracing the need for self-governance and the desire to articulate policing appropriate for their community. In the past many aboriginal police services were subject to the authority of a senior police service, such as the RCMP, OPP, or Sûreté du Quebec, and were limited to by-law or band law enforcement. Currently, aboriginal police officers generally have full powers of arrest and enforce the criminal code, federal and provincial statutes, and band by-laws within the jurisdiction of reserve lands.

Federal Policing

The concept of federal policing more accurately refers to the broad tasks that the RCMP undertakes as a branch of the federal solicitor general's office. Unlike other police officers, RCMP officers have jurisdiction in all provinces and territories; they enforce federal statutes in all regions, police federal property as required, and have the powers of both peace officers and customs and excise officers. And while the RCMP has national jurisdiction, it does not enforce provincial or municipal statutes in the provinces of Ontario and Quebec.

The RCMP is tasked with a range of policing responsibilities that include the operation of a number of specialized directorates serving the needs of police services nationally. For example: The RCMP's L Directorate operates crime detection labs across the country, offering identification services such as DNA analysis, fingerprinting, criminal history files, etc. Its V Directorate operates the Canadian Police Information Centre (CPIC), the computerized information system that provides police services with instant criminal records, vehicle information, stolen property data, missing persons information, etc. The P Directorate serves as the international liaison with Interpol and foreign services. The RCMP is also the lead organization in the national partnership with the Canadian Association of Chiefs of Police and the National Research Council in the development of the Canadian Police Research Centre. This centre is responsible for the development and evaluation of high-technology products for police services. This array of common services provides continuity throughout Canada's law enforcement community.

Training and Education

Training and education is regulated by a combination of federal and provincial legislation. These regulations, acts, and by-laws set out the provisions for police training facilities, funding, and basic training requirements and provide the authority to develop curriculum and training programs. A police officer's training occupies an important aspect of his or her career and learning path. This learning path is broken into four main categories: recruit/basic training, orientation/field training, in-service training, and advanced training.

Recruit training provides new officers with the skills and competencies required to achieve a specific level of operational performance.

Field training occurs after the recruit has successfully completed basic training. This enables recruits to apply the skills and competencies they have learned in previous training under the supervision of a senior officer.

In-service training occurs throughout the career of a police officer. The objectives of this training are to ensure that officers' skills are maintained, to ensure that they remain current with changing legislative and operational practices, to assist in the career development of individuals, etc.

Advanced training focuses on the development of specialized skills and knowledge designed to achieve a level of expertise in a given area of policing.

As with Canadian policing in general, training and how it is delivered varies by jurisdiction, consistent with provincial and federal responsibility. There are seven police schools and academies across the country: the Canadian Police College, RCMP Training Depot, the Ontario Police College, the British Columbia Police Academy, the Saskatchewan Police College, Ecole Nationale de Police du Quebec, and the Atlantic Police Academy. The Provinces of Alberta and Manitoba do not have provincial recruit training sites, and as a result the municipal police services (e.g., those in Edmonton, Calgary, Lethbridge, and Winnipeg) in these provinces that do not contract with the RCMP for policing operate their own training. (As of the fall of 2006, the Alberta solicitor general and public security minister has begun planning and development for a provincial police and peace officer training academy.) Many of the police colleges are regionally mandated and are thus limited to training officers within specific provincial jurisdictions. The exception to this is the Canadian Police College, which provides experienced police personnel at the federal, provincial, and municipal levels with specialized training. As well, varying levels of in-service and advanced training is undertaken by large municipal and provincial police services. While there are no national training academies, there are organizations such as the Canadian Association of Police Educators and the Police Sector Council that seek to set informal national standards and common training strategies. The legislation governing police training is shown in Table 12.1.

Table 12.1   Legislation Governing Police Training

Jurisdiction	Legislation
Federal	• Royal Canadian Mounted Police Act 1985 • Commissioner's Standing Orders
Alberta	Police Act/Police Act Service Regulation 1998
British Columbia	Police Act 1996
Manitoba	City of Winnipeg and City of Brandon Bylaws
New Brunswick	Police Act/Regulations 1996
Newfoundland	Royal Newfoundland Constabulary Act 1992
Nova Scotia	Police Act 1989
Ontario	• Police Services Act 1990 • Adequacy and Effectiveness of Police Services Regulation 3/99
Prince Edward Island	Police Act 1988
Québec	Bill 86 Police Act
Saskatchewan	Police Act 1990-91

_____ Community-Based Policing and Shifting Models

There is little question that community policing has become the official philosophy so to speak with respect to policing in Canada. Nor is there doubt that it has had a monumental effect on those who have sought to improve police operations, management, or relations with the public. And yet, while there is a consensus about community policing's potential and the fact that it is a radical shift from the professional model of policing, there is little consensus on a specific definition of the concept. This problem of definition is due, in part, to the fact that both academics and practitioners have struggled with the definition of community-based policing. The vagaries of definition have been shown to haunt police practitioners and their efforts to implement community-based policing in a consistent manner. In some instances the essence of community-based policing remains elusive and therefore hinders future efforts at application.

More recently, police policy makers and strategists have begun to build on the foundation of community-based policing and problem solving in an effort to achieve greater levels of efficiency and effectiveness. These operational strategies are based on the concept of proactive policing. Examples of this strategic orientation can be noted in the Metropolitan Toronto

Police Service's Crime Management Program, in the Edmonton Police Service's Project Archimedes, and in the RCMP's Criminal Intelligence Program. Here, the term *proactive policing* (or *intelligence-led policing* as it is referred to in various jurisdictions) applies to both a style of policing and to specific targeting actions. Interestingly in a post–September 11 environment, alternate formulations of proactive policing have begun to take shape. More specifically, the concept of *integrated policing* has received great attention. In this context police services are to work in a cohesive and collaborative manner in terms of "exchanging strategic and criminal intelligence, sharing tactical and operational knowledge, planning joint and individual actions" (RCMP 2004, p. 1).

One example of this shift toward integrated policing is the renewed reliance upon Integrated Border Enforcement Teams (IBETs). The RCMP argues that its expanded national security mandate of "identifying, investigating and interdicting persons and organizations that pose a threat to national security or engage in other organized crime" reinforces both the importance of and the need to expand IBETs in a post–September 11 environment (RCMP, 2004). From the perspective of integration, IBETs are a partnership of six national agencies: the RCMP, Canada Customs and Revenue, U.S. Border Patrol, U.S. Customs Service, Citizenship and Immigration Canada, and the U.S. Coast Guard. Interestingly, prior to September 11, there were four IBETs operating in Ontario, Quebec, New Brunswick, and British Columbia; currently there are 22 teams covering 15 regions with the expectation that this number will increase.

Similarly, the creation of Integrated National Security Enforcement Teams (INSETs) replicates the trend toward integrated policing, building upon a need to collaborate across numerous organizational and operational jurisdictions. The role of INSETs is "to share and receive resources and intelligence with other RCMP operations as well as international, national, provincial, regional and local agencies who are working to counter terrorism" (RCMP, 2004, p. 2). Other examples of joint operations are the Canadian Intelligence Services within each province, the Integrated Child Exploitation (ICE) units, and the Integrated Response to Organized Crime (IROC) units. The underlying premise of these collaborative efforts is for police agencies to work together to ensure the creation of communication, shared resources, and intelligence networks in an effort to support national security, reduce crime, and combat terrorism (RCMP, 2004). Unfortunately, the backdrop to this shift in collaboration was a governance trend in the late 1990s toward a fragmented and pluralized network of security, wherein citizens may in fact not articulate broadly shared security interests, nor achieve equitable levels of security. It was a trend that undermined the importance of state coordinated security as a fundamental example of a public good. The provision of security was couched in the economic rhetoric of efficiency, effectiveness, and creation of private goods, not the public good.

Conclusion

Within current Canadian policing, the question we grapple with is how might the state (re)formulate principles of accountability and regulation in an effort to address not only broadly shared policing interests but the governance of a disparate multiorganizational security landscape. And while this may in fact indicate a potential shift in governance, it does not suggest that the dichotomy between private and public interests no longer exists, nor is there a renewed appetite for a heavy handed regulatory regime ensuring public security. What it does suggest is an evolving governance environment wherein the provision of goods (i.e. public safety) may be achieved through the cooperative actions of multiple stakeholders. This has a distinct importance for Canadian policing, as more and more agencies pursue coherent policing policies that require high levels of coordination and cooperation (Law Commission of Canada, 2006).

Although the provision of a secure environment is reliant upon the joint actions of various players, it is also reliant upon the state's ability to coordinate the organizational apparatus of the integrated, multifunctional security and policing providers. Moreover, it is incumbent upon the state to "bring reflexive coherence and forms of democratic accountability to the interorganizational networks and multi-level political configurations within which security and policing are situated" (Loader & Walker, 2001, p. 27). An alternative model is one wherein the previously accepted state centered responsibility of dispensing and governing security is replaced with a model that connects both state and nonstate nodes in the process of governance (Johnston & Shearing, 2003; Shearing & Wood, 2003). "Within this conception of governance no set of nodes is given conceptual priority" and the level of contribution of each node is developed via negotiation or collaborative processes (Johnston & Shearing, 2003, p. 147). Johnston and Shearing argue, "By emphasizing that the state is no longer a stable locus of government, the nodal model defines governance as the property of networks rather than as the product of any single centre of action" (2003, p. 148). In terms of the Canadian landscape, this representation has a particular currency, as there is a robust trend toward a complex continuum of policing.

The concern that this landscape raises is whether or not we have any assurances that these partnerships and collaborative efforts may in fact serve the desired outcome of enhanced security. What is interesting about the current examples of collaborative or networked operations is that they are more than mere emergent trends but serve as the operational framework of future police and security governance. The concern that arises from these shifts is whether or not they will facilitate the full participation of citizens and thus enhance the democratic character of future policing partnerships. This is of particular interest in Canada, as policing is "no longer the sole purview of the uniformed municipal, provincial or federal police officer. Our daily lives are now inundated with the complex mix of public and private policing activities" (Law Commission of Canada, 2006, p. 1).

Note

1. In January 2004, CBC News obtained surveillance video tapes taken by police officers in September 1995, one of which contains racist remarks made by police officers the day before George's death.

References

Bartle. (1994). 33 C.R. (4th) 1 (S.C.C.).

Blandford, S. (2003). *The impact of adequacy standards upon Ontario police services.* Unpublished manuscript.

Brodeur, J.-P., & Viau L. (1995). Police accountability in crisis situations. In R. C. Macleod & D. Schneiderman, *Police powers in Canada: The evolution and practice of authority* (pp. 243–308). Toronto, ON: University of Toronto Press.

Canadian Centre for Justice Statistics. (2007). *Police personnel, police/civilian personnel ratio.* Statistics Canada. Retrieved January 16, 2007, from http://www.statcan.ca/english/Pgdb/legal15.htm

Charter of Rights and Freedoms. (1982). Constitution Act, 1982, Part I, Sch. B., ch. 11, as reprinted in R.S.C.

Collins. (1987). 56 C.R. (ed) 193 (S.C.C.).

Commission for Public Complaints Against the RCMP. (2003, October 23). *News release.* Retrieved November 21, 2006 from http://www.cpc-cpp.gc.ca

Commission for Public Complaints Against the RCMP. (2004, January 24). *Media advisory.* Retrieved November 21, 2006 from http://www.cpc-cpp.gc.ca

Department of Justice. (2001). *Royal assent of Bill C-36: The anti-terrorism act.* Retrieved December 10, 2006, from http://canada.justice.gc.ca/en/news/nr/2001/doc_28217.html

Griffiths, C., Whitelaw, B., & Parent, R. (1999). *Canadian police work.* Toronto, ON: ITP Nelson.

Hunter v. Sotham, Inc. (1984). 2 S.C.R 145, 41 C.R (3d) 97 (S.C.C).

Jain, H. (1995). An assessment of strategies of recruiting visible-minority police officers in Canada: 1985-1990. In R. C. Macleod & D. Schneiderman, *Police powers in Canada: The evolution and practice of authority* (pp. 138–164). Toronto, ON: University of Toronto Press.

Johnston, L., & Shearing, C. (2003). *Governing security: Explorations in policing and justice.* London: Routledge.

Law Commission of Canada. (2006). *In search of security: The future of policing in Canada.* Ottawa, ON: Minister of Public Works and Government Services.

Loader, I., & Walker, N. (2001). Policing as a public good: Reconstructing the connections between policing and the state. *Theoretical Criminology, 5*(1) 9–35.

Ministry of Human Resources Development. (2000). *Strategic human resources analysis of public policing in Canada.* Ottawa, ON: Queen's Printer.

Murphy, C. (1998). *Policing postmodern Canada.* Unpublished manuscript.

O'Malley, P. (1996). Risk, power and crime prevention. *Economy and Society, 21*(3), 175–192.

Quigley, C. (2004). Police under fire. *MacLean's Magazine, 117*(5), 36–41.

Royal Canadian Mounted Police (RCMP). (2004). *Integrated police.* Retrieved January 4, 2007, from http://www.rcmp-grc.gc.ca/priorities/integrated_e.htm

Shearing, C., & Wood, J. (2003). Nodal governance, democracy and new denizens. *Journal of Law and Society, 30*(3), 400–419.

Simpson. (1993). 20 C.R. (4th) 1 (ONT.C.A).

Stenning, P. (2003). Policing the cultural kaleidoscope: Recent Canadian experience. *Police and Society, 13,* 13–47.

Stuart, D. (1996). *Charter justice in Canadian criminal law.* Toronto, ON: Carswell.

Topp, L. (2003). Recent research: Policing issues regarding multiculturalism in Canada. *The Canadian Journal of Police and Security Services, 1*(2), 150–162.

Further Reading

Freidland, M. L. (1995). Reforming police powers: Who's in charge? In R. C. Macleod & D. Schneiderman (Eds.), *Police powers in Canada: The evolution and practice of authority* (pp. 110–118). Toronto, ON: University of Toronto Press.

Forcese, D. (1999). *Policing Canadian society.* Scarborough, ON: Prentice-Hall Canada.

Loader, I. (1999). Consumer culture and the commodification of policing and security. *Sociology, 33*(2), 373–392.

13

Democracy's Double Edge

Police and Procedure in the United States

Anders Walker

F ew historians consider law enforcement in the United States to be a direct manifestation of American democracy. Yet, policing in the United States has always been, and continues to be, remarkably democratic. Americans, for the most part, have never feared a centralized, secret police. Nor has the United States ever possessed a national police force capable of operating entirely free from democratic control. Much of this has to do with the constitutional structure of American government, and in particular the diffusion of power within America's federal system, an arrangement that has limited centralized power, guarded states' rights, and preserved, to a remarkable degree, local municipal control over law enforcement. Popular resistance to centralized authority, further, helps explain why American policing has not followed centralized European models and why local police have dominated, and continue to dominate, the American policing experience (Harris, 2005).

One consequence of this experience, an unfortunate one for both minorities and proponents of police professionalism, is that local police have enjoyed relative freedom from centralized standards, procedures, and rules. Attempts to curb this freedom, whether by exclusionary rules, civilian suits, or other means, have proven difficult. In fact, a brief survey of police history suggests that local majorities have often sided with local police, meanwhile opposing attempts at reforming or standardizing police procedure. Ties between democracy and discretion, not surprisingly, have proven particularly problematic for racial and ethnic minorities who have generally been the most frequent victims, not to mention most vocal critics, of police misconduct.

To underscore the decentralized, democratic nature of American police, this chapter will proceed in five parts. The first part will provide a brief overview of the historical evolution of police and police procedure in the United States. It will discuss the long-standing relationship between law enforcement and local politics in America. It will also suggest that police procedure has only become a national political issue insofar as electoral minorities, whether politically threatened elites or disenfranchised racial groups, have made it so. Even a cursory glance at U.S. history suggests that the majority of American voters have, for the most part, not been concerned with police misconduct, as evidenced by a glaring absence of congressional, state, and local legislation on the subject.

Instead, the dominant regulatory apparatus of police conduct has been the federal courts, the least democratic branch of the federal government, and arguably the most limited in terms of actual, regulatory power. Bound by jurisdictional limits written into the U.S. Constitution, the federal judiciary did not develop a constitutional theory conducive to regulating police misconduct until the 1960s, and then only through relatively cumbersome devices like exclusionary rules and civilian lawsuits. Within a decade of their inception, these innovations fueled widespread anger at judicial activism, increased popular support for law enforcement, and discouraged popular willingness to fund legal representation for criminal defendants, all forces that have made the task of police regulation through the courts a complex, convoluted one. The end result, though frustrating for advocates of reform, has been the perpetuation of a highly decentralized, remarkably discretionary, and fundamentally democratic American police.

The second section focuses on the subject of minorities and policing, suggesting that for the most part, American police have enjoyed popular support precisely because they have mirrored the demographic makeup of local majorities. The one great exception to this has been racial minorities. Since the founding of the United States, racial minorities, and particularly African Americans, have traditionally been excluded from police hiring, alienated from local police departments, and shut out of local politics. Not only that, but for years local police, beginning with slave patrols, were used expressly to maintain racial order and subordinate black populations. This led, invariably, to police abuses of black civilians. Though such abuses began, arguably, during slavery, they attracted little popular attention. In fact, it was not until the 1960s that police-minority conflict became a matter of national concern. Much of this had to do with the televised broadcasting of urban riots, many of which were triggered by police action in heavily black ghettos.

The third section discusses the implications that racial tensions have had for police organization and strategy in the United States, focusing on the evolution of alternate attempts to discipline the police, aside from the courts, in the 1960s and 1970s. These include, for example, the development of civilian review boards, the expansion of formal procedures for filing complaints, the implementation of internal accountability mechanisms, and changes in recruitment strategies.

Perhaps the most notable police reform to come out of the 1970s, and the focus of the fourth section, is community policing. While scholars have been tempted to frame community policing as a "radical revolution" in law enforcement, the concept reflects a return, in many ways, to America's longstanding tradition of locally controlled, democratic police (Barlow & Barlow, 1999). Yet, there are differences. Perhaps the biggest difference is that community policing seeks to do what policing has never done in the United States, namely to develop positive relationships between disenfranchised minority communities and police. For some, this makes it "a new tool in the drama of control" (Manning, 1991). Meanwhile, for others, it makes community policing a useful device for improving law enforcement, and police service, to the communities that most need it (Harris, 2005). Modern proponents of community policing, consequently, mimic old forms in so far as they aim to reestablish local ties to local police, yet diverge from them insofar as they seek simply to engage in "image management" of police (Bayley, 1994; Platt et al., 1988).

The final section concludes the chapter by discussing the significant challenge that global terrorism has posed for America's decentralized, locally controlled, democratic police. In fact, this section suggests that the terror threat has already begun to push the evolution of policing in new, more aggressive, more centralized directions. One example of this is the liberalization of search and seizure requirements under the Patriot Act. Another is the expansion of paramilitary policing. Finally, because of its ability to mobilize popular opinion in favor of increased size and centralization, terrorism has arguably facilitated the rise of a new era of predatory policing. That such an era is sanctioned, or at least not bitterly opposed by a majority of voters, suggests a new shift in police history, one that runs contrary to long-standing American trends.

The History and Political Context of Policing in the United States

The burden of law enforcement in America, beginning with the colonial era, has rested largely on the shoulders of local, community volunteers (Walker, 1998). During the seventeenth and eighteenth centuries, for example, community leaders and volunteers banded together for the purposes of investigation, trial, and sentencing, often free from any formal procedures or rules (Brown, 1969). Evidence of such practices emerged in northern colonies like Massachusetts, southern colonies like South Carolina, and western frontier regions as well (Hindus, 1980; Brown, 1969).

Following the American Revolution, community control of policing continued as citizens called for the dissolution of the military, the perpetuation of volunteer-based militias, and the conversion of local sheriffs from agents of the British crown to democratically elected public servants (Walker, 1998). Still influential in many rural portions of the United States, sheriffs enjoyed broad discretionary powers and performed a variety of duties, including the running of jails, serving of subpoenas, apprehension of offenders, and performance of various, informal, public services. In fact, due to their democratically elected status, sheriffs served, in large part, as little more than armed agents of local majority control (Walker, 1983/1999).

As cities and towns grew in size over the course of the nineteenth century, the relationship between local majorities and police became more complex but not necessarily less democratic. In larger cities, for example, night watch systems emerged, usually manned by members of local communities who were charged with raising alarms but otherwise operated free from any type of centralized regulation or control (Monkkonen, 1992; Walker, 1998). Less-democratic agents of law enforcement also emerged, as for example, constables, who demanded fees for services, and private police forces, which were often hired by wealthy elites to protect capital and discipline labor (Ferdinand, 1980; Morn, 1982). However, neither constabularies nor private police agencies ever assumed a dominant role in American policing, even in urban settings. In fact, both succumbed to the rise of organized, hierarchical police departments, particularly in metropolitan centers (Monkkonen, 1992).

While it was a seemingly undemocratic phenomenon, the rise of organized, hierarchical police departments was itself closely tied to democratic politics. For example, elected officials called for such departments only after electoral majorities expressed concern over rising rates of urban unrest, social disorder, and rioting in the nineteenth century (Monkkonen, 1992). Much of this disorder was profoundly political in nature and reflected attempts by electoral minorities to exercise power and control over electoral majorities outside the framework of the formal political process (Gallman, 1988; Gilje, 1987; Schneider, 1980). Consequently, the invocation of professional policing became linked, in a relatively direct sense, to larger questions of preserving majority rule and controlling minority dissent (Liebman & Polen, 1978).

To suppress urban, minority unrest, elected officials in New York, Philadelphia, Boston, and other cities began to look abroad for more formal, centralized models of police control (Gallman, 1988; Steinberg, 1989; Walker, 1998). The most appealing of such models came from England, where, as early as 1829, officials began to develop a centralized, professional police force linked directly to the national government. Though New York and other cities adopted facets of the British model, they made no effort to link these models to federal authority. In fact, the era during which these cities adopted formal police models, roughly 1820 to 1840, was characterized by a radical democratization of American politics and a general move away from centralized, federal control (Remini, 1988). Consequently, police departments retained close ties with local elected officials, particularly mayors, who not only encouraged police to be responsive to majority demands but used policing positions as political plums to be handed out to constituents (Monkkonen, 1992).

Failure to break the bonds between local politics and police compromised efforts to impose unified, professional rules onto American law enforcement (Miller, 1977). Not surprisingly, advocates of police reform often shared an interest in breaking local, majority rule. For example, progressive police reformers in the 1880s and 1890s, many of whom came from educated, Protestant backgrounds, advocated reining in the rampant nepotism, machine politics, and community-level corruption of big city police departments, then dominated by Catholic, largely Irish immigrants (Monkkonen, 1992; Rousey, 1983). Not coincidentally, they also advocated a much grander, "progressive" effort to impose Protestant, Anglo-Saxon values onto Catholic communities, including the establishment of settlement houses in Catholic neighborhoods, the teaching of English to immigrant children, and the shuttering of Irish and Italian saloons (Boyer, 1978; Crocker, 1992).

Perhaps one of the most celebrated agents of progressive police reform, Theodore Roosevelt, took widely publicized steps to break bonds between local ethnic majorities and police while serving as police commissioner of New York from 1895 to 1897 (Morris, 1979/2001). Not surprisingly, Roosevelt's failure to break these bonds foreshadowed his support for a centralized, federal police agency. Indeed, once elected president, Roosevelt endorsed one of the first American attempts to form a professional, federally controlled police force, an organization that would come to be known as the Federal Bureau of Investigation, or FBI. Yet, the FBI enjoyed little popularity, remained crippled by constitutionally mandated jurisdictional restraints, and became relegated, for many years, to the ignominious job of preventing interstate trafficking in prostitution (Morris, 1979/2001).

Despite the efforts of progressives like Theodore Roosevelt to reform big city police departments, progressives failed to break the local, community oriented political machines that controlled police hiring. Big city policing, consequently, remained deeply tied to local politics, and big city police remained, in large part, manned by local, immigrant, ethnic majorities. Corruption, according to progressives, continued and even worsened during the opening decades of the twentieth century. Yet, this corruption retained a decidedly local, democratic flair. For example, police often proved reluctant to enforce laws against crimes that they themselves thought should not be illegal activities. This became particularly clear during Prohibition, when progressives and rural voters in the South and West outlawed alcohol, prompting big city police to side with local Catholic majorities, turning a blind eye to the perpetuation of deeply rooted, culturally popular practices like drinking. The ensuing crime wave in the 1920s and 1930s, itself a type of popular, arguably democratic protest, became legendary—prompting renewed, centralized, federal interest in crime, crime control, and police professionalism (Walker, 1998).

A similar phenomenon emerged in the context of labor. Just as many local police departments in major cities like Boston, New York, and even New Orleans were manned by Irish Catholics, so too were many rural police departments manned by members of the working class (Johnson, 1976). During the first two decades of the twentieth century, as strikes threatened to disrupt industry and unions like the International Workers of the World gained remarkable popularity, business interests struggled to drive a wedge between local, working-class communities and police (Walker, 1977). One answer to this problem was the formation of private police agencies, like the Pinkerton Detective Agency (Morn, 1982). Another answer, popular in heavily industrialized states like Pennsylvania, was the formation of a centrally organized, professional, state police force (Walker, 1977, 1998).

A third group of people interested in police reform, besides industrialists and progressives, were African Americans. Beginning in the 1920s, the National Association for the Advancement of Colored People, or NAACP, began to file lawsuits in federal courts in the American South to remedy police abuses against African Americans (Klarman, 2000). Though the NAACP achieved significant victories, local majorities did little to enforce federal rulings, even when they emanated from the United States Supreme Court (Klarman, 2002). Indeed, it wouldn't be until the 1960s, as the judiciary intensified its reform efforts, that it would make a significant impact on the centralized regulation of police (Powe, 2000).

No discussion of police reform in America would be complete without at least some mention of police who sought to reform departments themselves, regardless of their general failure to do so. For example, California police chief August Vollmer achieved national acclaim for transforming Berkeley, California's police department between 1905 and 1932. Vollmer advocated a variety of technical innovations, including the use of bicycles, motorcycles, and eventually automobiles, not to mention the adoption of fingerprinting. Vollmer also shifted hiring strategies away from members of the working class and toward middle-class college graduates (Vollmer, 1920–1921). Ironically, this innovation, together with the use of technology, achieved the same basic goals that reformers from the Progressive Era onward had sought, namely the isolation of police from their local communities (Walker, 1977).

Though Vollmer gained national attention, and helped make the idea of professionalism a national goal, he failed, for the most part, to reform American police departments. Again, local politics, local ties, and local community norms prevailed. This was true in rural areas as well as big cities. Though supervisory commissions formed in Cleveland, Chicago, and Missouri in the 1920s, big city police departments all remained closely intertwined with local politics and, presumably, local corruption. In fact, Vollmer himself attempted to transform the Los Angeles Police Department (LAPD) by serving as its police chief in 1923, only to quit in despair after a year. Vollmer's failure to reform the LAPD, in many ways, mirrored the larger failure of reform to win popular support nationally. Despite, or perhaps because of, links between local politics and police, popular interest in police corruption remained minimal for most of the nineteenth and twentieth centuries. In fact, very little federal, state, or for that matter local legislation regulating police procedure emerged during this period (Walker, 1977).

Yet, changes did occur. While August Vollmer's recommendations for reform failed to mobilize voters, his ideas about technology contributed to a significant transformation of police practice. In particular, Vollmer's support for the use of the automobile gained currency as O. W. Wilson, an early proponent of the idea that police should concentrate on crime prevention, began advocating motorized patrol (Walker, 1984). In fact, Wilson made vehicular patrol, coupled with speedy responses to calls for service, a central part of his larger theory of police management. Wilson articulated this theory in *Police Administration,* a book that inspired police officials and helped shift policing strategies nationally away from community-oriented foot patrols toward roving, rapid-response vehicular patrols (Walker, 1984; Wilson, 1950).

This shift in patrol coincided, in a manner that is suggestive of continued ties between American democracy and police, with an increased popular interest in targeting serious as opposed to mid-level or minor crimes. Much of this interest came, perhaps ironically, from sensationalized accounts of mob related violence in the 1920s, violence that big city police departments arguably did little to prevent. Indeed, the primary advocate of controlling violent crime in the 1930s was not a local police chief at all, but a federal officer in charge of the FBI named J. Edgar Hoover. In 1930, Hoover developed an index of the seven major violent crimes known as the Uniform Crime Reports (UCR). He then used the UCR both to increase the legitimacy of the FBI and to spread fears that America was in the grips of a violent crime wave. President Herbert Hoover, also a federal official, directed federal resources toward investigating this crime wave in 1929 by creating a federal Commission on Law Observance and Enforcement popularly known as the Wickersham Commission. The Wickersham Commission produced several substantive reports, among them a report on police professionalism written by August Vollmer and another report on police brutality and corruption written by several lawyers affiliated with the American Civil Liberties Union, or ACLU.

Yet, little happened. States did not take drastic measures to increase regulation of police. Nor did voters demand substantive reform. Arguably, this was because voters did not see a need to reform police, even though they did become more interested in targeting violent crime. In fact, popular fear of violent crime probably reduced popular interest in reining in law enforcement. Sadly, police brutality, corruption, and misconduct continued, falling most heavily on the shoulders of disenfranchised minorities who possessed little say in electoral politics.

Racial and Ethnic Context

Tensions between racial minorities and police became particularly acute in the latter half of the twentieth century. Even though the United States fought a bitter war against a racist regime in Nazi Germany in the 1940s, popular majorities proved reluctant to end formal, racial discrimination at home. As late as 1948, virtually every state in the union continued to uphold racially restrictive covenants in property ownership; meanwhile at least 13 states continued to practice formal racial segregation in public schools. Eleven states, all in the South, continued to obstruct black voting rights, not to mention the right to sit at lunch counters, ride buses, and even go to the same public restrooms as whites. Though less formal arrangements limited black economic opportunities nationwide, most states tolerated racially discriminatory hiring practices, not only in the private sector but also in public positions, not least of them police departments (Klarman, 2004).

Massive migrations of African Americans out of the South during the 1940s and 1950s exacerbated tensions between local black communities and police in the North and the West. Factors that contributed to this included the concentration of African American immigrants, aided by restrictive covenants, in isolated, urban ghettoes. This problem worsened when, as northern and western ghettoes grew, local police departments resisted hiring blacks, transforming themselves not into extensions of local, community control, but racially distinct, occupational forces. This development was arguably a new phenomenon in northern cities, which had traditionally adjusted to demographic shifts at the local level. Not surprisingly, it led to popular black perceptions of police as armed agents of white oppression, not to mention a lack of sensitivity on the part of white police toward local black majorities.

Evidence of clashes between local black majorities and white police emerged, prominently, in the federal courts. The NAACP, coupled with other civil rights groups like the ACLU, intensified its attack on police abuses beginning in the late 1950s. Already interested in ameliorating racial inequality in the United States, and not as beholden to white majorities as its state counterparts, the federal judiciary responded. In 1961, the Supreme Court of the United States resurrected a Reconstruction-era statute (initially designed to control the Ku Klux Klan) allowing citizens to sue police for misconduct (*Monroe v. Pape,* 1961). That same year, it resurrected the Fourteenth Amendment (initially passed to protect freed slaves) and used it to incorporate Fourth Amendment restrictions onto *local* police departments, ordering them to jettison evidence that had been collected without a warrant (*Mapp v. Ohio,* 1961). This constituted a substantial reinterpretation of the United States Constitution, which held that the Fourth Amendment was designed to control federal, not state or local power. Regardless, the Supreme Court continued to reinterpret the Constitution and, in 1963, incorporated the Sixth Amendment (also designed to limit federal power), forcing local police departments to grant suspects the advice of counsel during police interrogations (*Escobedo v. Illinois,* 1964). In 1966, the court incorporated the Fifth Amendment, using it to force local courts to disregard confessions in cases where police failed to warn criminal defendants of their constitutional rights (*Miranda v. Arizona,* 1966). In all of these cases, the plaintiffs belonged to racial minorities, the very people shut out of police hiring, local politics, and popular rule.

Even as the federal judiciary tried to compensate for the failure of local police departments to treat black communities fairly, tensions exploded in 1964 and 1965, as urban riots broke out in black ghettoes, triggered by instances of police misconduct. The rise of television, arguably, contributed to these riots, as it expanded black awareness not only of conditions in other cities, but also of conditions in the American South. There, beginning in 1963, civil rights strategists broke the veil of systematic white domination by orchestrating dramatic confrontations between black demonstrators and police, leading to national outrage and unprecedented federal interest in civil rights (Eskew, 1997; Garrow, 1978). Meanwhile, antipolice riots continued in the North and West through the 1960s, leading to a national crisis and unprecedented federal interest in disciplining police. One outcome of such interest was a federally sponsored recommendation that departments hire more black police officers to ease tensions between black majorities and white police, a logical solution given the positive impact that police hiring had traditionally had on police-community relations in the United States (Walker, 1983/1999). Other recommendations, sometimes calling for changes in organizational structure, emerged as well.

Organizational Structure and Issues

Across the country in the 1960s, major police departments encountered demands from civil rights groups like the ACLU and others that complaints of police misconduct be subjected to rigorous civilian review. This led, in cities like Philadelphia and New York, to formal civilian review boards, assigned to investigate allegations of police misconduct. However, civilian review boards failed to gain significant police support, and in fact came to be seen as bastions of minority special interests, leading to their temporary demise in the 1970s (Skolnick & Fyfe, 1993; Walker, 1998).[1]

Dissatisfaction with notions of civilian review, not to mention increasingly intrusive federal court rulings, led police departments to develop their own mechanisms for improving professionalism and accountability. Major police departments in cities like New York, Chicago, and Los Angeles began to engage in more expansive hiring of minorities, not to mention more aggressive hiring of college graduates (Walker, 1983/1999). Departments also expanded preservice training programs, which had been nonexistent in many localities prior to the 1960s, and instituted procedural guidelines for officers on the street (Walker, 1983/1999). Often, these coincided with the development of internal affairs units assigned to investigating misconduct independent of outside interference.

As police departments developed internal modes of control, so too did external controls emerge as well. In 1979, an organization emerged that certified police departments that lived up to a specific set of rigorous, professional standards known as the Commission on Accreditation for Law Enforcement Agencies (Walker, 1983/1999). To further enforce professionalism, many states established Peace Officer Standards and Training Boards, or POSTs, at roughly the same time. These led, in turn, to new disciplinary possibilities, including the decertification of officers found guilty of misconduct (Goldman & Puro, 1987).

Even as states developed more sophisticated modalities of ensuring police accountability, however, significant disparities continued to exist between urban and rural departments (Weisheit, 1996). In fact, extremely rural departments remained, in many ways, substantially isolated from reforms taking place in urban areas. Some of this had to do with the smaller size of such departments, along with lower budgets, lower numbers of recruits, and closer contacts with the local community (Weisheit, 1996). Of course, what constitutes a rural department was, and remains, partially unclear. In 2004, there were over 17,000 state and local police agencies in the United States (BJS, 2007). Out of those, over 50 percent had fewer than 10 officers. However, many of these were small municipal departments, not necessarily rural ones. In fact, small town police make up the majority of law enforcement officers in the United States (Falcone, Wells, & Weisheit, 2002).

What kind of training do they receive? In 2000, only 15 percent of local police departments, presumably the largest ones, required some degree of college level work (BJS, 2007). Further, recruits in departments serving over 100,000 people were required to undergo twice as much training (1,600 hours) as recruits in departments serving fewer than 2,500 people, who were required to undergo roughly 800 hours of training (BJS, 2007). One conclusion to be drawn from this is that training, and by extension professionalism generally, plays a greater role in large urban departments than in small town or rural ones.

Community Policing

Perhaps the greatest reform initiative to come out of the post–civil rights era was community policing. First proposed in the 1970s, community policing sought to reorient police away from aggressive surveillance of minority communities toward a more problem-oriented, quality-of-life approach. Manifestations of this included a return to the foot patrol, not to mention an expansion in the scope of police responsibilities away from crime prevention and toward solving community problems dealing with housing, sanitation, and so on. Particularly successful forms of community policing focused on developing preventive strategies for dealing with patterns of crime in certain low-income areas, like public housing projects (Harris, 2005).

In a manner that is important to understanding long-term democratic trends, community policing represents, in certain ways, a return to old forms. Urban police traditionally participated in community politics and performed functions far beyond the apprehension of criminals. Modern community policing seeks, in theory, to reestablish such ties precisely where they have broken down (Harris, 2005).

Perhaps the most effective means of establishing local ties between communities and police is hiring. Interestingly, cities that have worked hard to hire officers out of local communities, and have then sent those officers back into their communities, have been able to take community policing to a new, more aggressive level: targeting small offenses of chronic offenders (Harris, 2005). In New York City, for example, community policing evolved into an aggressive, zero tolerance campaign against minor, quality-of-life crimes like graffiti painting, turnstile jumping, and public drunkenness. However, thanks at least in part to minority hiring, such campaigns did not breed the type of localized resistance that one might otherwise have come to expect from heavily police minority communities (Walker, 1983/1999).

Perhaps not surprisingly, the rapid rise of community policing in the United States coincided, suggestively, with an equally rapid backlash against liberal, federally mandated police reform (Graham, 1970). In the 1970s and 1980s, for example, substantial percentages of white voters rebelled against judicial attempts to regulate the police. While much of this resistance stemmed from police departments themselves, it spread to electoral politics, fueling the candidacies of conservative law-and-order candidates like Richard Nixon in 1968 and 1972 and Ronald Reagan in 1980. Such leaders successfully linked judicial activism to rising crime and disorder, laying the foundation for a conservative backlash against judicially sponsored, federal police regulation that would last, arguably, through the end of the twentieth century. In fact, some scholars have concluded that this backlash culminated in a type of "penal populism" that has since led to unprecedented incarceration rates for racial and ethnic minorities (Roberts, Stalans, Indermauer, & Hough, 2003; Tonry, 2004). Majority voters, who may have felt that intrusive federal regulation placed their communities at risk, reduced funding to public defenders, endorsed mandatory sentencing schemes, and tacitly approved an overbroadening of criminal codes (Stuntz, 2001). One consequence of this push was a modification, if not retraction, of many of the bold regulatory decisions produced by the Supreme Court in the 1960s (Walker, 1998).

Terrorism

Popular resistance to federal regulation of local police flagged, briefly, in the aftermath of organized, terrorist attacks on landmarks in New York City and Washington, D.C. in September 2001. Within weeks of the news that terrorists had hijacked passenger jets and flown them into prominent buildings, Congress gained popular support for a significant enlargement of federal power in local affairs. This enlargement, delineated in the 2001 Patriot Act, expanded federal abilities to monitor private communications, seize private assets, and investigate allegations of terrorism. In April 2002, the Justice Department added to this by pressuring local police departments into enforcing federal immigration law (Harris, 2005). Not surprisingly, this engendered a certain amount of local resistance by police departments engaged in community policing of local Muslim and even Mexican communities (Harris, 2005).

If terrorism threatened aspects of community policing, it encouraged the development of other disciplinary modalities, perhaps most noticeably aggressive, paramilitary style police units. In fact, the development of heavily armed, police paramilitary units (hereinafter PPUs) coincided with early fears of terrorism in the 1970s (Kraska, 2001). Reasons for their emergence included hostage-style kidnappings, as well as urban rioting and other types of violent, crisis situations (Kraska, 2001). Ironically, the law enforcement campaign against drugs in the 1980s and 1990s dramatically increased the use of PPUs, usually for warrant delivery, no-knock entries, and confiscatory raids (Kraska, 2001). And PPUs benefited from funding designed for community policing, particularly in cities where PPUs were used to stage aggressive patrols targeting quality-of-life issues among specific populations (Kraska, 2001).

The rise of PPUs and the convergence of interest shown by local and national law enforcement agencies in preventing terrorism might help shift the traditionally idiosyncratic, democratic nature of policing in the United States toward a more unified, integrated national model. Before September 11, for example, localism had served the majority of Americans well. Under local, democratic policing, Americans had been able to transform the armed fist of the centralized state into an armed wing of local, popular control. This had been true from the founding of the country up to the dawn of the twenty-first century. Only electoral, and in particular racial, minorities had reason to fear the police, viewing them as oppressive agents of state domination and control.

Following September 11, however, it remains to be seen whether local, decentralized, democratic rule can meet the threat of globally sponsored terrorism. Many of the provisions of the Patriot Act, for example, point to a need for centralized law enforcement power, particularly in terms of surveillance and seizure of assets. This is particularly true given the mobile nature of the terror threat, not to mention the opportunities that jurisdictional and geographic constraints provide to criminals willing to transgress local, national, and even international boundaries. Not surprisingly, the FBI has become the primary law enforcement agency responsible for handling the terror threat.

Note

1. Despite a brief moment of unpopularity, and against the wishes of newly formed police unions, citizen review procedures reemerged in the 1980s and 1990s, particularly in major, urban departments (Walker, 1983/1999).

References

Barlow, D., & Barlow, M. H. (1999). A political economy of community policing. *Policing: An International Journal of Police Strategies and Management, 22,* 646.

Bayley, D. H. (1994). *Police for the future.* New York: Oxford University Press.

Boyer, P. M. (1978). *Urban masses and moral order in America, 1820–1920.* Cambridge, MA: Harvard University Press.

Brown, R. M. (1969). Historical patterns of violence in America. In H. D. Graham & T. R. Gurr (Eds.), *Violence in America: Historical and comparative perspectives* (pp. 35–64). New York: Bantam.

Bureau of Justice Statistics (BJS). (2007). *Census of state and local law enforcement agencies, 2004.* Retrieved August 17, 2007, from http://www.ojp.usdoj.gov/bjs/abstract/csllea04.htm

Crocker, R. H. (1992). *Social work and social order: The settlement movement in two industrial cities, 1889–1930.* Urbana: University of Illinois Press.

Escobedo v. Illinois, 378 U.S. 478 (1964).

Eskew, G. (1997). *But for Birmingham: The local and national movements in the civil rights struggle.* Chapel Hill: University of North Carolina Press.

Falcone, D. N., Wells, L. E., & Weisheit, R. A. (2002). The small town police department. *Policing, 25,* 371–384.

Ferdinand, T. N. (1980). Criminality, the courts, and the constabulary in Boston, 1702–1967. *Journal of Research in Crime and Delinquency, 17,* 190–208.

Gallman, J. M. (1988). "Preserving the peace: Order and disorder in Civil War Pennsylvania." *Pennsylvania History, 55,* 201–215.

Garrow, D. J. (1978). *Protest At Selma: Martin Luther King, Jr. and the Voting Rights Act of 1965.* New Haven, CT: Yale University Press.

Gilje, P. A. (1987). *The road to mobocracy: Popular disorder in New York City, 1763–1834.* Chapel Hill: University of North Carolina Press.

Goldman, R., & Puro, S. (1987, Fall). Decertification of police: An alternative to traditional remedies for police misconduct. *Hastings Constitutional Law Quarterly, 15,* 45–80.

Graham, F. P. (1970). *The self-inflicted wound.* New York: Macmillan.

Harris, D. A. (2005). *Good cops: The case for preventive policing.* New York: New Press.

Hindus, M. S. (1980). *Prison and plantation: Crime, justice, and authority in Massachusetts and South Carolina, 1767–1878.* Chapel Hill: University of North Carolina Press.

Johnson, B. C. (1976). Taking care of labor: The police in American politics. *Theory and Society, 3,* 89–117.

Klarman, M. J. (2000). The racial origins of modern criminal procedure. *Michigan Law Review, 99*, 48–97.

Klarman, M. J. (2002, June). Is the Supreme Court sometimes irrelevant? Race and the Southern criminal justice system in the 1940s. *Journal of American History, 89*, 119–153.

Klarman, M. J. (2004). *From Jim Crow to Civil Rights: The Supreme Court and the struggle for racial equality.* New York: Oxford University Press.

Kraska, P. B. (2001). *Militarizing the American criminal justice system: The changing roles of the armed forces and the police.* Boston: Northeastern University Press.

Liebman, R., & Polen, M. (1978). Perspectives on policing in nineteenth century America. *Social Science History, 12*, 346–360.

Manning, P. K. (1991). Community policing as a drama of control. In J. Greene & S. Mastrofski (Eds.), *Community policing: Rhetoric and reality* (pp. 27–45). New York: Praeger.

Mapp v. Ohio, 367 U.S. 643 (1961).

Miller, W. (1977). *Cops and bobbies: Police authority in New York and London, 1830–1870.* Chicago, IL: University of Chicago Press.

Miranda v. Arizona, 384 U.S. 436 (1966).

Monkkonen, E. H. (1992). History of urban police. *Crime and Justice, 15*, 547–580.

Monroe v. Pape, 365 U.S. 167 (1961).

Morn, F. (1982). *"The eye that never sleeps": A history of the Pinkerton National Detective Agency.* Bloomington: Indiana University Press.

Morris, E. (1979/2001). *The rise of Theodore Roosevelt.* New York: Modern American Library. (Original work published 1979)

Platt, T., Frappier, J., Gerda, R., Schauffler, R., Trujillo, L., Cooper, L., et al. (1988). *The iron fist and the velvet glove: An analysis of the US police.* San Francisco: Synthesis.

Powe, L. A., Jr. (2000). *The Warren court and American politics.* Cambridge, MA: Belknap Press.

Remini, R. V. (1988). *The life of Andrew Jackson.* New York: HarperCollins.

Roberts, J., Stalans, L., Indermauer, D., & Hough, M. (2003). *Penal populism and public opinion: Lessons from five countries.* New York: Oxford University Press.

Rousey, D. C. (1983). Hibernian leatherheads: Irish cops in New Orleans, 1830–1860. *Journal of Urban History, 10*, 61–84.

Schneider, J. C. (1980). *Detroit and the problem of order, 1830–1880: A geography of crime, rioting, and policing.* Lincoln: University of Nebraska Press.

Skolnick, J. H., & Fyfe, J. J. (1993). *Above the law: Police and the excessive use of force.* New York: Free Press.

Steinberg, A. (1989). *The transformation of criminal justice: Philadelphia 1800–1880.* Chapel Hill: University of North Carolina Press.

Stuntz, W. J. (2001). The pathological politics of criminal law. *Michigan Law Review, 100*, 505–600.

Tonry, M. (2004). *Thinking about crime: Sense and sensibility in American penal culture.* New York: Oxford University Press.

Vollmer, A. (1920–1921). Practical method for selecting policemen. *Journal of American Institute of Criminal Law and Criminology, 11*, 571–581.

Walker, S. (1977). *A critical history of police reform: The emergence of professionalism.* Lexington, MA: Lexington Books.

Walker, S. (1983/1999). *The police in America: An introduction.* Boston: McGraw-Hill. (Original work published 1983).

Walker, S. (1984). Broken windows and fractured history: The use and misuse of history in recent police patrol analysis. *Justice Quarterly, 1*(1), 77–90.

Walker, S. (1998). *Popular justice: A history of American criminal justice.* New York: Oxford University Press.

Weisheit, R. A. (1996). *Crime and policing in rural and small-town America.* Prospect Heights, IL: Waveland Press.

Wilson, O. W. (1950). *Police administration.* New York: McGraw-Hill.

14

International Cooperation in Policing

A Partial Answer to the Query?

Maria (Maki) Haberfeld, William McDonald, and Agostino von Hassell

Here is an attempt to find a partial answer to the query of how one attains a democratic form of policing. Policing as such is not a democratic activity—it is paramilitary in nature. International police cooperation can be used as a framework for a police organization flourishing inside a democracy and adhering to principles of democracy. The model of international cooperation in policing, however, is only a partial answer for achieving more democratic policing, especially given the fact that the five main themes identified in this volume can be much more successfully addressed from a global, rather than local, perspective. Many local impediments can and may be overcome by creating international standards that will serve as the blueprints for each and every country that wishes to democratize its police systems or enhance the process that is already in place.

History of Policing in a Democratic Form of Government

One cannot turn back the clock and establish a democratic system of government in every country dating back hundreds of years. But one can trace the evolution of policing as a profession in every country. For hundreds if not thousands of years, policing was seen as a vocation rather than as a career. It is possible to identify a baseline of expectations that, when adhered to, transform the outlook of this institution.

Policing is a paramilitary undertaking that evolved from the military (Haberfeld, 2002), and it is somewhat puzzling why it departed so far from the admiration and respect that societies often hold for their armed troops. A closer look at the two organizations—military and police—reveals that the problem is in the perceptions of the population receiving the services of these two uniformed services. While the military is designated to fight the external enemy, the police face the enemy within. The problem with this concept, especially in the more democratic environments, is the definition of the enemy within. Similar to the terrorist in the cliché, "One person's terrorist in another person's freedom fighter," one's "enemy within" is another person's family, friend, supplier of goods and services, symbolic figure, or just a plain hero. The preceding concept lies at the bottom of the problem in which we find ourselves adoring our troops at times (although not always, such as when we criticize their performance, especially during times of war) and despising our police at the mere hint of perceived misconduct.

The more democratic we become as a society, the more we resent the concept of the use of force against us, be it on the level of central government or the level of local law enforcement. In our zeal to further human rights and the protection of each individual, we fail to acknowledge the existence of those who do not subscribe to the same moral and ethical values as the majority. We turn a blind eye to the primary reason policing was originally conceived—"Something ought not be happening about which something should be done NOW!" (Bittner, 1970).

Corruption Within Governmental Organizations and the Oversight Mechanisms in Place

The level of corruption within governmental structures definitely affects the level of corruption within police organizations. It is possible, through the creation of oversight mechanisms that meet international standards, to set apart the police profession from other forms of executive government. Interpol, for example, has an elaborate set of mechanisms to deal with various instances of corruption. The 186 countries that are currently Interpol members can easily benefit from adapting these tools to deal with corrupt behaviors in their own institutions, including their police organizations.

Scope of and Response to Civil Disobedience

The manner in which the police, as a proxy of a larger government, deal with civil disobedience is a clear indication of the level of democracy in a given country. Of course, the operational side of the response can become much more extreme and aggressive in nature than what was allowed for in the planning process. The manner in which a police organization becomes accountable after a violation of the procedures serves as an indicator of the level of its accountability and hence, democratization. A good example occurred in Los Angeles when police officers responded violently to a demonstration held by supporters of illegal immigration (Glazer, 2007). Two high-ranking police commanders were disciplined and reassigned without the need for members of the public to file a complaint. The Los Angeles Police Department's chief of police immediately responded to the account of the events. It certainly bolstered the perception of democratic policing working effectively, though it can be argued that the rapid decision sacrificed the police officers' right to a thorough investigation of the event. As Haberfeld (2002, p.119) posits, "Police officers are *guilty until proven innocent*, and even when proven innocent, by a *jury of their peers, still perceived as being guilty*" (emphasis added). But this is, unfortunately, the price that police officers are still asked to pay in the most democratic of our societies.

_____ Organizational Structures of Police Departments

Organizational structures of police departments reflect the level of professionalization of these institutions. The practices involved in hiring, recruitment, selection, supervision, discipline, and operational deployment are the best indicators of professionalization in any profession, and especially in the police profession. When a police organization places a significant amount of effort on recruitment, selection, and training of men and women who represent the highest standards, it sends a clear message that the police profession is not for everybody but only for the few best. The intricacy inherent to international cooperation in policing paired with technological advances and high-tech approaches to crime fighting require a sophisticated and well-educated workforce.

The following pages, which describe the levels of complexity and finesse involved in various joint operations of international law enforcement agencies in their various modalities, serve again as a model for democratization for local police organizations. The high standards of performance that become mandatory in the environment of international cooperation ultimately force the transition from a vocational orientation of policing toward a real profession. (This professionalism is also reflected in some periodicals that Interpol and Europol produce; they can be easily regarded as peer reviewed publications; indeed many of them surpass many of the existing peer reviewed publications in this field.)

Operational Responses to _____ Terrorism and Organized Crime

Interpol and Europol presently lead the way in joint efforts to tackle the phenomena of terrorism and organized crime. The various task forces and color coded notices disseminated by the two organizations enable police agencies around the world to concentrate on local problems from a more global perspective and to seek the expertise and knowledge of the larger law enforcement community.

It is within this context that any given country should look at the structures and mechanisms created by the international law enforcement agencies and aim to adopt a similar mode of response on a local level. Countries like Israel or the United Kingdom no longer feel isolated and misunderstood in their fight against local terrorist activities. Nowadays a terrorist event in Israel or in the United Kingdom generates a global flurry of activities. Such an event becomes a problem that is no longer perceived as a problem of one country or another but as a worldwide threat. The title theme for this concentrated and joint effort can be easily summarized in the cliché, "The enemy of my friend is my enemy" with a slight adaptation: "The enemy of one country is the enemy of the remaining 185."

There is hardly any country today that endorses or supports human trafficking, sexual exploitation of children and women, or drug trafficking. However, efforts to combat these heinous activities will remain futile if international forces do not exchange and share their intelligence resources and do not pull together to curb and eradicate these plagues of the twenty-first century. Similar to the medical profession, which is making efforts in combating and eradicating contagious diseases that have plagued the world for centuries, law enforcement as a profession must be capable of learning and appreciating the common standards that apply to international cooperation. The quality of these standards will pave the way to a wider acceptance and support of the idea of policing.

Looking at international cooperation in law enforcement, we can see the seeds of change toward a much more democratic form of policing, one that will be more acceptable to human rights champions who view policing as a necessary evil rather than an organization whose existence enables human rights to flourish.

Through the overview of existing international police cooperation structures, the authors would like to endorse the idea of this cross-pollination in order to further and advance the concepts inherent in democratic policing.

The Concept of International Police Cooperation

International police cooperation, both formal and informal, has an extensive history. This chapter provides an overview of the two most prominent organizations embodying such cooperation, Interpol and Europol. An overview of their histories, missions, goals, and activities familiarizes the reader with the basic tenets of global information and intelligence exchange related to law enforcement.

By necessity, law enforcement has to take a more global approach to thwart various sophisticated groups of criminals. This could not have been more clearly illustrated than in the intense global investigations after the terror attacks of September 11. The only practical and efficient way to combat terrorist actions, as well as the entire host of spin-offs such as money laundering or trafficking in weapons of mass destruction, must come through mutual cooperation among law enforcement agencies around the world.

The feasibility of such operational cooperation will also be illustrated by an overview of the role of police in peacekeeping missions. Such cooperation, currently limited in scope and authority, provides a baseline for creative solutions in areas subject to a variety of disasters. Whether one looks at the Balkans or, more recently, at Iraq, it is quite clear that international police cooperation cannot be confined to clearinghouse (exchange of information) operations only. Today proactive and reactive global law enforcement responses are the only way to address the international nature of crime. Modern crime, transcending borders, cultures, languages, and legal systems, must be met with an effective response. The organizations and task forces discussed here assist in providing such a response.

The information presented is based on a compilation of available data, primarily downloaded from the Internet, without any content analysis of the sources; therefore this text differs in its vocabulary and sentence structure from the preceding and final pages of this chapter. It is a calculated presentation, based on the notion that the official Web sites of Interpol, Europol, and the United Nations provide the most valuable source for research on international police cooperation and that their information should be presented with minimum editorial changes, as its operational significance is best reflected in least edited content. Later in the chapter, the authors provide critical analyses of the effectiveness and perceived efficiency of these organizations and entities.

Interpol

Interpol is the byname of the International Criminal Police Organization, an organization established to promote international criminal police cooperation. The name Interpol, once the telegraph address of the organization, was officially incorporated into the formal name adopted in 1956: International Criminal Police Organization–Interpol (abbreviated to ICPO–Interpol or, more frequently, Interpol).

History

The history of Interpol goes back to the 1920s. After World War I, Europe faced a great increase in crime. One of the countries most affected was Austria, which in 1923 hosted a meeting of police representatives from 20 nations. This meeting led to the 1923 establishment of the International Police Commission (Interpol's predecessor), headquartered in Vienna. From

1923 until 1938, the commission flourished. When in 1938 Austria became part of Nazi Germany, the commission, along with it all of its records, was moved to Berlin.

The outbreak of World War II brought the activities of the commission to a halt. After that war, France offered the International Police Commission new headquarters in Paris, together with the services of a number of French police officials to form the general secretariat. A complete reorganization was needed, because all of the organization's prewar records had been lost or destroyed. The commission again became very active, and by 1955, the number of affiliated countries had increased from 19 to 55.

A modernized constitution was ratified in 1956, and the name was changed to the *International Criminal Police Organization* (retrieved August 17, 2007, from http://interpol.int/Public/ICPO/LegalMaterials/constitution/constitution).

Member Countries

By May 2007, Interpol was the second largest international organization in terms of membership after the United Nations, with 186 member countries (see the complete list at http://www.interpol.int/Public/Icpo/Members/default.asp; retrieved August 21, 2007). There are still a few countries that are not members; North Korea is one example.

Every member country has an Interpol office called a National Central Bureau, which is staffed with the country's own police officers. This bureau is the single point of contact for foreign governments requiring assistance with overseas investigations and information on the different police structures in other countries.

Contrary to popular belief, Interpol officers do not travel around the world investigating cases. Each country employs its own officers to operate on its own territory and in accordance with its own national laws. Each country may also send officers to serve a tour at Interpol Headquarters in Lyon, France.

Mission

Interpol's Web site states that its mission is "to be the world's preeminent police organization in support of all organizations, authorities, and services whose mission is preventing, detecting and suppressing crime" (retrieved August 21, 2007, from http://www.interpol.int/Public/Icpo/Members/default.asp).

Interpol seeks to achieve this by providing a global perspective and a regional focus; exchanging information that is timely, accurate, relevant, and complete; facilitating international cooperation; coordinating operational activities of the members; and making available know-how, expertise, and good practice.

The core services are: (1) a unique global police communication system, (2) a range of criminal databases and analytical services, and (3) proactive global support for police operations (retrieved May 3, 2004, from http://www.interpol.int/Public/Icpo/default.asp).

Because of the mandated political neutrality, Interpol's constitution prohibits any involvement in the investigation of crimes that do not affect several member countries or any engagement in activity of a political, military, religious, or racial character. Interpol's work focuses primarily on public safety and terrorism, organized crime, illicit drugs, weapons smuggling, human trafficking, money laundering, financial and high-tech crime, and corruption (retrieved May 3, 2004, from http://www.interpol.int/Public/Icpo/FactSheets/FS200101.asp).

Organizational Structure

Interpol has two interrelated governing bodies, the General Assembly and the Executive Committee. Major decisions on policy, budget, working methods, finances, and activities are made by its General Assembly, which meets annually. It is composed of delegates appointed by the member countries. Each country represented has one vote (retrieved August 21, 2007, from http://www.interpol.int/Public/icpo/governance/default.asp).

The Executive Committee supervises the execution of the decisions of the General Assembly and the work of the secretary general. The committee has 13 members: the president (who chairs the committee), four vice presidents, and eight delegates. The members are elected by the General Assembly and should represent different countries. The president and the four vice presidents must come from different continents. The president is elected for four years and the vice presidents for three.

At the time of writing, the president is Jackie Selebi, serving a term from 2004 to 2008. He has held the position of national commissioner of the South African Police Service since January 2000 and is the former vice president of the African region (retrieved August 21, 2007, from http://www.interpol.int./Public/icpo/Governance/PR/selebi.asp).

Decisions and recommendations adopted by the two governing bodies are implemented by the General Secretariat. The (2007) secretary-general, Ronald K. Noble, is the first non-European and the first U.S. national to hold the position. A native New Yorker and long-serving prosecutor, he has held senior law enforcement positions in the U.S. treasury and justice departments and, most recently, was a professor of criminal law at New York University (retrieved August 21, 2007, from http://www.interpol.int/Public/ICPO/Governance/SG/noble.asp).

A key Interpol unit is the Command and Co-ordination Centre (CCC), which links the General Secretariat with National Central Bureaus in all 186 countries and regional offices. It operates around the clock using Interpol's four official languages and serves as the first point of contact for any member faced with a crisis or incident. Another key CCC function is the coordination of the deployment of incident response teams (IRT) to the sites of major disasters or terror attacks (retrieved May 9, 2007, from http://www.Interpol.int/Public/CCC/default.asp).

Financing

Interpol is financed by annual contributions from its 186 members. They are calculated on a sliding scale according to the gross national product of each country. Interpol is taking on a multibillion-dollar crime problem with an annual budget of only €44.5 million in 2007 (about US$60 million; retrieved May 7, 2007, from http://www.interpol.int/Public?ICPO/Fact Sheets/G101.pdf).

Public Safety and Terrorism

Terrorists often seek to justify their acts on ideological, political, or religious grounds. That might seem to place terrorism outside of Interpol's reach because, as noted earlier, Interpol needs to remain politically neutral. Yet Interpol responds to terrorism because those acts—regardless of their motivation—constitute a serious threat to individual lives and freedom.

Interpol's role in fighting terrorism aims at preventing acts of international terrorism and, if these are carried out, to ensure that the perpetrators are brought to justice. It does this through formally and informally exchanging information.

To help member countries report on suspect individuals, Interpol has issued a number of practical guidelines to its member countries on the type of information needed. This includes information about suspect individuals and groups, modi operandi, evidence from scenes of the crime, and the use of new technologies by terrorist groups.

Since September 11 Interpol has issued 55 so-called Red Notices (explained in more detail below) regarding terrorists suspected of having committed or being connected to global terrorist attacks. Interpol has also increased the number of so-called Blue Notices (requests for information about the location of a suspect); 19 had been issued for the presumed September 11 hijackers at the time of publication of this book (Deridder, 2001).

Fusion Task Force

The FTF was created by Interpol in September 2002 as an operational investigative support body whose primary objectives included the following:

- Identify active terrorist groups and their membership.
- Solicit, collect, and share information and intelligence.

- Provide analytical support.
- Enhance the capacity of member countries to address the threats of terrorism and organized crime.

Because terrorist organizations' far-reaching activities are inextricably linked, the FTF investigates not only attacks, but also organizational hierarchies, financing, methods, and motives. Four regional task forces have been created in regions considered to be particularly susceptible to terrorist activity: Project Pacific (Southeast Asia), Project Kalkan (Central Asia), Project Amazon (South America), and Project Baobab (Africa). As of November 15, 2004, over 7,176 profiles of suspect individuals were in the FTF registry (retrieved May 7, 2007, from http://www.interpol.int/Public/FusionTask Force/default.asp). (Since that date, the FTF has not disclosed figures.)

Bioterrorism is another focus of Interpol. Evidence shows that terrorist organizations have heightened interest in the use of biological weapons, establishing terrorist support cells in different regions around the world with the ability and motivation to carry out attacks.

Interpol's Weapons Projects

Interpol has two major initiatives relating to conventional weapons (firearms and explosives): the Orange Notice and the Interpol Weapons Electronic Tracing System (IWETS). The Orange Notice provides a warning about weapons when there is reason to believe that it will help law enforcement and security officials identify a threat they might not normally detect. The Orange Notice also covers parcel bombs and information about radiological, chemical, and biological threats. Over 39 Orange Notices had been issued by Interpol as of August 2007.

Fugitive Investigations

Interpol's activities in respect to international fugitives have been part of its core business since the creation of the organization. At the request of its member countries, Interpol circulates international electronic notices, called Red Notices, containing identification details and judicial information about wanted criminals. A number of countries have given Interpol's Red Notices legal status, and they provide a basis for provisional arrest (retrieved May 5, 2004, from http://www.interpol.int/Public/Wanted/ Fugitives/Default.asp).

The General Secretariat of Interpol offers its member countries direct automatic search facilities and responds to queries concerning wanted persons. Although these are important tools in the hunt for fugitives, they are not sufficient. Interpol believes that its member countries need a proactive approach to locating and hunting fugitives at the international level.

That is why, in an effort to further assist its member countries in apprehending fugitives, the secretary general has established a new investigative service at the General Secretariat that deals exclusively with matters related to fugitives. The Fugitive Investigative Support Sub-Directorate, as it is known, actively encourages the international search for and arrest of fugitive offenders wherever they may hide. It coordinates and enhances international cooperation in the field, collects and disseminates best practices and expert knowledge, offers direct investigative support and specialized knowledge, conducts and coordinates relevant research, serves as a global point of reference for fugitive-related information, and develops and promotes training (retrieved August 21, 2007, from http://www.interpol.int/Public/Wanted/fugitiveInvest/serv.asp).

The International Notices System

One of Interpol's most important functions is to help the police of its member countries in communicating critical crime-related information to one another. In practice, this is done primarily through Interpol's system of notices, which help the world's law enforcement community exchange information about missing persons, unidentified bodies, persons who are wanted for committing serious crimes, and criminal modi operandi. In addition, Interpol notices are used by the International Tribunals for the Former Yugoslavia and Rwanda to seek persons wanted for serious violations of international human rights laws (retrieved August 21, 2007, from http://www.interpol.int/Public/Wanted/Default.asp).

Each notice gives full details of the individual concerned and the relevant national arrest warrant or court order, and it specifically requests that the fugitive be traced and arrested or detained with a view to extradition. Interpol issues seven types of notices; a recent addition is one for groups and individuals who are the targets of UN sanctions against al-Quaeda and the Taliban (retrieved August 21, 2007, from http://www.interpol.int/Public/Notices/default.asp). The other six types are as follows:

- Red Notices, based on a national arrest warrant, are used to seek the arrest and extradition of suspects.
- Blue Notices are used to seek information on the identity of persons or on their illegal activities related to a criminal matter. Such Blue Notices are used primarily for tracing and locating offenders when the decision to seek to extradite them has not yet been made and for locating witnesses to crimes.
- Green Notices are used to provide warnings and criminal intelligence about persons who have committed criminal offenses and who are likely to repeat these crimes in other countries.
- Yellow Notices are used to help locate missing persons, including children, or to help people (especially those severely ill or injured) to identify themselves.

- Black Notices are used to determine the identity of deceased persons
- Orange Notices address weapons issues, including radiological, chemical, and biological threats.

Child Abuse and Human Trafficking

Interpol's involvement in the investigation of offenses against children began in 1989 following the adoption of a UN convention. A specialized Trafficking of Human Beings Sub-Directorate was set up at Interpol headquarters, and the combating of crimes against children became Interpol's highest priority. Furthermore, Interpol's Specialist Group on Crimes Against Children (formerly known as the Standing Working Party on Offences Against Minors) brings together law enforcement officers from every continent to exchange information, develop working relationships, and agree on and implement operational matters. These semiannual meetings now attract more than 100 police officers from some 40 countries. The specialist group deals with child prostitution, child pornography, missing children, and trafficking in children, and it has recently taken on the issue of the management of sex offenders, which reflects the reality that to protect children, known sex offenders need to be prevented from reoffending. The specialist group has also produced the *Interpol Handbook of Good Practice for Specialized Officers Dealing with Crimes Against Children*. This handbook has been circulated to all member countries (Cameron-Waller, 2001).

Interpol is also deeply engaged in combating the increasing amount of child pornography, especially that distributed over the Internet. Interpol's General Secretariat has set up an automated image comparison database that is capable of linking series of images to provide investigators with the tools necessary to rapidly analyze data seized from persons suspected of involvement in child pornography.

Interpol maintains a database on missing and abducted children on behalf of the 186 member countries. The only children appearing on this Web site are those about whom the respective law enforcement authorities have requested that Interpol circulate information on an international basis. That is why, out of the thousands of children who go missing each year, only a few hundred appear in the database (retrieved May 5, 2004, from http://www.interpol.int/Public/Children/Missing/Default.asp).

In June 1999, Interpol's General Secretariat, at the request of member countries, initiated Project Bridge to facilitate more effective and efficient collection of information on organized crime groups and associations involved in the smuggling of immigrants and to improve the combating of this form of crime by undertaking adequate prevention and investigative measures (retrieved May 5, 2004, from http://www.interpol.int/Public/THB/PeopleSmuggling/Bridge/Default.asp).

Interpol is a partner within the Virtual Global Taskforce (VGT), which is an alliance of law enforcement agencies from around the world working

together to fight online child abuse. (For more information, see http://www
.virtualglobaltaskforce.com.)

Criminal Organizations and Drug Control

Interpol's Criminal Organizations and Drug Sub-Directorate is located
within the Criminal Intelligence Directorate of its General Secretariat. This
sub-directorate is the central repository of professional and technical expertise in drug control within the Interpol framework and provides assistance,
for example, to National Central Bureaus. Essentially, it acts as a clearinghouse for the collection, collation, analysis, and dissemination of drug-
related information. It also monitors the illicit drug situation on a global
basis, seeks to identify international drug trafficking organizations, coordinates international investigations, and maintains liaison with the United
Nations, its specialized agencies, and other international and regional organizations involved in drug control activities.

Interpol's Criminal Organizations and Drug Sub-Directorate seeks to
enhance cooperation among member countries and to stimulate the
exchange of information among all national and international enforcement
bodies concerned with countering the illicit production, traffic, and use of
narcotic drugs and psychotropic substances. In addition to responding to
international drug investigation inquiries and coordinating international
drug investigations where at least two member countries are involved, the
sub-directorate organizes working meetings involving two or more countries where common links have been identified in cases being investigated in
those member countries. The sub-directorate also organizes either regional
or worldwide meetings on specific drug topics, on an annual or ad hoc
basis. The aims of these meetings on specific topics include assessing the
extent of the drug problem in question, the exchange of information on the
latest methods of investigative techniques, and the further strengthening of
cooperation within the law enforcement communities.

Financial Crimes

Some transnational crimes are clearly financial in nature (e.g., money
laundering), but even those without an obvious link to money will likely
involve illicit financial transactions as an integral aspect of the crime.
Because of its capacity to facilitate the cooperative efforts of police, international institutions, and the private sector, Interpol has an important role
in responding to financial crime.

On September 17, 2001, a Financial and High-Tech Crime Sub-
Directorate was established within the Specialized Crimes Directorate of
ICPO–Interpol. Police officers in the sub-directorate also deal with offenses

relating to money laundering, counterfeit currency, payment cards, and intellectual property. The sub-directorate seeks to provide National Central Bureaus with expertise in specialized areas and enhance partnerships with relevant organizations, develop and coordinate best practices, and increase the flow and exchange of information related to these forms of crime (retrieved May 5, 2004, from http://www.interpol.int/Public/FinancialCrime/Money Laundering/default.asp).

Counterfeiting

The internationally waged battle against counterfeiting is led by the Counterfeit and Security Documents Branch (CSDB) of Interpol's General Secretariat. This body has fostered relationships with such entities as the U.S. Secret Service (USSS) and Europol as well as the European Anti-Fraud Office (OLAF), the European Central Bank (ECB), the Central Bank Counterfeit Deterrence Group (CBCDG), leading law enforcement and banking agencies, and innovative leaders in private industry. Interpol activities in this field encompass, among others things, exchange of information using the I-24/7 global police communication system, training classes, dedicated publications (for example, a regularly updated *List of Currencies* of all 186 member countries), working group meetings, and global and regional conferences (for instance, an International Conference on Protection of the Euro against Counterfeiting, which Interpol organized in cooperation with Europol and the European Central Bank; Interpol, 2007a, 2007b).

Payment Cards

Interpol assumed responsibility for counterfeit currency as a result of an international treaty, the 1929 International Convention for the Suppression of Counterfeiting Currency (known as the 1929 Geneva Convention), but there are no similar arrangements for counterfeit payment cards, and it is unlikely that there will be such arrangements in the near future. Payment cards are increasingly being used as a substitute for cash. With the growth of debit card activity and the emergence of electronic applications, the trend is likely to increase rather than diminish. Although it is difficult to be specific about the quantity of counterfeit currency in circulation, which varies considerably from country to country, its monetary value is thought to be far less than the millions of dollars in losses a year as a result of payment card counterfeiting (retrieved May 5, 2004, from http://www.interpol.int/Public/CreditCards/Default.asp).

In the year 2000, Interpol created a central database to allow for the classification of altered or counterfeit cards submitted by certified law enforcement and industry experts through forensic analysis. The database is currently accessible to member countries and has proved to be a useful tool for the law enforcement community (retrieved May 9, 2007, from http://www.interpol.int/Public/CreditCards/Default.asp).

Money Laundering

The international police community is aware that there is a need to achieve major results in the struggle against the financial criminal activities related to organized criminal groups. During the past 20 years, Interpol's General Assembly has passed a number of resolutions that have called on member countries to concentrate their investigative resources on identifying, tracing, and seizing the assets of criminal enterprises.

These resolutions have also called on member countries to increase the exchange of information in this field and have encouraged governments to adopt laws and regulations that would allow police access to the financial records of criminal organizations and would also allow the confiscation of proceeds gained by criminal activity. A concise working definition of money laundering was adopted by Interpol's General Assembly in 1995: It is defined as any act or attempted act to conceal or disguise the identity of illegally obtained proceeds so that they appear to have originated from legitimate sources.

Another important innovation in combating money laundering is the IMOLIN (International Money Laundering Information). This is an Internet-based information network that serves as a clearinghouse for money-laundering information for the benefit of all national and international anti–money laundering agencies. The IMOLIN database is administered by the Global Program against Money Laundering of the United Nations Office on Drugs and Crime for the United Nations and other international organizations, including Interpol (retrieved May 9, 2007, from http://www .interpol.int./Public/FinancialCrime/MoneyLaundering/default.asp).

Intellectual Property Crime

This particular area of crime covers an array of offenses from trademark and patent right infringements to software piracy, and it affects a vast range of products— from medicines to aircraft and vehicle spare parts, from clothing to music CDs and computer software. The total losses caused by this form of crime add up to hundred of billions of U.S. dollars globally every year. Interpol has recognized the extensive involvement of organized crime and terrorist groups in intellectual property crime. In 2000, the Interpol General Assembly mandated the Interpol General Secretariat to take action not only to raise awareness of the problem but also to provide a strategic plan in close cooperation with private industry (retrieved May 5, 2004, from http://www.interpol.int/Public/FinancialCrime/Intellectual Property/Default.asp).

Interpol's first international conference on intellectual property crime (Lyon, France, November 15–16, 2001) led to the establishment of a Group of Experts on Intellectual Property Crime, bringing together representatives of all the key stakeholders, including customs authorities, international agencies, and the private sector. The Group of Experts functions as a forum for the exchange of information and facilitates investigations into intellectual property offenses. It will also offer support through tailored training programs. This is a multiagency group, drawing its membership from public and private sectors (retrieved August 21, 2007, from http://www.interpol.int/Public/FinancialCrime/IntellectualProperty/Default.asp). The first meeting of the Group of Experts took place on July 23, 2002, and the group adopted the name *Interpol Intellectual Property Crime Action Group* (IIPCAG) (retrieved May 9, 2007, from http://www.interpol.int./Public/FinancialCrime/IntellectualProperty).

Corruption

Interpol's International Group of Experts on Corruption (IGEC) was established in 1998. Its membership consists of law enforcement representatives from eight countries (including the United States), a representative of Interpol's General Secretariat, and seven other persons representing a variety of international organizations, the international financial services community, and academia. This group was mandated to develop and implement an anticorruption strategy with the objectives of not only raising awareness of the major issues but also, and in particular, improving the capacity and effectiveness of law enforcement in the fight against corruption (retrieved May 5, 2004, from http://www.interpol.int/Public/Corruption/IGEC/Default.asp).

Among its activities, the IGEC prepared a code of ethics and a code of conduct (subsequently adopted by Interpol's General Assembly in 1999), a survey of police integrity in its 186 member countries, and global standards to combat corruption in police forces and services (adopted by Interpol's General Assembly in 2002). These global standards consist of several principles and numerous measures designed to improve the integrity of police forces and services, to improve their efficacy in combating corruption, and to represent an ideal toward which the Interpol member countries should strive. These standards have been well received by the international law enforcement community and mark the beginning of a proactive approach for law enforcement in combating corruption (retrieved May 5, 2004, from http://www.interpol.int/Public/Corruption/IGEC/Default.asp).

Among the many initiatives of the IGEC, the most important seem to be the following two: the Global Standards to Combat Corruption in Police Forces/Services, institutionalized by the Interpol General Assembly held in Cameroon in October 2002; and the Library of Best Practice, published in

2003, which is designed to aid individuals investigating corruption cases (retrieved May 9, 2007, from http://www.interpol.int./Public/Corruption/IGEC/Default.asp).

Publications

Interpol's primary publications include the *International Criminal Police Review* and *International Crime Statistics*. The *International Criminal Police Review*, which was published between 1946 and 2001, is not currently in production as Interpol reassesses the publication's role. Interpol has published *International Crime Statistics* every two years since 1950 and every year since 1993. Since 2000, the publication has been available electronically on a country-by-country basis.

The data are provided by the National Central Bureaus, and Interpol publishes them as submitted, without any attempt to process them. Due primarily to the legal and procedural differences in the different countries and the differences in statistical methods, the statistics cannot be used for comparative purposes. Police statistics reflect only reported crimes, which represent only a fraction of the real level of crime. Furthermore, the volume of crime reported to the police depends, to a certain extent, on the action of police and can vary with time, as well as from country to country. Consequently, the data (available to authorized users only) published in the current set of statistics should be interpreted with caution (retrieved September 27, 2004, from http://www.interpol.int/Public/Statistics/ICS/default.asp).

In addition, a sample of very valuable Interpol publications include the following titles:

Interpol: An Overview	*Crime Against Children*
Notices	*Interpol and Drug Trafficking*
Connecting Police	*DNA Gateway*
Databases	*Disaster Victim*
Terrorism	*Identification*
Bioterrorism	*Intellectual Property Crime*
People Smuggling	*Money Laundering*
Trafficking In Human Beings	*Project Geiger*

All of the above fact sheets (available on the Internet in portable document format [pdf]) are published in four languages: Arabic, English, French, and Spanish, which are Interpol's official languages. Interpol's *Annual Report* is also published in these languages; at the time this book was published; the most recent report had been issued in May 2007 and covered the year 2005. Interpol also issues the following guides and manuals:

Bio-terrorism Incident Pre-Planning Guide—2006

DNA Handbook

As well as the following posters:

Most Wanted Works of art

Most Wanted

And the following leaflets and brochures:

For a Safer World

Mind/Find

There is also a work on CD/DVD: *Stolen Works of Art.* All of these publications are available through Interpol's Web site (retrieved May 6, 2007, from http://www.interpol.int/Public/Icpo/Publications/default.asp).

Regional Activities

In 2001, the Interpol General Secretariat set up the Directorate for Regional and National Police Services. It is comprised of five sub-directorates: one each for Africa, the Americas, Asia and the South Pacific, Europe, and the Middle East and North Africa; there is also a subregional coordination bureau. The directorate design recognizes that practical law enforcement needs in each region vary to some extent. By promoting a network of regional institutions and developing effective strategic alliances with other institutions, Interpol seeks to provide better-tailored assistance through its National Central Bureaus (retrieved May 5, 2004, from http://www.interpol.int/Public/Region/Americas/Default.asp).

All Interpol National Central Bureaus in the Americas are connected to the I-24/7 communication system (retrieved May 9, 2007, from http://www .interpol.int.Public/Region/Americas/Default.asp).

Europol

The European Union was originally established largely to promote the economic integration of its member states. Economic integration, however, brought with it new opportunities for offenders, above all the ease with which they could transcend national borders. Because crime was being organized increasingly at a European level rather than on a national or local level, politicians agreed that an organization was needed that could coordinate the law enforcement resources of member states to effectively tackle crime on a pan-European level (a level that as of May 1, 2004, encompassed

25 countries).[1] As of August 2007, the number of member states had increased to 27. In 1992, the Maastricht Treaty established Europol's predecessor, the European Drugs Unit. It formally began operations on January 3, 1994. The European Drugs Unit had a rather limited mandate; it was focused on supporting each member state's fight against illicit drugs and the associated money laundering.

The Convention on the Establishment of a European Police Office (the Europol Convention) was adopted on July 26, 1995, and by 1998 had been ratified by all the member states. On July 1, 1999, Europol formally took over the work of the European Drugs Unit. It is based in The Hague, in the Netherlands. Its responsibilities have grown from drug policing to include areas of serious crime as diverse as terrorism, drug trafficking, human trafficking, illegal immigration, trafficking in radioactive and nuclear substances, trafficking in stolen motor vehicles, counterfeiting, and money laundering associated with international criminal activities (British Broadcasting Corporation, 2003; see also http://www.europol.eu.int/index .asp?page=facts&language=en, retrieved May 3, 2004).

Mission

As is the case with Interpol, Europol is (at least at present) not an operational entity, in that Europol staff members do not have police powers in the individual member states. Thus, they do not, for example, investigate offenses or question suspects. Instead, Europol seeks to support the law enforcement agencies of all its member states primarily by gathering and analyzing information and intelligence specifically about people who are members or possible members of international criminal organizations. This information is received from a variety of sources, such as national police forces as well as other international crime-fighting organizations (such as Interpol), and is entered into computers for processing and analysis. When Europol identifies information that requires action by national law enforcement agencies, such as connections identified between criminal offenses, it notifies the appropriate authorities without delay.

Europol is also charged with the task of developing expertise in certain fields of crime and making this expertise available to the member states when needed (retrieved May 3, 2004, from http://www.europol.eu.int/ index.asp?page=facts&language=en and from http://www.europol.eu.int/ index.asp?page=faq&language=en). Europol thus serves as a link between the law enforcement agencies of the member states of the European Union. On October 16, 1999, a unit called Eurojust, which may be said in broad terms to be parallel to Europol, was created to serve the same function among the prosecution authorities of the member states. To foster closer cooperation between Eurojust and Europol—necessary in particular because of the key role that prosecutors have in many member states in guiding the course of police investigations—Eurojust also has its headquarters in The Hague, in the Netherlands (Eurojust, n.d.).

Organizational Structure, Management, and Control

Europol is above all a body for the coordination of international law enforcement. The police officers working at Europol fall into two categories: regular staff members and liaison officers. The regular staff members (some 590 as of May 2007) take care of the joint activities, such as planning and analysis. The liaison officers (some 90 as of May 2007) represent a variety of national law enforcement agencies: the police, customs, gendarmerie, immigration services, and so on. Their function is largely to work together on individual cases that affect their national law enforcement interests. For example, if an analysis of data shows that a case may have connections with Germany and Spain, the German and Spanish liaison officers will meet to discuss how to deal with the case. They will then liaise with the competent national or local law enforcement authorities to ensure follow-through (retrieved May 10, 2007, from http://www .europol.europa.eu/index.asp?page=facts).

Europol is accountable to the European Union Council of Ministers for Justice and Home Affairs (retrieved May 3, 2004, from http://www .europol.eu.int/index.asp?page=mgmtcontrol&language=en). The council is responsible for the main control and guidance function of Europol. It appoints the director and deputy directors and adopts the budget. It also adopts regulations related to Europol's work. Each year, the council forwards a special report to the European Parliament on the work of Europol. The European Parliament is also consulted if the Europol Convention or other Europol regulations are amended.

Europol's management board is composed of one representative of each member state. Each member has one vote. Members of the European Commission (the executive branch of the EU government) are also invited to attend the meetings of the management board with nonvoting status.

The management board meets at least twice a year to discuss a wide range of Europol issues that relate to its current activities and its future developments. It adopts a general report on Europol's activities during the previous year, as well as a report on Europol's future activities, taking into account the operational requirements of member states as well as the budgetary and staffing implications for Europol. These reports are submitted to Europol's Council of Ministers of Justice and Home Affairs for approval (retrieved May 3, 2004, from http://www.europol.eu.int/index.asp?page= mgmtcontrol&language=en).

Europol is headed by a director appointed by the council acting unanimously, after obtaining the opinion of the management board, for a five-year period. The director's mandate may be renewed once for a further period of four years. The director is responsible for the day-to-day administration of Europol, the performance of its tasks, personnel management, and other tasks assigned to him or her by the Europol Convention or by the management board. The director is assisted by deputy directors, also appointed by the council for a four-year period, renewable once.

After the events of September 11, Europol was partially restructured. The three departments—Investigation Support, Intelligence Analysis, and Organized Crime—were combined into one single department called Serious Crime, thus combining information exchange, analysis, and expertise.

Cooperation With Third Countries and International Organizations

Europol has improved its international law enforcement cooperation by signing bilateral agreements with the following non-EU countries and international organizations: Iceland, Norway, the United States, the European Central Bank, the European Monitoring Centre on Drug and Drug Addiction, Interpol, and the World Customs Organization. In the sprit of cooperation, Europol has opened a liaison office in Washington D.C. (retrieved May 3, 2004, from http://www.europol.eu.int/index.asp?page=facts&language=en).

The Europol Computer System (TECS)

The Europol Convention calls on Europol to establish and maintain a computerized system to allow input of, access to, and analysis of data. The convention lays down a strict framework for human rights and data protection, control, supervision, and security. The Europol Computer System (TECS) has three principal components: an information system, an analysis system, and an index system (retrieved August 18, 2007, from http://www .europol.europe/eu/index.asp?page=facts).

Strict data protection legislation in many member states of the European Union prompted the Europol Convention to set up a special body to ensure compliance with such legislation: the Joint Supervisory Body. This body is composed of two representatives from each of the national supervisory bodies, each appointed for five years by each member state. Each delegation has one vote. Its task is to review the activities of Europol to ensure that the rights of the individual are not violated by the storage, processing, and use of the data held by Europol. It also monitors the permissibility of the transmission of data originating from Europol. Every European citizen has the right to request a review by the Joint Supervisory Body to ensure that the manner in which his or her personal data have been collected, stored, processed, and used by Europol is lawful and accurate (retrieved May 3, 2004, from http://www.europol.eu.int/index.asp?page=mgmtcontrol&language=en).

Financing

Europol is funded by contributions from the member states, calculated on the basis of their gross national products. The budget for 2007 was

€67.9 million ("Budget for Europol," 2006), which is approximately US $91.7 million. The annual accounts of Europol are subject to an audit, which is carried out by the Joint Audit Committee (retrieved August 18, 2007 from http://www.europol.europa.eu/index.asp?page=mgmtcontrol)

Activities

Europol is deeply involved in combating all kinds of major crimes taking place in the member states. The results of its activities are published in detail in the *Europol Annual Reports*. The following is a presentation of selected Europol activities based on its annual reports for 2001 and 2002 (retrieved August 20, 2007, from http://www.europol.eu.int/index.asp?page=publar2001 and from http://www.europol.eu.int/index.asp?page=publar2002).

Combating Terrorism

Following the events of September 11 and the subsequent decisions taken by the EU Council of Justice and Home Affairs Ministers on September 20, 2001, Europol together with the member states set up a Counter-Terrorism Task Force (CTTF) to implement a comprehensive set of measures. The CTTF consists of experts and liaison officers from the police forces and services of member states as well as their intelligence services in an unprecedented exercise of cooperation and collaboration.

In addition to creating the CTTF, Europol has provided several products and services related to counterterrorism. The exchange of counterterrorist information between member states by way of the Europol liaison officers and the network of national units has expanded. A special conference on terrorism was held in Madrid (January 29–February 2, 2002). Several directives were updated—for example, on the counterterrorism responsibilities at the national level within each member state, counterterrorism legislation in member states, and counterterrorism competencies/centers of excellence in the member states.

The *Open Source Digest* on terrorism-related activity is disseminated to the member states on a weekly basis. Also provided is the *Glossary of Terrorist Groups,* containing basic details about these groups' origins, ideologies, objectives, leadership, and activities.

Periodical trends and situation reports are provided on topics related to terrorism, based on open sources of information that are reported by member states to Europol. The first report, *EU Terrorism Situation and Trend Report TE-SAT 2007,* was presented at the European Parliament in Brussels by Europol director Max-Peter Ratzel (TE-SAT, 2007).

This document provided an analytic overview of the phenomenon of terrorism in the EU. The report for the first time collated detailed statistical data on terrorist attacks and plots in the eleven member states, covering all the 498 attacks in 2006. Among the several annexes, one describes implementations of the Framework Decision on Combating Terrorism in Member States, an agreement that provided Eurojust with information on court convictions of terrorists. *TE-SAT 2007*, being a public document, allows EU citizens to get acquainted with major Europol activities that normally are not publicized due to their confidentiality (retrieved May 10, 2007, from http://www.europol.europa.eu/index.asp?page=news&news= pr070410.htm).

Financial Crimes and Other Crimes Against Property and Public Goods, Including Fraud

In the area of financial and property crime, Europol's activities currently focus on providing strategic support while preparing for more operational activities in the immediate future. In the field of money laundering, Europol has begun to systematically collect information on suspicious transactions that have been identified by law enforcement and judicial authorities of the member states. Further strategic support includes the issuing of information bulletins on specific matters related to financial investigations and assistance in an initiative to create a *European Manual on Money Laundering*. An EU "situation report" is updated periodically in the area of combating credit card fraud. The result of this work is used to define a common EU strategy to fight this phenomenon.

The Financial Crime Information Centre was further developed with a view to providing member states with secure access to Europol's Web site. This Web site includes a library of information related to financial matters and various technical subjects related to financial investigations.

In 2001 Europol was involved in three operations concerning trafficking in stolen motor vehicles in Europe. Europol supported these operations by providing analytical support, coordinating international cooperation, and coordinating the information exchange. Europol also initiated several bilateral investigations among third countries and member states.

In cooperation with German and Austrian authorities, Europol developed the international European Vehicle Identification Database. This database was developed and translated by Europol and is now available in German, English, and French. Europol also developed the Blanco Documents Database containing stolen blank vehicle registration documents of various countries.

Vehicle theft is still one of the most common crimes in Europe. The scope of this problem can be illustrated by the fact that in the EU countries alone, 771,745 vehicles were stolen in 2004 (retrieved May 11, 2007, from http://www.europol.europa.eu.publications/SeriousCrimeOverviews/2005/ overview).

Combating Drug-Related Criminality

Europol took over the tasks of the Europol Drugs Unit on July 1, 1999. It is responsible for combating drug trafficking within the European Union and works to improve police and customs cooperation between member states ("Action Plan," 2005).

Europol has supported operational projects against, for example, Turkish, Latin American, and indigenous criminal groups. There has been an improvement in both the quality and quantity of information supplied to Europol. This has led to the identification of criminals, new common targets, and links between investigations, as well as improvement in cooperation among the member states based on intelligence and analysis supplied by Europol.

During 2001, Europol assisted law enforcement teams in three member states in the dismantling of nine illicit laboratories and the collection of evidence. Europol's efforts contributed to seizures of synthetic drugs and laid the groundwork for the arrests of several suspects. Currently, there are two expert systems related to drugs in place at Europol: the Ecstasy Logo System and the Cocaine Logo System. These systems improve law enforcement cooperation in member states by identifying links between all seizures of ecstasy tablets and all seizures of cocaine, primarily based on certain particularities of the seized drugs.

Following a ban on opium poppy cultivation in Afghanistan and the events of September 11, Europol drafted a report on the status of opium production in that country, the world's largest producer of opium. Within the framework of its Joint Action on New Synthetic Drugs, Europol, together with the European Monitoring Centre for Drugs and Drug Addiction (EMCDDA), drafted joint progress reports on GHB (gamma-hydroxybutyrate, a "rape drug"), ketamine, and PMMA (polymethyl-methacrylate). As a direct result of the EU Action Plan on Drugs 2000–2004, a Collection Model for drug seizure statistics was drafted by Europol in close cooperation with experts from member states and the EMCDDA. A Model of Parameters for the Assessment of the European Drugs Strategy, drafted by Europol in cooperation with experts from member states and the EMCDDA, was adopted by the Horizontal Working Party on Drugs and was implemented in 2002.

During 2001, under the Synthetic Drug Assistance Program within PHARE (Poland and Hungary Assistance for Economic Restructuring), Europol organized and gave training courses to law enforcement officers, forensic scientists, and public prosecutors from several East European countries on the dismantling of illicit laboratories. In addition, training was provided to specialist teams in the Netherlands. Europol also assisted French authorities in a joint training program on synthetic drugs and their precursors for law enforcement staff from Latin American countries.

Fulfilling its mission of combating drug trafficking and other drug-related crimes, Europol is the main cooperation partner EMCDDA. This institution, established in 1993 and based in Lisbon, is one of the European Union's decentralized agencies. EMCDDA's Annual Report 2006, is available in 23 languages (EMCDDA, 2006).

According to Max-Peter Ratzel, director of Europol, a special focus has been given to the preparation of Europol's first Organized Crime Threat

Assessment (OCTA) report. The goal is to identify crime trends and to give decision makers a better basis for prioritization (retrieved August 21, 2007, from http://www.interpol.int/Public/ICPO/InterpolAtWork/iaw2005.pdf).

Further developments in the area of operational agreements and strategic relationship with key partners were made in 2005. Both the U.S. Secret Service and the Federal Bureau of Investigation (FBI) stationed liaison officers within Europol. Following the signing of an operational agreement with Canada, the Royal Canadian Mounted Police (RCMP) included their representatives.

The progress in cooperation between Europol and various countries can be illustrated by the fact that during only two months, from January 16 through March 15, 2007, four bilateral agreements on strategic cooperation were signed. The agreements were signed between Europol and Australia, Moldova, Albania, and Macedonia, and a multilateral agreement on witness protection was signed as well (retrieved May 10, 2007, from http://www.europol.europa.eu/index.asp?page=news&language).

Peacekeeping Operations: The Police Component _____

From 1948 up to the present, more than 65 international peacekeeping missions or operations have been established worldwide,[2] primarily, but not exclusively, under the flag of the United Nations. All these operations have included the contribution of law enforcement agencies, which so far have come from a total of 89 countries. Nonetheless, the main components of these peacekeeping forces have been military units, and the police components usually played only a minor part.

A few examples illustrate the role of the police in peacekeeping operations. The UN peacekeeping operation in the territory of the former Yugoslavia (the UN Protection Force), which lasted from 1992 to 1995, involved 37,795 military personnel and only 803 police officers.[3] The UN peacekeeping operation in Cyprus, which began in 1964 and continues at the time of publication, has involved 1,373 military personnel and only 35 police officers.

This ratio of police to military was more weighted toward the police component in the peacekeeping operation in Namibia from April 1989 through March 1990. The operation involved 4,493 military personnel and 1,500 police officers.[3] The more recent UN peacekeeping operation in East Timor, which began on May 20, 2002, is being carried out by a contingent of 5,000 troops and 1,250 police officers from 33 countries.[3]

In the sections that follow, peacekeeping operations that have involved a sizable police force component are examined more closely, in chronological order.

The UN International Police Task Force in Bosnia and Herzegovina

The first peacekeeping operation involving a sizable police force component followed the work of the UN Protection Force mentioned above. This was the UN Mission in Bosnia and Herzegovina (UNMIBH), which included the UN International Police Task Force (IPTF). UNMIBH began in January 1995 and continued until the European Union took over the responsibility from the United Nations in January 2003 (in the form of the EU Police Mission in Bosnia and Herzegovina).

Since IPTF was an organic component of UNMIBH, understanding the place and role of the IPTF requires a description of the organizational structure, the scope of the mission, and the other components of UNMIBH.[4]

Background

In 1946, the Socialist Republic of Bosnia and Herzegovina (BiH) became part of the Federal People's Republic of Yugoslavia. The population of the republic (almost 4 million) was and remains ethnically diverse. According to the 1991 census, 44 percent of the population were Muslims, 31 percent were Serbs, and 17 percent were Croats. For many years, a seemingly endless conflict had been carried out among these ethnic groups in the fields of religious, economic, cultural, and political life. As long as Yugoslavia was under communist rule under the leadership of Marshall Tito, these conflicts were hidden. The post-Tito regime in Yugoslavia was not able to deal with these and other, no less important, conflicts, which beset all six federal republics that made up Yugoslavia (Bosnia, Serbia, Slovenia, Croatia, Herzegovina, Kosovo). As a result of growing tensions in Bosnia and Herzegovina, on April 7, 1992, a civil war broke out. Serb paramilitary forces started firing on Sarajevo, and the bombardment of the city by heavy artillery began soon thereafter.

During this war, which spread to all the parts of the territory of BiH (about 20,000 square miles) and lasted until November 1995, approximately 200,000 people died and more than 2 million were driven from their homes.

The member states of the United Nations were unable to agree on military intervention, although the United Nations did send troops to facilitate the delivery of humanitarian aid. This mandate was later extended to the protection of a number of territories declared by the United Nations as safe areas. A ceasefire negotiated in December 1994 generally held until mid-March 1995.

In May 1995, North Atlantic Treaty Organization (NATO) forces launched air strikes on Serb targets (70 percent of the territory of BiH was then under Serb control), after the Serb military refused to comply with a UN ultimatum to remove all heavy weapons from a 12-mile exclusion zone around Sarajevo. Further NATO air strikes against Serb targets and a new offensive by the BiH and Croatian military helped to bring about U.S.-sponsored peace talks in Dayton, Ohio, in November 1995. Formalized in Paris in December of the same year, the subsequent agreement called for a federalized BiH in which 51 percent of the land would constitute the Croat-Bosnian federation, and 49 percent would constitute the Serb Republic (Republika Srbska).[5] The Dayton-Paris Agreement,[6] which contained 15 detailed articles and 11 annexes, covered a broad range of issues, from the military aspects of the peace settlement and the delineation of a boundary between the Federation of Bosnia and Herzegovina and the Republika Srbska to the holding of democratic elections, the protection of human rights, and assistance to refugees. Part of the Dayton-Paris Agreement called for the withdrawal of the UN Protection Force and the deployment of the NATO-led multinational Implementation Force (IFOR), and in this connection also the establishment of the IPTF.

On December 20, 1995, IFOR replaced the UN Protection Force. On the next day, December 21, the UN Security Council set up the IPTF and the UN Civil Affairs office, brought together as the UNMIBH, originally for a period of one year. The Security Council renewed the UNMIBH mandate on several occasions, the last one extending the mandate to December 31, 2002, at which time UNMIBH was terminated (UN Peace and Security Section, 2003a).

UNMIBH's mandate was to contribute to the establishment of the rule of law in Bosnia and Herzegovina, to assist in reforming and restructuring the local police, to monitor and audit the performance of the police and others involved in the maintenance of law and order, and to monitor and investigate police compliance with human rights (UN Peace and Security Section, 2003b).

Components

The main components of the UNMIBH were the IPTF, the Civil Affairs unit, and the Division of Administration, which included the work of the UN Trust Fund (three separate trust funds were established by the UN secretary-general: a fund for the restoration of essential public services in Sarajevo in March 1994, a fund for a police assistance program in December 1995, and a fund for emergency assistance trust projects outside Sarajevo in 2001). UNMIBH had a nationwide presence with regional headquarters in Banja Luca, Bihac, Doboj, Mostar, and Tuzla and a district headquarters in Brcko (UN Peace and Security Section, 2003a).

Personnel

The IPTF had an authorized strength of 2,057 police officers representing 43 countries, approximately 336 international civilian staff members from around 48 countries, and 1,575 locally recruited staff members. As of October 10, 2002, the largest contingents in the IPTF came from the United States (200 police officers) and Jordan (147). Other countries that contributed large numbers of police officers included Bulgaria (34), Egypt (47), France (93), Ghana (97), India (94), Ireland (28), the Netherlands (54), Pakistan (89), Poland (48), Portugal (30), the Russian Federation (32), Sweden (27), Turkey (30), Ukraine (28), and the United Kingdom (70). During the seven years that the IPTF was in existence, due to the rotation of police officers, more than 8,000 police officers from these 43 countries took part (UN Security Council, 2002).

Mandate Implementation Plan (MIP) 2000–2002

The Mandate Implementation Plan (MIP) was a consolidated strategic and operational framework for the completion of UNMIBH's core mandate in Bosnia and Herzegovina. On the basis of the relevant Security Council resolutions, the MIP identified the objectives of the mission and the programs and modalities used to achieve those objectives. With the support of international partners and the full cooperation of other international organizations,[7] UNMIBH established the following goals (UN Peace and Security Section, 2003b):

That all law enforcement personnel must meet internationally determined standards of professional competence and personal integrity

That all civilian law enforcement agencies must meet internationally determined standards of organizational capability and institutional integrity while progressively meeting the bench marks for multiethnic representation

That the institutional, legislative, and operational requirements for effective civilian police and judicial cooperation in law enforcement must be in place

That the State Border Service (SBS) must be fully established and that there is effective cooperation between law enforcement institutions at interentity, state, and international levels

That the public and the police must know their respective rights and duties and how to exercise them

That BiH must be supported in playing a full role as a member state of the United Nations

The Police Component (IPTF)

The IPTF monitored and advised local police with the objective of changing the primary focus of the police from the security of the state to that of protection of the individual. In so doing, IPTF helped to restructure and reform the local police to create democratic and professional police forces that were multiethnic, effective, transparent, impartial, accountable, and representative of the society they serve and that facilitated the return of refugees and displaced persons.

IPTF aimed to create a professional police force that met international standards and accurately reflected the ethnic composition of the population according to the 1991 census in the federation and the 1997 election results in the Republika Srbska and by encouraging female recruitment. IPTF registered some 25,278 local police personnel.

Special Trafficking Operations Program (STOP)

This program was established in June 2001 to address the issue of the trafficking of women and girls for prostitution in Bosnia and Herzegovina. STOP teams (IPTF staff together with the local police) throughout the country actively coordinated their efforts with the relevant entity and cantonal authorities to ensure that all establishments determined to be involved in using trafficked women and girls for prostitution were closed and that traffickers and brothel owners were brought to justice (Human Rights Watch, 2002).

The End of the Mandate

On December 31, 2002, the mandate of the UNMIBH, including its police component (the IPTF), was successfully completed. This mission and the IPTF made up the most extensive police reform and restructuring mission ever undertaken by the United Nations.

On a global scale, when we take into consideration the approximately 8,000 police officers from 43 different countries who served in the IPTF during the seven years of its existence, the task force was unprecedented. The service of so many police officers in the BiH was quite fruitful. The UNMIBH and its main component, the IPTF, left behind a legacy of democratic law enforcement, ensuring a secure environment for returning refugees. Independent local police structures were established in the country, with approximately 16,000 law enforcement officers certified after a comprehensive verification process. All local police officers were trained in basic standards of democratic policing. Progress was made on minority recruitment and gender balance through the two police academies established by the UNMIBH and the IPTF.

It is highly symbolic that the police forces from various countries that served in the UN Integrated Mission in Timor-Leste (UNMIT) included a team of police officers from Bosnia and Herzegovina, who developed under the help and supervision of the IPTF in that country. As of March 31, 2007, the UNMIT is composed of 10,027 military troops from 70 countries and a contingent of 651 police officers from 43 countries ("August 2007 Timor-Leste," 2007).

The UN Liaison Office in Sarajevo

The UN Liaison Office in Sarajevo was established in January 2003. Its main task was to ensure a seamless transition from the UNMIBH and its IPTF, which completed their mandate on December 31, 2002, to the European Union Police Mission (EUPM).

The UN Liaison Office assists the EUPM in the implementation of its mandate. The aim is to preserve and build on the achievements of the UNMIBH in police reform and restructuring. The Liaison Office provides the institutional memory of the UNMIBH mission to EUPM to ensure continuity in the democratization process of law enforcement agencies.

Another task of the Liaison Office is to maintain close contact and continue the political dialogue with the authorities of Bosnia and Herzegovina on the state and entity levels. In addition, the office continues communication and close liaison with the Office of the High Representative, the Organization for Security Cooperation in Europe, the Office of United Nations High Commissioner for Refugees, and other international organizations.

The UN Trust Fund, after the successful implementation of its projects to equip the local police, continues with the implementation of a number of projects in Bosnia-Herzegovina aimed at the rehabilitation of the devastated infrastructure and the restoration of essential public services. The Liaison Office has assumed the role of observing the implementation of UN Trust Fund projects and organizes media coverage when projects are completed (UN Liaison Office Sarajevo, 2002).

The European Union Police Mission (EUPM) in Bosnia and Herzegovina

The establishment of the European Union Police Mission was endorsed by both the Peace Implementation Council Steering Board (an international board established to observe and streamline the agreement between Bosnia and Herzegovina) and by the United Nations Security Council (Resolution 1396). The mission was established for a period of three years. Its annual budget was €38 million, of which €20 million came from the EU budget.

The EUPM began operations on January 1, 2003, following the departure of the IPTF. The mission was part of a broad approach followed by the EU and other actors that included activities to address the whole range of rule-of-law issues.

The refocused EUPM follow-up mission will have a duration of two years (from January 1, 2006 until the end of 2007). It supports the national police reform process and continues to develop and consolidate local capacity and regional cooperation in the fight against major and organized crime. The number of EUPM personnel in the follow-up mission is substantially reduced in comparison to 2003. As of May 4, 2007, the force was composed of 157 police officers and 29 civilian specialists from 32 countries, including 25 from the European Union (European Union Police Mission in Bosnia and Herzegovina, n.d.)

The Multinational Police Specialized Unit of the Kosovo Force (KFOR)

Kosovo lies in southern Serbia and has a mixed population, of whom the majority are ethnic Albanians. Until 1989, the region enjoyed a high degree of autonomy within the former Yugoslavia. In 1989, the Serbian leader Slobodan Milosevic altered the status of the region, removing autonomy and bringing the region under the direct control of Belgrade, the Serbian capital. The Kosovar Albanians strenuously opposed the move.

Military and paramilitary forces from the Federal Republic of Yugoslavia and the Kosovo Liberation Army were fighting day and night. Ethnic tensions were high and claimed the lives of many. More than 1,500 Kosovar Albanians were killed. Nearly 1 million people fled Kosovo to seek refuge.

Under the UN Security Council mandate (Resolution 1244 of June 10, 1999) the peace-enforcing Kosovo Force (KFOR) was set up. The objectives of KFOR were to establish and maintain a secure environment in Kosovo, including maintaining public safety and order; monitoring, verifying, and when necessary, enforcing compliance with the agreements that ended the conflict; and providing assistance to the UN Mission in Kosovo (NATO, 2003, 2004).

KFOR has two main components: a military component, consisting of five multinational brigades, and a police component, the Multinational Specialized Unit (MSU). In total, the KFOR troops come from 30 NATO and non-NATO nations. As of May 2007, NATO has approximately 16,000 troops deployed in Kosovo (NATO, n.d.b).

The MSU is a police force with a military status and an overall police capability. It consists of a regiment of the Italian Carabinieri (police), a contingent of the French Gendarmerie (militarized police), and a platoon of the Estonian Army (NATO, n.d.a).

The MSU has substantial experience in combating organized crime and terrorism. It possesses the human resources and dedicated investigative tools needed to analyze the structure of subversive and criminal organizations. It also provides prevention and repression resources to be used as KFOR assets.

The MSU conducts general patrolling operations to maintain a regular presence within KFOR. Such operations are in support of KFOR routine patrol activity and allow the MSU to interact with the local community while deepening their overall knowledge of evolving criminal and security threats in each area. Each detachment in KFOR has a different strength depending on the public order and security situation of the area.

The primary tasks of the MSU are to maintain a secure environment and establish a presence through patrolling, attend to law enforcement in close cooperation with the UN Mission in Kosovo, gather information, police civil disturbances, gather and analyze criminal intelligence on organized crime, conduct antiterrorism and VIP escort operations as well as special police operations, and investigate crimes related to military security (Bureau for International Narcotics and Law Enforcement Affairs, 2003; NATO, 2003; n.d.a).

The Next Steps

The deployment of the police in peacekeeping missions originally occurred, exclusively, under the auspices of the United Nations and the European Union, which continue to recognize the primacy of the UN Security Council for the maintenance of internal security. Increasingly, however, the United Nations calls on regional organizations to take responsibility for civilian crisis management in trouble spots closest to them. In June 2000, at a meeting of the European Council at Santa Maria da Feira, the member states of the European Union agreed that by 2003 they should be able to provide up to 5,000 police officers for international missions across the range of crisis prevention and crisis management operations. Within this goal, member states also took upon themselves the task of identifying and deploying, when the needs arises, up to 1,000 police officers within 30 days as part of a so-called European Union Rapid Reaction Police Force (Lindborg, 2001).

The unexpected mass looting in Baghdad, Basra, and other Iraqi towns in April 2003 placed a new and very urgent task on the agenda of the police forces: preparing and setting up new well-armed and specialized antilooting police detachments. According to the Geneva Convention, in wartime the armed forces are responsible for the safety and security of hospitals, museums, banks, and the like in operational areas. The lessons from the recent war in Iraq are that the army alone is not capable of effectively preventing and combating mass looting. It should be supported with well-trained and highly specialized antilooting police units acting, where possible, in cooperation with the local police forces. Until now, police force detachments that participated in war operations were not brought into action until some time had passed since the liberation of towns. However, in Baghdad, organized gangs of looters broke into several museums including the National Archaeological Museum. Libraries, banks, and even some hospitals were looted almost simultaneously with the arrival of U.S. tanks and troops. Thus in the future, police antilooting detachments should be prepared for action and positioned with forward combat detachments. For example, the Italian Police (Carabinieri) have already started forming such antilooting detachments (Gruner, 2006).

Future Trends

The future of international police cooperation can and should be evaluated from the perspective of the assessment of the two supranational law enforcement organizations, Interpol and Europol. Despite their quite impressive geographical mandate, these organizations remain nonoperational and serve more as clearinghouses for the exchange of information rather than as fully operational entities. To fully assess the potential of those two organizations, we must also look at the hybrid creations: international police task forces, which currently are the only actively operational solution to global law enforcement–related problems.

To target, effectively and efficiently, increasing transnational criminal activity, we need to identify operational responses. Even though Interpol and Europol are not operational in the traditional sense, they can serve as a very important backup system for operational agencies around the world. The key word, however, is *can*.

Recently the authors have seen an increased number of opinions and proposals for the establishment of international operational joint military-police combat units, with a rapid reaction status. For example, Canadian newspaper columnist Olivia Ward proposed that the United Nations establish a 15,000-strong force as quickly as possible. It should be composed of military, police, and civilian international staff, including medics and conflict transformation experts, who would be based at designated UN sites and ready to deploy with 48 hours notice (Ward, 2006).

It is rather obvious that a number of problems emerge as an outcome of such multinational cooperation. First, to borrow from the terminology used in literature dealing with terrorism, "One person's terrorist is another's freedom fighter." The membership, especially of Interpol, is open to virtually all countries, give or take a few. Among those members, one can find many countries that do not have friendly relations with one another about a variety of issues. Sharing information about potential terrorist threats with a country that harbors terrorism might prove to be quite challenging. Sharing information with the police force of a country that is well known to be infiltrated by organized crime doesn't seem prudent, either. Finally, making sense of statistical data that are grouped and defined in a somewhat archaic manner won't contribute an efficient response to the particular crime. For example, for statistical purposes, Interpol still groups murder and attempted murder in the same category.

Finally, here are a few recommendations for the future of international police cooperation. First, the need for an efficient and effective operational force, such as an international police task force, is a priority, especially given the recent developments in Iraq and Afghanistan. Such a task force needs a well-developed support system in the form of valid intelligence, and this could and has to be supplied by organizations such as Interpol or Europol. However, the composition of such a task force has to be very carefully defined, and it remains to be seen who could be put in charge of such decision-making processes. Second, the existence of numerous international law enforcement academies, not discussed in this chapter, will further some informal cooperation among law enforcement agencies, and such friendly cooperation is frequently more valuable than a reliance on formal entities. Finally, the exchange of police representatives among allied countries similar to what was established by the

New York Police Department after the September 11 attack will continue to facilitate formal and informal cooperation.

What we now need is a clearly defined policy for international police cooperation, information exchange, and operational assistance. The answer to the question of who will be in charge of this remains open for now.

Notes

1. At the time of the establishment of Europol, in 1999, the European Union consisted of 15 countries: Austria, Belgium, Denmark, Finland, France, Germany, Greece, Ireland, Italy, Luxembourg, the Netherlands, Portugal, Spain, Sweden, and the United Kingdom. Additional states that had joined as of August 2007 included Bulgaria, Cyprus, the Czech Republic, Estonia, Hungary, Latvia, Lithuania, Malta, Poland, Romania, Slovakia, and Slovenia. Already in advance of the accession of these new member states to the European Union, agreements were drafted on cooperation to form Europol. The first such agreement was signed on March 21, 2001, with Poland. As of August 2007, The European Union comprised 27 states, including recently joined Romania and Bulgaria, while Europol, as of May 2007, had 34 member states.

2. See, for example, the *European Foreign and Security Policy Newsletter,* Issue 9, April 2002, page 9, which lists 20 UN peacekeeping missions in which the Irish Garda (the Irish police force) has participated. For a full list of UN peacekeeping missions from 1945 until the present, see http://en.wikipedia.org/wiki/List_of_UN_peacekeeping_missions.

3. Regarding all the UN peacekeeping missions in East Timor, including UNMIT (United Nations Integrated Mission in Timor-Leste), UNMISET (United Nations Mission in East Timor), UNTAET (United Nations Transitional Administration in East Timor), UNAMET (United Nations Mission in East Timor), and all other related topics see the following sources:

- August 2007 Timor-Leste (2007). Retrieved August 20, 2007, from http://www.securitycouncilreport.org/site/c.glKWLeMTIsG/b.3041225/k.275/August_2007BRTimorLeste.htm.
- UN Security Council 5516th Meeting (AM). (2006, August 25). Retrieved August 21, 2007 from http://www.unmiset.org/UNMISETWebSite.nsf/60325cf 12626b2a3.
- The very essential (many useful links) Wikipedia source retrieved August 21, 2007 from http://en.wikipedia.org/wiki/List_of_UN_peacekeeping-missions

4. All information about the UNMIBH and the IPTF, unless specified otherwise, is taken from the UNMIBH official Web site at http://www.un.org/Depts/dpko/missions/unmibh/mandate.html, retrieved August 21, 2007.

5. This Serb Republic in the territory of Bosnia and Herzegovina should not be confused with the Serb (Belgrad) and Montenegro Republic, which recently officially replaced the former Socialist Federal Republic of Yugoslavia.

6. The full text of the Dayton-Paris Peace Agreement is available at http://www.oscebih.org/essentials/gfap/eng, retrieved August 21, 2007.

7. See OSCE (n.d.).

References

Action Plan to Combat Drugs (2000–2004). (2005). Retrieved August 20, 2007, from http://europa.eu/scadplus/leg/en/lvb/l33092.htm

August 2007 Timor-Leste. (2007). Retrieved August 20, 2007, from http://www.securitycouncilreport.org/site/c.glKWLeMTIsG/b.3041225/k.275/August_2007 BRTimorLeste.htm

Bittner, E (1970). *The function of the police in modern society*. Washington, DC: U.S. Government Printing Office.

British Broadcasting Corporation. (2003, December 2). *Crime fighters: Policing—Europol*. Retrieved May 3, 2004, from http://www.bbc.co.uk/crime/fighters/europol.shtml

Budget for Europol for 2007. (2006, August 2). *Official Journal of the European Union, C180, 49, 1–9* [Electronic version]. Retrieved August 20, 2007, from http://eur-ex.europa.eu/JOIndex.do?year=2006&serie=C&textfield2=180& Submit=Search.

Bureau for International Narcotics and Law Enforcement Affairs. (2003, January 10). *United States participation in international police (CIVPOL) missions*. Retrieved April 18, 2003, from http://www.state.gov/g/inl/rls/fs/16554.htm

Cameron-Waller, S. (2001, December 17). *Interpol statement: Second world conference on commercial exploitation of children*. Retrieved March 21, 2003, from http://www.interpol.int/Public/Icpo/speeches/20011219.asp

Deridder, W. (2001, October). *16th annual Interpol symposium on terrorism*. Retrieved May 5, 2004, from http://www.interpol.int/public/ICPO/speeches/20011022b.asp

Eurojust. (n.d.). *Welcome to Eurojust's website*. Retrieved May 3, 2004, from http://www.eurojust.eu.int/index.htm

European Monitoring Centre for Drugs and Drug Addiction (EMCDDA). (2006). *Annual report 2006: The state of the drugs problem in Europe* [Electronic version]. Retrieved August 20, 2007, from http://ar2006.emcdda.europa.eu/en/home-en.html

European Union Police Mission in Bosnia and Herzegovina. (n.d.). *Overview*. Retrieved May 12, 2007, from http://www.eupm.org/Overview.aspx

Glazer, A. (2007, May 8). *LAPD brass reassigned after May 1 clash*. Retrieved August 19, 2007, from http://abcnews.go.com/US/wireStory?id=3149965

Gruner, S. (2006). Italy's special Carabinieri unit fights art looting. *WSJ.com opinion journal from the Wall Street journal opinion page* [Electronic version]. Retrieved August 20, 2007, from http://www.opinionjournal.com/la/?id=110008219

Haberfeld, M. R. (2002). *Critical issues in police training*. Upper Saddle River, NJ: Prentice-Hall.

Human Rights Watch. (2002). Hopes betrayed: Trafficking of women and girls to post-conflict Bosnia and Herzegovina for forced prostitution. *Bosnia and Herzegovina, 14(9[D])* [Electronic version]. Retrieved August 21, 2007 from http://www.hrw.org/reports/2002/bosnia/

Interpol. (2007a). Counterfeit currency. Retrieved October 26, 2007, from http://www.interpol.int/Public/FinancialCrime/CounterfeitCurrency/

Interpol. (2007b). Financial and high-tech crimes. Retrieved October 26, 2007, from http://www.interpol.int/Public/FinancialCrime/Default.asp

Lindborg, C. (2001). *The EU rapid reaction force: Europe takes on a new security challenge.* Basic paper no. 37. Retrieved August 21, 2007, from http://www .basicint.org/pubs/Papers/BP37.htm

North Atlantic Treaty Organization (NATO). (2003). *KFOR information.* Retrieved August 19, 2007, from http://www.nato.int/issues/kosovo/index.html

North Atlantic Treaty Organization (NATO). (2004). *Kosovo force.* Retrieved August 19, 2007, from http://www.nato.int/kfor/structur/units/msu.html

North Atlantic Treaty Organization (NATO). (n.d.a). *Multinational specialized unit.* Retrieved August 18, 2007, from http://www.nato.int/kfor/structur/unOOits/ msu.html

North Atlantic Treaty Organization (NATO). (n.d.b). *NATO in Kosovo.* Retrieved May 12, 2007, from http://www.nato.int/issues/kosovo/index.html

Organization for Security and Co-operation in Europe (OSCE). (n.d.). *Mission to Bosnia and Herzegovina.* Retrieved August 18, 2007, from http://www.oscebih .org/security_cooperation/?d=4

TE-SAT: European terrorism situation and trend report. (2007). [Electronic version]. Retrieved August 20, 2007, from http://www.europol.eu.int/index.asp?page =publar2001

UN Liaison Office Sarajevo. (2002, December 31). *About us.* Retrieved August 19, 2007 from: http://www.un.org/Depts/dpko/missons/unmibh.pdf

UN Peace and Security Section. (2003a). *Bosnia and Herzegovina: UNMIBH— Background.* Retrieved May 7, 2004, from http://www.un.org/Depts/dpko/ missions/unmibh/background.html

UN Peace and Security Section. (2003b). *Bosnia and Herzegovina: UNMIBH— Mandate.* Retrieved May 7, 2004, from http://www.un.org/Depts/dpko/ missions/unmibh/mandate.html

UN Security Council. (2002). *Report of the Secretary-General on the United Nations Mission in Bosnia and Herzegovina.* Retrieved May 18, 2004, from http://216.239.51.104/search?q=cache:ZjDRIz7mTTcJ:www.womenwarpeace .org/bosnia/docs/sgreptosc5jun02.pdf+iptf+ghana&hl=en

Ward, O. (2006, June 15). United Nations "army" proposed. *Toronto Star* [Electronic version]. Retrieved August 20, 2007, from http://www.global policy.org/security/peacekpg/reform/2006/0615army.htm

Further Reading

European Union Police Mission. (2003). *European Union police mission in Bosnia and Herzegovina.* Retrieved May 7, 2004, from http://www.eupm.org/ index.html

Interpol. (1999, February 17). *Drug control.* Retrieved May 5, 2004 from http://www.interpol.int/Public/drugs/Default.asp

Interpol. (2003, March). *Interpol's international notices system.* Retrieved May 5, 2004, from http://www.interpol.int/Public/Wanted/Fugitives/Default.asp

Interpol. (n.d.). *Brief history of Interpol.* Retrieved May 3, 2004, from http:// www.interpol.int/public/ICPO/history.asp

Appendix A

Atlas of Regional Maps

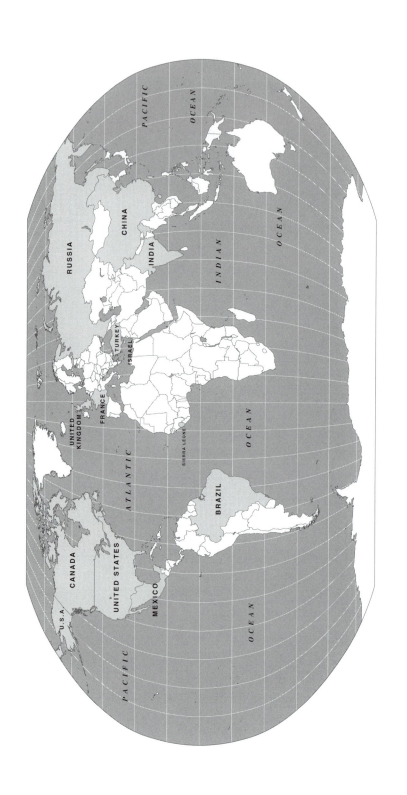

Map 1   The World. See Chapters 1 and 14.

Map 2   Asia. See Chapters 2, 6, and 7.

Map 3   South America. See Chapter 3.

Map 4 North America. See Chapters 4, 12, and 13.

Map 5   Africa. See Chapter 5.

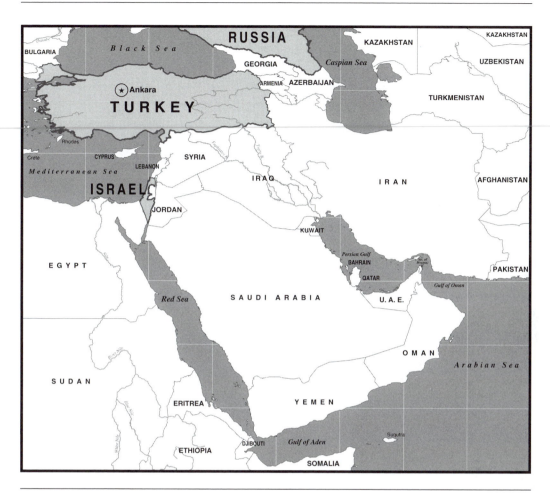

Map 6   The Middle East. See Chapters 8 and 9.

Map 7   Western Europe. See Chapters 10 and 11.

Index

About the Editors

Maria (Maki) Haberfeld is a professor of police science and chair of the Department of Law, Police Science, and Criminal Justice Administration at John Jay College of Criminal Justice, City University of New York. She was born in Poland and immigrated to Israel as a teenager. Prior to coming to John Jay, she served in the Israeli Defense Forces and left the army at the rank of a sergeant; she then joined the Israel National Police and left the force at the rank of lieutenant. She also worked for the U.S. Drug Enforcement Administration in its New York field office as a special consultant. She holds two bachelor of arts degrees, two master's degrees, and a PhD in criminal justice.

Her recent publications include a book that she wrote on police training entitled *Critical Issues in Police Training* (2002), two books that she coedited—*Contours of Police Integrity* (2004) and *Encyclopedia of Law Enforcement, the International Volume* (2005), another book that she authored, *Police Leadership* (2005), and a book she coauthored, *Enhancing Police Integrity* (2006).

For the last six years (2001–2007), Dr. Haberfeld has been involved in developing, coordinating, and teaching in a special training program for the New York City Police Department. Currently she is also an academic coordinator of the Law Enforcement Executive Police Institute for the state of New York, where she oversees the delivery of the training modules and teaches leadership courses. She is involved in two major research studies, one on the use of force by the police in 10 different countries and the other on training police in counterterrorism response post–September 11, which also involves comparative studies of a number of countries around the world.

Ibrahim Cerrah graduated from the Turkish National Police Academy and was appointed as a police sergeant to Ankara Police College in 1986. He worked there until he was transferred to a civilian/academic position at the Turkish National Police Academy in 1989.

Between 1990 and 1995, he completed his MA and PhD studies at the Scarman Center for the Study of Public Order, University of Leicester, UK.

Since then he has been teaching as a member of the full time faculty of the Turkish National Police Academy.

During 2001–2002, 2004, and 2007, he visited the John Jay College of Criminal Justice, City University of New York as a Fulbright fellow and taught several courses such as Introduction to Law Enforcement, Police Administration, Comparative Police Systems, Police Ethics, and Terrorism.

His study and teaching interests/areas include police ethics, police subculture, police education, democratization of policing, and issues involving domestic security. He has authored and edited a number of books and other publications, both in Turkish and in English. He is the founding editor-in-chief of a bilingual journal, *Turkish Journal of Police Studies*. Since 2001, he has been working as the director of the Institute for Security Science in Ankara, Turkey. He became a full professor in 2006. He is married and has three children.

About the Contributors

Curtis Clarke is an associate professor and coordinator of the criminal justice program at Athabasca University. He has carried out empirical studies on the implementation of community-based policing, on police organizational and managerial change, on intelligence-led policing, and on the shifting boundaries between private and public policing. Professor Clarke has completed research for the Canadian Association of Chiefs of Police, the Federal Solicitor General, Health Canada, the Edmonton Police Service, the Metropolitan Toronto Police Service, the Alberta Association of Chiefs of Police, and the Law Commission of Canada. Dr. Clarke currently chairs a research subcommittee for the human resources department of the Alberta Association of Chiefs of Police, and he is treasurer for the Canadian Association of Police Educators. At present Dr. Clarke is seconded to the Alberta Solicitor General and Public Security Ministry, where he is overseeing the development and coordination of the provincial police and peace officer training strategy.

Stuart Cullen completed a 32-year police career in 1995, having attained the rank of superintendent. For the past 15 years he has been an associate tutor to major international command and leadership programs at the International Faculty, Leadership Academy for Policing, Bramshill, England. He has also been extensively involved in international police training and reform programs in Africa, Eastern Europe, Latin America, and the Caribbean. His clients have included the United Kingdom Foreign and Commonwealth Office, Department for International Development and the European Union. He has special experience working on reform programs in postconflict societies and societies in transition. Stuart Cullen is author or coauthor of a number of chapters and books on comparative international policing, human rights, and democratization and policing.

Benoît Dupont is professor of criminology at the Université de Montréal and deputy director of the International Centre for Comparative Criminology there. He is also the holder of the Canada Research Chair in Security, Identity, and Technology. His areas of interest include the governance of security (especially the functioning of security networks), the impact of new technologies on policing, and the impact of mass surveillance on privacy. He recently coedited a book with Jennifer Wood entitled *Democracy, Society and the Governance of Security* (Cambridge University Press, 2006).

Ruth Geva, a freelance organizational consultant, specializes in community policing, crime prevention, and emergency management. For almost 30 years, she was employed by the Israel Police and by Israel's Ministry of Public Security in various operational and management positions, retiring in 2001 with the rank of chief superintendent. Ms. Geva initiated and set up the National Crime Prevention Council in Israel, was the Israeli delegate to the UN Crime Prevention Division, coordinated the international relations of the ministry, and was part of the team that implemented community policing in Israel. A graduate of the University of Toronto (BSc) and the Hebrew University in Jerusalem (MA in criminology), she is also a graduate of the Home Office Crime Prevention Centre in the UK and has a diploma in organizational management. Ruth Geva is the author of over 70 professional publications and 2 textbooks on crime prevention. For the last four years, Ms. Geva has acted as coordinator of a project to set up Community Emergency Centers in all Jerusalem neighborhoods.

Lior Gideon, currently a full time professor at the Department of Law, Police Science, and Criminal Justice Administration at John Jay College of Criminal Justice, City University of New York, earned his PhD from the Faculty of Law, Institute of Criminology at the Hebrew University of Jerusalem. He received a postdoctoral fellowship at the University of Maryland at College Park. His main research interests are comparative criminal justice and rehabilitation, reintegration, and reentry issues for criminal offenders, in particular examining offenders' perceptions of their needs. Additionally, he specializes in correction-based program evaluation.

Farrukh Hakeem is an associate professor of criminal justice in the Department of Social Sciences, Shaw University, and teaches criminal justice courses. He has also taught at John Jay College of Criminal Justice, City University of New York and at The College of New Jersey. He teaches courses in the areas of law enforcement, corrections, comparative laws, and computer applications. After completing his graduate work in sociology and law at Bombay University, he was admitted to the Indian bar in 1979. While practicing law at Bombay High Court, he attended evening classes and completed an LLM in property law and matrimonial law at the University Department of Law, Bombay University. He obtained a fellowship to complete an MA in sociology at the University of Arizona. He then earned a PhD from the Graduate School and University Center of the City University of New York. His dissertation focused on the socioeconomic determinants of punishment. His current research interests are in the area of comparative law, international policing, disparities in punishment, and health. He has published articles in the *International Journal of Comparative and Applied Criminal Justice, The Encyclopedia of Law Enforcement,* and *Public Health Reports.*

Sergio Herzog is a senior lecturer at the Faculty of Law, Institute of Criminology at the Hebrew University of Jerusalem. He received his bachelor's degree in psychology and his PhD in criminology (direct track) from the Hebrew University of Jerusalem. His research interests lie in the areas of criminology, criminal justice systems, and social psychology. He conducted empirical research on the serious phenomenon of police violence in Israel; he collected and analyzed data on use-of-force complaints against police officers, their historical trends, the functioning of the civilian board in Israel that has handled these complaints, and the personal attitudes of suspected police officers, complainants, and civilian investigators concerning the roots, situations, and treatment of police violence. He has published six articles that have added both to the theoretical understanding of the phenomenon and to the specific treatment of public complaints against police officers by both internal (police) and external (civilian) complaints boards.

Matt Long is senior lecturer in criminology at Nottingham Trent University. He has previously worked at Sheffield Hallam, Manchester, and East London Universities. Between 1998 and 2004, he lectured at the national police training college at Bramshill. In 2002 he was appointed visiting professor in law and police science at John Jay College of Criminal Justice, City University of New York. He continues to act as a police trainer in a consultant capacity.

Yue Ma is a faculty member in the Department of Law and Police Science at John Jay College of Criminal Justice, City University of New York. He received his PhD from Rutgers University. Dr. Ma also holds a JD from Rutgers University Law School and an LLM from University of Minnesota Law School. Dr. Ma is interested in the comparative study of legal and criminal justice issues. He has published articles exploring a wide range of legal and criminal justice issues in the cross-nation context. Among the topics covered by his research and articles are the development of criminal justice standards in Europe under the European Convention on Human Rights, comparative analysis of exclusionary rules, comparative analysis of prosecutorial discretion and plea bargaining, comparison of lay participation in criminal trials, comparative study of the law of interrogation, and the judicial role in supervising the exercise of prosecutorial discretion. Dr. Ma has also published articles and book chapters on China's criminal justice system.

William H. McDonald is the founder and dean of the School of Criminal Justice at Monroe College, Bronx, New York. He holds a PhD in criminal justice and a master's in philosophy from the City University of New York, a master of science degree in public safety administration from Central Connecticut University, a graduate certificate in criminal justice education from the University of Virginia, and a bachelor of science degree in criminal justice from American University. He is a Neiderhoffer Fellow, a graduate of the FBI National Academy, and a former visiting professor at Bramshill, the police college for England and Wales. In addition to having taught for years, he was the director of public safety for Connecticut State University, a special agent with the U.S. Treasury Department, and a senior homicide detective with the Metropolitan Police Department of Washington, D.C. He has served as a technical consultant to a number of domestic and foreign criminal justice agencies.

Benjamin Nelson Reames holds a PhD in political science from Columbia University and a master of public policy from the University of Michigan, where he also earned his BA in social sciences. He is currently working for the U.S. Department of State in Asia. (He wrote his chapters for this book independently, prior to his employment with the State Department, and none of his views reflect U.S. policy or opinions on any matters, in any way). Previously he has been an anticorruption specialist at Partners of the Americas, a Fulbright-Hays fellow researching police reform in Brazil, a senior associate working with the Lawyers Committee for Human Rights (now Human Rights First) on their Mexico Policing Project, and a consultant to the UN Development Programme's country office in Guatemala on police reform. He was also a senior research associate for the Civilian Complaint Review Board of New York City, which investigates complaints against the police department.

Peter Roudik is a senior legal specialist at the Law Library of Congress, where he is responsible for doing research on laws of the former Soviet states. He joined the Law Library in 1996 after 10 years of academic experience, during which he wrote and lectured extensively on constitutional law issues. He authored a volume on Russia and the Commonwealth of Independent States for the *World Legal Systems Cyclopedia*. He has testified frequently before the U.S. Congress, and his legal commentaries have been broadcast by the Voice of America, Radio Liberty, and C-SPAN. Before coming to the United States, he worked as a legal advisor to the Russian government where he was involved in drafting legislation.

Agostino von Hassell spent his formative years in the United States, studying European history at Columbia University and graduating with a BA in 1974. He then attended Columbia University Graduate School of Journalism and graduated with awards in 1975. He is the president of The Repton Group LLC, a business consulting firm. von Hassell has extensive expertise in national security matters, high-level investigations around the globe, terrorism and military issues, and global trade problems. He has published numerous books on military history, including *Alliances of Enemies* about the U.S. Office of Strategic Services and Germany's Abwehr in World War II. That book was published by St. Martin's Press in November 2006.

Anders Walker, who is currently an assistant professor at the Saint Louis University School of Law, is interested in the relationship between democracy and law, particularly the manner in which popular politics can influence legal doctrine. A graduate of Duke University School of Law, Walker first became interested in clashes between popular politics and law while pursuing a JD/MA in history at Duke. He pursued this interest as a PhD candidate in African American Studies and History at Yale, focusing on the manner in which African American history, read as the story of a disenfranchised electoral minority, actually casts into stark relief a much larger story of the excesses of populist rule in democratic societies, a force that law is often unable to influence.